CULTURAL CONTINUITY IN ADVANCED ECONOMIES

Cultural Continuity in Advanced Economies

Britain and the U.S. Versus Continental Europe

GUSTAV SCHACHTER
Northeastern University, Boston, USA

SAUL ENGELBOURG
Boston University, USA

Routledge
Taylor & Francis Group

LONDON AND NEW YORK

First published 2005 by Ashgate Publishing

Reissued 2019 by Routledge
2 Park Square, Milton Park, Abingdon, Oxon, OX14 4RN
52 Vanderbilt Avenue, New York, NY 10017

Routledge is an imprint of the Taylor & Francis Group, an informa business

A Library of Congress record exists under LC control number:

ISBN 13: 978-0-8153-8839-5 (hbk)
ISBN 13: 978-1-138-35679-5 (pbk)
ISBN 13: 978-1-351-16044-5 (ebk)

Contents

Preface

Gustav Schachter and Saul Engelbourg correctly contend that the concept of capitalism has varied according to each nation's cultural and historical heritage; it has continued to be different in Anglo-American countries (Britain and the United States) from Continental European countries (here represented by Germany, France, and Italy). Over the last three centuries the Anglo-American model has been based on *laissez faire*, economic liberalism that stresses the role of the individual as the primary decision-maker of economic behavior. The Continental European model has modified capitalism by an unwritten but widely accepted social contract. The Anglo-Americans have opted for the individualist and minimalist State while by and large Continental Europeans have favored the Interventionist State.

Anglo-American capitalism envisions that business firms aim to maximize profits; wages reflect marginal productivity of labor and workers are replaced or terminated when not needed. But also workers have mobility to change employers whenever they find better opportunities. In Continental Europe changing jobs has been a far less prevalent phenomenon than in the United States or in Britain. What the Germans have called the *Soziale Marktwirtschaft*, social market economy, explains that the State can be a moderator between labor and management. In Europe, the State has both overtly and covertly interfered in the economy and occasionally has subsidized various sectors. Although at the end of the twentieth century France, Germany, and Italy have privatized many public enterprises, State ownership of productive enterprises has remained much larger than that of Britain and the United States.

The British model of capitalism provided the basis for the market economy and a minimalist State. The British classical economic school of thought (Smith, Ricardo, Malthus) advocated economic liberalism as the best path for economic development. By the nineteenth century, the British industrial revolution was well under way, and London became the principal European *entrepôt* and the most sophisticated financial market in the world. Owing to the high level of wealth and income, London soon developed a thriving capital market, able to readily mobilize funds at low cost. This allowed the development of the infrastructure, roads, canals and railroads, by private business. By the twentieth century, while Britain declined as a world economic power, economic liberalism preserved its allure although with lasting deviations from *laissez faire*.

After the American Revolution, the United States proved to be even more individualistic than Britain. Colonists in British North America came mainly from Britain; they brought with them British economic values and political institutions. While opposing the mother country's mercantilist policies towards the colonies, with independence the United States introduced mercantilist regulations to protect the domestic economy. Subsequently, some Americans have questioned the entire mercantilist argument, and have vouched that free trade might be more efficient even though the State has often imposed high tariffs. U. S. policy makers have defended individualism, and pragmatically have accepted limited State intervention, such as promotion for the construction of roads, canals, and railroads.

Different from Britain and the United States, French, German, and Italian intervention has been much more intrusive. Under the absolutism of the *Ancien Régime*, France accepted a central role for the State in the domestic and foreign markets. Preferring a strong State presence in the economy, French policy makers practiced mercantilism, known as *Colbertisme*, protecting domestic industry until post-World War II. The State not only developed infrastructure, but also pursued direct productive initiatives. From the seventeenth century *Colbertisme*, the French Revolution, and Napoleon, through the twentieth century, the nation that coined the term *laissez faire*, adopted economic *dirigisme*. The French culture accepted *l'état* as a social partner different from that of Britain and the United States but similar to Germany and Italy.

Until the mid-nineteenth century, Germany and Italy remained politically and economically fragmented among numerous mini states and city-states. Prussia emerged as the main German state. To finance wars and foster economic growth, Prussia pursued *Cameralist* policies, a variant of mercantilism. By the 1870s Germany became the dominant power in Central Europe and pursued mercantilist policies. Notwithstanding the Nazi aberration, during the twentieth century, policy makers adopted the *Soziale Marktwirtschaft*, a modified economic liberalism, based largely on Bismarck's social legislation of the nineteenth century.

During the eighteenth century, Italian states by and large practiced mercantilism. The Enlightenment and the French Revolution as well as British liberal economic ideas influenced the Italian states. While some Italian economists have strongly advocated free trade, until the mid-twentieth century the conventional wisdom has accepted public regulation and protectionism as the most effective means of building a strong domestic industry. From unification in 1861 through the twentieth century, the State has provided incentives, subsidies, and has supported domestic industries, as well as becoming an entrepreneur after the economic crisis of the thirties.

Gustav Schachter and Saul Engelbourg present a compelling historical background of three centuries of continuity of policy and thought in advanced economies. I agree with the Authors' thesis that notwithstanding some deviation from the trend, the Anglo-Americans have defended the minimalist State, have viewed *étatisme* and planning as coercive and anti-democratic, and have vouched for the infallible economic man and private enterprise. *Au contraire*, Continental European culture has included the active State at the level of thought and policy. In France, Germany and Italy the political absolutism of the eighteenth and part of the nineteenth centuries brought political democracy in the twentieth century, but no significant change in the role of the State in the economy.

Beniamino Moro
Department of Economics, University of Cagliari (Italy)
December 2004

Acknowledgements

We are grateful to John Q. Adams of the University of Maryland and Northeastern University, John Munro of Simon Fraser University and Andrew Sum of Northeastern University, who read and commented on our numerous drafts, and to Beniamino Moro of the University of Cagliari for contributing a Preface to this book. We are also indebted to the late Luigi de Rosa of University of Naples and the late Charles P. Kindleberger of the Massachusetts Institute of Technology for commenting and making suggestions on earlier drafts. We want to give special thanks to Cheryl Noakes Fonville of Northeastern University Department of Economics for her patience and grace. This book is an outcome of the steady encouragement and editorial support of our wives, Francine N. Schachter and Charlotte Engelbourg. We are gratefully indebted to Shelley Hamilton and Levanto G. Schachter for their technical and editorial help; we could not possibly have completed the project without their assistance. We apologize to anyone we forgot to acknowledge. While all of the above were helpful, we assume full responsibility for errors and omissions.

Chapter 1

Introduction

We explore the role of the State in the process of economic development since the eighteenth century in five major industrialized western countries. We chose Britain and the United States of America as examples of the Anglo-Saxons[1] and France, Germany, and Italy, as representing Continental Europe respectively.[2] These countries have been major players in the world economy and their public policies frequently have been reasonably consistent and path dependent, that is, the path once chosen strongly influences what follows for good or ill.[3] There are no insuperable problems in generalizing the historical path of Britain and France, integrated nation-states for the period under study. Problems arise, however, concerning the United States, Germany, and Italy. The Thirteen Colonies gained independence from Britain in 1776 and then established the United States, Italy unified in 1861 and Germany in 1870. This disparity is reflected in this Introduction.

There has been continuity of thought and action in the role played by the State in Britain and the United States compared with Continental Europe. The specific institutional and intellectual legacies of the Anglo-American and Continental European countries have persisted in substantial degree from the eighteenth century to the present. The Anglo-American model has been based more or less on *laissez faire*, that is, economic liberalism that stresses individuals as the primary decision makers in determining the performance of economic functions.[4]

In contrast, the Continental model has been based on State intervention. The justification for government intervention includes: nation building, economic growth and development, and rent seeking by producers or consumers as well as price and employment stability. These multiple, and at times competing goals affect public policy; furthermore, dissonant and disparate government actions may have unintended as well as intended consequences. Hence, the State governs both by design and accident. As an eminent twentieth-century economist observed that one is struck by the minimal role of the State in the process of industrialization of

---

1   Anglo-Americans represent by and large the Anglo-Saxon countries, which in addition to Britain and the United States include such other countries as Australia, Canada, and New Zealand.
2   For a contemporary overview of the economic history of each of the five countries see: *Oxford Encyclopedia of Economic History*, 2003, Vol. 2, pp. 200-210, 360-379, 404-417, 449-439; Vol. 3, pp. 173-185; Vol. 5, pp. 159-174.
3   See: Engelbourg and Schachter 1999.
4   Grampp 1965, p. viii.

Britain. 'On the Continent, where industrialization came later than in England and where the philosophy of natural liberty never cut quite so wide a swath, the role of the state in economic development was much larger.'[5]

Recently, an economic historian attributed the continuation of these specific models to differences in 'values'; his assertion is based on the hypothesis that socio-psychological factors play a role in the process of economic development.[6] These 'values' (either as embodied in an institutional and intellectual framework or as socio-psychological factors) have been deeply ingrained over many generations as part of the general cultural milieu.

Philosophically, if not always in practice, the Anglo-Americans abhor the State's role while the Continentals sustain the State even under market-oriented regimes. In Britain and the United States the individual conceptually has been the supreme actor as envisioned by Adam Smith in the late eighteenth century; one need no more than recall the atomistic principle of the economic man in Smith's classical economic model. Smith's economic man is rationally motivated to maximize his material welfare and, through the harmony of interests, the welfare of the State as well. In Britain and the United States public welfare has constituted a summation of individual welfare, or the Smithian atomistic view of society. In contrast, in Continental Europe, Smith's dictum has been assisted (or ignored) by the State that has pursued public goals in unison with the private sector. For instance: 'the difference between EU and US markets is that the phrase 'social partner', which the EU uses to describe the management and unions... has no counterpart in the United States. Mention social partner to Americans and people think of square dancing in Texas, not business and labor'.[7]

The evolving nature of the State in Britain, France, Germany, and Italy has its roots in the exit from feudalism; the United States never experienced feudalism. In Britain, the process of change from feudalism, through absolutist regimes, to a representative system allowed the slow, even if uneven, development of a balance between the State and various national or local interest groups. This occurred while a parallel individualistic evolution developed in the civil society.[8]

In Britain, as a result of the 1688 Glorious Revolution (also known as the Bloodless Revolution) the king no longer controlled either the army or public finances. The British individualistic movement remained embedded in the old

---

5   Mason 1960, p. 637. Also, Alexander Gerschenkron in *Economic Backwardness in Historical Perspective* in 1962 contended that at the onset of industrialization backward countries depended on the State to supply the needed inputs, such as infrastructure and investment, as well as a proper economic climate, when the market failed.

6   Crouzet 1985, p. 37

7   Freeman 2004, p. 36.

8   The English revolutions took place during the seventeenth century, but there is nothing in British history that resembles the Night of August 4, 1789, or the *Declaration of the Rights of Man and Citizen* later that month. The French Revolution of 1789 overthrew despotism but, nevertheless, failed to create a durable political system.

aristocratic structure and had a limited impact on social reforms. The oligarchy accepted freedom to trade or *economic liberalism*, and later during the nineteenth century, *political liberalism*, that is, enfranchising most male citizens. Britain adopted a complementary juridical and pragmatic vision of the State whereas in France the individual has had a more positive perception of the State.

British philosophers differed from their French counterparts with regard to the role of the individual in society. In interpreting the English Revolutions of the seventeenth century, John Locke (1632-1704) argued that civil society should exist according to the social compact wherein the majority rules; later David Hume (1711-1776) contended that the initial social compact everywhere was obtained by force or usurpation without, necessarily, the voluntary consent of the ruled.[9] The 'social contract' remained in Locke's and Hume's times a theoretical concept rather than a policy model.

Britain had a landed aristocracy with the apex represented in the hereditary House of Lords; however, by the end of the seventeenth century, the House of Commons prevailed. In the United States, all adult males signed the Mayflower Compact of 1620 and both Thomas Jefferson and John Adams in the early nineteenth century discussed a 'natural aristocracy' and defended elite government.[10] The uniqueness of the American system stems in part from the 'frontier' and that America never had a feudal society. While one hardly can be cavalier about the institution of slavery, social ascendancy was furthered by geographic mobility. Indentured servants disappeared into the population either after a term of several years or certainly in the next generation. Widespread property ownership in land resulted in adult males voting on a large scale even before the American Revolution.

While Thomas Jefferson was a disciple of Locke, he was also a slave owner. He did not envision any contradiction in inserting in the *Declaration of Independence* 'government derives its just power from the consent of the governed'; it took more than another century for the New Deal to institute a social contract in the United States. This can be observed from legislation protecting the working class, the poor, the aged, and the disabled, an aberration for a country where rugged individualism had been prevalent since its foundation. On the other hand, regardless of political overtones and notable deviations since the late nineteenth-century, the Continental countries have followed New Deal-type policies. Over the long run, both the Anglo-Americans and Continental Europeans implemented to some degree social legislation.

Anglo-American political theory separates the government from the people; the government is an agent of the people but is not identical with the people. The assumption is that by administering less, one governs better, or, as Jefferson

---

9   Locke 1967, p. 57; see also, Locke 1975, pp. 164-166; Hume 1967, pp. 151-152.
10   When Abraham Lincoln was elected president in 1860, he was among the richest men in Illinois. While the mythology portrays him as a defender of the poor that is not how he made his money. As a lawyer, he represented some of the most important business enterprises in his state.

contended, that government governs best which governs least.[11] The Anglo-Americans attempt to influence the State, in accordance with the harmony of interests of contending power centers, and perceive the State as a necessary evil. The United States Constitution is based on the principle of limited government, while Britain with no written Constitution, has no such written limitation. The French see the State, *l'état*, as a symbol of French power, one could call the State a metaphysical independent institution that has acquired the authority to unify society.[12] Germany and Italy, both before and after unification, substantially adhered to and reinforced the French model of State intervention.

During the eighteenth century the French *philosophes*[13] could not easily break with the old order, even though in the abstract they preached liberal political and economic policies and scarcely appreciated the up-and-coming moneyed class. Also, the emerging laic State weakened the Church by dividing the loyalty of a basically Roman Catholic population. For a generation after the Revolution, the disorganization of society mandated an almost continually reinforced French State.

The 'social contract' proposed in 1761 by Jean Jacques Rousseau (1712-1778) constituted an integral element of the eighteenth century Enlightenment.[14] His general concept was that a nation needed a central authority (perhaps a king) with limited power; however, the nation's laws should be based on the will of the people. By implication, if the people choose their government, there should be a symbiosis between the people and the State since their respective interests would coincide.[15] Rousseau perceived the institution of government as an intermediary between the ruling class and the ruled, aiming to maintain the law and cohesion in society, that is, a 'social contract'.[16]

While eighteenth century France never achieved political liberalism, it debated a philosophy that gained credence over time. Pre-revolutionary France had no effective institution to restrain the monarch even though the resurgent aristocracy limited Louis XV and Louis XVI; privilege fractured society and there was no equality before the law. Moreover, some historians contend that neither the

---

11   Locke 1995, p. 14; Rosanvallon 1989, p. 512.

12   Zysman 1979, p. 194.

13   During the eighteenth century, such French intellectuals as d'Alembert, Diderot, Montesquieu, Necker, Quesnay, Rousseau, Turgot, and Voltaire, as well as others, were known as '*philosophes*', most of whom contributed to the *Encyclopédie*.

14   Rousseau visualized a democratic State that transferred the rightful sovereignty of the population at large to a higher authority. Dobbin 1994, p. 102; Rousseau 1967, p. 222.

15   Rousseau's 'social contract' could be described in the following way: 'all of us put in common and all his power to the supreme direction of the general will; and we receive as a body each member as a part indivisible from the whole'. In 1762 authorities condemned Rousseau's *The Contrat Social* as subversive'. Goulemot and Launay 1968, p. 187.

16   Rousseau 1966, pp. 50-52. At the beginning of the twenty-first century the French had a *Ministre de l'Emploie, du Travail et de la Cohésion sociale* (Ministry of Employment, Labor, and Social Cohesion).

common workers nor the landless peasants were in positions of leadership or even foot soldiers of the Revolution.[17]

Both before and after the 1789 Revolution, the weight of the French State has been greater than in Britain.[18] The assumption has been from the *Ancien Régime* into the twentieth century that the State can mobilize resources for the public will.[19] 'Centralized institutions served both monarchical and republican rule in France. Core characteristics of political culture and state structure survived revolutionary changes in state purposes.'[20]

With its highly technocratic bureaucracy, the State has provided guidance, wanted as well as unwanted, to the various economic sectors. In France, Germany, and Italy, the State has been expected to lead by appropriate policies, which some observers call *dirigisme*, that is, overt state control of the commanding heights of the economy. 'Private economic actors followed the lead of public officials.'[21]

Few dispute the continuity of French policies such as *Colbertisme*, mercantilism, and *dirigisme* from the seventeenth to the twentieth century. 'The French dirigiste model, based on a strong and ambitious state, at once the creator of riches and the guarantor of equality, retains a tight grip on the French mind.'[22] While significant inequality prevailed before and after the French Revolution of 1789, the State remained the final arbiter in socio-economic relations.

The policies of the five countries considered here varied over time but were consistent to each one's institutional and cultural mode. While in the Anglo-American countries the approaches have often been different, the underlying philosophy was similar. The State in Britain has been comparatively non-intrusive, that is, the State has been less likely to own, regulate, or tax and spend. A mercantilist State at the end of the eighteenth century, owing partially to the strictures of Adam Smith as well as to having become the workshop of the world, Britain adopted free trade during 1846-1931. On the other hand, Britain instituted protection during the depression of the 1930s, only to restore free trade during the second half of the twentieth century even before joining the Common Market. Similarly, after World War II, Britain nationalized several key industries and then, only a few short years later, privatized many of the same industries. This is not to say that the British economy reverted to the *status quo ante bellum* as of 1939, much less that of 1914. One could make the same observation concerning British social policies.

No one would suggest that the United States has ever embodied extreme *laissez faire* policies. The record is replete with illustrations of State promotion of the economy in addition to having a protective tariff policy until 1934 and more or less free trade since. Still, the United States has been different and has relied more on the market (regulated to be sure) rather than on the State. The federal system

---

17   Halperin 1997, pp. 54-55.
18   Rosanvallon 1989, pp. 497-502.
19   Hayward 1986, p. 19.
20   Dobbin 1994, p. 96.
21   Kuisel 1981, p. 277.
22   *The Economist*, 5 June 1999.

resulted in a polycentric polity; the individual states at times imitated and pursued rival state mercantilism but also restrained each other. Social policy originated in the states with the federal government entering the scene only in the 1930s.

The Continentals have been contending that the State is and should be an endogenous participant in the market place. By recognizing this symbiotic partnership, Continental Europe has welcomed the State's overt initiative and cooperation in the economy and society. France's *dirigisme* extended from Louis XIV through the twentieth century while Germany's *Der Staat kann* (the State can) remained valid permanently. Italy's example, with a polycentric government that emphasizes *clientelismo*,[23] represents just such an exaggerated version of what happens in every relationship between the State and society.

The European Continental countries present many similarities in economic policies and social legislation. France followed a path in which absolute monarchs developed a mercantilist economic policy as an adjunct to State building; mercantilism endured as economic policy regardless of the form of government. Since the State built major canals and roads under the *Ancien Regime*, France proceeded to construct its railroads with critical State participation; one should also note the importance of railroads as a crucial element in military strategy as contributing to State railroad policy.

Also, with a fair degree of consistency, until after World War II, France employed the protective tariff to shelter both agriculture and industry. In addition, the *Banque de France*, the central bank, acted as an agent of State economic policy rather than as an autonomous check on government decision-making. While the 'social contract' has furnished a theoretical framework for all governments, the State has been increasingly active in protecting, and some will say over protecting individuals or groups in need.

Eighteenth and nineteenth centuries German philosophers interpreted the 'social contract' within the political theory of the State, *Staatszwecklehre*. German political philosophy was based on their version of natural law that legitimized the existence of the State, founded through a 'social contract'. According to the German philosophers the State, that is, the ruler defined the common good. In contrast, Locke, writing within the British historical context, emphasized individual liberty and property. German philosophers viewed the social contact in a one-sided fashion with the State (the sovereign) making the rules, and the individual citizens necessarily obeying.[24] 'In Germany as a rule the model of the social contract and natural law were used to support absolutism and provide a theoretical justification for it right up to the end of the eighteenth century.'[25]

Moreover, during the eighteenth century the multiple German states, by and large, adhered to *Cameralism*, a variant form of mercantilism. In the nineteenth century Friedrich List rejected Smith's free trade as inappropriate for any nation but for advanced industrialize Britain. Prussia-Germany, like France, utilized

---

23   *Clientelismo* could be defined as a situation in which it is expected that, as a rule, administrators or bureaucrats cater to special interest individuals or groups.

24   Klippel 1999, pp. 73-76

25   Klippel 1999, p. 74.

protective tariffs to stimulate industrialization. The German State was instrumental in building the railroads and nationalized them fairly early. Germany invested heavily in education from the elementary through the university levels. Furthermore, much of Germany's success in chemical, electrical equipment, and steel during the nineteenth and twentieth centuries can be attributed to State funding for scientific research.

Whereas the United States adopted an antitrust policy to restrain the excesses of large-scale enterprise in an effort to preserve a free market, the German State eagerly embraced and legalized cartels for many sectors of the economy. Germany assumed leadership in social policy late in the nineteenth century. Since World War II the State has continued to play a pivotal role in the economy with an eye to promoting social and political stability by protecting small-scale enterprise.

Pre-unification Italy, unlike Germany, presented deep socio-economic differences; after unification, regional disparities continued to plague Italy. To finance railroad construction, of necessity Italy relied on foreign capital, just as it did in banking. The State encouraged railroad investment primarily with an eye to nation building rather than economic considerations; Italy nationalized its railroads early in the twentieth century. Heavy industry depended substantially on State support in the form of protective tariffs and State defense procurement. The desire to become a great power provided the impetus for the State's activist economic policy.

During the depression of the early nineteen thirties Italy rescued numerous large-scale banks and industrial enterprises and established a State holding company still in existence. By the mid-twentieth century, the State owned the largest share of the economy among the western European countries. By the end of the century many but not all State enterprises had been privatized, while the State has persisted as a dominant force in the economy.

Before unification the Italian component states varied in enacting social legislation but since unification, Italy's welfare state has expanded through an active public policy for health, education, and welfare. The role of the State has been particularly accentuated in the South, Italy's most backward region; the State has allocated massive funds and enacted special legislation to increase the level of southern economic activity and well being in a vain effort to narrow the perennial regional dualism.

We recognize potential objections to our thesis. Over the last three centuries the Anglo-Americans were not purist economic or political liberals. The British had the Poor Laws as well as the State meddling in the public utilities debate. In the United States, the individual states played an important role during the canal building era and a lesser role in railroad construction. The federal government encouraged settlement by granting land to individuals and railroads. Also, one could cite the interventionist New Deal as a counterfactual to *laissez faire*. On the other hand, the Continental countries witnessed few aberrations such as the short-lived French economic liberalism at the beginning of the 1789 Revolution or the corporative policies of the Vichy government during World War II. Similarly, Nazism in Germany and Fascism in Italy could be considered exceptions to our thesis. Yet over the last three centuries, as a rule, path dependency prevailed. The main political and economic philosophy of the Anglo-Americans has been *liberalism* while the *social contract and state-oriented* philosophy have prevailed in Continental Europe.

Chapter 2

The Eighteenth Century

During the first half of the eighteenth century, some traces of feudalism still prevailed in France, Germany, and Italy. While Britain had already become a parliamentary kingdom, vestiges of seigneur-serf relationships remained on the continent. Depending on the definition, one could place the end of French feudalism at the fourteenth century when the State became more centralized and the king gained control over his vassals. A broader definition would set the end of feudalism in the seventeenth century, when Louis XIV made the aristocracy dependent on his will and kept the subordinated nobles 'captive' at Versailles. While some form of serfdom (the *barons* in Sicily and the *Junkers* in Prussia) lingered, the end of feudalism is associated with the French Revolution of 1789, even though in some places vestiges of feudalism lasted longer.

By the end of the eighteenth century, Britain and France constituted the European superpowers; Germany and Italy were only unified a century later. Moreover, the economies of Germany and Italy lagged far behind the level of income and wealth of Britain and France.[1] By the second half of the eighteenth century Britain defeated France on land and sea, in Europe, Asia, and North America. Victory enhanced the British Empire and foreign commerce, while leaving France to ponder why.[2]

The British economy of the eighteenth century reflected emerging capitalism influenced by the mercantile-industrial entrepreneurs; the State preserved and protected the rules of the game as substantially construed by these entrepreneurs. The British model provided the basis for the capitalist market economy, with a

---

1   Frederick the Great of Prussia (1712-1786), built a strong army, with the financial support of Britain who needed allies against the French. Italy was fractured into a dozen or so individual mini states that were partially controlled by foreign powers and consequently played a minimal independent role in European affairs.

2   During the Middle Ages both Britain and France achieved the consolidation of their respective nations. England became a unified state in 1066. During the Hundred Years War (1337-1453) between England and France, the English king claimed the dynastic right to be king of France and held much French territory. The English retreated from France thus enabling Louis XI (1461-1483) to expand the land under his control. The war weakened the feudal lords and furthered the consolidation of France as a kingdom. A century later, the Wars of Religion (1562-1598) witnessed the disintegration and the reconstruction of France culminating with Henry IV who issued the Edict of Nantes in 1598 that allowed the Huguenots limited religious toleration.

minimal role for the State, and British economic thought and policy represented one pole. Britain underwent its political revolution during the seventeenth century and progressed to individualism at least a century earlier than in France. In 1776, Adam Smith (1723-1790), as well as his predecessors, argued that economic liberalism, with few exceptions, such as public works and security beyond the scope of private enterprise, should be the model for the economic growth of nations.[3]

The North American Thirteen Colonies prospered, but for reasons that had relatively little to do with economic policy making. Prosperity seems to have derived more from the efficient use of abundant natural resources seized from the natives (the frontier), combined with best practice of the western world. After the American Revolution, the United States proved to be even more individualistic than Britain. Also, it continued to have a colonial economy in the sense that the umbilical cord remained firmly attached to the former mother country. Colonists in British North America came mainly from Britain; they brought with them religion, values (including a desire to escape from what they judged to be excessive and unwarranted economic regulation), language, legal codes, and political institutions representative government.

During the colonial period, each of the Thirteen Colonies exercised considerable economic autonomy with the caveat of serving the mother country. Before and after the Revolution mercantilism prevailed; each colony pursued an active policy of promotion and regulation.[4] American economic thought and policy, as well as prosperity, not surprisingly, derived from Britain, the mother country. British North America, and later the United States, consciously and unconsciously, modeled itself rather closely on Britain, modified by the profound influence of the frontier.

Most American exports after the Revolution still went to Britain and British lenders anchored the credit chain. Given the historic roots as well as the specific economic circumstances of British North America, including the desire of individuals to get rich quickly, there was little alternative but to follow path dependence. However, during the pre-revolutionary debate (1750-1775) many Americans, even while accepting mercantilist regulations in the domestic sector, questioned the entire mercantilist argument. In accordance with their individual interests, they contended that international free trade might be preferable to British mercantilist regulation.[5]

Different from Britain and the United States, Continental Europe supplied an alternative standard that advocated (and practiced) an enhanced role for the State in

3   Smith 1937, passim.
4   Such active policy inevitably leaves footprints in the sand of time but historical events and historical records are not necessarily identical. The historian therefore may discover proportionately more evidence of government intervention since such evidence tends to survive. Spengler 1949, p. 440.
5   McCusker and Menard 1991, pp. 331-332; Williams 1958, p. 419; Matson and Onuf 1990, pp. 15-25.

forging national economic policy.[6] Under the *Ancien Régime* of the seventeenth and eighteenth centuries, the State in France was absolutist and yet limited in its administrative ability to make its will effective. France instituted the *intendant* (directorat) system in a vain effort to achieve absolutist centralization since it retained too many administrative units and overlapping jurisdictions.

Jean-Baptiste Colbert (1661-1683), principal minister under Louis XIV, epitomized French mercantilist economic policies. At a time when Britain long had had a unified national market, Colbert pushed for a free internal market that was geographically segmented by tariffs thus counter productive for expanding commerce. While he protected industries via intricate mercantilist policies, Colbert subsidized foreign commerce through State-sponsored overseas trading companies. In contrast, British mercantilism left individuals greater scope for initiative than the French.

During the mid-1700s, while Britain gradually developed capitalist agriculture and industry as well as domestic and foreign commerce, France still debated agricultural marketing policies. French policy makers and theoreticians had a general awareness of the rise in population and the consequent pressure on food prices especially as resulted from the crisis years of 1763, 1766, and 1774.[7] Francois Quesnay (1694-1774), an agricultural fundamentalist, had presented a blue print for *limited* economic liberalism that advocated free trade for (only) farm products and *limited* political freedom for everybody.[8] As remarked by the sociologist Emile Durkheim (1858-1917), in France 'individualism has marched through history *pari passu* with étatisme'.[9] According to Durkheim, the State, in a sense, liberates the individual; its order and rules allow the individual to develop.[10]

It seems that in the seventeenth and eighteenth centuries France, the divisions by class and region required a strong central power to achieve a consolidated State. Regions furthest from Paris, and frequently added to French central control last, enjoyed the greatest autonomy, preserving their legal and judicial identity, provincial estates, local tariffs, and a favored position in national taxation. These conditions prevailed from the death of Louis XIV (1715) to the French Revolution (1789). To consolidate the nation and, in the search for efficiency and continuity in public administration, the French established the system of *les grandes écoles*

---

6   During the first half of the seventeenth century, the nobility attempted to rebel against the central power only to be definitively defeated in 1648 by Louis XIV (1643-1715) who became an absolute monarch. Louis XIV, an astute despot, controlled the nobility at Versailles at great expense. When he revoked the Edict of Nantes in 1685, France was weakened by the flight of numerous Huguenots to Britain, Germany and Holland, many of them skilled artisans.

7   The fall of the Bastille on July 14, 1789 was partially occasioned by the bad harvest of 1788 and the severe following winter as well as the cyclical movement of prices in the spring of 1789.

8   Schachter 1991, pp. 314-315.

9   Durkheim 1975, p. 171.

10 Rosenvallon 1989, p. 498.

(equivalent to schools of public administration) to provide trained administrators and high-level public servants.

Unlike France, during the eighteenth century Germany remained politically fragmented among hundreds of states, mini states and city-states.[11] During the eighteenth century Prussia emerged as the main German state challenging the power of Austria. The War of the Austrian Succession (1740-1748) brought the conflict over supremacy in the German orbit to a head and the Seven Years War (1756-1763) confirmed Prussia as a power of equal weight with Austria.[12] During the eighteenth century, Prussia emerged as the most influential German state, among the numerous other territorial entities that would form Germany in the next century.

Two monarchs ruled Prussia during almost the entire century, providing continuity: Frederick Wilhelm I (1712-1740) and Frederick II (the Great) (1740-1786). Frederick Wilhelm wanted to emulate Louis XIV of France in assuming absolute power but not in copying Louis's opulent Versailles living style, being parsimonious but also because Prussia lacked the resources. To compete with the major powers, Britain, France, and Austria, he devoted most of the public revenue to the army. Yet, his long reign provided stability and prepared the way for Prussia's expansion. His follower, Frederick II, combined the qualities of a warrior king with that of an enlightened despot; he was probably better educated and more intellectual than the other crowned heads in Europe. Neither Frederick William I nor Frederick II distinguished between the State and the dynastic monarchy.[13]

In conjunction with monarch's avarice under Frederick William and extravagance under Frederick II, wars generated fiscal problems. State policies were designed to raise revenue in accordance with the dominant theory of *Cameralism* (from *Kammereramt*, German word for treasury) a variety of mercantilism. Pursuing *Cameralist* policies, the State introduced new industries and expanded old ones in the hope of stimulating economic growth, increasing tax

---

11 By the mid-seventeenth century the Holy Roman Empire had become a sham and a hindrance for the multitude of states, kingdoms and principalities that were supposed to be subordinates. With the Treaty of Westphalia (1648) signed after the Thirty Years War, the Holy Roman Empire recognized the independence and sovereignty of the various constituent parts of the Empire. While the Empire nominally lingered until 1806, it had ceased to be an effective force a century and a half before that.

12 Austria was only partially German since it included Austria, Bohemia, and Hungary as its major constituents; in addition, the Italian duchy of Tuscany, where the Medici family died out in 1737, was controlled by proxy by a Habsburg duke related to the Austrian ruling family.

13 Frederick the Great waged wars against Austria; the Prussia-Austria struggle translated also in the more or less continuous warfare between the British and the French. In 1746, during the Dresden peace negotiations, after the Second Silesian War between Prussia and Austria, Frederick succeeded in gaining relative independence for the Prussian part of the shaky Holy Roman Empire by obtaining the privilege called *non-appellando* that freed the kingdom's courts from the imperial's courts jurisdiction. Asprey 1986, p. 366 notes.

income, and meeting domestic demands for goods that would otherwise have to be imported; the State also attempted to promote domestic commerce through a program of road improvement.

The largest of the German princedoms, Prussia hardly possessed a native commercial class, while the population was sparse especially in the newly conquered lands. To encourage immigration, the Prussian State established mortgage loan banks to provide agricultural credit (a State Bank was founded in 1765) and engaged in land reclamation. In other sectors, the State's roster of activities included subsidies, monopolies, tariffs, export restrictions, and the abolition of internal tolls, which stimulated industry and domestic trade. The State also engaged in mining and lumbering and became the largest grain producer on its own land.

Prussia's economy was hardly wholly in private hands but consisted of enterprises owned and/or administered by the State. Throughout the eighteenth century, the northern German States practiced mercantilism. Liberal economic policies were tried more often in southern states such as Baden, Bavaria, Saxony, and Wurttemberg. Recognizing that expanding the market would result in positive economic consequences, the Prussian monarchy attempted to expand the free trade area within Prussia but Germany was so splintered that free trade between and among the multitude of German states was hindered by border impediments.[14]

Italy had experienced similarities and many differences from Germany. During the eighteenth century Italy was a conglomerate of independent, semi-independent and dependent states.[15] Venice, Florence, and Milan as well as other city-states held their own for various periods of time. These city-states contributed to the stability and socio-economic development of northern Italy; many of the Italian city-states expanded into the surrounding countryside and those controlled from abroad attempted to achieve independence. The Italian Renaissance weakened papal and imperial authority while facilitating an intellectual and cultural explosion in the city-states of the North. The South developed differently when in the fifteenth century the mainland South and Sicily became Spanish possessions and the quasi-independent Kingdom of the Two Sicilies under the Spanish Bourbons, after 1729,

In 1522, Francis, *Il Milanese*, lost the Milan area, to Spanish rule, that lasted until 1714, when Milan was transferred to Austria. During the eighteenth century, the Austrian Habsburg dynasty's (1282-1918) dominions, included among other central and eastern European possessions, Lombardy, Parma and in the South, Naples and Sicily. In the early eighteenth century the duchy of Savoy (Piedmont) added the island of Sardinia and established the Kingdom of Sardinia in 1720.

---

14   Fear 1997a, p.136, citing Sheehan 1989, p. 40.
15   The disintegration of the Roman Empire triggered the evolving self-governing political entities in the Italian peninsula; political and social fragmentation during the Middle Ages and the Renaissance persisted and individual cities or communes successfully asserted their independence.

Piedmont-Sardinia acted in a similar way to Prussia in Germany, if less powerful as a catalyst in the Italian unifying process, for a century and more thereafter.[16]

During the eighteenth century, the French enlightenment and liberal ideas from Britain spread to Italy, breaking traditional values and institutions and eventually bringing about profound convulsions, and ultimately progress. While mercantilism exemplified State economic policy, regardless of the exceptions, the debate focused on grain trade restrictions. Aware of English and French thinking, Italians were influenced by Adam Smith and the classical economists. Some Italian economic writers proposed free trade grain policy adapted to Italian circumstances; others accepted public regulation as normal and therefore viewed protection as a special case.

Italy continued to be divided among several individual political entities until the middle of the nineteenth century and, therefore, could not easily compete with the rising national monarchies. It had a backward economy during the eighteenth century, at least in part because of political fragmentation and military invasion, but also because of the shift of trade from the Mediterranean Sea to the Atlantic Ocean. Furthermore, foreign powers, Austria, France, and Spain controlled much Italian territory directly or indirectly. Italy had to wait another three quarters of a mere century before becoming other than a geographic expression.

Britain

The English national market originated in 1066 with the Norman Conquest, when William I the Conqueror (1027-1087), subjugated much of the then Saxon-Scandinavian island.[17] William I transformed the contested land into a country with a French-speaking aristocracy and a social and political culture strongly influenced by that of northern France. He placed local governments firmly under his control. In his Domesday Survey of 1086, William asserted rights over his subjects as a feudal lord over his vassals. Furthermore, the Domesday Book compiled a property register for tax assessment.[18] Among other things, the Domesday Book surveyed and recorded the widespread use of water mills, which, of necessity, concerned water rights adjudicated through the Royal courts. From

---

16   By the terms of the Treaty of Utrecht (1713) Sardinia was awarded to Austria and Sicily to Savoy, but Sicily and Sardinia were exchanged in 1720. The Kingdom of the Two Sicilies was thereby reconstituted. Savoy came to be called 'Sardinia'.

17   Neither Wales nor Scotland initially constituted part of Great Britain. England conquered Wales in the thirteenth century. James VI of Scotland became James I of England upon the death of Queen Elizabeth (1603); the union of England and Scotland adopted the name of Great Britain.

18   Royal commissioners collected information in this 'book' as to size, resources, and present and past land ownership. The Domesday Book supplied a unique record as a basis for taxation and administration; for example, the Domesday Book recorded 5000 water wheels (water power).

that time on, England constituted the first European national centralized political entity with fairly well defined boundaries, more so than any other medieval political entity.[19]

Winston Churchill declared that England owed its good government to its bad kings. Certainly, such events as the Magna Carta (1215), the Petition of Right (1629), and the Bill of Rights (1689) constitute milestones in the evolution of the restraints imposed on the monarch. As a consequence of the fiscal revolution of the seventeenth century, the landed aristocracy tamed the king. When George III attempted to 'be a king' (1760-1820), he had to work through Parliament. One century after the Glorious Revolution (1688-1689) neither ideas nor actions stood much chance of adoption unless acceptable to the small minority holding economic and political power.

Britain's island status obviated a large peacetime standing army or expensive fortifications and therefore burdened less the State's treasury less. On the other hand, throughout the Second Hundred Years War (1689-1763), Britain served as the paymaster for its allies; its subventions, as well as its diplomacy, kept allied armies in the field. By 1700, Britain was wealthy enough and had a sufficiently effective taxation system so that it could bear the burden without undue strain. While tax farming prevailed in France and elsewhere on the Continent until the French Revolution in 1789, Britain bureaucratized the central Treasury administration and terminated the tax farming of customs in 1661, that is, before the Glorious Revolution. Britain's more rapid communication and transportation systems, owing among other things to its smaller size than France, favored earlier bureaucratization.[20] Thus, when Smith inveighed against mercantilism, Britain could be simultaneously mercantilist and minimalist. In short, political freedom, as well as a flourishing House of Commons to which men were elected as individuals rather than as members of an estate, minimized the role of the State in the economy.

---

19 A century later, Henry II (1154-1189) founder of the Angevin (Plantagenet) dynasty, restored and extended royal authority and instituted legal reforms. In particular, the royal court sent judges on circuit with increasing regularity. These itinerant judges formed a rudimentary national judicial system, which centralized the English polity and political economy. The 'baronial' class claimed the right to participate in the government and intensified pressures to restrain the power of the monarch. These constraints began with the Magna Charta (1215), which the barons forced on King John (1167-1216). During the War of the Roses of the second half of the fifteenth century two noble houses contested for the right to succeed to the throne. This dynastic struggle ended in 1485 with the establishment of the Tudor dynasty and the coronation of Henry VII (1485-1509) whose government was both modern and national. Henry VIII (1509-1547) broke the papacy's hold on England thus setting an independent course for the nation, which allowed the king to govern free of external claims; consequently, the State became a still more cohesive entity.

20 Kiser and Kane 2001, pp. 189, 217.

National Economic Integration

Local transit tolls disappeared in England by the end of fifteenth century, which resulted in the largest integrated European market. The Tudors and the Stuarts were forced to rule through Parliament, which originated during the thirteenth century and gradually asserted its right to control taxing and spending. The outcome of the two seventeenth century revolutions was a constitutional monarchy with a sharing of political power between the monarch and the propertied minority who controlled Parliament. By the late seventeenth century, the monarch could no longer use public funds without the consent of the Parliament. Having trimmed the power of the monarchy, Parliament declared its supremacy, though the State intervened less in the economy than heretofore. Furthermore, a centralized, but not definitely absolutist, Britain had a constitutional monarchy with a long-established parliament dominated by the landed aristocracy. Control of taxing, spending, and commercial policy rested in the hands of the House of Commons elected by a comparatively small number of wealthy taxpayers.[21]

Although inheriting certain institutions and policies from the Middle Ages, Britain allowed the market considerable scope, even if it meant the ultimate demise of vested interests through creative destruction. Having originated during the early thirteenth century, the guilds reached the end of their economic usefulness to society as a whole by the sixteenth century; until then the guilds controlled apprenticeship and therefore entry into various occupations.   However, the Elizabethan Statute of Artificers (otherwise known as the Statute of Apprentices) of 1563, while recognizing the already existing guilds, placed them under public authority and instituted statutory apprenticeship.

The innovation of the domestic or 'putting-out' system meant that industry moved outside towns and therefore beyond the reach of the guilds and the local governments. This system stemmed from varied organizational and technological innovations and the market forces unleashed by the absence of minute regulations. Both the guilds and the later domestic system prescribed some industrial practices and proscribed others.   While the guilds stressed the traditional and the maintenance of the status quo, the domestic system, for example, in the wool textile industry, brought to the fore merchants who advanced capital and sub-divided tasks to reduce the cost of production, and augmented profits.

If only because the monarchy had lost the ability, State enterprises constituted a relative rarity in Britain during the eighteenth century. In contrast with other countries, which initiated state enterprises to manufacture selected luxury products such as crystal, porcelain, and tapestries, a British state enterprise built warships for the navy. Henry VIII (1509-1547) founded the Royal Naval Dockyard, in 1514, comparable to the Arsenal in Venice, which survived as a naval base until the early 1980s.

---

21   Sée 1926, pp. 107-110.

Development of British Capitalism

During the eighteenth century, the archaic system of guilds and apprenticeship began to dissolve. Legislation governing apprenticeship was repealed and in some cases town corporations ceased to enforce the licensing practices. In 1756, Parliament declined to extend apprenticeship regulations to the rapidly growing textile industry and similar action applied to other industries in later years. The final demise of apprenticeship in 1814 seems not to have been directly related to Adam Smith's polemic in the *Wealth of Nations* against mercantilist policy although he inveighed against apprenticeship as an impediment to the functioning of the labor market.[22] Smith argued that low wages, which stemmed from the apprenticeship system, led to inefficient workers because these apprentices were not always well trained. Furthermore, the hardly impartial justices of the peace from the Tudor era (1485-1603) until the mid 1700s controlled wages and prices. By the 1800s, the State no longer regulated wages as it had since the Statute of Laborers (1351), enacted in the wake of the Black Death.

Despite multitudinous rules and regulations (some nominally fell under the rubric of consumer protection), the domestic sector of the British economy during the eighteenth century became and remained relatively free, with some unintended aid to industry. On the other hand, a mixture of incomplete *laissez faire* and mercantilist policies were introduced. No grand theory could possibly account for permitting the miller a range of decision-making denied to the baker. The size of bread (regulated according to standard) prevailed in many towns. Furthermore, in 1758 the law specified how many loaves of bread must be baked from a quantity of flour.[23]

No wonder that Smith found the laws circumscribing the baker such an easy target. What others ascribed to the watchful eye of the government, Smith credited to the harmony of interests between the baker and his customers. Nevertheless, opinion, law, and a weak bureaucracy (justice of the peace exercised administrative functions but it was a part time position) exercised less influence than earlier. The market became more important while respect for laws and public opinion declined.[24] In that place and time, 'government was both corrupt and inefficient'.[25] This duo may have induced Smith to undervalue government intervention as against the market.[26]

22 Rule 1992, pp. 314-315; Lane 1978, p. 85. The message of the *Wealth of Nations* spread rapidly in Continental Europe with translations in German (1776), French (1778-1779), and Italian (1790). In the young United States, Alexander Hamilton was cognizant of Smith and directly, but without mentioning Smith by name, rebutted Smith in his *Report on Manufactures* (1790).
23 Ashton 1955, p. 55.
24 Ashton 1955, p. 65.
25 Robbins 1976, p. 177.
26 Kindleberger 1976, p. 12; Lane 1978, pp. 92-93.

The Agricultural Revolution

Starting in the sixteenth century land tenancy began to change institutionally. Under the traditional medieval system of landholding, the units of cultivation were both scattered and quite small. The community exercised considerable control over the agricultural practices of the individual cultivator, resulting in low productivity and consequent dearth. During the sixteenth century a number of large landowners were allowed to enclose common lands if all owners agreed voluntarily. Under the cover of these exemptions, limited areas were enclosed during the sixteenth and seventeenth centuries, but the general rule confining the right to enclose still prevailed.

By the eighteenth and nineteenth centuries, privately lobbied acts of Parliament conferred the power to enclose on the majority of owners, which accelerated the number of acres enclosed. An enclosure act took a village's commonly farmed open land and parceled it out to individual owners, who could then fence the land and farm as they chose. Enclosure encouraged the market in land to flourish and induced and/or drove the dispossessed from the land to work in industry. The price of wheat in Britain increased substantially during 1760-1790, offset by importation from Ireland. Relatively unimportant in the Agricultural Revolution, enclosure eventuated in larger agricultural units, which resulted in scale economies, innovation in process and product, increased productivity and yield, and a market in both land and products of the land that collectively eased the grain shortage.[27]

Private Enterprise

National interest and policy shaped economic activity at home and abroad. The creation of the public debt, as a result of the financial revolution of the seventeenth century, immeasurably strengthened public credit enabling the British government to borrow at a comparatively low interest rate. By securing the right of private property, the public debt fostered saving and investment. In addition, between the second half of the sixteenth and the early seventeenth century, Britain chartered and conferred monopolistic trading privileges on half a dozen overseas trading companies and granted them the power to mobilize military forces to protect these privileges against all comers. The most successful of these private enterprises, the East India Company (1600) survived for two and a half centuries. Only in 1793 were interlopers, that is, British subjects, allowed to trade with the subcontinent controlled by the East India Company although legal and illegal traders sometime hampered this monopoly.[28] One observer claims that in 'Corporate Britain', the State shored up the monopolies in international trade, through high tariffs, heavy duties, and subsidies.[29]

---

27   Thomas 1985, p. 141; Ambrosoli 1997, p. 412.
28   Ashton 1955, p. 130.
29   Vries 2002, p. 73.

A self-sufficient empire remained a constant objective of British statecraft. Having defeated its rivals, Britain emerged as the major European power during the eighteenth century. Even in 1700, Britain was an economic force to be reckoned with and British institutions and resources combined with relatively relaxed mercantilist policies to improve its economic standing. Britain ranked highest among the eighteenth century world powers with regard to domestic product, per capita income, and economic growth, and excelled in productivity in virtually every single sector.

Mercantilism and Laissez Faire

Britain relied heavily on foreign commerce, which the State regulated much more closely than domestic commerce. For instance, starting in the mid-seventeenth century, Britain began to use the power of the State to regulate international economic relations. Britain placed limitations on the export of technology and the emigration of skilled workers. Starting in the late seventeenth century, Britain forbade the export of specific machinery; complete free trade for machinery was not established until 1843. Britain introduced the Navigation Acts that obliged empire shippers to use only British carriers. Economic nationalism or mercantilism also governed trade between Britain and its far-flung empire.

The two seventeenth century Navigation Acts, in particular the Navigation Act of 1651, deliberately weakened the grasp of the Dutch as Europe's chief carriers and middlemen and combined to transfer the *entrepôt* from Amsterdam to London. This successful British mercantilist policy helped surmount the Dutch lead by 1750 at the latest. Adam Smith defended the Navigation Acts because these acts helped Britain overcome Dutch maritime supremacy despite his overall critique of such interference with natural law. Thus, regardless of ideology, political goals transcended economic considerations; the State adopted mercantilist policies when deemed strategically necessary in the pursuit of power politics. Only long after it had achieved industrial leadership during the nineteenth century did Britain replace protection and regulation with *laissez faire*.

The Board of Trade

Britain founded the Lord Commissioners of Trade and Plantations, commonly known as the Board of Trade in 1696. Parliament established the Board of Trade, an investigatory and advisory body subordinate to Parliament, to exercise general jurisdiction over colonial and international trade affairs. The Parliament required the Board of Trade to consider carefully the balance of trade with each particular country and to advise on means for correcting unfavorable and securing favorable balances. The entire trade policy, with all its complicated system of treaties, restrictions, and drawbacks was devised to accomplish this goal.

The Board of Trade, composed of mercantilist members who represented the merchant class, gave merchants an institution through which they could express their views and it recognized the power of the merchants. On the other hand, offsetting the vested interests of the merchants, the Board of Trade included experts who weighed the lobbyists versus the claims of public policy. Among the early members of the Board of Trade we find such notables as Sir Josiah Child, merchant, Governor of the East India Company and economist (1630-1699), Charles Devenant, Inspector of Foreign Trade (1656-1714), and John Locke, philosopher (1632-1704).

The mercantilist Board of Trade was charged with the duty of making the colonies and, for that matter, foreign trade profitable to Britain. This forum assuredly acknowledged the influence of the merchants in the polity; Adam Smith, for one, noted that merchants influenced the councils of State. The evidence is overwhelming that the middle class could exert enough political suasion so that frequently its interests, viewed as consistent with the national interest, proved decisive in the formation of economic policy.[30]

Market Intervention

On the other hand, indicating a willingness not to regulate the totality of colonial commerce after the final defeat of France in 1763, Britain created Caribbean free ports, which allowed trade between the French and Spanish West Indian islands and the Thirteen Colonies.[31] Britain formulated a mercantilist policy that affected the Thirteen Colonies both positively and negatively. Also, the State played an important role in protecting mercantile endeavors. British expenditure on the military between 1680 and 1815 equaled the amount of British exports (or imports) for the period.[32] True enough, in 1786, England and France signed the Eden Treaty; according to this trade agreement, France lowered its rates on British textiles and Britain reduced its duties on French wines to the level of those of Britain's traditional ally wines on Portugal.

British economic policy reflected moneyed class interest bias, with the State nominally seeking to promote economic growth, if only as an adjunct to nation building. However, if necessary, Britain did not hesitate to regulate the domestic market. Probably because of pressure from British owners of colonial plantations as well as the productivity differential, Britain fostered tobacco growing in the Thirteen Colonies and prohibited the cultivation of tobacco in Britain. Also, the fishery sector was protected and regulated as the nursery of the navy. Furthermore, the Monopolies Act of 1624 granted monopoly for a limited number of years for inventions. In 1681 the infant industry argument became an integral part of economic policy.[33]

---

30   Nettels 1938, pp. 374, 553-556; Wilson 1968, p. 167.
31   Appleby 1978, p. 103; Koehn 1994, p. 199.
32   Vries 2002, p. 79.
33   Clapham 1963, pp. 265, 269; Lipson 1959, p. 170.

To assist its textile industry, Britain subsidized the production of indigo, a plant that yields a blue dye stuff, in British North America; after the American Revolution, Britain obtained indigo on the open market at lower cost. Also, the Iron Act of 1750 prohibited the erection of new iron finishing mills in the British North American colonies although allowing existing facilities to continue production. Similarly, Britain later added iron to the list of enumerated commodities that could be exported only to Britain, which aided the expansion of semi-finished iron production in British North America.

To foster shipbuilding and shipping for both maritime and naval supremacy, Britain treated colonial-built ships as if they had been built in the Mother Country. London was developed as an *entrepôt* to encourage European goods to pass through England and English customs en route to British North America. Collectively these measures enhanced the British carrying trade and, as mentioned, London emerged as the *entrepôt* by the mid-eighteenth century. On the other hand, prior to the American Revolution, competition from the low cost lumber of the Thirteen Colonies adversely affected the British shipbuilding industry; after the American Revolution, the shipbuilding industry in Britain recovered.[34]

Essentially no internal trade barriers existed within Britain after the Act of Union (1707), which economically united England with Scotland. The Union had some important economic results, for example, by bringing Scotland inside the ambit of the Navigation Acts. It encouraged a free flow of ideas, particularly in agriculture, and gave limited state assistance to the linen industry.[35] During the eighteenth century Britain and its colonies constituted the world's largest customs union. The British population had the highest standard of living in the world, mainly because workers received higher wages than on the Continent. This stemmed partly from the choice of specialization and quantity production, by far more prevalent than in France.[36]

The State's Role in Developing Transportation Networks

The evolution of the British transportation system always has been constrained by the country's pivotal geographic features. Not only is Britain an island but also the island is small enough so that no point is more than 150 miles from the coast. Britain developed its canals relatively late, being well endowed with rivers and therefore having ready access to coastal shipping. These factors combined to enhance the importance of coastal shipping relative to the much higher cost of overland commerce.

Although an isolated event, the construction of the Exeter Ship Canal (1564-1566) is surely worth examining. Exeter lies on the river Exe about ten miles above this river's entry into the English Channel but by the thirteenth century sea-

34   Clapham 1963, p. 276; Rule 1992, pp. 127-128.
35   Rae 1974, pp. 62-63.
36   Crouzet 1985, pp. 41-42.

going vessels could no longer come this far up the river. The city corporation obtained a private act from Parliament and built this canal. From the fifteenth to the eighteenth centuries, Exeter thrived as a cloth making and cloth-trading town. One of the ten historic regional centers, Exeter's population doubled from 5,000 in 1500 to 10,000 in 1700, and increased to 17,000 in 1800, owing in part to the canal which afforded Exeter improved access to the English Channel.[37]

The Canal Age (1760-1830) in Britain began in the middle of the eighteenth century. These small-scale critical improvements were undertaken largely by private voluntary initiative, with little or no direct government finance or, indeed, encouragement. Instead, Britain experienced non-governmental projecting and financing of transport improvements. Local property owners (and others) initiated canal projects motivated by public spirit.

General incorporation is universally a nineteenth century phenomenon; like other European countries, Britain did not have a general corporation (joint stock company) law until the mid-nineteenth century. Therefore, prior to that time, the organization of each corporation required a separate private bill, which had to be submitted to Parliament and then steered carefully through the legislative process. Typically, Parliament chartered each corporation to build a canal in a private bill and conferred the privilege of limited liability and the power of eminent domain but imposed various restrictions on the tolls and the rates of return.[38]

In 1759, Parliament chartered the Duke of Bridgewater to build a canal from Worsley to Manchester without the power of eminent domain; since the canal interfered with the private property of others, the Duke of Bridgewater had to negotiate with individual property owners without the aegis of the State. Completed in 1761, the Bridgewater canal extended deep into the coalfields. Exceptional as a canal owner as well as a carrier, the State fixed maximum freight rates for the Duke as well as the selling price of coal. The Bridgewater canal proved that canals could be directly profitable as enterprises as well as through induced externalities.[39]

Contemporaneously with canals, turnpikes were also constructed by local voluntary initiative and by the private sector rather than by the State. The vital difference was that canals depended on water sources (rivers) while turnpikes could be constructed any place. During the eighteenth century, Parliament designed and sanctioned individual turnpike trusts by private acts, given the

---

37   Hadfield 1968, pp. 19, 33, 45, 209.
38   Hadfield 1968, p. 78; Ward 1974, p. 78; Hawke and Higgins 1981, p. 232, Rule 1992, p. 150.
39   In 1759, the Duke of Bridgewater, the founder of British inland navigation, built the Bridgewater canal from his estates at Worsley to Manchester as an alternative to river transportation and horse-drawn wagons. The Duke constructed this ten-mile canal, the first to take a route independent of any river, supplying part of the capital himself and borrowing the remainder. In 1776, he extended the canal from Manchester to Liverpool, an additional 30 miles. Lipson 1959, p. 232; Ashton 1955, pp. 74-75, 82-83, 88; Chaloner 1953, pp. 181-185.

absence of a general incorporation law, typically with a life span of twenty years. These trusts undertook to build and maintain relatively short, about thirty miles or so, stretches of improved roads, which charged users tolls, thus ending the traditional right to travel free on the king's highway. Turnpike trusts were not commercial profit-oriented enterprises but were initiated and managed by local public-spirited trustees who sought better access to markets by selling trust bonds. 'The great majority of trust income was derived from the tolls granted by local acts, the trustees often mortgaged these tolls...to provide funds for initial road improvements.'[40]

Parliament authorized the first toll road in 1663. By 1707, one witnessed the first true turnpike administered by trustees rather than by the local justice of the peace. The turnpike trusts could take land by eminent domain with the price ultimately determined by the justice of the peace. The general Turnpike Act of 1773 supplemented these private acts. During the turnpike era the public and private worked hand in hand; the public enabled, while the private invested, owned, and managed. The central government regulated, rather than initiated, by restricting profits as well as mandating wagonloads, wheel dimensions, and horsepower. Private initiative proved critical with a minimalist State.[41]

Social Classes and Social Welfare

Owing in part to primogeniture, only the eldest son inherited the title and the younger sons had to make their way in the world as best as they could, members of the aristocracy took an active (or, if necessary, a silent) part in economic activity without incurring the loss of social status. In addition, the exclusion of the Dissenters from the Anglican Church, the army, and the government left business enterprise as a viable option for the ambitious, the talented, and the venturesome. Thus, by the end of the seventeenth century, at least a small but significant segment of the middle class, both rural and urban, made its voice heard directly, as well as indirectly, in the political arena.

After the Glorious Revolution and throughout the eighteenth century all owners of land that yielded at least 40 shillings a year elected the members of the House of Commons. Towns with varying suffrages elected the bulk of members. Out of the combined English and Welsh population of perhaps six to seven million, only 250,000 (or less than a half percent of the total) adult males had the suffrage. Even in the absence of a party system, the existence of political factions provided an entering wedge for all manner of common interests to express themselves to the ruling oligarchy.

By the standards and values of a much later era, Britain did not accomplish much regarding welfare legislation. Prior to the Reformation, the poor had been the

---

40 Albert 1972, p. 93.
41 Ashton 1955, pp. 79, 81-83, 87; Pawson 1977, pp. 26, 84-85, 161, 169; Pawson 1979, p. 145; Rule 1992, pp. 222-223.

concern of the Catholic Church; the Reformation confiscated the financial resources of the Church while augmenting those of the State. Under the Tudors, the State acknowledged its social responsibility for welfare and adopted paternalistic social legislation designed both to force people to work and to relieve absolute destitution. The Elizabethan Poor Law of 1603 supplemented the voluntary charity of individuals distributed by the Anglican Church; the State through taxation transferred some money from the rich to the poor. Later characterized as the 'Old Poor Law', Elizabethan Poor Law of 1603 lasted for more than two centuries.[42] Britain increased poor relief during the 1790s in response to, among other causes, the French Revolution.[43]

Conclusions

During the eighteenth century the major difference between the Anglo-Americans economic liberalism and the Continental limited economic liberalism pivoted on the role of the State. The Anglo-American version posited a minimal role for the State, with markets relatively unhampered and goods and services moving comparatively free of obstacles, in spite of a plethora of health and safety regulations, many inherited from an earlier era. Hardly an ideologue, Smith acknowledged that private individuals acting through the market could not perform certain activities efficiently; the State set regulations and rules, as well as providing education, defense, and some infrastructure; true enough, Britain's infrastructure in the eighteenth century stemmed mostly from private voluntary initiative.

Different from France, a greater symbiosis prevailed between British scientists and scholars and early industrialists. The British founded the Royal Society of London, the oldest scientific society in Britain, in 1662; during the seventeenth century less than half of this Society's papers were devoted to pure science while more than half were related to socio-economic needs. In France, the State attempted to influence a plethora of intellectuals and the so-called '*philosophes*' that were prone to abstractions rather than practical pursuits.[44] The king of France encouraged and founded such associations, whereas in Britain, individuals voluntarily founded such groups, the crown playing a purely nominal role, if that. A century later, that is, during 1766-1791 the Lunar Society of Birmingham, a key manufacturing center, and the home of the Boulton and Watt steam engine enterprise, actively promoted science and its application to industry.

British mercantilism was less comprehensive than the French counterpart. It appears that during the eighteenth century, the role of the State in the British economy was marginal but by no means trivial. For one, the central government employed 16,000 civil servants (many engaged in the tax collection bureaucracy which helped Britain to end tax farming), the largest number per capita for the

---

42   Fraser 1973, p. 93; Appleby 1978, p. 131.
43   Lindert 1998, pp. 112, 128-129, 134.
44   Musson 1972, pp. 20, 50; Crouzet 1985, p. 38.

period.[45] Britain had a greater ability to tax than France owing to the existence of an effective Parliament; considerable overlap prevailed between the wealthy taxpayers and the restricted number of voters and, furthermore, no tax-exempt class existed as in France before 1789.

There were rare instances of direct State intervention but there were no State manufacturing enterprises Owing to the financial revolution of the preceding century, in 1700, Britain, a relatively rich nation possessed a well-developed financial market with a prevailing low rate of interest, which facilitated capital accumulation and thereby reducing the cost of capital-intensive investments. The comparatively small scale and local nature of social overhead capital projects generally did not exceed the financial resources of local investors.

No one of these factors, in and of itself, proved decisive in defining the scope of the State in the British economy. All, however, were longstanding and fundamental in defining the parameters within which the State dealt with the economy; never at arm's distance, equally the embrace of the State never smothered the individual or the market. More to the point, the State's limited reach antedated Adam Smith's economic theory as well as the accompanying *laissez faire* ideology.[46]

Even though the bulk of the middle class, living in towns, lacked the vote it had a voice in the House of Commons, The House of Commons was accessible to the broad currents of popular opinion, especially since the younger sons of the aristocracy did not inherit land or title, thus lessening the degree of social stratification. Also, intermarriage took place between merchants and landed aristocracy – more common than elsewhere, perhaps because Britain had a weaker military tradition and as an island nation, a much smaller army than France; although the British sent relatively few troops to the Continent, they subsidized the armies of their allies. Finally, the boroughs (incorporated towns) had representatives in Commons and the towns elected the bulk of the members.

United States

Both before and after independence, United States economic polices closely followed economic thought developed from John Locke (1632-1704) to Adam Smith (1723-1790). These ideas included economic individualism that is, equal opportunity, sanctity of contracts, property rights, competition, as well as limited government.[47] People assumed that the forces unleashed by an unhampered individualism could control external forces and nature itself, contributing to the betterment of the self and consequently increase the well being of society. Since

---

45   Vries 2002, p. 105.
46   Pawson 1979, p. 225.
47   The constitutions of both the federal government and the states are based on this
       limited government concept.

individual rights and private property were deemed sacrosanct, the State, or the government representing the State, existed to defend these rights.[48]

During the seventeenth century, with the singular exception of Georgia (established in 1732), British chartered overseas trading companies, which founded colonies in North America. For example, the Virginia Company, and proprietors such as William Penn and George Calvert, combined with lower and middle class individuals seeking land and economic opportunity as well as refuge from political, economic, or religious oppression, founded the Thirteen Colonies in British North America. The passive British government essentially provided 'hunting licenses' the various colonies, individually or collectively, adopted diverse economic policies constrained by the particular frontier conditions, blended with the British mercantilist example to enhance their prosperity.

These policies were subject to British imperial rules, consistent with their charters and in accordance with interests of the property holding voters and the various and sundry colonial governments adopted policies that promoted and regulated their individual economies.   For instance, the colonies encouraged exports and discouraged imports.   A very high proportion of adult males, many more than in Britain, owned enough property to vote in the two most populous colonies, Massachusetts and Virginia.   The Mother Country's policy of 'salutary neglect' (1721-1742) left the Thirteen Colonies, by and large, to their own devices. Although British mercantilist regulations affecting the Thirteen Colonies began in the mid-seventeenth century, the colonists felt increasingly pinched a century later.

As a whole, the Thirteen Colonies individually enacted consumer protection legislation as well as laws aimed at attracting entrepreneurs, capital, and labor. The Thirteen Colonies grew wheat, tobacco, corn, rice, and indigo, among other crops, for both local consumption and export.   In addition, since the colonists desired to replicate the European world they had known, they produced a wide variety of manufactured goods.   High land transportation costs dictated that most manufactured products be consumed locally or shipped to nearby areas.

The Colonies, the State, and Slavery

The southern colonies prospered with a plantation economy based on slavery even though most whites did not own either plantations or slaves. To be sure, slaves had been obtained from Black Africa from time immemorial, both by the Roman Empire (a majority of the city of Rome's population was made up of slaves or former slaves from conquered lands) and later by Moslems, both of which enslaved blacks and whites indiscriminately. Also, slavery existed in Medieval Europe; in particular, slavery prevailed in Mediterranean Europe during the fifteenth century, that is, before the Age of Discovery. Slavery existed in the Iberian world as well as France, and Italy and the slaves comprised North Africans, Greeks, Turks, Slavs, and Black Africans.

---

48   Lodge 1986, pp. 9-12, 100.

The State circa 1500 and before in Western Europe (and elsewhere) recognized the legitimacy of slavery. Slaves were property, seemingly sanctified by the Bible, as well as the example of ancient Greece and Rome. Through at least the nineteenth century many religious doctrines insisted that masters and slaves accept their status, because some men were born to be free and some were born to be slaves. Spain introduced African slaves in the Western Hemisphere in 1501, and everyone followed suit.

The establishment of colonial empires in North and South America dramatically altered the circumstances. Plantation agriculture, especially cotton, sugar, and tobacco, relied on slavery. In the sixteenth century neither Catholic nor Protestant Churches objected to slavery, which they justified as a secular institution. Spain imported about one hundred thousand African slaves to its empire in Mexico, Peru, and elsewhere in the New World by 1560. Also, slaves furnished the labor in France's West Indian sugar colonies. Owing to the 1789 Revolution, the French temporarily abolished slavery in their colonies in 1794; Napoleon reinstated colonial slavery, only to be permanently abolished after the 1848 Revolution.

The situation in Britain profoundly affected British North America. The Royal African Company (1672), a chartered company, held a monopoly of English trade with Africa between 1672 and 1698, and governed the English possessions on the West African coast until 1750. This Company supplied slaves to Spanish America after 1713, thus initiating the most active period of the British slave trade. John Locke, the preeminent seventeenth century English liberal political theorist, invested in the Royal African Company, thereby by inference endorsing slavery. Like the French West Indian sugar colonies, the British counterparts depended on slave labor.[49]

In 1772, Lord Chief Justice William Mansfield ruled in the Somerset case that English law did not support slavery, thus laying the basis for freeing England's 15 thousand slaves. Adam Smith espoused antislavery views in his *Wealth of Nations* and therefore placed slavery beyond the bounds to which *laissez faire* applied. Finally, 1833 witnessed the abolition of slavery in the British colonies. In short, the State initially could construe *laissez faire* so as to implicitly justify the ownership of one person by another and then explicitly deny that right. The end of slavery in the British Empire contributed to the later emancipation in the United States. Society establishes property rights as well as destroys them.[50]

Colonization began in Virginia in 1607; slavery followed in 1619, the same year as the founding of the Virginia House of Burgesses (the colonial legislature). Some contend that although slaves existed, slavery as an institution did not develop until half a century later, but before the end of the seventeenth century the legal

---

49   Spain granted Britain the *asiento*, that is, the lucrative privilege of providing the Spanish colonies with African slaves. Much of the wealth of Bristol and Liverpool was built upon the slave trade.

50   Davis 1984, pp. 118, 433-435, 487.

status of slavery as property had been solidified. Slavery became much more important economically and numerically in the eighteenth century than in the seventeenth. In 1776, British North America had 500,000 slaves, mostly south of Pennsylvania, although slavery existed in all of the Thirteen Colonies. In addition to working as manual laborers and servants, slaves proliferated in the commercial cultivation of indigo, rice, and tobacco as cash staple crops.

The arduous and prolonged process of ending slavery in the United States commenced with the American Revolution. In 1778, Virginia prohibited the further importation of slaves, and by 1790 most of the other states had done likewise. However, South Carolina, which in 1787 had prohibited the importation of slaves, reopened its ports to the slave trade in 1803. In accordance with the Constitution, by 1807, Congress prohibited the further importation of slaves. The Massachusetts Constitution of 1780 declared that all men are free and equal by birth; a judicial decision in 1783 interpreted this clause as having the effect of abolishing slavery. Similarly, in 1799 New York passed a gradual emancipation law, with the final abolition of slavery occurring in 1827. All states north of Delaware gradually abolished slavery by about 1820.

Land Policy

Large-scale agriculture existed both before and after the Revolution, using slaves, indentured servants, and wage laborers. However, the sheer abundance of land coupled with the need of state governments to maximize revenue, resulted in land being sold in small tracts. The patroon system, which sold land only in large tracts to settlers, retarded the growth of New York before the Revolution. The American Revolution did not result in a vast land redistribution program but, nevertheless, had several consequences, which favored small farm settlement. First, the estates of Loyalists who fled to Canada and Britain, after the Revolution, were confiscated and sold at auction. Second, entailed primogeniture ended. Lastly, small farm settlement was favored in the conflict between statute law and frontier custom as was indicated by squatters' rights.

No general British land policy prevailed before the Revolution and each colony fended for itself. Land, that is, raw unoccupied land existed on such a prodigious scale that every proprietor, private or State, had to market land aggressively to derive any income from land either in rents, sales, or taxes. After the Revolution, the federal government, keeping in mind its revenue needs, had land disposal and management of the public domain as one of its principal tasks. Under the Articles of Confederation, an Act (1787) fixed the auction price minimum at $1 per acre. The Federal Act of 1796 set the price at $2 an acre for 640 acres while that of 1800 kept the price the same but halved the minimum acreage to 320 acres. Finally, in 1862 the Homestead Act granted 160-acre allotments virtually free to settlers.

State Intervention by the Mother Country

The economic success of the colonies drew the attention of competing interests in the Mother Country, which did not have a uniformly benign attitude towards potential competition. Starting in the 1650s and revised administratively and comprehensively in 1696, Britain imposed new mercantilist rules and regulations on colonial exports and imports as well as on colonial manufacturing. All imports had to originate in Britain and a small but ever-increasing number of 'enumerated' products had to be shipped first to Britain and then re-exported. After 1691 Britain pursued a naval stores and forest policy to supply naval stores and ship masts for the navy. Some products, nevertheless, benefited from these regulations. For instance, Britain provided a bounty to indigo producers; with the cessation of the bounty after independence, indigo cultivation withered away.[51]

Similarly, the availability of low cost resources resulted in the development of two world-class manufacturing industries. Taking advantage of the availability of low-cost lumber, the colonies started to build ships early in the seventeenth century (1631). By including colonial-built ships in the British registry, the British promoted the colonial shipbuilding industry to such an extent that by 1775 one-third of the British mercantile marine had been built in the Thirteen Colonies, much to the detriment of the British shipbuilding industry. The loss of this British market after independence negatively impacted the United States shipbuilding industry.

Iron manufacturing commenced in the mid-seventeenth century and boomed during the eighteenth century. By 1700, the Thirteen Colonies produced one-seventieth of the world's iron output and by 1775 one-seventh. In 1750, the British introduced the Iron Act, which decried the growth of the colonial iron industry at the expense of its British equivalent, and soon thereafter declared iron an enumerated commodity. The Iron Act did not significantly affect the colonial iron industry either absolutely or relatively, and encouraged the production of pig iron and semi-finished iron products by allowing colonial iron entry into the British market while limiting the production of finished iron products.

The colonial iron industry benefited from low cost resources (iron ore and wood for fuel) but suffered from high cost labor. The Iron Act therefore did not divert the iron industry from its most profitable endeavor. By providing an outlet for the colonial iron industry, the Iron Act promoted the prosperity of the iron industry. Also, the British never adequately enforced the 1750 law, which prohibited the erection of new finishing facilities, and which required a greater infusion of high cost capital and labor. After independence, as was in the case of the shipbuilding industry, the end of British encouragement of the colonial iron industry and the limitations of the local market, brought about partially by high cost land transportation, caused the iron industry to decline temporarily.

---

51   For a brief current exposition of this topic, see McCusker 1996, Vol. I, pp. 357-362.

Like other European imperial nations such as France, Portugal, Spain, and Holland, and especially in an effort to wrest commercial supremacy from the Dutch, Britain adopted mercantilist legislation to convert the British Empire into a largely self-sufficient entity.   The burden of this legislation on the Thirteen Colonies in some ways diminished as Britain became more efficient as a manufacturer and as a provider of commercial and financial services. However, Britain prevented colonial growers from selling tobacco, an enumerated commodity directly to Continental Europe. The loss was offset in part because Britain prohibited its farmers from growing tobacco.   Yet, after independence, Britain continued to be the *entrepôt* for United States foreign trade; only tobacco was exported directly to Continental Europe in any appreciable amount.

Colonial Public Policy

Government promotion of the economy was widely accepted and pursued in all quarters; certainly, the consensus was private as well as public.[52] From the outset there had been discussion of how the economic freedom of individuals in the market place could enhance the economic welfare of the community. Also, public policy makers were concerned with how the State could create a favorable climate for entrepreneurs.[53] For instance, while the great Puritan migration to Massachusetts of the seventeenth century was being discussed, a series of draft proposals circulated among the leaders of the movement. One emphasized the economic considerations and welcomed the 'free adventure of particular persons'.[54]

To foster economic growth, provincial and local governments adopted a broad array of measures to increase economic activity as well as to protect specific economic interests. For example, governments limited the number of firms and set entry requirements in some industries or sectors; to this day, local, state, and federal government regulation determines the 'proper' number of banks and liquor establishments.   Craft separation (segmentation) and apprenticeship declined during the eighteenth century; *laissez faire* here followed British policy.[55] Also, government used the police power to fix prices and quality standards for the protection of the consumer. On occasion, other and more self-interested motives intruded. For instance, following the example of Virginia, Maryland passed the Tobacco Inspection Act (1747), which aimed at quality improvement for this most important export and therefore an increased price through product differentiation.[56] A century earlier, that is, during the seventeenth century, Virginia, Maryland, and Carolina had attempted unsuccessfully a government-sponsored control of tobacco

---

52   Dorfman 1959, p. 570.
53   Goodrich 1950a, p. 3.
54   Winthrop Papers 1931, Vol. II, pp. 145-147.
55   Morris 1946, pp. 152-153.
56   McKinney Schweitzer 1980, p. 551.

production.[57]   Mercantilism therefore could discourage as well as encourage production.

Most provincial governments provided for State or publicly supported roads, ferries, and bridges. In one variant, the colony of New York and New Jersey in 1706 granted a monopoly for a stage line between Amboy and Burlington, New Jersey, and a ferry between Burlington and Philadelphia, thus providing a route between New York harbor and Philadelphia. Similarly, the Thirteen Colonies supplied intra-colonial postal services. Since no single colony could deal with inter-colonial postal service, Britain authorized such a service in 1753 and appointed Benjamin Franklin as postmaster general.

These types of legislation reflected the British mercantilist heritage.[58] At times, in the absence of investors willing to risk private capital, the colonies resorted to public ownership and operation to promote private enterprise. Similarly, following the British example, the colonies instituted bounties, that is, prizes for American entrepreneurs. Although by the 1760s Benjamin Franklin, colonial agent in Britain (1764-1775) and influenced by the ideas of the Physiocrats and Adam Smith, espoused a *laissez faire* viewpoint, he stood out as an exception with little effect on policy.[59]

The American Revolution had both intended and unintended consequences. The formation of the United States surely constituted an initially unintended consequence. However, apart from ending British mercantilist controls on the economy, the American Revolution resulted in more continuity than change. During the so-called 'Critical Period' (1781-1789) the Articles of the Confederation constituted the first try at a federal system. Under the Articles of the Confederation each state cast a single vote and a unanimous vote of all states was required. Highly decentralized with economic decision-making in the hands of individual states, the Articles of the Confederation proved to be unworkable and abortive.

Mercantilism and Domestic Regulations

Individual states within the United States enacted tariff acts for both revenue and protection. Ferries operated where the State allowed and the State also fixed the rates. Prompted by both the economic conditions of the day as well as history, both merchants and artisans demanded State aid and the various states responded to the popular will with trade and navigation acts. Although the *Wealth of Nations* was readily available in the United States, Americans rejected Smith. While some individuals opposed regulation in theory, they accepted it in practice. Nevertheless, both during the Revolution and the Confederation eras people

---

57   Saloutos 1946, p. 45.
58   Hughes, 1976, p. 4; Hughes 1991, p. 16.
59   Heath 1954, p. 21; Dorfman 1959, p. 570; Nash 1964, pp. 12-16; Hartz 1948, pp. 5, 37.

invoked *laissez faire* reasoning to challenge wage and price controls, occasioned by the massive use of fiat money to pay for the Revolution and the consequent inflation.[60]

Those who possessed large economic interests as well as large vision executed what might be characterized as a *coup d'état*. Some fifty men convinced of the need for an alteration in the balance between the center and the periphery convened in 1787. Key compromises proved necessary before a deal could be struck within the Constitutional Convention; agreement was much greater within the Convention than in the country at large since those who opposed increased centralization absented themselves from the Convention.

The drafters of the Constitution provided for adoption by nine of the original thirteen states indicating both the rejection of the principle of unanimity of the Articles of Confederation and the recognition that ratification might not be easy to achieve. This prediction proved to be on the mark: six states ratified easily and quickly but three pivotal states, Massachusetts, New York and Virginia divided sharply and ratified only after contentious debate. While no state decided permanently against entering the Union, North Carolina and Rhode Island entered the Union late and only after threats of coercion followed persuasion.

The Constitution (1789) conferred significant additional economic powers (for example, interstate and foreign commerce and taxation) on the federal government, which, among other things, undertook to regulate immigration as well as to reserve the coasting trade for ships (*cabotage*) of American registry. In contrast, the Articles of the Confederation had given the individual states the power to regulate domestic and foreign commerce. Just as the various states under the Articles had imposed tariffs, so they had controlled immigration such as it was. The United States imposed a prohibitive tax on foreign built and owned ships in 1789 (the Tonnage Act) to preserve the coasting trade for American shipping. Later, the 1817 Navigation Act excluded foreign ships from coastwise competition.[61]

During the American Revolution, the central government undertook the manufacture of gunpowder; Washington selected Springfield, Massachusetts, as the site of the first arsenal. The Springfield Armory was built in 1794 while the arsenal in Harper's Ferry, Virginia, was constructed in 1795.[62] The State's arms manufacturing facilities interacted with their private counterparts but any initiative from the State to the private sector constituted an unintended consequence rather than a conscious and deliberate policy decision. Another of the enumerated powers of the Constitution enabled the federal government to create a postal service; as a public service, the Post Office Act (1792) set fees for delivering newspapers at extremely low rates. The policy of subsidizing the propagation of

---

60   Jensen 1956, pp. 282-301; Morris 1946, pp. 117-118.
61   Nettels 1962, p. 111.
62   Others were erected, at various times, until, in 1900, the federal government had
       seventeen arsenals.

the media was thought to aim at the national interest by the dissemination of information on business and public affairs.

The State and Private Enterprise

George Washington (1732-1799) epitomizes, as well as any one-man can, the economy of late eighteenth century America. In addition to being Commander-in-Chief of the Revolutionary Army and first President of the United States, Washington was a very rich man with his hand in diverse economic activities. A planter merchant and slaveholder, he also became an entrepreneur who at various times was a land speculator, manufacturer of bricks, linen, woolen, and cotton cloth, and a flour mill and a saw mill operator as well as a landlord and moneylender. As owner of western lands needing low cost transportation to enhance their value, during the 1780s Washington became the first president of two canal companies: the Potomac Company and the James River and Kanawha Company. In short, Washington carried on many businesses with little or no government participation but other business ventures necessitated considerably more State intervention.

Alexander Hamilton, Washington's Secretary of the Treasury and the first as well as undoubtedly the greatest Secretary of the Treasury, has been variously characterized as a 'minister of planning' or a 'minister of finance' in the broadest possible sense. His reports encompassed all aspects of the American economy and he grounded his argument on the best available information. His *Report on Public Credit* (1790) had the incidental consequence of tying the holders of the public debt (that is, the moneyed class) to the federal government as against the states. Similarly, his *Report on a National Bank* (1790) resulted in the establishment of the Bank of the United States (1791-1811) as a government-backed partially owned institution, with branches eventually in all principal commercial centers. Hamilton's *Report on Manufactures* (1791) prompted the enactment of a tariff with at least mildly protective features. Like Washington and many others, Hamilton definitely thought the State should cooperate with private enterprise.

Individual States Market Intervention

During the years immediately after the American Revolution, the overwhelming share of State intervention in the economy took place at the state rather than at the federal level. During this decade the states, of necessity, converted their colonial charters into constitutions, which gave them broad police power concerning the economy. Virtually without interruption, the states resumed the promotion and regulation policies that had prevailed prior to the American Revolution. Thus, the state governments dictated number, entry, price, and quality.

The Massachusetts constitution of 1780 reflected the common concern of that state with all aspects of the economy. Soon after, Pennsylvania, Georgia, and other states followed Massachusetts's example. Before the Revolution, owing to the

British Currency Act (1764), as well as the weak commercial sector of the colonial economy, no chartered commercial banks operated in the Thirteen Colonies. During the 1780s the states chartered banks in the principal commercial cities: Boston, New York, and Philadelphia; by 1795 the states had chartered some twenty such banks.[63]

According to the Constitution, as well as the contemporary climate of opinion, health, education, and welfare were delegated to the individual states with no role for the federal government. Those poor judged deserving by their families and their local communities, that is, the lame, the halt, and the blind, received the care of their families and their immediate communities. The larger society presumably did not bear any such responsibility.

Similarly, education was a function reserved to the individual states, and assigned by them to the various localities; the emphasis was on local control of financing and spending. Schooling and political participation were invariably closely connected since public opinion assumed that the electorate should be literate in a democracy.[64] In addition, to supplement the colleges under private auspices, several territories/states chartered state colleges between the end of the Revolution and the turn of the century. The idea of a national university, despite having being endorsed by George Washington, died stillborn since the constitutionality of such an idea seemed dubious.

Controls and Regulations

Throughout the waterpower era, the land was dotted with mills to manufacture a wide spectrum of diverse semi-finished and finished products. However, the rights of navigation as well as the rights of riparian owners upstream and downstream inhibited the construction of mills. Riparian owners challenged mill builders in the courts. To limit the vested rights of these property owners, the colony of Massachusetts enacted the first Mill Act in 1713 and the state of Massachusetts built on the colonial precedent in 1796. Milldam statutes enacted by other colonies and states, which emulated Massachusetts, authorized enterprises to exercise eminent domain for manufacturing and other purposes on behalf of the common good. Similarly, the State extended the eminent domain power to private turnpike, bridge, and canal companies; eminent domain assumed a public purpose which, in turn, justified regulation.[65]

During the American Revolution Massachusetts fixed prices, controlled supplies, and regulated labor. While hardly *laissez faire* in intent, these measures were not necessarily war inspired. After the Revolution, the government of Massachusetts used mercantilist policies; during the Critical Period, Massachusetts

---

63   Nash 1968, p. 18; Hughes 1976, pp. 4-6; Handlin and Handlin 1969, pp. 59, 71; Hartz 1948, pp. 4, 9; Heath 1954, p. 359.

64   Also, some communities founded schools for girls after and because of the Revolution.

65   Horwitz 1977, p. 47; Scheiber 1973, p. 234.

set minimum standards and inspected lumber, fish, meat, and other products and also protected specific industries. Although aware of *laissez faire* beliefs, by rejecting the view that the State should be inactive, Massachusetts, an economically and politically significant state, denied that people could rely on individual self-interest. In 1790, when the United States took its first census, Massachusetts had the second largest population of any state and a decade later ranked third. Its leading city and seaport, Boston, was the third most important United States seaport in both 1791 and 1801.[66]

While unincorporated enterprises conducted the overwhelming share of economic activity, that is, sole proprietorships or partnerships, corporations chartered by the State functioned where the good sense of the community judged them to be absolutely necessary. Thus, of the individual colonial legislatures, individually, chartered seven corporations before 1775 and the states chartered somewhat more than three hundred between 1780 and 1800 for banks, canals, turnpikes, bridges, insurance, public water supplies, and manufacturing, all deemed to possess a public purpose. For instance, in 1792, Pennsylvania chartered the Lancaster pike, a private enterprise linking Philadelphia to Lancaster, a munitions center seventy miles to the west.[67]

Taxation and Representation

A non-ideological explanation may supplement the ideological. Before the American Revolution, Britain bore the burden of defense as well as all other imperial-related expenses. The Thirteen Colonies were much more lightly taxed than Britain and extremely lightly taxed in world terms. Even so, the revolutionary slogan demanded 'no taxation without representation'. Reflecting this heritage, under the Articles of the Confederation the central government deliberately had no taxing power; there was considerable opposition to taxation, even with representation. Much of the sizeable opposition to the ratification of the Constitution stemmed from just this concern about taxation and with good reason. The Constitution granted the central government (as well as the states) the power to tax. Government at all levels became more energetic and per capita tax rates rose substantially after 1789.

In a society with relatively widespread suffrage and property ownership, 'we the people' paid taxes. Much of the opposition to a State with a grand design stemmed from a generalized opposition to taxation regardless of the purpose to which the spending would be directed. Such opponents defined the objectives of government minimally and asked not much more from the State than to be left alone to allocate their income unimpeded. Freedom, in this light, meant freedom from government.

---

66   Handlin and Handlin 1969, pp. x, xi, 53-54, 63, 65.
67   Nettels 1962, pp. 252, 290-292; Hurst 1970, p. 14.

Conclusions

To acknowledge this role of government as a promoter and regulator of the economy in the years immediately following independence in no way suggests that Americans were either ignorant of or oblivious to the arguments of Adam Smith in particular and *laissez faire* thought in general. Continuing policies in vogue before the Revolution, Americans sought to combine the public interest and the interests of particular interest groups.[68] The Constitution inaugurated a central government endowed with the specific enumerated powers to regulate and to tax interstate and foreign commerce.

Given the nature of the American economy in the late eighteenth century dominated by small-scale enterprises and high cost land transportation, most economic activity took place locally and without the benefit of State intervention. Therefore, economic activity fell within the purview of the individual states, which possessed concurrent jurisdiction and, above all, the police power. Most Americans were farmers and the State had nothing to say regarding farm prices, which resulted from the interaction of buyers and sellers in the market.

Within this perspective, Hamilton was cognizant of the new government's need for a source of revenue to meet ordinary expenses as well as pay interest on the combined debt of the federal and state governments. When advocating a protective tariff, and not mentioning Smith by name, Hamilton used Smith's ideas as a straw man which he then proceeded to knock down, if only on purely pragmatic grounds. Even those who advocated some version of the *laissez faire* argument were pragmatic rather than philosophical, and specific rather than general. Men could change sides as their specific individual and regional interests mandated.[69] Thus, certain projects became private rather than quasi public or public only because the efforts of one project in a region offset the efforts of another and similar project to obtain State funding.

In a world with high cost land transportation relative to water transportation, the physical horizon of many people frequently circumscribed their economic horizon. Only those situated on navigable water or adjacent thereto participated fully in the wider market. Consequently, individuals called upon the State to charter or subsidize private corporations, which could then build bridges, canals, and roads and then other individuals demanded that the State do the same on behalf of their parochial interests. The federal government represented anything but a prime mover in this entire process. Given the relatively low level of taxation, it is obvious that the State could not spend very much on any such projects, however worthwhile.

The United States during the Age of Washington hardly adhered to *laissez faire* in the most extreme form each policy decision was made pragmatically on a case-by-case basis rather than with regard to the abstract slippery slope doctrine.

---

68   Johnson 1962, pp. 435, 442, 444.
69   Henrich 1943, pp. 51, 53.

Although the revolutionaries had criticized mercantilism before the Revolution, when they had their chance to govern, they drew upon their mundane experience, rejected *laissez faire* and instead augmented the role of the State in the promotion of the economy.[70] The principle of limited government as embodied in the various constitutions resulted in a State that while not minimalist to the nth degree left the individual substantially to his own devices.

France

France entered the eighteenth century as a more or less consolidated State with substantially stable borders and as the most populous European State, about twenty million out of a total European population of hundred million. France had one of the highest per capita income in Europe, but with the State's finances in a shambles. By the middle of the seventeenth century, the struggle between the nobility and the king as well as the earlier religious wars had resulted in an absolutist monarchy.[71] Louis XIV (1643-1715) consolidated the nation but wrecked the State's finances; the heritage of the seventeenth century included wars, high royal living partially to tame the nobility, restrictive trade policies, and fiscal mismanagement.

Eighteenth century France suffered a financial panic immediately after the death of Louis XIV. Under the Regents, Louis XV, and Louis XVI, despotism continued while protectionist policies, weakened briefly late in the seventeenth century, prevailed during most of the eighteenth century. While economic growth was rapid and sustained in the first part of the century, it lessened by half during the second part of the century. The State vainly struggled to straighten its finances by juggling taxes and through various financial schemes, to increase revenue.

The eighteenth century witnessed the rise of the bourgeoisie while simultaneously the Enlightenment and economic liberalism challenged the established institutions and culminated with the 1789 Revolution. The Physiocrats and the contributors to the *Encyclopédie*, a financially and intellectually successful publication, influenced public policy and stimulated commercial capitalism. The movement of ideas 'denoted intellectual communication and economic trading'.[72] Those economic policies and institutions, developed throughout the seventeenth century still endured up to and even after the Revolution. During the eighteenth century the French State's economic policies continued to include: an archaic system of taxation, excessive protection of domestic producers, control of the internal and external grain market, and participation in manufacturing enterprises.

---

70 Handlin and Handlin 1969, p. 242; Johnson, 1973, pp. 10, 162; Matson 1996, p. 371.
71 Different from France, the seventeenth century British revolutions never challenged the integrity or the sovereignty of the State; instead, the British transferred power from the monarch to an oligarchy.
72 Jones 2002, p. xxiii.

Seventeenth Century Colbertisme

France achieved institutional and political cohesion considerably later than Britain. Cardinal Armand Jean du Plessis Duc de Richelieu (1565-1642), chief minister (1622-1642), under Louis XIII (1601-1643), secured royal domination of the nobility. Jean-Baptiste Colbert (1661-1683) strengthened the basis of the mercantilist economic system under which France attained a more centralized government during the reign of Louis XIV. Since the sixteenth century France has been traditionally mercantilist, inferring State interference in the economy and protectionism.

French mercantilism, known as *Colbertisme*, was much more interventionist than British mercantilism; it emphasized protection for incipient industry through tariffs or other measures and a strong State presence in the economy. Mercantilists claimed that the State's economic health would affect the well being of its citizens. The State not only took the initiative in infrastructure development (canals and roads) but also initiated productive activities. Yet, *Colbertisme* never became a set of coherent principles of political economy but rather constituted *ad hoc* decisions taken at the center of power.[73]

In contrast to Britain, France was absolutist and centralized but not economically integrated. While in Britain, some subordinated policies were formulated and implemented at the local level, in France, local and regional institutions and privileges mitigated centralization. The *Ancien Régime*, the pre-1789 French government, supported policies emanating from the centre in order to achieve a cohesive State, but not necessarily an integrated economy; internal economic integration was postponed until the advent of Napoleon.[74] From Colbert to the French Revolution serious but unsuccessful attempts were made to integrate the internal market.[75] Colbert instituted the Five Great Farms, a tariff union in central France in which the tolls were collected by tax farmers. The area of these Farms encompassed a sizeable free trade area.[76] Yet, French *octrois* (customs duties at city gates) persisted until the coming of the automobile in the twentieth century. These internal trade barriers fragmented the French market despite the efforts of Colbert as well as of those ministers who followed during the next century.[77]

Beginning with Colbert in the seventeenth century, the State acted to build canals linking major rivers and the rivers to the sea thereby extending the market. In order to integrate the economy, Colbert built the Lanquedoc Canal that joined the Atlantic Ocean with the Mediterranean Sea via the Garonne River as well as

---

73   Gueslin 1997, pp. 26, 29; Goubert 1970, Vol. 2, pp. 351-358.
74   Geiger 1994, p. 35.
75   With no internal tariffs, with an insignificant guild system, and with monopoly not allowed within the country, except for inventions, Britain had the largest free trade area in Europe.
76   The size of the Five Great Farms area was almost as large as England.
77   Schaeper 1995, Vol. 2, p. 763.

another canal that connected the Seine and the Loire rivers. Owing to geography French canals were longer than those in Britain.[78]

French canals were a species of military engineering; the State trained engineers. In contrast to semi-literate British engineers, French military engineers learned science and mathematics, and built roads, bridges, canals, and fortifications.[79] Not surprisingly, before the Revolution, Arthur Young (1741-1820), a noted eighteenth century British agronomist and traveler, admired the magnitude of the French state canal projects and was dazzled by the 'commerce, wealth, and magnificence of the cities'.[80] On the other hand, returning after the Revolution (1792) Young deplored the conditions of the French infrastructure.[81]

Les manufactures royales

Colbert believed that the State, that is, the king, had to be strong; to be strong meant to be rich. Wealth meant gold and silver that France did not produce; therefore, by necessity, it needed a favorable balance of trade to achieve this objective. Colbert encouraged state enterprises; *les manufactures royales*, subsidized dependencies of the crown, which produced such luxury items as porcelains, crystals, and tapestries. In 1665, Colbert was instrumental in bringing twenty Venetian glass blowing workers to Paris. They set up glass and silvering mirror shops and furnished the famous Hall of Mirrors for the Versailles palace.[82]

The State enterprises were prosperous when they received State subsidies (in part these subsidies consisted of purchases by the crown without regard to cost), but experienced losses as soon as the subsidies were suspended. These enterprises hardly survived Colbert but were encouraged again under Louis XV. Many of *les manufactures royales* probably were not expected to be profitable but were expected to glorify the 'Sun King', in which case profits were almost irrelevant.

Under the *Ancien Régime*, a large share of the industrial sector was highly dependent on the crown. Some *manufactures royales* were directly or indirectly under the management of the king; others needed royal authorization to be established. The State encouraged those industries with subsidies, such as interest free loans. In some instances, the State constituted a significant purchaser. In addition, these enterprises received aid from the provincial and local governments. Some of the textile enterprises were given monopoly power. In certain industries,

---

78   France was larger and the interior of France was much further from the sea than that of Britain.

79   Langins 2004, pp. 168, 432.

80   Arthur Young (1929) *Travels in France in the Years 1787, 1788, 1789*, Edited by C. Maxwell, Cambridge, Cambridge University Press, pp. 58, 151, cited by Jones 2002, pp. 166, 410.

81   Young also criticized the Physiocrats' land tax on the *produit net* as ineffective; the National Assembly briefly imposed such a tax. Young 1942, pp. 349-366.

82   Scoville 1950, pp. 23, 27. *Les manufactures royales* at Saint Gobain led in the production of plate glass and mirrors.

the State just did not permit competing enterprises to operate. Industrial organizations and operation were strictly regulated. The State determined the quality and nature of raw materials, their utilization, and the processing procedures, as well as the quality of the manufactured products.

The State and the Risk-Adverse Frenchmen

During the late 1600s Colbert attempted to unify the economy by eliminating impediments to the free flow of goods in the domestic market, he believed in State intervention. 'Colbertism remains a popular term for pervasive government initiative at the microeconomic level.'[83] The upper classes as well as the upper hierarchy of the clergy enjoyed a life of wealth. The middle class (lower bourgeoisie) was mainly in trade while the upper bourgeoisie turned towards banking that, as in many places, seemed to be somehow more prestigious. The significance of the anti-economic prejudice, however, cannot easily be quantified or verified.

It was more prestigious to be in the upper ranks of the civil service than in trade. Since Henry III (1574-1589), the French State's need for money often had been met by selling positions in the government's bureaucracy. This practice, in its origin a purely financial expedient, skillfully exploited the vanity of the Third Estate, the desire of the commoner to hold some public office. Indeed, the craving to secure a place in the bureaucracy became a second nature with the Frenchman, and had much to do with the servile state to which the people were reduced and the revolutionary movement.[84]

The 'risk-adverse' culture prevailed through the Revolution. It is worth noting differences between the nobility in Britain and in France. As noted above, in Britain only the eldest son inherited (still true) the title and became a member of the nobility, while the others had to turn to the Church, the army, or, heaven forbid, business to make their careers; thus many younger sons went to America or India to make their fortunes. However, in France all sons became members of the nobility, which may have made a difference.[85] To no one's surprise, French personal conservatism, as hoarding gold under the mattress, did not encourage the development of financial institutions. French banks were more cautious in their investment choices, than their British counter parts, with many lost opportunities because of minimizing risk.[86]

---

83   Adams 1989, p. 46.
84   Tocqueville 1955, p. 104. It is also true that Louis XIV granted pensions and not employment to lure the nobility to Versailles.
85   Guerard 1969, p. 183.
86   Hoffmann 1963, p. 6.

The Role of the State in Science and Culture

The *Ancien Régime* the Old Order, encouraged science and culture in order to pursue its political objectives. The State intervened in the cultural field to propagate institutional models in the service of the State and to glorify the Sun King. The protection and limited freedom granted to intellectual development was motivated by mercantilist objectives. Colbert hoped that artistic, technical, and scientific developments would increase French industrial potential and therefore improve the balance of trade.

The State, Louis XI (1461-1483), and Henry IV (1553-1610), financed irrigation and flood control. Following the example of Italy (Padova 1525 and Pisa 1544) and Montpellier (1593), Louis XIII authorized royal gardens in Paris. Under Louis XV, in 1739, this culminated with France being renowned for its outstanding botanist, Georg Louis Leclerc Buffon (1707-1781). Also, other scientific and cultural institutions were encouraged as dependencies of the State. Charles IX (1560-1574),[87] and Henry III promoted the Academy of Music and Poetry. Cardinal de Richelieu, head of the government, followed suit with the Academy of France a model for an academic institution dependent on the State.[88] Aiming to have a centralized State, France developed an innovative civil service that succeeded in perpetuating control of policy implementation and political power. Under the *Ancien Régime*, France achieved formal training for civil servants through the *corps* and the *écoles*.[89]

Attempts to Modify Mercantilism

The French overseas trading companies, chartered by the State, were unable to withstand the competition of the British and the Dutch. Yet, these trading companies were important for French imperial strategy. Overseas, France failed in its struggle with Britain in part because it limited emigration to French North America only to French Catholics; as a result, by 1763 French North America had only 80,000 European colonists while British North America had 2,000,000. Also,

---

87 But also during his reign, the Massacre of Saint Bartholomew took place, when numerous Huguenots were killed.

88 In succession, we have: the Painting and Sculpture Academy (1648), the Belles-lettres Academy (1663), the Academy of Sciences (1666), the Music Academy (1669), the Architecture Academy (1671), the Surgery Academy (1731), and the Medicine Academy (1776). Colbert encouraged the expansion of academies in the provinces. Consequently, under Louis XIV, a dozen academies and under Louis XV about twenty academies were created. Descimon and Guery 1989, Vol. II, pp. 320-321.

89 For instance, under Louis XIV in 1697, the *Corps de Genie*, a cadre of military engineers, and the *Corps des Ponts et Chaussées* for bridges and roads was established in 1716. In 1775, the *Ecole des Ponts et Chaussées*, a cadre of civil engineers came into being. Weis 1982, p. 1.

the French East India Company could not withstand the political non-commercial objectives of the French State.

During the seventeenth century France tried continuously, and with some success, to expand its frontiers. Louis XIV dreamt of a so-called 'natural frontier' on the Rhine and the Alps, and in 1667, he claimed the Spanish Netherlands. The Dutch and the Austrian Habsburgs stopped the French; the Habsburgs lost territory to the French but the Dutch retained their territory intact. When the English joined the Dutch against Louis XIV, after William of Orange married Mary Stuart, niece of the king of England, Louis XIV ended the war in 1676.

Under pressure, Colbert had to sign the Treaty of Nimegue (1678) that reversed many of the mercantilist policies that he had instituted.[90] By the beginning of the eighteenth century, perhaps as a consequence of this treaty, but also because of currency depreciation (stemming from uncontrolled State debt) and low wages (compared with Britain), French manufactured exports became competitive. International trade expanded; exports doubled in a decade and maintained a rate of growth of four percent to mid-century, quite a feat if one considers that *Colbertisme* prevailed. Most of the exports gains were in high quality manufacturing. For instance, earlier Colbert had praised the Lyon fashion industry as being the gold mines of France.[91]

Post-Louis XIV Financial Bubble

With the death of Louis XIV in 1715, France underwent a traumatic period. His temporary successor, the Regents, Philip II Duc d'Orleans (1715-1723) and Hercule de Fleury (1723-1726), attempted to resolve the financial mess and the debt France inherited, while still maintaining the absolute monarchy. John Law (1671-1729), an exiled British subject, a monetary theorist and a banker, offered his services to the Regent. In 1716, Law established the private *Banque Générale*, nationalized in 1718 and named the *Banque Royale*. Baron de la Brede e de Montesquieu (1689-1755), a contemporary French *philosophe*, argued, based on the experience of the Bank of England established in 1694, that a central bank is incompatible with an absolutist regime since it cannot act autonomously.[92] But for a while Law did very well with the Royal Bank, succeeding in paying the French national debt by 1719. Consequently, the Regent appointed him Minister of Finance in 1720.

As a speculator, Law introduced various schemes by creating a monopoly, the *Compagnie des Indes*, that traded in Canadian furs and falsely claimed to trade in

90   Unlike the French spelling, the English spelling is Nimwegen and the Dutch spelling is Nijmegen. Goubert 1970, Tome II, pp. 354-5.
91   The State was quite severe in maintaining quality control through periodic inspection of factories, shops, and stores. Jones 2002, pp. 159-162.
92   Note that Montesquieu favored the British system of government rather than the French; his comment on banking is only one element in his more general critique of absolutism.

gold, silver, lead, quicksilver, tobacco, and rice. With great expectations, the company's stock traded at nearly forty times its face value within the year, at a time when people believed that face value had more than nominal value or significance.[93] When he could not repay short-term notes, a financial panic ensued. Law's financial manipulation triggered inflation (prices doubled within one year) but also reduced unemployment.[94]

The ensuing financial crisis left the State with empty coffers again. The gainers were the aristocrats since inflation allowed them to repay their debts and the peasant proprietors who had more money to spend and invest because of higher farm prices. These gains also brought an inflation driven economic expansion. In closing a brief but spectacular financial and political career, Law fled the country after unintentionally inducing a complete collapse of financial markets and a French distrust of banks.[95]

Dirigisme and Enlightened Despotism

Dirigisme could be defined as a political economy in which the State gives general direction to the economy. A noted economic historian maintained that 'most continental countries had long traditions of state paternalism or étatisme'.[96] The French Enlightenment favored individual freedom but advocated a pivotal role for the State in the form of an enlightened despot to promote economic growth. 'French policy makers of all persuasions. . .[were] more likely to approve *dirigiste* style intervention than the British counterparts.'[97]

Francois Quesnay (1694-1774), a physician, and the main exponent of the Physiocrat philosophy, advocated limited free trade for agriculture. Quesnay favored Enlightened Despotism, based on top down reform. However, the despotism of eighteenth-century France was never enlightened and therefore meaningful economic reform never occurred before 1789.[98] In practice, State economic policies stemmed more from the lack (in comparison with Britain) of private entrepreneurs than from the State overtly replacing the market.[99]

Even after the overthrow of the traditional despot (1789), political freedom proved sporadic. Not until the 1870s, and only after several revolutions, France

93 Investors held that view in the United States until the early twentieth century; in 1912, New York State legalized the sale of no par value stock.
94 Unwittingly, he pursued Keynesian policies before their time, although hardly for the same reasons.
95 Norberg 1994, pp. 276-282; Bordo 1987, p. 143. Andrew Jackson's opposition to the Second Bank of the United States was motivated in part by his having read about the South Sea Bubble in Britain which occurred about the same time as Law's collapse. In France, this financial disaster probably induced risk-adverse behavior detrimental to capital mobilization.
96 Cameron 1997, p. 293.
97 Hall 1986a, p. 279.
98 Schachter 1991, pp. 315-317.
99 Geiger 1994, p. 43.

established a parliamentary system based on universal manhood suffrage and ministerial responsibility to the legislature. During the eighteenth century France's political, social, and economic institutions differed greatly from those of Britain. France remained an absolute monarchy, and vestiges of feudalism and serfdom survived in France until the Revolution; for example, the aristocracy (the nobility and the clergy) was exempted from taxes. Also, those peasant proprietors who possessed, but did not own, land paid a *cens* (*quitrent*), a fee to the original landowner; this limited land held in freehold, and, although peasants had freedom of movement, these peasants still paid feudal dues.[100]

Wealth Accumulation, Taxation, and Representation

Privileges of all sorts segmented French society, much more than in Britain, from the wealthy to the poor as well as from province to province. Pre-Revolutionary France financially favored those connected with the regime; the aristocracy was tax exempt and had more wealth and income than only a handful of merchants. Under Louis XIV and Louis XV, the wealth accumulated in the service of the king was far larger than the wealth derived from commerce. For instance, it is estimated that Cardinal Jules Mazarin (1602-1661), who inherited Richelieu's political position, was worth 50 million *livres*, which made him the richest man in France; his successor, Colbert, left a large estate, but less than his predecessor, about one million *livres*.[101]

Throughout the eighteenth century the merchants and the emerging business class attempted but did not succeed in amassing the wealth that up to 1789 the land owning class possessed. On the other hand, about 1700 merchants connected with the regime reaped huge profits from contracts to supply the armies. With the blessing of the State, entrepreneurs succeeded in organizing enterprises just for this purpose. The *Compagnie des fermes générales* (Company of General Farms) was established in 1718 with a capital of 100,000,000 livres representing 100,000 shares. It appears that under the *Ancien Régime*, the only big business was State business and sometimes the king participated as a significant owner.[102]

Under the *Ancien Régime* the system of taxation was far from equitable with the nobility and the clergy not taxed at all. The King was concerned with revenue not equity and taxes were added as the need arose. The *vingtième*, a five percent tax, introduced in 1749, in principle constituted a levy on income applicable to everyone similar to an early *dixième*, a ten percent tax, was imposed periodically.

---

100 The French term is *cens*—a feudal rent; one who held land on such a basis before the abolition of feudal tenure in 1789 was called a *censier*. By the end of the *Ancien Régime* the *cens* had little monetary value but retained an honorific value indicating the subordination of the tenant to the lord. Quinn 1985, pp. 162-163.

101 There is no way to translate this amount into present day value but, if the value was measured in gold, 50 million and even one million *livres* constituted a colossal fortune.

102 Leon 1970a, pp. 616-617, 623-631.

These taxes through which the king attempted to overcome the fiscal immunities and tax exemptions were not accepted lightly by the privileged class and proved almost impossible to implement. The *taille*, a poll tax, the most onerous tax, financed wars and was not paid by nobles and clergy. From time to time France introduced other direct taxes depending on the needs of the treasury. The capitation tax and the *vingtième* were levied arbitrarily, often in proportion to the *taille* and to rent earned.[103] Two other problems increased the inefficiency of the tax system: entrusting local agents to collect taxes proved to be very expensive and the assessment of taxes encouraged not only fraud but also decreased production because farmers withheld production from the market to avoid taxes.

Alexis de Tocqueville (1805-1859), nineteenth century author and statesman, noted that during the eighteenth century the fiscal system in Britain contained less inequality than in France. In Britain the poor were often exempted form taxations while in France the rich noblemen and Clergymen were exempted.

> The English aristocracy voluntarily shouldered the heaviest public burden so as to be allowed to retain its authority; in France the nobles clung on their exemptions from taxation to the very end to console themselves from having lost the right to rule.[104]

While it is reasonable for a government to be in debt, during the eighteenth century, owing to wars and living in a style beyond the State's means, neither the Crown nor its ministers hesitated to go heavily into debt. Two thirds of State expenditures were for wars or to service the public debt.[105] The loans were usually in the form of *rente perpétuelle*, a perpetual annuity loan or a *rente viagère*, a life annuity loan. Under Louis XIV, Lorenzo Tonti, a Neapolitan banker, introduced the *tontine*, a kind of life insurance. The king would receive cash and in exchange would establish a life annuity according to actuarial calculations. This method of raising funds for the government was in force between 1689 and 1770.[106] By contrast, owing to the seventeenth century Financial Revolution, the creditors of the State controlled the British political process. During the eighteenth century the British paid higher taxes than the French and also Britain could borrow at a lower interest rate than France. This affected private financial markets; the cost of capital was higher in France than in Britain.

Jean-Jacques Rousseau (1712-1778), a French *philosophe*, agreed with assertion that taxation should be tied to representation. He went further by arguing that the State must treat the citizens equitably and in the process protect the poor. Since inequity destroys freedom, taxation should be used as a social policy for income redistribution, that is, eliminating tax exemptions. As an economic historian concludes: 'fiscal demands here are not just a part of the bargain between

---

103 Aftalion 1990, p. 13.
104 Tocqueville 1955, p. 98.
105 Gueslin 1997, p. 9.
106 Norberg 1994, pp. 271-275.

the ruler and the ruled; they are an instrument of social equity and an important part of modern liberty'.[107] During the French Revolution, policy makers attempted to introduce a 'fair' tax system but soon after, to finance the State treasury, they had to return to the taxation system (with fewer exemptions) inherited from the *Ancien Régime*.[108]

The Physiocrats

With the high costs of horse and wagon transportation and an underdeveloped canal system (despite a few canals individually that dwarfed those in Britain), even a minor grain shortage aroused the fear of localized famine in France. The movement of grain from one province to another had been restricted to protect the local inhabitants. For this reason, France, probably a net importer of grain in the mid-eighteenth century, adopted free trade in grain as a short-run expedient during the crop crises of 1754, 1763, and 1774. Indeed, the Physiocrats, epitomized by Francois Quesnay (although one could easily cite half a dozen others), focused on agriculture and started to advocate a freer market for grain since they believed that this commodity, above all others, was needed for survival. The Physiocrats influenced economic policies under Louis XV and Louis XVI; for instance, in 1760, by tilting economic policies towards agricultural development, some land reclamation was started, agricultural cooperatives were encouraged, and a Ministry of Agriculture was established.[109]

Most Frenchmen, however, opposed free trade in grain and preferred protectionism. The ever-present fear of famine presumably justified State control to protect the poor and thereby avert civil disorder. Anne Robert Jacques Turgot (1727-1781), another leading Physiocrat, argued that 'the freer, the more animated and the more extensive trade is, the more swiftly, efficaciously and abundantly can the people be supplied'.[110] Turgot contended that the mechanism of supply and demand, without too much regulation or government interference, could forestall famine and poverty. While Minister of Finance from 1774 to 1776, Turgot decreed domestic free trade on grains, only to be reversed upon his dismissal. Based on this experience, a present-day economic historian remarked, 'French liberalism rarely flourishes enduringly'.[111] Some economic historians believe that Turgot was more influenced by the predecessors of Adam Smith than by the Physiocrats.[112] After all, the Physiocrats emphasized agriculture while Smith focused on commerce.[113]

---

107 Norberg 1994, p. 298.
108 Gueslin 1997, p. 58.
109 Schachter 1991, pp. 315-317.
110 *Oeuvre de Turgot*, ed. G. Schell (5 volumes, Paris 1913-1923) vol. IV, p. 204, quoted by Jones 2002, pp. 295-296.
111 Adams 1989, p. 251.
112 Groenewegen 1987, Vol. 3, pp. 216-218.
113 Napoleon later caustically referred to the British as 'a nation of shopkeepers'.

The French economy moved precariously between the *Ancien Régime* and the emerging capitalism. The pre-Physiocrats, for example, Pierre Le Pesant, Sieur de Noblesse de robe Boisguillebert (1646-1714), believed that a deep economic depression around 1700 occurred owing to bad public policies that allowed the price of grain to fall and thus the income of farmers to drop. France was basically an agricultural society so that, as elsewhere, the majority of the population depended on the well being of farmers.[114] Later, the Physiocrats contended that agricultural exports would increase total demand and thus induce an increase in French agricultural productivity, which was less than that of Britain. Small sized farms in France could not achieve scale economies or become capital intensive. While France pursued agricultural protection, the Physiocratic critique of French regulation of the internal grain trade, however revolutionary for continental Europe, was hardly profound and only asked that France adopt an economic policy long existing in Britain, namely, free trade in the domestic grain market.

According to some economic historians, the Physiocrats advanced the idea of competitive markets before Smith – the heyday of physiocracy occurred around the 1750s some two decades before the publication of Adam Smith's *Wealth of Nations*. Anticipating the thinking of two centuries later, they claimed that competition would equalize prices not only among regions but also among nations with benefits accruing to both sellers and buyers. Also, prices would be equalized over time because good years with good weather would make up for the bad years with bad weather. The Physiocrats manifested no evident interest in other marketable goods besides grains.[115]

The 'nature' core of physiocracy was akin to the religious belief in determinism. In order not to run afoul of the Church, the impression that nature and God are identical was tacitly accepted.[116] The French State had mixed feelings regarding the progress of physiocracy and economic liberalism.[117] Perhaps Quesnay's friendship with Louis XV (as the King's personal physician) helped to assure a relatively unhampered flow of liberal ideas. Nevertheless, Voltaire was exiled to Ferney at the Swiss border for being a maverick, in the sense that he did not adulate the king and criticized government corruption.[118]

The counterweight to Turgot was Jacques Necker (1732-1804), a wealthy Swiss financier who was virtually in charge of the State's financial well being

---

114 Labrousse 1970, pp. 368-370.
115 Schachter 1991, pp. 315-317.
116 A contemporary social critic, Abbe Galiani, accused the exponents of Physiocracy of advocating quasi-religious theorems harmful to much of the population. Jones 2002, p. 220.
117 Labrousse 1970, pp. 373-383.
118 In the 1770s, with the secret encouragement of Turgot, briefly in charge of the Ministry of Finance, Voltaire, joined others in 1776 to challenge the feudal lords who were in control of the *Parlement*. He proposed the abolition of feudal rights defended by nobles, the church and magistrates since a majority of the members of *Parlement* possessed a fiefdom. Sée 1967, p. 50.

during the 1780s. In order to obtain revenue for the crown, Necker tried lotteries, borrowing from the provincial estates, and lifetime annuities, *rentes viagères*. In addition, himself a Protestant, Necker tapped the émigré Huguenot international financial market with some success. His stroke of genius was to publicize the government accounts and forecasts to build confidence and thus improve the State's credit standing. These attempts came to naught and with finances in disarray, the system collapsed in 1789.[119]

Laissez Faire and Protectionism

During the second half of the eighteenth century the government instituted some liberal economic legislation, only to be countermanded in a power struggle at the Court. In 1786, through a peace treaty with their archenemy Britain, the French signed the Eden Treaty, a commercial agreement. The lower tariffs on manufactured goods created problems for French that lagged in productivity and had higher costs, thus unable to compete with Britain, where the Industrial Revolution was developing rapidly. Some contend that this treaty together with the social, political, and military problems that ensued, induced France to adopt protectionist policies more or less continuously until 1860.[120] France probably would have adopted mercantilist policies since it had been traditionally protectionist.

By mid century, the *Ancien Régime* industrial policies contravened the economic doctrines of the time. The Physiocrats, such as Quesnay, attempted to break the absolute hold of the centralized State on economic policies. During the second half of the eighteenth century, under the influence of Gournay, the Bureau of Commerce refused to authorize exclusive privileges for enterprises. As a young administrator, Turgot attempted to convert the physiocratic theory into policy, with some measure of success.

Turgot in his *Eloge de Gournay* recounted an anecdote from the previous century. At a reunion of tradesmen with Colbert, one of them said '*Monseigneur laissez-nous faire*', Sir, let us do. Gournay (1712-1749) adopted this utterance in the phrase *laissez faire* that became famous for centuries to come.[121] Philosophically the French so-called *laissez faire* theorists seem to have been in reality national economists who 'placed emphasis upon state rather than individual interests and...lauded political economic actions'.[122]

---

119   Jones 2002, pp. 310-317.
120   Catherine and Gousset 1965, pp. 89-90.
121   Meuvret 1971, p. 34.
122   Clough 1939, p. 363.

Socio-economic Classes and the State

The moneyed bourgeoisie believed that the nobles lodged in Versailles were parasites and futile. But, the aristocracy was hardly ready to fraternize with the 'inferior' classes. Voltaire asserted that: 'all the poor are not necessarily unhappy, the majority were born in these conditions, and the continuous work makes them unaware of their situation'.[123] Turgot fully agreed that extreme income inequality was not a bad thing at all.[124] Following some physiocratic tenets, the bourgeoisie argued that Mother Nature had decreed inequality and according to each one's aptitude this natural inequality was indispensable to the social order.

One has to remember that the Catholic Church, regardless of political changes and vicissitudes, remained a strong player in French public policies. The Church condemned the incipient capitalism and did not want to accept any hint of social transformation. During the early eighteenth century, a priest, *l'abbé* Lambert, exhorted the workers not to expect or accept increased remuneration for serving their masters; they would be better off by placing their hopes on the happiness the next world. Furthermore, public assistance to the poor was mainly left to voluntary philanthropy but increasingly it became obvious that the State would have to accept responsibility. In the wake of the downfall of the *Ancien Régime*, State assistance to the poor became recognized as a natural right.[125]

Workers attempted to organize with little success, not different from Britain and the United States. Strikes were generally condemned to failure because of a lack of a united front, limited participation, and often strikes were localized in a single place. On the other hand, industrial employers joined forces against worker associations to clamp down on wages and to intimidate those employers persuaded to break ranks. As in other mercantilist states, the State acted to keep labor costs (wages) down to keep French products competitive to fostering exports.

The State acted strongly on behalf of the employers because it assumed an identity between employer interest and national interest. It appears that the State was hostile to workers' demands and penalized workers who quit an employment without the agreement of the employer. No other employer could hire someone who did not have a labor identity card stating that the former employer had discharged the worker. Organized labor was viewed as a conspiracy against the well being of the society. At the convocation of the *Etats Généraux* (the Estates-General), the few industrial workers were not asked to participate, while their employers were, along with landlords and landless peasants. It seems that the workers were not yet aware of worker class-consciousness, rather their concern was limited to their poverty, insecurity, and their search for ways to survive. They

---

123   Leon 1970a, p. 646.
124   A famous contemporary French architect, Jacques François Blondel (1705-1774) maintained that there have to be some people who serve other people.
125   Bloch 1974, p. 450; Leon 1970b, p. 677; Duby and Mandron 1958, Vol. 2, pp. 170-179.

did participate in the 1789 Revolution not as workers, but as angry paupers and, more often, in Paris as a mob.

The Rise of the Bourgeoisie

Between 1700 and 1789, a handful of financiers and merchants succeeded in accumulating fortunes amounting to hundreds of millions of livres. In the hundred years before the Revolution, an institutional change took place slowly but steadily. Some members of the bourgeoisie, towns people, who had influence with the government at the local level were charged by the central government with various local tasks such as collecting taxes, applying rules and regulations, and signing contracts in the name of the State. These positions were often abused and influenced the spread of corruption although the majority of these intermediaries were able financiers who became quite wealthy. Many of these financiers emulated the king by supporting letters and encouraging talent and therefore by subsidizing the development of the arts. While the State depended on the bourgeoisie, still the ruling class felt that the bourgeois class was comprised of riff raff. The *philosophes*, the Church, and even the political class had no respect for these parvenus. Consequently, by the time of the Revolution there were no commoners in any high Church positions.[126]

By controlling finance and administration, the bourgeoisie became very powerful and attempted to challenge the State, that is, the king.[127] Anecdotally, it was reported that the old Duc de Richelieu told Louis XVI: 'Under Louis XIV one was silent, under Louis XV one dared to whisper, under you one speaks aloud'.[128] The economic, political, and social structure of the *Ancien Régime* was weakened beyond redemption. The fall of Bastille in 1789 symbolized the revolt against the *Ancien Régime*. The Revolution represented an epic break of the system, (equality before the law, the end of tax exemptions and much more), but in post-revolutionary France, the State continued in its pivotal role.

---

126 Sée 1967, pp. 56-63, 124-126, 143-147. The noble clergy, not different from other nobles, lived sumptuously, mainly in Paris, and rarely visited their parishioners. Only a minority of this high clergy cared about poverty, charity, and sickness; this miniscule minority helped in public assistance and the building of hospital. Yet the bulk of the clergy, the so-called lower level parish priests and vicars were, in the main, poverty stricken and associated more with the rest of the population from which they originated. It is estimated that during the 1750s there were 80,000 noble families comprising 400,000 individuals. The ecclesiastics accounted for 1.8 percent of the population but owned five to six percent of the land, mostly in scattered small parcels. But, in northern France, the clergy also owned urban real estate; they owned almost the entire town of Rennes. These contemporary estimates were made by the Reverend Coyer in *Noblesse commerçante* and by Marquise de Bouille in his *Mémoires*. Sée 1967, p. 72.
127 Leon 1970a, pp. 642-5; Sée 1967, p. 55.
128 Descimon and Guery 1989, p. 292.

The Revolution of 1789

It took a hundred years to arrive at the financial crisis, which preceded the French Revolution. France fought four wars (1689-1763) against Britain and its allies in an effort to extend the eastern frontier to its so-called natural boundary of the Rhine and the Alps. France lost every time but, nevertheless, gained control of Alsace and Lorraine. In an effort to seek revenge against Britain, France aided the Thirteen Colonies in North America in their struggle for independence. Wars were expensive, especially lost wars. The French Revolution stemmed, in part, of the inability of the royal treasury to put France's finances in order.

Several times during the eighteenth century the State wrote down the amount of its indebtedness, which alienated its bourgeois creditors. In 1787, France needed to borrow or increase taxes, but could do neither since the State defaulted and the bourgeoisie would not lend money again without some protection for the creditors. The aristocracy (Assembly of 'Notables' including the prelates and noblemen) in 1787 refused to yield on a new tax or end tax exemptions and insisted on sharing in control of the government on taxation and public spending. In a sense, both the bourgeoisie and the aristocracy shared a common objective, trimming the absolute power of the king. A weak monarch, Louis XVI, had no choice but to call the Estates-General, a nominally and quite limited representative institution that had not been convened since 1614.[129]

The Estates-General were convened to resolve the fiscal crisis but this opened the Pandora box of injustices of the *Ancien Régime* that could no longer be kept in check. The new nobility, made up of the bourgeoisie who were buying fiefs, was trying to maximize returns on its investments with deleterious effect on peasant income.[130] The Revolution had immediate economic consequences such as the depletion of the treasury and run-away inflation by printing worthless money, *assignats* to pay for the wars against Britain and its allies. From a social point of view, the abolition of the privileged orders profoundly altered land tenure and promoted peasant ownership. This produced a long run transformation regardless of the political changes that ensued.

All institutional or structural changes entail a cost, be it economic, political and/or social. For instance, enclosures helped make British agriculture much more efficient, measured in output per acre or man-hour, than French agriculture. Before the Revolution, British-type enclosure was introduced in France, which possibly increased poverty for the short run in the countryside, but enclosure never took hold in France to the same extent as in Britain. The French Revolution converted France into a nation of small peasant proprietors.[131]

---

129 In fact, the *Parlement* of Paris, one of the several supreme law courts, ruled in September 1788 that the Estates General should meet.

130 Aftalion 1990, pp. 11-30.

131 While it remains debatable, the 'push theory' claims that enclosures did not necessarily increase poverty in the British countryside, nor did it result in small proprietors, but instead created an urban labor reserve army living in abject poverty

The State in the Process of Industrialization

The abolition of trade associations encouraged the development of industry. The Schneider family initiated coke smelting in France during the 1780s, thanks to the proximity of coal and iron as well as that of royal support.[132] Perhaps because of the shortage of domestic high-grade coal, despite the war economy and the demands on the armament industry, French heavy industry failed to develop immediately after the Revolution and had to wait for the Napoleonic regime.[133] Some French historians observe that the period witnessed a process of *étatisation* (becoming state dependent). This assumption of control was completed through the extension of privileges to the urban society, including the nobles, by the new political order and by substituting the State for the Church in education and welfare.[134]

In the process of industrialization, the French State during and immediately after the Revolution, contributed significantly to the advancement of science by developing public higher education. During the revolutionary years, France established the *Ecole Polytechnique*, Polytechnic School, an engineering college, in 1794 and under Napoleon, the *Ecole des Arts et Métiers*, the School of Arts and Trades, in 1804. During the Revolutionary era the decimal and the metric systems, that eventually became almost universal, were adopted.[135] One cannot minimize these actions of the seemingly chaotic State in affecting technological progress and economic expansion.

The *philosophes* believed that the people could seize control of their destiny, but they did not preach revolution nor did they have a blue print for its aftermath. The consequences of the 1789 Revolution have been enormous for centuries. According to the Marxist view, the French Revolution was the corner stone of the political triumph of bourgeois capitalism. Others maintain that the Revolution

---

which in the short run compared unfavorably with rural poverty where the inhabitants could find rudimentary shelter and food. The 'pull theory' claims that opportunities in the cities attracted underemployed peasants to become potential industrial laborers.

132 Unfortunately, they went bankrupt by 1835 but finally succeeded in 1848.

133 Sée 1942, p. 67.

134 To withdraw the Church's control of the masses, the Constituent Assembly's Mendacity Committee proposed a welfare state scheme that would have made the Church's charity unnecessary. It failed for lack of structure and funds. Jones 2002, p. 452.

135 In 1794, the Convention voted the complete separation of Church and State. Wishing to cover his flank, Napoleon signed the Concordat of 1801 but the separation of religion and State did not take place for another one hundred years. It took Italy even longer; the Lateran Pact of 1929 reversed Cavour's 'a free Church in a free State'. On the other hand, Britain has never undergone this separation; the Commonwealth of Massachusetts was the last state in the United States to maintain an established official Church.

retarded capitalist development in France.[136] During the eighteenth century, France probably experienced a high rate of economic growth not different from that of the British economy.[137]

Capitalism and Social Change

The development of capitalism contributed greatly to the social transformation during the second part of the eighteenth century. The Revolution abolished all juridical distinctions that existed between classes and established *l'égalité de droit*, equality in the face of the law. Thus the abolition of juridical class privileges together with the advance of capitalism had the unintended effect of re-enforcing the continuing role for the State.[138]

An economic historian argued that, during the 1790s, notwithstanding revolutionary abuses (including execution by revolutionary tribunals for opposing the temporary majority), the French briefly may have enjoyed fuller political liberty than any place in Europe, arguably, Britain included. Most scholars would agree that the French Revolution in the long run occupies a prime place in the history of freedom.[139]

Social policies, perhaps unwittingly, contributed to institutional changes that might have enhanced economic development. If one assesses the policies adopted by the National Assembly, the successor to the Estates General, in the year immediately after the start of the Revolution, one would have to conclude that the 'libertarians' were in charge. Not much different from the British House of Commons or the United States Congress, the National Assembly represented powerful interest groups. The majority of those representing the nobles were military men and large landowners; parish priests represented the clergy.[140] Some claim that during the eighteenth century, in a similar way, but more so in Continental Europe than in the Anglo-American countries, governments aimed at increasing the wealth of the nation as much as increasing the power of the State.[141]

Under the *Ancien Régime*, organized crafts were dependent on the State that chartered guilds, which were an arm of the State and acted according to the implied

---

136 A few economic historians contend that the Industrial Revolution had begun in France and not in Britain. It is difficult to accept this statement because of the paucity of data for the specific period and the accepted conventional wisdom that the Industrial Revolution began in Britain. Cobban 1971, p. 168.

137 Komlos 2000, p. 308.

138 Sée 1967, pp. 181-184.

139 Norberg 1994, p. 254.

140 The 611 deputies of the Third Estate included functionaries (45 percent), lawyers (25 percent), magistrates and holders of various offices, seventy six merchants, forty landowners, doctors and professional men, eight industrialists, and one banker; many of the revolutionary leaders were intellectuals, for instance, Danton and Robespierre were lawyers while Marat was a physician. Aftalion 1990, p. 50.

141 Vries 2002, p. 74.

authority.[142] In line with the Physiocrats who believed in the rule of nature, in 1776, Turgot, while minister, had issued an edict that forbade associations of trades, laborers, and employers as restraining freedom. The edict encountered strong opposition. Turgot's dismissal followed soon thereafter and the edict remained a dead letter until 1791. The Allarde Law of 1791 attempted to eliminate guilds by prohibiting any professional association that aimed at defending the interests of its trade.[143] Similarly, Chambers of Commerce were prohibited in 1791 and business corporations were prohibited in 1793 (Le Chapelier Law). The decree drafted by Isaac-Rene-Guy Le Chapelier (1754-1794), an ex-nobleman and a deputy to the National Assembly from Rennes in northwestern France, read 'there shall be neither voluntary nor obligatory professional, craft, nor trade association'. To be sure, despite the Allarde Law, under Napoleon and subsequent regimes, the guilds revived, expanded, and maintained a monopolistic position for most of the century.[144]

During the spring of 1791, workers in Paris joined together in a series of strikes in an attempt to negotiate with their employers. In Le Chapelier's eyes, the workers tried to reassert the guild spirit of the old regime, a corporate interest incompatible with revolutionary principles and the public good; furthermore, *les manufactures royales* were dismantled confirming the *laissez faire* convictions of the National Assembly. The Le Chapelier Law also soothed the tension between the Assembly and the people of Paris as workers' demands for a controlled economy grew in greater political force. The Law remained in effect until 1884. Legislation enacted between 1789 and 1791, affirmed the free movement of people and goods within the whole of France. In the spirit of Adam Smith, Le Chapelier believed that a democracy had to allow free competition and bargaining between employer and employee and that all organized groups represented a threat to the State.[145]

French labor policies paralleled some of the policies adopted in Britain and the United States. In Britain, the Combination Act of 1799 prohibited organized labor; as late as 1901, the British courts threatened British unions in their very existence. The Taff Vale decision held a union financially responsible for business losses incurred by an employer during a strike; however, Parliament overruled the Taff Vale decision with new legislation in 1906. Similarly, the *Commonwealth vs. Hunt* (1842) decision in Massachusetts, legitimized unions; still as late as the beginning of the twentieth century a Supreme Court Justice declared that peaceful picketing is an oxymoron equivalent to chaste vulgarity.

---

142   Coornaert 1970, pp. 124-127.
143   Sée 1967, pp. 106-107.
144   Fohlen 1970, p. 204.
145   Sibalis 1985, pp. 576-578.

Liberalism French Style

By 1791, to make occupational entry free to everyone, all agriculture and industry regulations and subsidies were abrogated. The philosophy adopted was one of liberalism–freedom, property as a natural right, security, resistance to oppression, and freedom of trade. But, the National Assembly changed composition so often that no clear long-term policy evolved. Theoretically, Physiocracy influenced the members of the National Assembly although they did not hesitate to introduce domestic regulations or impediments to movement of people and goods.[146] Institutionally the 1791 legislation was directed towards the individual and not the State (apparently akin to Adam Smith's precepts). For an instant some French visualized a utopian freedom that never took hold, rather for the short run, to save so called revolutionary principles, the leaders of the French Revolution resorted to terror.[147]

For once, the intellectual libertarians made common cause with the masses for free markets. The libertarians believed that free markets would induce economic development; the masses were against any monopolies or privileges that they felt to have pauperized them. A French economic historian agrees that 'under the *Ancien Régime*, the State economic and social intervention in matters of industries and professions was biased towards the upper classes'.[148]

Already by 1792 the revolutionary government, *le Comité de Salut public*, prohibited exports of grains and by 1793, many products were rationed. Maximum prices were instituted and wages and salaries were capped without mitigating inflation. Freedom of movement for the masses was curtailed in 1792 and made even stricter in 1795. These prohibitions and regulations resulted in the public sector dominating France after 1792 and French *dirigisme* to be reinforced by events, culminating with Napoleon's *coup d'état*.[149]

---

146 Catherine and Gousset 1965, pp. 90-93.

147 Economic historians have summarized the principles of the reforms of 1791 as follows: 1. Economic equilibrium is based a natural laws that policy makers cannot change; 2. Natural laws are beneficial to all because economic forces left alone do better than when they are regulated by the government; 3. Best policy is to let all factors of production free to act and interact; 4. Freedom of contracts implies also rigorous implementation of contracts so that the system should function; 5. Economic forces set prices; there are no just or unjust prices, they have to be left to the market to be set; 6. Through this system, everyone is paid according to the quantity and quality of his contribution, if one performs well is well paid, if one errs, he merits the ruin; 7. Money must be stable as a store of value so that one can use his money freely and the property he acquires to be sacred; this is a tenet of liberty that is included in the *Droit des hommes* (the rights of men) of 1789; 8. The system does not worry about social consequences that can propel large wealth concentration in a few hands and much poverty for the masses; 9. Competition can take place when there are large numbers of participants; any collusion is prohibited, this is why all labor, professional and business grouping are not allowed; 10. Consequently the role of the State is that of an arbiter that supervises if all the rules of the market are in place. Catherine and Gousset 1965, pp. 94-97.

148 Rosanvallon 1989, p. 563.

149 Catherine and Gousset 1965, pp. 97-103.

Napoleon I, a dictator but also a son and heir of the Revolution, while instituting an absolutist regime, included libertarian principles in the Civil Code of 1803 and the Commercial Code of 1807. These Codes served as a model for many countries in years to come, and most of Europe adopted them at one time or another. Their implementation in France became difficult because of the intervening wars, the main source of perennial scarcity.

Conclusions

In the late eighteenth century France was the second largest European country after Russia; twice as populous as Britain (England and Scotland), France may have been the wealthiest country in Europe, although not per capita. While less industrial than Britain, because of its greater population, France figured as a major industrial center of Europe, and French exports to Europe were larger than those of Britain.

A contemporary French economist remarked that the French State had always had a small head and a large body, that is, the administrators and the enterprises created by the State. While under the *Ancien Régime* and continuing through the Revolution, the leaders proclaimed a libertarian philosophy, the State intervened in the market. The liberal *philosophes* exercised an intellectual influence but State intervention in the French economy did not change regardless of regime or political inclination.[150]

Incidentally, the *philosophes* did not agree as to what kind of political system would benefit the population or/and the State. Quesnay advocated a benevolent despot, Montesquieu and Rousseau favored limitations on the powers of the executive, and Voltaire, while preaching majority rule, maintained that a wealthy elite should formulate the policies of the State.[151] As a result of possessing more or less uncontrolled absolute power, the kings succeeded in squandering the national wealth and creating financial and economic chaos for the State. The outcome was the1789 Revolution.

Many would say that the leaders of the Revolution tarnished the ideals developed during the Revolution. The free movement of people, goods, and services, *laissez faire* (while advocated by some during the early phases of the Revolution) was not a doctrine accepted by most of the leaders or, for that matter, the conventional wisdom. In international trade, the State maintained control, through the *Ancien Régime*, the Revolution and the Revolutionary Wars, by overt or covert protection.[152] On the domestic front, before and after the Revolution, the State instituted quality and price control on may products. The State continued to

---

150　Jean Bouvier, 'Le capitalisme et l'Etat en France', *Recherches e Travaux*, IHES, Paris I Bulletin No. 15 December 1986, pp. 47-63, cited by Gueslin 1997, p. 22.

151　Catherine and Gousset 1965, pp. 87-88.

152　One could easily argue that France had a permanent war economy between 1789 and 1814.

play an important role not only in agriculture, contrary to what the Physiocrats had advocated, but also in most branches of industry and commerce.

Germany

During the eighteenth century, Germany had not yet come into existence as a territorial nation State. Instead, there were two categories of German speaking nations. One consisted of the polyglot, multiethnic Austrian Habsburg Empire, while the other comprised a multitude of German territories, among them the larger kingdoms of Baden, Bavaria, Prussia, Saxony, and Württemberg. Just before the French Revolution, the territory that would eventually become Germany consisted of about eighteen hundred (some estimate twenty five hundred) independent and semi-independent territorial units of varying size.[153] The eighteenth century witnessed the rivalry between an emerging Brandenburg-Prussia and Austria for control of Central Europe.[154] Prussia gradually gained hegemony as the dominant central European power and formed the core of German unification in the nineteenth century.[155]

The Protestant movement proved to be a key to the economic development of northern German entities, if only because the State superseded the Church in authority and, advocated public education.[156] Luther preached for the hegemony of the State rather than that of the Church, and he insisted that the State had an obligation to provide universal education so that individuals could read the Bible without an intercessor. Indeed, the Prussian rulers introduced compulsory

---

153 As they evolved into the eighteenth century, parts of Germany were nominally within the long defunct (476) Roman Empire revived in 962. This political entity received the appellation of the Holy Roman Empire during the twelfth century, reflecting the nominal acceptance of the Roman Church's spiritual control of Catholic Europe during the Middle Ages. In 800, for almost a century, Charlemagne (742-814), King of the Franks, succeeded in restoring the Western Roman Empire (known as the Carolingian) that lasted to 925. In 962, through an agreement between Pope John XII (955-964) and Otto I (912-973), King of Germany and the Holy Roman Emperor (962-973), the Empire was revived with a German emperor. During the ensuing centuries, the emperor shared an uneasy power relationship with the papacy. By about 1500, the emperor surrendered much of his grip on his constituencies, a heterogeneous mass of princes, kings, barons, and castle owners. That unruly crowd attempted to create a federal system but did not want to yield individual territorial sovereignty. The Thirty Years War (1618-1648) all but terminated the Holy Roman Empire's shadowy power.

154 While better off economically than Prussia-Brandenburg, Saxony and Bavaria, attempted alliances with the prospective winner.

155 The Hohenzollern princes first ruled over Brandenburg (1415) and added Prussia in 1525.

156 The Reformation, the revolt against the Catholic Church, starting with Jan Hus (1369-1415) in Bohemia and culminating with Martin Luther (1483-1536) in Saxony, precipitated a century or more of religious conflicts.

education; more generally, the State everywhere also had an important role in developing higher education.

For most of the eighteenth century, enlightened despots ruled Prussia, the largest, German entity, leaving aside the polyglot Austria. During the seventeenth and eighteenth centuries *Cameralism*, a variant of mercantilism, was taught in many German universities. While some German rulers toyed with economic liberalism, mercantilism generally prevailed. The State in various German territories intervened in the market with rules and regulations and did not shy away from rendering financial assistance to private enterprises. The struggle for political and economic control between eastern landowner, *Junkers*, and western business interests continued to affect economic policies and compromises ensued.

Setting the Future Germany

The Treaty of Westphalia (1648) transformed the Holy Roman Empire into a loose confederation of about 300 independent principalities and about fifteen hundred quasi-sovereign territories and individual fiefdoms. Some of the city-states were in reality self-governing towns controlled by the local elite or by a trade association (guild). These elites varied among states or localities; in Nuremberg, for instance, the leading families held official position by hereditary right. The *bürgerliche* (bourgeoisie) leaders of Hamburg were composed of craftsmen and merchants who disdained the aristocracy. However, cities like Berlin (Brandenburg-Prussia) or Munich (Bavaria) exercised considerably less independence because their respective territorial States controlled them.[157]

During the seventeenth and eighteenth centuries the basic unit in central Europe was the *Land* that represented a collection of laws, mores, and institutions. In various cities, guilds, aristocratic landowners, and the Church shared authority within the *Land* and there was little distinction between private and public institutions. Authority and willingness to obey were derived from traditional customs and often from brute force or from the fear of brute force. *Herrschaft*, the individual lord and master, who put the onus on economic, political, and social power on the individual rather than the institution, denotes this. A vivid example is the power of the *Junker*, the landed East Prussian aristocracy over the serfs.[158]

Cameralism

Cameralism, a variant of mercantilism, developed during the seventeenth and eighteenth centuries to restore order out of the chaos created by the Thirty Years

---

157 Borchardt 1985, pp. 19, 23-24; Henning 1974, pp. 253-254; Wehler 1989, pp. 36-43; Sheehan 1989, p. 133.
158 Sheehan 1989, pp. 25-26; Wehler 1989, pp. 254-256. After World War II, while institutional relationships were different, the German states reverted to the traditional *Länder*.

War (1618-1648), which had impoverished the German states.[159] *Kammer*, derived from the Greek and Latin *camera*, initially was used to define sovereign place, while *Kameralwissenschaft* translates as *Cameralism* or the science of economic administration. Frederick Wilhelm I of Prussia (1712-1740), in 1727 established a chair on *Cameralia und Oeconomia* at the University of Halle.[160] By 1750, *Cameralism* was taught in all thirty-one German universities as a course in administrative economics.[161]

Some German intellectuals and policy makers toyed for while with the physiocratic ideas. Carl Frederick, the ruler of Baden-Durlach corresponded with Mirabeau and employed Du Pont de Nemours as an adviser.[162] Experimentally, Carl Frederick introduced the 'single tax' system on land, only to abandon it as too difficult to implement since no reliable estimate of land value was available.[163] Freedom of trade in agricultural products never took hold in the economies of the German states. Adam Smith's ideas were repugnant to the government and social structure that existed in Prussia; the State controlled agriculture, industry, and foreign trade.[164]

By the end of the eighteenth century German intellectuals and policy makers classified as utopian even the physiocratic philosophy. The ideas of *laissez faire*, economic freedom, did not have a place in the *Cameralist* society. German economies were backward with respect to Britain and France and the sovereigns tolerated little intellectual freedom. The intellectuals vacillated between the *Cameralist* State order and the physiocrat *laissez faire* philosophy; there was never a clear-cut resolution to the debate. Despite this, the French enlightenment influenced German economic and political thought.

Cameralism assumed a primary role for the State. By extending the State controls and prerogatives, *Cameralism* allowed the extension of bureaucratic power, eventually giving way to the *Nationalökonomie* during the nineteenth century. *Cameralists* believed that this could be accomplished through the establishment of state economic enterprises and the development of infrastructure. They also wanted to remove internal trade barriers but this had to wait until the nineteenth century. *Cameralism* originated in the paternalistic character of centralized fiscal policy of the government in the process of development.[165] We question the contention that *Cameralism* aimed not only at increasing tax revenue

---

159 'The economic theory of mercantilism was modeled on the absolutist doctrine, and assumed that the state should also enjoy absolute directorial power in the economic sphere.' Munch 1996, p. 213.
160 Kellenbenz 1977, p. 303.
161 Tribe 1988, p. 6, note 12; Abel 1967, pp. 281-283.
162 Honore Gabriel Riquetti Mirabeau (1749-1791), head of the French National Assembly (1789-1791); Pierre Samuel Dupont de Nemours (1739-1817), a leading French Physiocrat.
163 Kellenbenz 1977, p. 299.
164 Behrens 1985, pp. 186-187.
165 Tribe 1988, pp. 10-11, 119-131; Abel 1967, pp. 283-285.

but also at improving the conditions of the people, in contrast to the view that British and French mercantilism aimed at only increasing the treasure of the crown.[166]

The State as Protagonist of Economic Progress

Various German states owned land, operated enterprises, and maintained a monopoly for certain commodities. Gustav Schmoller, a noted nineteenth century German economic historian, claimed that when the old medieval order stagnated, only the State, as represented by a strong enlightened despot, could induce change and that the State could serve as an instrument for social progress. Not all observers believe that direct State involvement in the market contributed substantially to German economic development, arguing that indirect government intervention, such as establishing an efficient legal system and building infrastructure, helped much more.

For example, starting in the seventeenth century, in Prussia-Brandenburg the State regulated wages and prices to fight inflation; also, financial assistance was given to private industry. During the eighteenth century, the Kingdom of Saxony developed a strong quality textile industry based on locally grown merino wool. Saxony did not hesitate to stop the export of native raw materials to avoid competition from abroad and prohibited the importation of manufactured goods thus giving local textile entrepreneurs a monopoly. Also, the State founded its own industries such as pottery at Meissen to produce 'Dresden China', akin to the French State owned *les manufactures royales* but economically viable.[167] Many German states took over much of the tax administration previously farmed out to private individuals. The *Unternehmerstaat*, the state entrepreneur, was important in manufacturing, domestic commerce, and foreign trade, in addition to the State's generally accepted functions such as police, defense, and education.[168]

The Junkers and the Absolutist Prussian State

Through the seventeenth century, many German rulers (kings, princes, dukes, barons, and counts) aimed at a life of leisure for themselves and their families; some also sought prestige, glory, territory and power. As *Herrschaft*, they did not differentiate between their dynastic power and the power of the State; they assumed that the State was an extension of their land.[169] After Frederick Wilhelm I ascended to the Prussian throne in 1712, Prussia begun emerge as the dominant

166 Recktenwald 1987, p. 313; Henning 1974, pp. 233-234; Wehler 1989, pp. 233-240.
167 Dorwart 1971, pp. 271-272; Hassinger 1978, pp. 608-629.
168 Borchardt 1985, pp. 25-26.
169 Sheehan 1989, p. 31.

German state, but the king was confronted with a power struggle with the *Junkers* East Elbian landed aristocracy, still very much in control of Prussia.[170]

King Frederick Wilhelm I believed in the heavy hand of the 'leader' to achieve greatness for Prussia. Perhaps by necessity, since Prussia was a poor country, he was parsimonious and dismantled the Versailles style of living at the royal palace as soon as he inherited the throne. Not different from other eighteenth century rulers (Britain excluded), he equated the wealth of the realm with his personal fortune. However, he was more extreme than other rulers in that he accumulated barrels of silver coins in the palace basement.

Prussian society was under the influence and control of the military; most agree that a militaristic culture developed that endured for centuries. The fiscal burden of military expenditures might have contributed to economic retardation. More than doubling the size of the army, and to overcome sparse population, Frederick Wilhelm encouraged settlements of religious refugees, such as the Huguenots from France (after Louis XIV revoked the Edict of Nantes in 1685), on wastelands (*wuste stellen*) that eventually became viable farms. Those colonists who settled in the newly acquired territories were exempt from the military draft.[171]

The East Elbian *Junkers* viewed this settlement policy negatively because it diminished their control of the countryside. Frederick William believed that a larger population gave a country more soldiers and productive peasants and therefore taxpayers. Prussia had a well-deserved inferiority complex; it could not compete on equal terms with Britain, France, and Spain or even the other important German states such as Austria, Saxony, and Hanover.

In line with the spirit of Louis XIV, Frederick Wilhelm I claimed that *l'état c'est moi*, 'I am the State', and behaved like a despot in formulating economic policies.[172] An absolute monarch, Frederick Wilhelm did not have any qualms about having the State as a leader or a partner in the market place. The debate in Prussia on the reform of the old feudal agrarian order centered between self-regulation and government intervention. The conventional wisdom assumed that the State was essential in any durable reform.

In the late eighteenth century, those who introduced Adam Smith's *Wealth of Nations* in Germany, Sartorius (1765-1828), for instance, were more inclusive and less defensive than Smith on the role of the State. In addition, to Smith's protection of property, national defense, and education, they included citizen welfare. Sartorius asserted that public policies should make possible that 'individual citizens might be able to earn an adequate income', and still result in enough funds for public expenditures. The modified economic principles of Smith

---

170 *Junkers* seems to derive from a Middle Age antonym, *junc-herre*, the *altherre* elder noble, versus young noble. Only with the introduction of limited democratic reforms during the nineteenth century did *Junkers* acquire a pejorative meaning. Rosenberg 1978, p. 25.

171 Busch 1981, pp. 21, 52, 61.

172 Asprey 1986, pp. 12-13.

and his followers were not readily accepted in Germany but they pushed government to reform.[173]

The Welfare State and Reformation

In addition to the economic debate, differences between religions probably played an important role in forging the role of the State in German entities. There is no consensus among social scientists that the widespread acceptance of Protestant doctrines in the northern German States was one of the causes of future economic expansion.[174] Also, since the Church controlled charity and social welfare before but not after the Reformation, the State had to fill the breach. The modern German 'Welfare State' has its origins in the Reformation with the emphasis on the role of the laic State in the socio-economy.

The Welfare State could be defined as limited in the provision of social services or in the post-medieval interpretation of the German *Polizeistaat* the power of the State to police or to interfere in the economy for the ostensible benefit of the population.[175] The latter interpretation indicates the strong role of the Prussia-Brandenburg state beginning with the seventeenth century in the education and health fields.[176] The *Polizeistaat* concerns a vast range of State intervention in Church affairs, industry, health and *Volkskorper*, the body of the nation. 'Everywhere, *Policey* involved regulation of both 'private' and 'public' concerns, indistinguishably'.[177] On the other hand, certain German states followed a previous British pattern, by forbidding begging; in Hamburg, a city-state and therefore different from the territorial states, according to the Protestant ethic, beggars were segregated in workhouses.[178]

Martin Luther and Education

Martin Luther argued that the secular State could be strengthened through the spread of literacy and education. Contrary to the medieval institutional framework that limited literacy to a few, Martin Luther believed that literacy must be universal, that is, every one should read the Bible, preferably in German, without

---

173   Zorn 1978, pp. 583-592; Kellenbenz 1977, pp. 315-320; Gagliardo 1969, p. 132; see also: G. Sartorius (1796) *Handbuch der Staatswirtschaft zum Gebrauche bei akademischen Vorlesungen, nach Adam Smith's Grundsatzen.* Berlin, pp. 14, 152-157, cited by Tribe 1988, pp. 164-168.

174   Max Weber in the early twentieth century ascribed the difference in economic progress of Germany between the Protestant North and East and the Catholic South and West to religion, especially Calvinism. Crouzet 2001, p. 49.

175   The theory and practice of *Policey* ('polity' or regulation), derived from Greek *politeia* and the Latin *politia*, refers to conditions of good order and means of securing it. Munch 1996, pp. 208-209.

176   Dorwart 1971, pp. 310-311; Gregg 1969, p. 4.

177   Munch 1996, p. 210.

178   Kellenbenz 1977, pp. 314-315.

needing clerical intercession.[179] If justice and reason were to guide civil society, Luther maintained that men needed to be educated; therefore the State had to organize public schools and compel parents to send their children to school. This requirement is in line with Luther's view that the State is the ultimate source of authority.

In Prussia-Brandenburg the schools were the responsibility of the towns, with the instruction in humanistic and theological subjects all in Latin. As elsewhere in Western Europe, the schools beyond primary level were meant to prepare men for the priesthood or public service. These schools were named *Klosterschule* (schools in cloisters), *Paticularschule* (private schools), or *Stadtschule* (state schools) and housed in former Augustinian or Franciscan cloisters, churches or other public buildings. While elementary education continued to be administered by the cities, the State assumed increasing responsibility.[180] Two Hohenzollern princes introduced compulsory education, especially in towns, emphasized German rather than Latin, and expanded the curriculum to include natural history and vocational training.[181]

The State's Role in Higher Education

Universities constitute a good proxy for cultural/economic development. Universities began in Italy and quickly spread to France and England before the end of the Middle Ages. The universities of Germany in general originated a century later than those of France, Britain, and Italy although the University of Heidelberg in the state of Baden was established in 1386. The University of Frankfurt was founded in 1506 and provided educated cadres for Prussia-Brandenburg for two hundred years; the University of Berlin was established as late as 1809.[182] The University of Halle eclipsed the University of Frankfurt in 1694 and consolidated the educational system from elementary to higher education in line with the spirit of the Protestant Reformation.

Public officials were very eager to attract the best teachers; accordingly, they offered monetary and other incentives. While they wanted to attract students from the aristocracy, most of the students came from families of intellectuals, the clergy, and bureaucrats.[183] Professors appointed by the government to teach in State

---

179 Before printing and paper were available after 1500, books were prohibitively expensive; since the clergy constituted the bulk of the literates, the Church had a quasi monopoly on publishing.

180 Dorwart 1971, pp. 146-147, 192-193.

181 Yet, as elsewhere (in Italy, because of the Piedmont Savoy connection, long after unification, in Russia to 1917) throughout the 1700s the language used at the European Courts remained French.

182 Frankfurt did not become part of Prussia until after the Austrian-Prussian War of 1866.

183 Dorwart 1971, pp. 144-147, 158-159; Sheehan 1989, pp. 138-139. See also a good discussion on the development of German universities in Wehler 1989, pp. 292-303.

universities, emphasized that the State was all-powerful and the source of all rights. To promote general welfare, the State 'had the right to interfere in any aspect of national and personal life'.[184]

As in the other countries of the day, the Prussian State also had a prominent role in medicine and public health. For instance, from the middle of the seventeenth century, the Brandenburg princes subjected public health to administrative regulations under the police power of the State. The *Collegium Medicum* (State Board of Medicine) was established in 1685 by the Elector Frederick Wilhelm as a response to the practice of medicine and distribution of medical remedies. The code of professional conduct was further expanded in 1725 when anyone applying to practice medicine was required to pass a stringent State test. A few years earlier, a *Collegium Sanitaris*, Board of Sanitation in 1720, gained jurisdiction over any activity that could harm the public such as the adulteration of foods, the burial of the dead, and cesspools polluting the Spree River running through Berlin. Thus the State, through occupational licensing, became the ultimate arbiter for the entire system of public and private health.[185]

Economic Liberalism

In 1791, Wilhelm von Humboldt (1767-1835), a political theorist and a reformer of Prussian education, called for a free society relegating the State to the protection of individuals and property from internal and external dangers. Distinguishing between the State and society, Humboldt argued that codified laws were needed to check on the State's transgressions. His proposals were attempted in Prussia but were not implemented because of strong opposition from elements of the bourgeoisie and the nobility.[186]

Public servants acted as a cohesive social group in the service to the State. It is remarkable that the staunchest supporters of economic liberalism were the public servants and not businessmen. One could, however, redefine their economic liberalism as using the power of the State to foster social and economic change by accepting a key role for the State in the market economy. The bureaucracy emulated the enlightened political absolutism.[187] Immanuel Kant (1724-1804) reasoned that enlightenment meant that people can discuss freely but, in the end, they have to obey the rules of the State.[188]

---

184 Since the State owed its existence to man, 'it had no right to require adherence to any particular form of religious belief or to limit freedom of thought on religious and philosophical matters', Behrens 1985, p. 179.

185 Britain lagged by a century (the late nineteenth century) in developing domestic public administration. Dorwart 1971, pp. 239-254.

186 Wilhelm von Humboldt (1960) *The Limits of State Action*, London, Cambridge University Press, pp. 43, 83, cited by Tribe 1988, pp. 153-154.

187 Brewer and Hellmuth 1999, p. 3.

188 Sheehan 1989, pp. 142, 196, 197, 202-203.

The Role of the State in the Larger Territories

Saxony Sharing a common cultural heritage with Prussia, Saxony (capital Dresden), the second largest German State outside Austria in the early eighteenth century, witnessed a close relationship between the local governments, that is, the guilds, and the entrepreneurs. Saxony encouraged industries and in 1754 an Augsburg master calico printer was recruited by the city of Plauen in central Saxony and given a monopoly until 1785 after which the printers organized in guilds. The State vacillated in its position, authorizing and denying monopoly power within the same trade; therefore, monopolies were dependent on the whims of the State. Even though Saxony adhered to mercantilism, the State permitted the use of domestic and imported raw materials.[189]

Württemberg In Württemberg, (principal city Stuttgart) in southwest Germany, public policies depended on State and non-State institutions. Among the larger German territories, Württemberg probably had the most arbitrary government. Duke Karl Eugen (1737-1793) spent extravagantly on palaces, mistresses, and court festivities, and especially on the military. He imposed heavy taxes collected by the army and also 'sold' soldiers into service. The central State became cohesive in the sixteenth century and thus could take charge of taxation, welfare, bureaucracy and control of the economy. The intrusive centralized State legislated guild privileges, wage ceiling, compulsory religious education, Sabbath observance, and community church courts.

Local Württemberg governments were even more meddling in the every day life of the citizenry. Towns and villages regulated minutia such as marriage, mobility, sexuality, leisure, and factor and product markets. They were empowered for their tasks through the support of the all-encompassing central State. Moreover, not different from other parts of central Europe, the non-State institution, the guilds in Württemberg possessed regional monopolies controlling many branches of commerce and handicraft industries until the end of the eighteenth century. As in other parts of Germany bordering France, Württemberg adopted the Napoleonic codes that modified but did not terminate bureaucratic absolutism.[190]

Baden The other two middle-sized states, Baden (capital Karlsruhe) and Bavaria (capital Munich) neighbored Württemberg and fought hard to retain their independence. Baden-Durlach represents the best example of eighteenth century German enlightened absolutism. In 1722, the Margrave Karl Wilhelm (1709-1738) issued an edict of religious toleration and assisted in building houses of prayers for Lutherans, Calvinists, Catholics and Jews. His son Karl Friedrich (1738-1811) continued with these progressive policies. Influenced by French

---

189 Tipton 1976, pp. 30-31.
190 Ogilvie 2003, pp. 19-21; Gagliardo 1991, p. 371; Hughes 1992, pp. 183-184.

Physiocrats, he attempted to implement their theories, without success in trade; however, these policies resulted in improvement in agriculture by using advanced farm techniques, better roads and canals and, most important, the abolition of serfdom in 1783. In addition, he encouraged education by introducing compulsory elementary education and founding seminars for training of teachers.[191]

Bavaria At the beginning of the eighteenth century, Bavaria was more or less a vassal of France but seeking the best deal shifted allegiances between France and Austria often. Different from Baden, Bavaria underwent continuous financial crises caused by poor public management. In an essentially agrarian economy, the State aimed to control business and trade but did not contribute to industrial development. One of the problems was that half the farm land was owned by Churches, the other was chaos in the State financing depending on three parallel, separated, and corrupted taxation conduits, directed by the Court Chamber, controlled by estates, and collection by tax farmers. Also, the State depended besides taxes, on revenue from State monopolies, and French subsidies. Like Wurttemberg and Baden and other German states, before and after Napoleon, Bavaria was a centralized bureaucratic absolutist State. Also, as in other States under France tutelage at the end of the eighteenth and beginning of the nineteenth century, Bavaria introduces Napoleonic civil and commercial codes that prescribed equality before the law, sanctity of property, and abolishing of guilds and feudalism. To be sure, as elsewhere, peasant entitlements were not successful because of lack of financial support for the newly freed serfs.[192]

Prussia Frederick II (the Great) of Prussia (1740-1786) maintained that the power of the State should rest on the economic welfare of its inhabitants. Not different from Saxony, Württemberg, Baden, and Bavaria, in Prussia, in every instance, government participation in the market, as a service to the citizens or setting rules of conduct, implied diminishing economic freedom and increasing the power of the bureaucracy. Freedom in Prussia and elsewhere in Germany hardly meant what it did in France, much less in Britain. Political freedom did not exist and economic freedom certainly was circumscribed; Frederick the Great decreed that 'all that is not commanded is prohibited'.[193]

Cameralism under Frederick the Great

From the middle of the eighteenth to the middle of the nineteenth century Prussia fought Austria for the hegemony of Germany. After two wars with Austria, Frederick the Great succeeded in annexing Silesia, a critical addition to the

191   Gagliardo 1991, pp. 372-373; Sheehan 1989, pp. 262-263.
192   Gagliardo 1991, pp. 282-285, Hughes 1992, pp. 125-126, 157; Sheehan 1989, pp. 267-272.
193   Sheehan 1989, pp. 123-124; 436-437; Tribe 1988, p. 19.

backward Prussian economy. Inheriting an unfavorable balance of trade, Frederick established a department in the General Directory (the Cabinet) to deal with industry, trade, and colonization. By adopting mercantilism, his fiscal policy discouraged imports and encouraged exports. Perhaps under the influence of *Cameralism*, Frederick the Great engaged in tariff wars with Austria and Saxony in order to disturb their foreign trade, a 'beggar thy neighbor' policy.

Frederick the Great's predecessors, Frederick Wilhelm and Frederick I, gave high priority to industrial endeavors, encouraging would-be entrepreneurs, giving incentives to artisans, accepting religious exiles (for example, the Huguenots, after Louis XIV revoked the Edict of Nantes in 1685), and investing State resources in industrial enterprises. Despite the efforts of his predecessors, Prussia was an underdeveloped country compared not only to Britain, France, and Austria but also relative to other German entities. Aiming to expand manufacturing and to make Prussia an industrial power, Frederick the Great dredged and reclaimed rivers and seaports and built three canals to improve communication and transportation among the various parts of Prussia.[194]

Frederick the Great improved communication within the realm, established many State enterprises, and gave incentives to entrepreneurs. Also, he attracted foreign skilled workers and offered them facilities to establish themselves in Prussia. The Hohenzollerns tried to attract, and at the same time resented the Jews, who were important financial intermediaries.[195] The Jews were present in finance and contributed to the economic development of Prussia and other German states.[196]

Aiming at social peace, Frederick retarded the introduction of British spinning machines so as not to increase the unemployment of textile workers. Secondary to wool and later cotton, he encouraged the development of the silk industry by establishing a special Central Industrial Fund to subsidize it.[197] The conversion of Germany into an industrial powerhouse during the nineteenth century originated in some measure with Prussia in the eighteenth century with the expansion of the State's role. Frederick the Great granted subsidies to industry, devoted crown lands for experimental farming, increased state monopolies for household necessities (salt, tobacco) and trade, and established a central (royal) bank.[198]

Participating in the debate of what makes a good leader in a well-organized State, Frederick the Great excelled as an enlightened despot. He corresponded with Voltaire; and even had Voltaire as an ungrateful guest. By and large, he

---

194 Behrens 1985, pp. 123-125; Kriedte 1996, p. 123.

195 Also, as practiced for over four centuries, Jews were used as cash cows by making them pay a per capita annual *schutzgeld*, 'protection money'.

196 All German rulers thought that the Jews could bring a contribution to the State. In Brandenburg especially, the rulers detested the Jews but at the same rulers found the Jews important for the State's financial and economic welfare. Dorwart 1971, pp. 112-142.

197 Henderson 1968, pp. 145-147.

198 Gagliardo 1967, pp. 36, 44-45; Ogilvie 1996, pp. 295-296.

followed the same *Cameralist* economic doctrine he inherited from his predecessors. He shunned the Physiocrats and the incipient British economic liberalism. Nineteenth century German economic historians emphasized that German eighteenth century mercantilism meant pursuing 'state making and national-economy making at the same time', that is, centralization of the bureaucratic State.[199]

By conquering valuable territory, Frederick the Great strengthened the Prussian economy. He followed in his father's footsteps by settling another 300,000 immigrants from Eastern Europe in 1200 new villages. These migrants worked the land and, of course, were used as fodder for Frederick's wars. While the army was large relative to the size of the economy and burdened the treasury, in time of peace, soldiers were free to attend to their lands for most of the year. The work on fortifications acted as a stimulus to the economy by giving employment to many.[200]

Prussia's Cameralist Effects on the Rhineland and Westphalia

In the beginning of the eighteenth century, Prussia could be considered an eastern European state. Centuries earlier, the merger with Brandenburg gave Prussia a more western orientation. Still, the capital, Berlin, was far from the Rhine, and the Rhineland and Westphalia were much more advanced economically. Prussia acquired some Rhineland territories even before the Seven Years War (1756-1763), and much more later at the Congress of Vienna in 1815.

Some historians contend that the central government's policies had little impact on the rate of economic growth of the Rhineland and Westphalia while the role of the State in Prussia was beneficial, notwithstanding the *Cameralist* policies of Frederick the Great. This debate is inconclusive, owing, if nothing else, to the paucity of data but there is a consensus among scholars that during the eighteenth century the absence of a unified German market put the economy of the individual states at a distinct disadvantage versus the more integrated countries of Europe such as Britain and France.[201]

The State as Entrepreneur

While the State owned major mines, in Saxony also small-scale entrepreneurs owned mines; indeed, in the seventeenth century, so successful were Saxon miners

---

199 Schmoller 1967, pp. 50-51.
200 As a result of the incorporation of Silesia, Frederick the Great endowed Prussia with an easier to defend frontier. Rents and income from public lands from conquest and land confiscated from nobles constituted between one third to one half of the government's revenue. While Prussia hardly had a debt to service, Frederick's goal to have enough reserves in bullion for a four-year war was thwarted by the Seven Years War. By 1763, he resorted to plundering foreign occupied lands and by debasing the coinage. Behrens 1985, pp. 79-81.
201 Tipton 1976, pp. 66-67.

that they were brought to England.[202] Certain historians maintain that wholly owned State industry constituted the exception; the government funded and occasionally managed enterprises, directly or indirectly.[203] Others observe that in Prussia, through the Overseas Trading Corporation (*Seehandlung*) and the Mining Office (*Oberbergsamt*), the State indirectly owned a number of manufacturing and mining businesses. Prussia established State-owned furnaces to produce coke-smelted pig iron. While in Britain and France the State also regulated foreign trade, in Prussia the State organized the minutia of foreign trade.[204]

A government (royal) engineer, *Direktionprinzip*, supervised public and private mine operations in Prussia and Saxony. In Prussia this arrangement lasted until the 1830s, and by 1865 only safety inspections were required. Furthermore, the kings and later the State claimed part of the product of the mines. By contrast, in Britain, the two seventeenth century revolutions trimmed the king's financial independence and his rights to mining output, while in the United States, which never had a monarchy or a feudal system, the ownership of surface land implied the ownership of subsurface with no residual claim from the State.[205]

The Economic Crisis of 1763-1764

Frederick the Great interfered in the market not only with macro policies but also with direct measures to achieve stated goals or correct specific market failures. At the conclusion of the Seven Years War in 1763, a crisis originated with increased credit transactions and speculation on commodities, currency and land. When the wholesale grain merchants did not listen to his advice not to hold their stocks of grains, he released his own stores of grains, held in reserve for war, bringing prices down. In the financial markets, the Hamburg[206] bankers rebuffed him when he wanted to save, by edict, the house of Gotzkovsky, a merchant, industrialist, and financier who had prospered during the Seven Years War. Before and during the war he assisted the king in numerous transactions that helped the kingdom as well as Gotzkovsky's own purse. By 1763, unsuccessful financial speculations brought his business to the verge of bankruptcy.[207]

The economic crisis of 1763-1764 stemming from the end of the war was a turning point for the kingdom. Frederick lost confidence in merchants and considered enlarging State ownership and control of business.[208] The State

---

202 Martin Luther's father worked first as a miner and then became the owner of several small mines, that is, a small-scale entrepreneur.

194 Gagliardo 1991, p. 191.

204 Dunlavy 1994, p. 16; Trebilcock 1981, pp. 22-26.

205 Cameron 1997, pp. 293-294.

206 Hamburg was a 'free city' of the Holy Roman Empire and, therefore, totally beyond Frederick's control.

207 Henderson 1968, pp. 49-55.

208 Rather the idea originated with a royal adviser, Calzabigi, who proposed to organize the whole economy into a single State corporation.

instituted the Royal Bank of Berlin, modeled on the Bank of England, the tobacco monopoly, and the State lottery. The emergency measures instituted by the King eased the crisis but many financial and industrial firms became bankrupt. While some State monopolies were eliminated at Frederick's death, many of the institutions created during Frederick's reign survived into the nineteenth century, such as the Mining Office, the Forestry Department, the Royal Bank of Berlin, and the Overseas Trade Corporation.[209]

Prussia's Fiscal Policy

Frederick attempted to reorganize the Prussian fiscal system but with limited success. For tax collection, he established a central *Régie* that took over excise collection from the local authorities. He would have preferred that the luxuries of the rich be taxed more heavily than the necessities of the poor. Economic historians argue that before the French Revolution the German peasant was viewed from a 'statist' fiscal point of view, that is, from the perspective of his contribution to the State. The peasant was considered the main input, besides land (capital input was not considered) in agricultural production.

The Prussian bureaucracy was interested in maximizing farm output that could be taxed and therefore increase the State (monarch) revenue.[210] The money collected by the *Régie* originated mainly with peasants, soldiers, artisans, farmers, and shopkeepers but not with nobles, officers, clergy, and merchants. As at any place and at any time, Prussian subjects hated the tax collector who was criticized at home and abroad; the *Régie* was in the hands of foreigners, French functionaries, the messengers of taxation. However, the king was happy since this arrangement guaranteed revenues for the State (king).

Perhaps the high excises retarded Prussian industrial expansion, yet on a per capita basis the tax burden of Prussia was less than that of Austria and France, richer, larger, and more powerful countries.[211] During the Seven Years War Britain subsidized Prussia, a much poorer country, to help keep the Prussian army in the field against France. After the war, Frederick levied contributions from defeated Saxony, and finally, in order to cover state expenses, he introduced a lottery based on the examples of the Italian cities. Furthermore, Prussia took advantage of the inherent weakness of neighboring Poland. During the seventeenth and eighteenth centuries, Poland had been a large and important nation. Given the power of the nobility, who usurped the power of the king, Poland was partitioned among its neighbors, Prussia, Russia, and Austria in 1772, 1793, and 1795. Prussia's expansionism was given a great spurt; Poland did not emerge again as an independent state until 1918.

---

209   Henderson 1968, p. 65.
210   Gagliardo 1969, p. 286.
211   Asprey 1986, p. 359.

Prussia's Serfdom during the German Enlightenment

The *Junkers* overtly and otherwise restrained East Prussia from industrialization. East Prussia remained basically agrarian to the close of the century while Silesia, economically more advanced, the territory newly acquired from Austria, experienced 'industrial feudalism'. In Silesia, the landowners established industries that employed serfs rather than wage earners.[212] In exchange, to yield political power to the monarch, some *Junkers* preserved their absolute manorial authority and their fiefdoms while continuing to hold the peasants as virtual serfs. The 'enlightened' Frederick maintained that agriculture is based on serf labor, and that abolishing serfdom would create chaos in agriculture.[213]

Education, Absolutism, and Welfare in Prussia

Hardly fond of the *Junkers*, Frederick the Great complained about the poor education of his officers and, for that matter, of his subjects more generally, but he discouraged education by limiting permission of students to go abroad. This policy was detrimental to social and economic betterment. In his later writings, Frederick the Great called for education, and established a rudimentary elementary system with refugee Jesuits as teachers. He has always been regarded a philosopher king, but his absolutist mantra inherited from his predecessors, remained in place.[214]

While he praised the French *philosophes* that esteemed Frederick highly, his 'enlightenment' did not make him less a despot.[215] A German historian has distinguished between the French and the German enlightenment. In France, supposedly the Physiocrats, *philosophes economistes*, allowed for the greater possible economic freedom. For Frederick the Great, the interest of the individual and that of the State coincided, and, in case of conflict, the individual must be sacrificed for the welfare of the State.[216]

Frederick's successors attempted to modify some of the policies introduced during his reign, a difficult endeavor since the 1789 French Revolution occurred soon after his death in 1786. The fiscal system was changed when the *Régie* was abolished and the restrictions on international trade were eased. However, the basic concept developed under Frederick the Great persisted; the State remained not only an agent of last resort but also an initiator and moderator in the market place.

---

212 Henderson 1968, pp. 160-165.
213 Behrens 1985, p. 83.
214 Asprey 1986, pp. 356-357.
215 Behrens 1985, p. 153.
216 V. Sellin 'Friedrich der Grosse und der angeklagte Absolutismus', in *Festschrift fuhr Werner Conze* (n. d.) cited by Behrens 1985, p. 177.

Conclusions

For most of the eighteenth century, like the French State, the German political units adopted mercantilism that came under one denominator, protection of industry and of foreign trade. In Prussia, *laissez faire* or the limited economic freedom proposed by the Physiocrats became academic. Under the *Cameralists* not even academia adopted Smith in its entirety. Sartorius, who translated the *Wealth of Nations*, and disseminated and commented on Smith's ideas, argued for a role of the State in the market place consistent with German official policy makers. In addition to protectionist polices, the State interfered in the market with macroeconomic policies and legislation to mitigate market failures. Furthermore, in Prussia and Saxony the rulers owned all or parts of industrial (a step ahead of handicrafts) enterprises.

While it is difficult to generalize the State in Germany (named as proxy here for the rather numerous political entities) played a direct and indirect role in forging economic development. The Protestant Reformation was influential in the development of northern German entities especially Prussia-Brandenburg, since Luther preached the precedence of the State over the Church. Due to Luther influence, the State introduced compulsory education. The emphasis on education spread German literacy inducing economic development and also strengthened the German bureaucracy.

The French Revolution had profound effects on all of Europe, including the German states. As an unintended consequence, the Revolution and Napoleon transformed the economy, society, and polity even though in the short run the changes were not always welcomed by the local inhabitants and, indeed, often avoided. In the Rhineland, Napoleonic armies overthrew land rulers and changes introduced in the legal system (the civil and commercial codes) affected every one for the next century. Napoleon 'ended seigneurialism, eliminated guilds, overturned monopolies, nullified privileges, emancipated the Jews, introduced religious toleration and secularized Church lands'.[217]

The 'freedom' brought by the Napoleonic armies was more acceptable to the nascent German bourgeoisie than to the peasantry or, in general, the lower classes, suspicious of breaks in tradition. To a great extent, the Napoleonic era served as a catalyst for the consolidation of the German states instigating the Prussian hegemony. Perhaps it is not that strange that the power of the State increased rather than diminished while economic policies suffered little change due, much like France, to a disciplined bureaucracy guarantors of continuity.

---

217   Blackbourn 1997, p. 71.

Italy

Circa 1300 the Italian peninsula was the most highly urbanized European region; of the fifty largest European cities, twenty were located in Italy north of Rome. From 1300 to 1700, these cities were at one time or another, wealthy and powerful, which gave the Italians a sense of superiority, and therefore rightly or wrongly, emulating the ancient Greeks, they characterized foreigners as 'barbarians'.[218] During the eighteenth century, Italy, like Germany, but to a much lesser extent, contained several territorial entities of varying sizes and degree of importance.

Unlike Germany, Italy did not have a State such as Prussia, which sought hegemony. The only comparable states were the Kingdom of Sardinia (Piedmont and Sardinia) in the north and the Kingdom of the Two Sicilies in the south. The other major entities included Lombardy, under the direct control of Spain and after 1713 of Austria, the Papal States, and Venice, independent until 1797. Austria governed Lombardy directly, and Leopold, brother of the emperor of Austria and grand duke of Tuscany (1765-1790), held the reins of power and exercised considerable autonomy. After 1764, the Spanish Bourbons dominated the Kingdom of the Two Sicilies, ruled by Charles III (1734-1759).

Early in the eighteenth century Italy witnessed a general economic decline compared with the preceding centuries. This decline originated with the discovery of America and the discovery of the all-water route to India and the rest of Asia that shifted trade patterns from the Mediterranean Sea to the Atlantic Ocean. In 1713, the Treaty of Utrecht changed the geopolitical configuration of Italy and facilitated the future hegemony of Piedmont, located in northwestern Italy, with Turin as the capital. Piedmont, the Kingdom of Sardinia after 1719, pursued mercantilist policies and became the most powerful independent state in Italy. Nevertheless, Lombardy, an eastern neighbor of Piedmont with the capital in Milan, was the most economically successful state, although subject to Austrian control.

Both Lombardy and Tuscany in central Italy attempted to apply certain *laissez faire* policies but with limited outcomes. Public policies in these states were more concerned with exports and stable grain supplies than an elusive 'economic freedom'. Ultimately, these states, as all the other Italian states, pursued mercantilist policies but freed the internal domestic markets. With new sea trade routes, the Republic of Venice in the northeast continued to decline politically and economically; Venetian policy makers were ambivalent concerning *laissez faire* since they accepted free trade in principle but vowed to protect domestic manufacturing. In 1797, the Republic of Venice lost its independence briefly to Napoleonic France and then to Austria.

During the Middle Ages and the Renaissance the unifying cultural force of the Italian territories was the Church and subsequently the evolving Italian language partly due to Dante, Petrarca, and Boccaccio. By the mid-1700s, the Papal States

---

218   Guerri 1992, p. 30.

comprised almost all of central Italy.[219] Attempts of the Papal States at economic expansion through limited free trade and subsidies to industry proved unsuccessful since the Papacy resisted modernization. The French Revolutionary and the Napoleonic interlude induced a further decline of the Papal States.

South of the Papal States, the Kingdom of the Two Sicilies (the Continental southern peninsula and the island of Sicily) confronted economic stagnation throughout the century. Economists and political scientists influenced public policies, but only to a limited extent. Parts of southern Italy were still dominated by *latifundia*, a continuation in some manner of the feudal/manorial system based on extensive agriculture on large landholdings. Policy makers argued for and against economic liberalism, but the State was probably too weak to introduce either. Industrial development was directed to satisfy the luxury needs of the court, not exports or satisfying ordinary internal demand. The brief tenure of the French administration brought turmoil but also some order in the economy, despite the volatile Napoleonic changes.

During the eighteenth century ambivalence on free trade prevailed, more often than not; mercantilist policies were preferred for many reasons. The overwhelming rationale was the perennial fear of famine and obtaining state revenue from tariffs; also, agriculture productivity was lower in most Italian states than in Britain or France. The State attempted to respond to these conditions, although not always successfully, through direct and indirect means.

Early Eighteenth Century Economic Decline

During the early eighteenth century, Italy's economy (as well as Germany's) declined as a whole compared to previous centuries and to the western European economies in particular Britain and France. Many foreign travelers remarked on the apparent decaying conditions of the cities and the countryside. Some correlated these dismal conditions with the power of the aristocracy and the lack of political and civil liberties. Economic historians maintain that the landed aristocracy constituted a dead weight, opposing any sort of change.

These aristocrats lived on the income from the land and enjoyed a life of leisure in the cities caring little for the agricultural laborer and rarely visiting their own lands. In absentia, these landlords ruled their holdings absolutely with no right of appeal, that is, the landed aristocracy had absolute power with no possible recourse of appeal to the State. The rural population suffered from increased taxes and periodically increased prices. As a result of the sharply askew system of political and economic power, as well as low agricultural productivity, rural poverty was rampant.[220] With few exceptions, the general decline can be seen in the intellectual life of the cities, both North and South. Universities founded in the Middle Ages

---

219 Also, the Italian states sought to capture the sources of Church financing.
220 Woolf 1973, pp. 23-32, 37, 43-44.

no longer attracted students from outside Italy and throughout the seventeenth century the number of students diminished from thousands to hundreds.[221]

Aside from the lack of adequate roads, the fractionalization of territories was detrimental to trade. The multiplicity of customs duties made life more expensive for the consumer but replenished each State's treasury. Not different from the United States during the nineteenth century, more public revenue was derived from custom duties than from other taxes. The restructuring of domestic taxation was attempted many times in the various states. The Kingdom of the Two Sicilies had a tax collection system similar to that of France where tax collection was entrusted to *fermiers*; only a small part of the collected taxes finally went to the State. The aristocracy opposed tax reforms that would adversely affect them. As a result, most of the states were heavily in debt. For example, in 1754, fifty percent of public expenditures of Lombardy were for interest on the public debt.[222]

Change in the Italian Geopolitical and Trade Position

Italy entered the eighteenth century weakened with the diminished prosperity of the northern cities; in particular, the trading advantages of Genoa and Venice had disappeared by 1700.[223] The Age of Discovery transferred the center of the commercial world from the Mediterranean Sea to the Atlantic Ocean. In addition, the development of powerful nation-states such as England (later Great Britain), France, and decadent Spain adversely affected Italy that still consisted of a dozen lesser states. Spanish mercantilist policies limited trade and increased taxes, and therefore were detrimental to the Italian economy, resulting in lowered living standards. Moreover, much agricultural land was abandoned, population decreased, and brigandage increased.

The Treaty of Utrecht of 1713 limited French expansion; Italy received a new and unstable political configuration. As a consequence of this treaty, the House of Savoy made significant territorial acquisitions. By 1748, Naples, Sicily, Parma, and Piacenza were under Spanish control; Austria ruled Lombardy, Tuscany, and Modena. The only independent states were the Papal States, Venice, Genoa, Lucca, and the Kingdom of Sardinia composed of Piedmont, Savoy, and Sardinia.

Piedmont

Victor Amadeus Asserts the Power of the State An 'enlightened despot', Duke Victor Amadeus II (1684-1730), established Piedmont east of the Alps, bordering

---

221 Luzzato 1967, p. 172; Vivanti 1991, pp. 243-283; Romano 1991a, pp. 342-343.
222 Woolf 1973, pp. 48-49, 57-58, 77-78.
223 The decline began with the struggle between Charles V, Holy Roman emperor, and Francis I, King of France that shattered the apparent political stability of the independent and quasi-independent Italian city-states. During the early 1500s, Francis I opposed Charles V, who dominated Europe and nearly encircled France by controlling Spain and much of Italy.

France. He also acquired the Kingdom of Sicily, united with Piedmont only up to 1719. It seems that Sicilians did not like the measures of efficiency brought by the Savoyards, thus they welcomed the Spanish. By far the superior military power, Spain took over Sicily without a fight. Piedmont was rewarded in exchange with the island of Sardinia. Rather than being a duchy, the combination of Piedmont and Sardinia combined as the Kingdom of Sardinia.

As in the German states and elsewhere, Duke Victor Amadeus slightly diminished the privileges of the nobles and clergy. For a while he protected the Valdese Huguenots but, under pressure from France, he drove them away, massacred or compelled them to convert to Catholicism. By demanding loyalty to the laic State, and granting civil rights to his subjects, he antagonized the papacy. Victor Amadeus insisted on his royal rights to name candidates for the Piedmont Church hierarchy; he also curtailed religious legacies to enhance the State's tax base. In 1715, Victor Amadeus moved to take control of the Church in Sicily. When Pope Clement XI issued an *interdict*, Victor Amadeus imprisoned hundreds of priests and replaced them with his own appointees, while expelling many clerics loyal to the Pope.

According to the 1727 Concordat with the Pope, Victor Amadeus took over the Inquisition and broke the tradition that the Church controlled education, establishing a university in Turin. This laic State institution was supposed to train civil servants but the curriculum also included engineering, surveying, architecture, and medicine. While many universities had been established in Italy centuries earlier, by 1730 the University of Turin enrolled 2000 students compared with Padua (the Veneto) at 1000 and Bologna (the Papal States) at 400. Also, to encourage persons who were not nobles to obtain an advanced education, Victor Amadeus, in 1720, established a residential college for nearly two hundred youths.

Financial Controls of the State In his expanded State, Victor Amadeus ordered a radical fiscal reform based on *perequazione*, a census of lands, to assess taxable valuation and income derived from production. It required over ten years to complete, but became a highly efficient bureaucratic success. As a result of this assessment, nobles were obliged to show land titles and the State dispossessed them if they could not prove title. Also, he eliminated local tax collectors and centralized tax assessments in Turin. Believing in the centrality of decision making, while following a policy of decentralization, Victor Amadeus enforced rigid State financial controls. These policies transferred some of the royal alliances from the traditional nobility to the bourgeoisie.[224]

Mercantilism and the Military-Bureaucratic State Victor Amadeus used the power of the State for mercantilist purposes such as encouraging manufacturing designed to generate taxes by reducing imports. While some silk spinning existed during the seventeenth century, manufacturing output quadrupled during the first half of the

---

224   Oliva 1998, pp. 301-303.

eighteenth century. Amadeus compares favorably with his Prussian contemporary counterpart, King Friedrich Wilhelm, for his efficiency and austerity for himself and his associates in advancing the cause of the State. In 1730, he abdicated in favor of his son, Carlo Emanuele III (1730-1773), who abolished the medieval remnants of serfdom and seigniorial dues.[225]

By the middle of the eighteenth century, Piedmont became the most efficient military-bureaucratic state in the peninsula but hardly as economically advanced as neighboring Lombardy. One of the impediments was that, similar to Louis XIV, the king distributed positions and privileges in order to retain his hold on the nobles. Piedmont sought to be strong militarily, to perfect a centralized administration, and to control the nobility. Some economic historians point out that the State gained the confidence of the population. The rigid central government control did not grant enough space for an intellectual debate. In fact, Carlo Emanuele III did not care about or did not understand the arts and sciences. To maintain control of the printed word, he established a state-printing house, and penalized those Piedmont subjects who printed abroad.[226]

Genoa

Rise and Fall of the Banking State While Piedmont's neighboring *Repubblica di Genova* still retained its independence in 1700, Genoa represented a special situation. As a political independent entity, Genoa constituted a small strip of land bounded by the Apennine Mountains and the Tyrrhenian Sea with no other big cities or natural resources. In the Genoese republic, there was little space for agriculture; however, during the Middle Ages and the Renaissance Genoa developed a banking system that rivaled Florence and competed in trade with Venice.

For two hundred years the Genoese bankers exploited the Spanish monarchy, developing 'usury capitalism'. The Genoese bankers (like other banking houses) did not invest in productive endeavors; they preferred public to private investments guaranteed by mortgages on anticipated tax revenue. Genoese banks survived the seventeenth century despite the chaos in Spanish public finances, even though the bankers were adversely affected by successive Spanish bankruptcies; the bankers were viewed as a pillar of support for the decaying Spanish nobility and monarchy, only to be wiped out by the French Revolution.[227]

Lombardy

Laissez Faire Attempts in Austrian Lombardy Under Spanish domination, Lombardy witnessed a period of decline during the sixteenth and seventeenth

---

225 Hanlon 2000, pp. 276-280, 314-315; Oliva 1998, pp. 298-299.
226 Oliva 1998, pp. 312-313, 323-324; Candeloro 1973, pp. 92-95.
227 Candeloro 1973, Vol. 1, pp. 102-105.

centuries. This deterioration stemmed from, among other reasons, the Spanish decadence, and the loss of the oriental markets after 1497, the shrinking of the silk industry, and, most of all, to the weakness of the entrepreneurial class. In Milan, and in some minor Lombard cities, the wealthy aristocrats preferred to live on revenue derived from land holding, less risky and requiring less effort. Therefore, after the Treaty of Utrecht, the change from Spanish to Austrian tutelage was quite welcome since the governing Austrian Empire was considered a more enlightened foreign power.[228]

The Austrian Habsburgs in 1765 appointed Pietro Verri (1727-1797), a Milanese economist, who eventually became converted to physiocratic ideas, to the Lombardy Supreme Economic Council. Verri argued that a unified market would facilitate economic development. Market unification meant eliminating all interregional impediments such as tariffs and regulations imposed by the guilds. Since tariffs brought revenue to the Austrian treasury, the Austrian rulers rejected these reforms fearing that the State would lose secure tariff revenue; Verri assumed the eventual replacement of tariff revenue by taxes on an anticipated enlarged output. Transit duties were terminated only in 1781 and customs duties were abolished in 1787. Even after that date, the State still continued to protect domestic industries by subsidies and tax exemptions.[229]

In 1769, in *Reflections on Restrictive Laws*, Verri had favored free internal grain trade limited to the home economy. On the other hand, he did not necessarily favor a single tax on land as the Physiocrats advocated. In his *Meditations on Political Economy* (1771), Verri claimed that such a tax could not be instituted without disallowing the importation of foreign products. Nevertheless, under the Austrian Habsburg empress, Maria Theresa (1740-1780), the State imposed a land tax, a *mensuale*, a 'monthly', inherited from the Spaniards, based on an earlier survey (1568) that included the nobility. This tax policy compelled the landowner to increase productivity and weakened the feudal system that, as a consequence of the French Revolution, was abolished entirely in 1797.[230] Verri, with Cesare Beccaria (1738-1794), a multifaceted social scientist from Pavia, and others established the *Accademia dei Pugni* (the Fists Academy) that promoted equity, free trade, and social justice. Verri strongly urged that the State design public policy in favor of the local nobility who were better educated.[231]

Pompeo Neri's Tax Reform in Lombardy In the 1750s, Pompeo Neri (1706-1776) a public administrator in Lombardy and Tuscany succeeded in instituting a commercial and personal tax in Lombardy. In order to encourage agriculture, the

228 Candeloro 1973, Vol. 1, p. 79.
229 Hanlon 2000, pp. 357-358.
230 Grab 1985, pp. 192-194, 198, 206-208; Woolf 1991, pp. 99-104; Di Scala 1998, pp. 4, 7; Klang 1977, pp. 54-55.
231 Candeloro 1973, Vol.1, pp. 88-89; Beccaria became famous and quite influential for modifying the penal code in many places in Italy and elsewhere with his 1764 *Essay on Crime and Punishment*. Hanlon 2000, pp. 320-321.

commercial tax law excluded proprietors, sharecroppers, tenant farmers, and salaried workers. The personal tax was imposed uniformly on all males between 14 and 60 with deductions allowed for the land tax. A general land census completed in 1757, and implemented in 1760, allowed a fairer and a more stable assessment for land values and corresponding taxation. It taxed individual landowners rather than communities and relied on the findings of professional surveyors and assessors. The tax was revolutionary because it did not take the nobles' declarations at face value. Neri also wanted to limit the power of the urban oligarchs, but was unsuccessful because of intramural politics.[232]

'Liberalism' in Lombardy   Gianrinaldo Carli (1720-1795), president of the Economic Council of Lombardy, managed the results of the census with little regard for local politics since he had the support of the dominant power in Vienna. In his 1776 opus *l'Uomo libero*, 'the Free Man', Carli contended that governments are meant to protect private property and that natural selection allows for the unequal distribution of land that divides the population between proprietors and laborers and that the servitude of the laborers is fair because the laborers (especially the landless) would starve if they did not work for the landlords. However, since landlords can be rapacious and selfish, he concluded that the monarchy with its impartial justice was the only institution that could reconcile these incongruities.[233] As an administrator, Carli was pragmatic, preventing food riots in late 1760s when acute shortages of grains occurred all throughout Italy and elsewhere.[234]

Another innovation in Lombardy in the 1770s was the State subsidy for apprenticeship in the silk industry. This subsidy aimed to satisfy the demand for silk, to avoid hiring foreign workers, and to create local employment. By the end of the eighteenth century, a Royal Commission on trade criticized industrial subsidies and protection. Only a few people benefited from the State's largess while the majority of small artisans, traders, and domestic consumers were hurt. In 1786, the State decided to protect only those industries using domestic raw materials and responding to consumer demand.[235]

Tuscany

Modified Laissez Faire in Lombardy and Tuscany   Pompeo Neri (1706-1776), a public administrator in Lombardy and Tuscany, believed that elites (noblemen) should govern but only by consent since otherwise despotism reigns. He defended *laissez faire* saying that the government should not interfere in the affairs of individuals. In line with the French Physiocrats, he argued that agriculture was the

---

232   Klang 1977, pp. 5, 23-34; Hanlon 2000, p. 356; Candeloro 1973, Vol. 1. pp. 84-86.
233   In a contradictory fashion, Carli agreed with the pre-Spanish-Peruvian Incas that the government should ban all private surpluses over one's subsistence.
234   Klang 1977, pp. 54-55, 69-82.
235   Vaussard 1963, pp. 175-176.

most important endeavor of Tuscany and the government should not hamper exports with the objective of helping the urban dwellers. Neri contended that landlords should be taxed when they do not use their surplus income for investment but for luxuries. As a precursor of 'trickle down' economics, Neri maintained that the accumulation of wealth among those who invest would benefit poorer people.[236]

Other Italian 'liberal' economists argued for a modified *laissez faire* policy in which the State would play an active role. They claimed that in Britain the State protected only the vested mercantile interests with no protection for others. Since the State plays a role in the economy, it should promote free trade but should act to adjust market failures.[237]

State Intervention under Pietro Leopoldo in Tuscany The belief prevailed, perhaps with good reasons that grain shortages meant famine, such as experienced in the Italian peninsula in 1764. Tuscany was probably the first political entity in Continental Europe to 'free' internal trade during the 1770s but still the State continued to regulate the grain trade. Here, more so than in France, public policy preceded Physiocratic theory. Generally, the various Italian states gingerly pursued freeing the markets under autocratic leadership. Unlike France, which responded only to recurring crises, in 1776 Lombardy, controlled by Austria, declared freedom of internal trade in grains and permitted their export in 1786.[238]

The economic crisis of 1765-1766 induced legislation in Tuscany that ended the prohibition of grain exports.[239] Grand Duke Pietro Leopoldo (1765-1790), a Habsburg, introduced extensive economic reforms in Tuscany. In 1768, Pietro Leopoldo also terminated the general farm tax, still persisting in France, that is, by halting tax farmers from collecting taxes for the State.[240] He allowed the unlimited export and import of agricultural products in 1775. Between 1766 and 1782 Pietro Leopoldo unified the tolls and customs of almost all of Tuscany, which expanded the domestic market. Pietro Leopoldo's free trade policy, unique in Italy, fulfilled the vision of free trade of the French Physiocrats.

Public policies were more concerned with exports rather than with the domestic market since tariffs, besides representing an important source for public revenue, were viewed as important tools for protecting home industries. In addition, Pietro Leopoldo insisted that it was the duty of the State to improve the infrastructure. Consequently, he made money available for bridges, roads, drainage canals,

---

236 Woolf 1973, pp. 95-96.
237 See for instance: G. D. Romagnosi (1836), *Collezione degli articoli di economia politica e statistica civile*, Prato, Italy, pp. 41-42, 53, 147, 392, and (1832), *Dell'indole e de fattori dell'incivilimento*, Milan, pp. 211, 251, 262, cited by Badaloni 1973, pp. 944-946.
238 Baumol 1987, pp. 139-140; Carpanetto and Ricuperati 1987, pp. 24-25; Gagliardo 1967, pp. 24-25; Candeloro 1973. Vol. 1, pp. 115-124.
239 Cochrane 1961, p. 218.
240 Cochrane 1973, p. 425.

hospitals, and public buildings. He streamlined his administration, decreasing the outlays by thirty percent and succeeded in having more control of the economy than before his reforms.[241]

Not a firm believer in unrestricted private property Pietro Leopoldo enacted legislation to curb *latifundia* and landlords absenteeism. The Latin *latifondo* denotes large landholdings extensively cultivated, that is, mainly with day laborers but also in places with sharecropping, with minimal investment or technology; typically, this form of agricultural organization is inefficient with low yields per acre. By curbing *latifundia*, Pietro Leopoldo hoped to increase farm output. Also, lands expropriated from suppressed religious orders, such as the Jesuits, were distributed to peasant small holders. In the mountainous areas he did not divide the common lands but rather protected them through *Communita della montagna*, the Mountain Community Agency, that awarded subsidies and tax exemptions. Leopoldo's reforms in Tuscany represented a model for reforms elsewhere in Italy although with limited success.

Further liberalization occurred, restrictions were abolished in the movement of foodstuff within Tuscany in 1775, and most goods were freed from duties in 1781.[242] Pietro Leopoldo changed the status of the free port of Livorno, abolishing legislation that heretofore had hampered the free movement of people and goods. To encourage international trade, Livorno was considered outside the State in terms of taxes and tariffs. After Livorno was acquired by Tuscany, for two centuries the Medici instituted liberal policies to help the development of their only port. The Medici abolished restrictions on foreigners and encouraged migration by granting housing subsidies, tax forgiveness, and improving the infrastructure. During the fifteenth and sixteenth centuries the Medici established in Livorno a limited free trade zone and after 1765, Pietro Leopoldo revitalized Livorno into an effective free port.[243]

Venice

Decline: The Difficult End of the Oligarchy Seventeenth century Italy witnessed the slow disappearance of Venice as a world power and trading center and the transformation from empire to small republic to non-entity. Starting in the preceding century, on the mainland, a middle class formed by merchants and artisans, emerged in the smaller cities. The capital of the Republic of Venice did not recognize this slow but definite change. The secular oligarchy acted as it had for centuries, assuming that the State still retained power.[244]

---

241 Woolf 1991, p. 90; Hanlon 2000, pp. 363-364.
242 Cochrane 1973, pp. 401, 425.
243 Marchi 1984, pp. 31-32, 101-103; LoRomer 1987, pp. 19-20.
244 Candeloro 1973, Vol. 1, p. 102.

In 1719, Austria designated Trieste, on the Adriatic Sea a free port, the only seaport and natural outlet for the Habsburg Empire; the rise of Trieste as an Austrian port helped curb Venice's influence. Accumulated capital was transferred from commerce to agriculture and used for building *ville* and *palazzi*, showy palaces. Unwittingly, Venice became a tourist attraction and an international intellectual center. By the middle of the century, twenty percent of the population was foreign. Both the city of Venice and the *Terraferma*, the hinterland, attracted many from abroad because of freedom (licentiousness). The citizens of Venice had economic freedom but could not participate in politics; this was reserved to the wellborn or parvenus 3500 nobles.

The noble families, not much different from the British counterpart, had only one inheritor. Of three brothers, the eldest became a politician and remained a bachelor, the second son married and lived a life of leisure, and the third joined the clergy or some public function as a sinecure. All the power resided in the city, while Venice deprived the *Terraferma* of policy participation; however, its inhabitants paid very few taxes.[245] Paolo Renier, a reformist political figure at the end of the eighteenth century, argued that Venice's major economic ills could be attributed to income and wealth inequality, making a few very wealthy while the majority lived in miserable conditions. In 1779, some reformers argued that the pauperization of the masses was connected with trade policies; they argued that it was fine to encourage exports but tariffs on consumer goods inevitably made life difficult for the lower income classes.[246]

Control of Foreign Trade Rapid urbanization during the Middle Ages of necessity brought public intervention in grain markets; often communes purchased and stored grains for emergency use. The size of its population and limited hinterland required the Republic of Venice, in particular, to control the grain market through regulated prices, trade, and distribution to protect the lower income classes from recurring shortages. By 1754, Venice allowed the free export of grains but still under State control.[247] Twenty years later, the government again imposed restrictions on exports and controlled the retail prices of flour and bread. The only grain product allowed for export was biscuits, thus encouraging the food transformation industry.

In 1770, wishing to promote the development of a domestic silk industry and to increase industrial employment, the State prohibited shops from selling imported silk. The Venetian policy makers were ambivalent about *laissez faire*. During the 1770s reformers accepted French ideas of free trade in principle but vowed to protect domestic manufacturing. During the 1790s the French influenced the dissolution of craft groups as an impediment to trade. These various policy

---

245 Hanlon 2000, pp. 264-265; Zorzi 2001, p. 442.
246 Zorzi 2001, pp. 452, 464-5.
247 Lane 1973, p. 59; Carpanetto and Ricuperati 1987, p. 306; Persson 1996, pp. 667-691; Waley 1988, pp. 60, 79.

distortions were the last gasps of a dying republic; the Republic of Venice ceased to exist as an independent entity in 1797.[248]

The 1797 peace treaty with Napoleonic France dismembered the republic, allowing the secession of the hinterland, the *Terraferma*, leaving only the city of Venice as a political entity until occupied first by France and thereafter by Austria. To face the peace requirements and continue public services the new government was obliged to impose a *una tantum* tax, one-time assessment, in addition to taxes on commerce and industry. These taxes together with the disruption of foreign trade triggered an economic and financial crisis. The central bank, *Banco Giro*, and the *Zecca*, the mint, were on the brink of insolvency for the first time since the Middle Ages.

An attempt was made at revival, the opening of a free port in 1806, only to become worthless when Napoleon promulgated the Continental Blockade against Britain. By far stronger than France's navy, the British navy sequestered all French ships it encountered, including those of Venice, again bringing the commerce of Venice to a standstill. In 1815, the Treaty of Vienna combined the Veneto together with Lombardy under Austrian tutelage.[249]

The Papal State

Increasing Limitations Central and northern Italian communities organized in city-states during the Middle Ages with not much economic interchange.[250] The unifying cultural force was the Church owing to the assumption that Church policies were overriding and that one could not distinguish between the Church and the State. The Rinascimento did not alter the institutional influence of the Church but gradually its political control was confined to the Papal States, located in central Italy in what is today Lazio, Emilia-Romagna, Umbria and the Marche.[251]

When 'progressive' Austria replaced 'retrograde' Spain as the controlling power in Italy, the Church maintained its strong social control having lost political power; the Austrian administration could not permit Church meddling. Compared with the Papal States, Austria constituted a model of economic and administrative

---

248 Venturi 1980, pp. 104, 116, 124; Venice ceded to France part of the navy and material, 20 pieces of artwork and 500 manuscripts (to be chosen by Napoleon) in addition to three million lire in cash. At the same time the public debt reached 40 million ducats. Zorzi 2001, p. 535.

249 Zorzi 2001, pp. 341-343, 367-368.

250 Upon the dissolution of the Western Roman Empire and rapidly filling the institutional vacuum, the Catholic Church assumed a secular role.

251 In 1592, in Rome, the papal seat, there was a priest (not counting nuns and monks) for every 81 people and by 1760, one for every 55 people. True enough, the clergy were the only literate class constituting almost the entire public bureaucracy including clerks, teachers, and scribes. Around 1600, other cities had a large number of clergy per capita: Reggio Calabria 250, Naples 200, Milan 266, Bologna 617, and Venice 277. Guerri 1992, pp. 141-146.

efficiency; no wonder the popes viewed any Austrian interference with suspicion.[252] In 1708, the last time the Catholic Church attempted to assert itself against the Catholic but laic Austria, it failed dismally.[253]

An important change was the abolition of the Church's monopoly on education and the replacement of the Church social charity with the State's social services.[254] The Italian states increasingly took over education and welfare, previously a Church prerogative. The laic State administrators realized that primary education is the basis of molding the population to be faithful to the State rather than to the Church. With the Church's diminishing financial resources, the laic State stepped in, even when there was no overt separation of State and Church and religious education continued in the State public schools. Welfare, that is, caring for the indigent, the poor, and the disable became public policy, even in the Papal States.

The Church's authority was increasingly eroded as Austria and other European Catholic States sought to capture sources of Church financing. Losing the source of income damaged the Papal States greatly; provincial townships were deeply in debt, agriculture was stagnating, and commerce in Bologna and Ancona languished. Internal tariffs exacerbated the economic conditions as domestic and international trade was impeded. The perennial inefficiency both in agriculture and limited industry, forced many to seek dole from the State. Economic historians maintain that the few entrepreneurs in agricultural and industry were crowded out by the State, thus lacking capital to expand.

Mercantilism The Papal States adopted limited mercantilist policies but to challenge Venice, established a free port in Ancona in the Marche, on the Adriatic Sea, that stimulated the economy. The Papal States pursued pragmatic policies; custom duties were not applied to grains and other consumer products that were lacking domestically. Commerce and industry were organized in corporate form that theoretically gave equal rights to employers and employees. In practice, however, barons controlled these corporations mainly in textile manufacturing. When they were accused of being greedy by maximizing profits to the detriment of everyone else, the barons retorted that the State was not helpful by limiting subsidies and not increasing custom duties.

The Papal States were hampered in their ability to act by the inflexible state structure and foreign (Austria and France) pressure to allow trade. Furthermore, the single provinces of the Papal States placed contradictory demands on the State.

---

252 In control of Lombardy, The Austrians did not view kindly the Church's ownership of 22 percent of Lombardy real estate (not much different from most European Catholic countries); in the Kingdom of Naples the ecclesiastic gross income was higher than the State's revenue.

253 Pope Benedetto XIV (1740-1758) implemented modernization policies of the Church and the State; upon his death, his successors reversed his policies. Guerri 1992, pp. 156-157.

254 Guerri 1992, pp. 157-158. See also Candeloro 1973, Vol. 1, pp. 136-159 for an analysis of the Papal States.

Bologna and the more economically advanced areas urged liberal economic policies while the Marche and Romagna, provinces with mini feudal estates and underdeveloped industry, asked that the State be active on their behalf.[255]

External Influences   At the close of the century, as all over Italy, Napoleon changed the Papal States institutions drastically. Townships could eliminate their debt by selling ecclesiastic property; during the brief Napoleonic interlude, the administration eliminated internal tariffs, built roads, and introduced Napoleonic commercial, civil, and penal codes. Romans were not enthusiastic about the reforms; apparently there was no uprising against the Papal States or, for that matter, against the French. The wealthy absentee landowners and Church-connected individuals did not enjoy being deprived of wealth and privileges; the poor, more attached to religion and now subservient to a foreign power, apparently did not live better under the French than under the Pope.[256]

The Kingdom of the Two Sicilies

Drive for a Laic and 'National' State in the South   In the southern part of Italy, that is, the peninsula south of the Papal States, as a result of the War of Spanish Succession, the Kingdom of Naples became independent under the Spanish Bourbon Charles IV (1735-1759). The reforms under his regime were mainly due to sophisticated intellectuals who participated in the government. During Charles' reign, *Monsignor* Celestino Galiani, in charge of the University of Naples, suppressed chairs in vogue of jurisprudence and scholastic theology and introduced a curriculum that included experimental physics, astronomy, botany, chemistry, and political economy.

The philosopher and jurist, Giambattista Vico (1668-1744), dominated Neapolitan intellectual life; he argued that if one were loyal to the State one was loyal to one's own interests. From the relationship between the State and men emerge principles that regulate the history of mankind. Vico believed that a nation is like a living organism, with an inevitable lifecycle of childhood, adulthood, and old age. This organic view of the nation was welcomed in Naples in 1725, when the first edition of, *Scienza nuova* (the New Science) was first published, since increasingly the population of Naples wanted regime change from the Spanish Bourbon dynasty.[257]

Italian universities achieved a breakthrough in 1755 when the Abbe Antonio Genovesi's (1713-1769) lectures on political economy at the University of Naples were delivered in Italian and not Latin. Genovesi argued that the supreme duty of the State is to educate the people, regardless of class. He maintained that

255   Carpanetto and Recuperati 1986, pp. 241-246; Valsecchi 1959, pp. 445-455.
256   Guerri 1992, pp. 152-165. By 1815, the Treaty of Vienna restored the Papal States to the *status quo ante bellum*.
257   Noether 1951, pp. 51-54.

economic justice would be accomplished through agricultural reform that included the redistribution of land. Besides the equitable distribution of property, Genovesi advocated the end of feudal laws, advanced medical practices, and work provided and required for all citizens. He believed in *laissez faire* in industry and commerce as long as it was not against the welfare of the State.

As a professor of political economy, Genovesi had many followers; his mentor, the Florentine economist Bartolomeo Intieri, held him in such high esteem that he dedicated his *Lezioni di Commercio, o sia d'Economia Civile*, Lessons in Trade or in Civil Economics, to Genovesi. Influenced by the French Physiocrats, Intieri attempted with this treatise to explain the laws that govern prices and championed free trade. On the other hand, in practice, Genovesi advanced a model of political economy centered on the State.[258]

Institutional Changes under the Bourbon Dynasty   At the beginning of the eighteenth century, the nobility in the Kingdom of Naples formed four percent of the population and received one third of the national income; also, the number of clergy was significant large. During the French Revolution, one sixth of Naples real estate belonged to the tax-exempt Church. The Bourbons pursued a policy of curtailing ecclesiastic authority and sought ways to overturn the *mortmain*, land legacy in perpetuity. The Concordat with Rome of 1741 allowed taxes on the clergy and granted royal rights over appointments on church courts.[259]

Early in the eighteenth century, Naples had one lawyer and/or notary for every 150 people. This occurred partially due to the lack of uniform civil and commercial codes since Naples had gone through so many conquests: Roman, Byzantine, Swabian, Angevin, Aragonese, and Spanish. The absence of uniform codes and liquid capital, as well as other obstacles to trade, handicapped industrial activity. With high tariffs and ineffective government, smuggling became endemic.[260]   Most Neapolitan economic activities consisted of middlemen, moneychangers, and private contractor for public projects, doctors, as well as an army of tax collectors. The most visible employer remained the State, and as in many Italian places, begging was a normal way of life, even in puritanical Genoa.

The kingdom had an unsustainable large foreign debt. Economic development could not occur because of: poor transportation facilities (inadequate road system), an educational system monopolized by the Jesuits to train youth mostly for the priesthood, as well as an outdated legal system. Furthermore, in Naples, neither the lawyers nor the medical doctors were well trained. As a result, by the end of the

---

258   Acton 1956, pp. 97-99; Noether 1951, p. 92; Campolieti 1999, p. 15; Carpanetto and Recuperati 1986, p. 1.

259   Vaussard 1963, pp. 67-88; Hanlon 2000, p. 341. The Kingdom of Naples (later the Kingdom of the Two Sicilies), with Spanish oversight, numbered 119 princes, 156 dukes, 173 marquises, 42 counts, and 445 barons. There were 12,000 ecclesiastics including 5,000 priests who served in 400 churches; the situation was not that different from other major Italian city-states.

260   Vaussard 1963, pp. 67-88, 175-179.

eighteenth century, industrial development in the Kingdom of the Two Sicilies continued in the pre infancy stage.[261]

Taxation and Liberalism Charles IV limited tax farming in the Kingdom of the Two Sicilies.[262] The Physiocrats congratulated themselves on their apparent influence on Charles, and subsequently Ferdinand. But, this chief minister, Bernardo Tanucci (1759-1776), was a noted Neapolitan reformer rejected the proposal of Antonio Genovesi, an outstanding Physiocrat, to free the grain trade and more generally eliminate government interference in the economy as a means of preventing such a terrible catastrophe as the famine of 1763-1764. Tanucci redistributed land confiscated from the Church, but peasants endowed with such land did not have financing for improvements or for seasonal sustenance; therefore, these peasants chose to sell their plots to wealthier farmers, thus, a new class of large landowners emerged. As the number of landless peasants increased, discontent spread and food riots often occurred.[263]

Liberal Genovesi vs. Mercantilist Tanucci As in France and Germany, a problem of the Kingdom of the Tow Sicilies remained the segmentation of markets. Many advocated a unified domestic market, that is, the removal of internal market impediments. Genovesi argued that the Kingdom of the Two Sicilies should not sign bilateral trade treaties because these are constraining; as long as the Kingdom of the Two Sicilies remained a less advanced nation, these agreements would only benefit the more advanced nation.

The dichotomy between the liberal theoretician Genovesi and the mercantilist policy maker Tanucci brought about reforms such as the redistribution of confiscated land to the peasants. As a strong anti-clerical, with the king's permission, and regardless of Rome's displeasure, Tanucci transferred power, loyalty, land, and revenue from the Church to the State. Upon Ferdinand's marriage to Maria Carolina, daughter of Maria Theresa of Austria, Tanucci was eased out in 1776 and replaced by students of Genovesi, more interested in economic reform through free trade than in confronting the Church.[264]

Progress in Sicily In a parallel manner, in 1781, King Ferdinand appointed a moderate anticlerical, Domenico Caracciolo, as Viceroy of Sicily. His attempts to dismantle the feudal and Church hold on the island and introduce an honest and efficient tax system gained him the hatred of virtually everyone of consequence; he had to be recalled soon thereafter. Caracciolo and his successors achieved a somewhat more equitable distribution of the tax burden, dismantled the institution of serfdom, by royal decree, and confiscated illegal fiefdoms for the crown.

---

261 Campolieti 1999, p. 49.
262 Charles IV, King of Sicily and Naples from 1736 to 1759, thereafter became Charles III of Spain (1759-1788), and the crown passed to his third son, Ferdinand.
263 Hanlon 2000, pp. 331-333.
264 Campolieti 1999, pp. 88-90, 162.

Ferdinand decreed that everyone in the realm have legal equality, and marriage had to have the consent of the parties but not of the parents while abolishing the dowry. He favored establishing technical schools under the aegis of the State to increase opportunities in manufacturing. Ferdinand also proposed opening hospitals, clinics, and cleaning the sewage system as well as lessening poverty.[265]

Economic Liberalism under Queen Maria Carolina   In 1780, Queen Maria Carolina, King Ferdinand's wife, appointed John Acton (1736-1814), an Anglo-French adventurer, as Minister of War, in 1782, Finance Minister, and, in 1786, Prime Minister. Acton rapidly dismantled the grain protection system attempted to dissolve guilds and monopolies, reduced protective tariffs, and signed bilateral commercial treaties; however, his fight against the feudal system was not wholly successful. To encourage private property rights and individualism, in 1791, he confiscated and distributed some feudal land to small holders. In 1792 communal lands were privatized and grazing rights were abolished. Only with the arrival of the French in 1806 could the State suppress the monastic orders, do away with fiefdoms, and transfer their revenue to the State.[266]

The Bourbon Royal courts were major consumers of luxury goods and established industries to satisfy the court's needs; Charles III built a tapestry factory on the Gobelin model and a porcelain factory, modeled after Meissen in Saxony. In addition, he established the Academy of Design in 1752 and the Academy of Architecture in 1772. The manufacturing industries created by Ferdinand IV such as silk, leather goods, cotton, and shipbuilding did not have enough capital or demand to survive unaided. On the other hand, the State protected industry put a damper on private enterprises. Both the silk and the woolen industries declined in the Kingdom of the Two Sicilies, as well as almost all over Italy, during the eighteenth century; woolen was being displaced by cotton goods and, it was difficult to withstand British competition.[267]

Sicilian Nationalism and the Latifundia   In forty years as ruler of the Kingdom of the Two Sicilies, King Ferdinand never visited Sicily. Nevertheless, in 1798, Ferdinand and Queen Maria Carolina sought refuge in Palermo, from the French invaders the capital of Sicily. The Sicilian barons, who ruled Sicily, did not recognize the authority of the central government over their fiefdoms. Both transportation and communication were almost non-existent, which did not allow for much regional interaction. Sicily was still in the Middle Ages socially; landlords lorded it over peasants and serfs. Palermo, the third largest city in the

---

265   Woolf 1991, p. 90; Noether 1951, p. 94; Hanlon 2000, pp. 342-350; Campolieti 1999, pp. 152-155.
266   Hanlon 2000, pp. 346-347; Woolf 1991, pp. 138-141; Campolieti 1999, pp. 187-197.
267   Hanlon 2000, pp. 334-337. See also Candeloro 1973, Vol. 1, pp. 136-159 for an analysis of the Kingdom of the Two Sicilies.

kingdom, had only very rich absentee landowners and masses of otherwise starving beggars.[268]

Of three hundred sixty Sicilian villages, two hundred lived under a seigniorial feudal system with the landlord possessing absolute power. With some rare exceptions, the serfs had to work without pay, *corvées*; they could not change domicile, and the landlord, not the State, acted as police, judge, and jailer. Sicilian patriotism was directed towards the barons while the king was considered a stranger; obedience to the king instead of the barons was considered treason. In northern Italy the barons joined the bourgeoisie by seeking public employment and eventually becoming entrepreneurs. Following the Spanish example, no such osmosis took place in Sicily, the wealthy city dwellers sought to enter in the baronial class and live a sumptuous life based on returns from newly acquired land. While Italy lagged vis-à-vis Britain and France culturally, Sicily was far behind the rest of Italy. Illiteracy was rampant, the University of Catania closed and an earthquake had destroyed the University of Messina at the end of the seventeenth century. When Palermo tried to fill the vacuum, Catania instituted three schools exclusively for the nobles so that the aristocracy maintained its privileges.[269]

More than virtually all European areas, Sicily depended on agriculture; usually the landlords lived in the cities, leaving the land management to bailiffs. Sicilian economic backwardness also stemmed from the lack of investment since the barons squandered the surplus in extravagant expenditure.[270] While in the North feudalism had started to disappear centuries before due to the strong influence of merchants and bankers in the powerful cities, nothing comparable was happening in the South, even though Naples was the second largest city in Italy. Furthermore, in the North intensive agriculture was introduced while in the continental South and Sicily, the mainly absentee landlords did not invest in land or labor improvement or technology.[271]

The Napoleonic Interlude in Italy

Public Administration and Fiscal Policy in the South Paralleling the events in northern Italy, Napoleon brought revolutionary changes in southern Italy under the aegis of his elder brother Joseph Bonaparte, King of Naples (1806-1808) and Napoleon's brother-in-law, Joachim Murat, King of Naples (1808-1813). The two kings attempted to reorganize the public administration according to the Napoleonic model. Since under the Bourbons the barons sought positions in the government at all levels, the civil service became bloated with unnecessary State functionaries. Consequently, Joseph Bonaparte and Murat attempted to trim the

---

268 Just before the Napoleonic conquest, the *libro d'oro*, 'the book of gold' proudly affirmed that Sicily was the 'land of the nobles', with 152 princes, 788 marquises, and 1500 dukes and barons.
269 Montanelli, 2001, p. 67.
270 Schachter 1965, passim; Montanelli 2001, pp. 63-80.
271 Malanima 1991, pp. 182-183; Schachter 1965, passim.

State administration in order to achieve efficiency. The French regime reorganized the civil service by eliminating a majority of the parasitic jobs.

In addition, Murat changed the fiscal system. Under the Bourbons, not different from the *Ancien Régime*, taxes were farmed out and middlemen appropriated the lion's share. In the Kingdom of Naples, there were 104 types of taxes under 30 administrative units to the delight of the civil service functionaries and fiscal intermediaries. Bonaparte's reform established a land tax equally applicable to large and small landowners as well as to ecclesiastic lands. Murat went further by abolishing internal tariffs and imposing protective measures for the rudimentary domestic industries.

Both Bonaparte and Murat aimed at the dissolution of the feudal system by auctioning lands owned by exiles and the Church. Their attempts were in vain since speculators acquired these properties, and enhanced the *latifundia* even further. All in all, the French regime adopted the foreign *dirigiste* model with reforms imposed from above; it did not have the time span or the support of the local groups in power to accomplish much. With the Restoration, the Old Regime reversed most of the reforms.[272]

Liberalism in the Cisalpine Republic Created by Napoleon in 1797, the Cisalpine Republic, with its capital in Milan, was weary of French liberalism. Nevertheless, the State condemned feudalism, confiscated Church lands, instituted civil matrimony, and declared gender equality. By 1802 Napoleon established the short-lived Italian Republic of the North, with himself as president and, it became the Kingdom of Italy in 1804. He chose Francesco Melzi d'Eril, a Milanese moderate liberal as vice-president. Under Melzi, the Napoleonic codes prevailed. Melzi's government brought stability and with it economic development, which equally benefited the large landowners and the bourgeoisie; this positive turn of events was suffocated by the Continental System, that is, the economic blockade and boycott of British goods.[273]

Influenced by the French Enlightenment, those Italians who wanted reform maintained that the duty of the State was to train workers to become more productive. To introduce greater efficiency, it was necessary to have more competition that would allow the optimum use of resources and result in lower consumer prices. Especially for the grain market, the reformers wanted to eliminate State constraints, which interfered with demand and supply and therefore with availability and price. They claimed that commercial legislation was needed to sanctify the contracts for sales, transfers, and investments. In various regions of Italy, not always recognized officially, the public notary had partially fulfilled this quasi-legal task since the twelfth century, but other reforms would take a long time to come to fruition.[274]

---

272   Anzilotti 1964, pp. 212-221.
273   Di Scala 1998, pp. 25-33.
274   Bianchini 1991, pp. 190-193, 198.

Like other Italian intellectuals around Melzi, Machiavelli and Vico influenced the southern nationalist Vincenzo Cuoco (1770-1823). Cuoco believed that a large educated population was necessary to achieve a national (unification) goal because education makes good citizens; Cuoco argued that the State should offer free basic education to everyone but since not all citizens are equal, higher education need not be free, and therefore he suggested that the State aid these needy students. Cuoco claimed that education creates public spirit, and public spirit in his view was nationalism.[275]

Conclusions

The eighteenth century witnessed radical changes within the Italian states and in their relationships with each other as well as with the outside world. While at times vacillating on the free trade issue, all Italian states almost always reverted to some control of international trade. The fear of famine in a world of extremely limited and high cost inland transportation dictated the states' policies. The British industrial revolution influenced all Italian states; while in Britain the State generally pursued hands off policy, the Italian states lent more than a willing hand to the incipient manufacturing industries. The State provided incentives, overt subsidies, and supported industries through the purchasing power of the State; also it did not shy away from becoming the entrepreneur.[276] During the 1780s and 1790s the State in both Piedmont and the Kingdom of the Two Sicilies invested in the textile industry.[277]

All Italian states practiced mercantilism during most of the eighteenth century; however, there were differences in nuances and in attempts at *laissez faire*. Piedmont gained political ascendancy in quest of the Italian hegemony, building a powerful military-bureaucratic state. Cavour's nineteenth century liberalism did

---

275 Noether 1951, pp. 153-162.

276 While more often than not connected with defense needs, in 1223 Venice had established the Naval Arsenal which produced ships, guns and, in 1303, hemp for manufacturing naval rope. The Savoy dynasty in Piedmont followed suit in 1570 with a modest arsenal while Naples dedicated large amounts to produce in State enterprises. During the sixteenth century, in many Italian states, easy access popular banks were established widely, which the population could trust because the State guaranteed deposits. Italian states established the *Banca di Palermo* (1551), *Banco di San Giorgio* restarted in 1586, *La Tavola di citta di Messina* (1587), *Il Banco della Piazza di Rialto* in Venice (1587), *Il Banco di Sant'Ambrogio* (1593) in Milan, and Il *Banco di Santo Spirito* (1605) in Rome. Perini 1991, p. 298.

277 The states were also instrumental, for instance, in establishing printing houses, the most famous was the one established during the Renaissance by Cosimo de Medici in Florence. Others followed especially in the Papal States in Subiaco near Rome in 1464. Naples initiated a State press circa 1487, and much later, the *Stamperia Reale*, the Royal Printing Press was established in Turin in 1740. While most printing initiatives were done by the State, Venetian private printing houses established in the late 1400s were highly successful. Perini 1991, pp. 299-303.

not impede Piedmont from subsidizing industry and imposing tariffs to reduce imports and to generate government revenue. On the other hand, the most economically advanced Italian state, Lombardy, had the political fortunes dictated by outsiders; under Spanish dominion, Lombardy's economy faltered until the Treaty of Utrecht assigned Lombardy to Austria. A number of economists influenced economic policy in both Lombardy and Tuscany (that Austria controlled by proxy) and succeeded in legislating an efficient, although not necessarily more equitable, tax system. While impediments in internal markets were abolished, Lombardy and Tuscany continued to protect industry and agriculture through tariffs, subsidies, and tax exemption.

Also, the Republic of Venice attempted to occasionally control grains trade during the eighteenth century. The Republic's economic fortunes were declining first because of shift in world trade direction and after 1719 because of competition of the Austrian free port of Trieste on the Adriatic. Policy makers were ambivalent on *laissez faire*; while accepting in principle French economic liberal ideas, they extended protection to domestic industry. When Napoleon dismembered the Republic between the city of Venice and the hinterland in 1797, the Republic was doomed and economic chaos ensued.

Further south, throughout the century, while occasionally and theoretically accepting *laissez faire*, both the Papal States and the Kingdom of the Two Sicilies generally practiced mercantilism. In the Kingdom of the Two Sicilies, the Crown directly built manufacturing industries for the court's needs. Attempts to eliminate the Sicilian *latifundia* were not successful, leaving Sicily especially behind compared with the rest of Italy. While on the mainland the controlled the economy, in Sicily, the local barons maintained their economic supremacy.

The Italian states were more than arbiters for social legislation, implementing it to protect the poor and disabled. As in Germany, the State took advantage of the weakening of the power of the Church. Even though the Reformation hardly affected Italy, in almost all of Italy Church land was at least partially confiscated and occasionally distributed to the landless peasants. Although significantly less than in Protestant Germany, the secular State made important inroads and took over the policy decisions and enfranchised a larger population. Solidifying further the role of the State in the economy, for better or for worst, the French Revolution brought in its wake a new social order.[278]

Eighteenth Century: Concluding Remarks

The eighteenth century closed as it opened, with mercantilism (however defined) still dominant although increasingly coming under intellectual challenge, thanks to Adam Smith and his predecessors as well as his successors. Each of the five countries under discussion utilized the State in an effort to bolster its economy and

---

278   Candeloro 1973, Vol. 1, pp. 163-168.

thereby engaged in nation building, although to widely varying degrees, in the boardroom and council chamber as well as on the battlefield. However, this broad generalization must be qualified by the specific economic and political circumstances of the Anglo-American and the Continental countries. Some scholars claim that eighteenth century primitive institutional State lacked the means or organization of the centuries to follow.[279]

A small island but with the largest overseas empire, after 1763 Britain closely regulated international commerce, much more so than the domestic sector although the combined shock of the American Revolution and Smith's scathing critique of mercantilism surely gave men pause. For instance, the Calico Acts (1701 and 1721) had a negative impact on the cotton textile industry of India but led to the growth of the cotton textile industry in Britain. From at least the mid-seventeenth century mercantilism helped propel Britain to the fore, the State's finger lingered on the scale, especially with regard to foreign trade, even though with less and less warrant, until the mid-nineteenth century. Totally unlike elsewhere, Britain built its roads and canals through private capital and initiative. Owing to the high level of wealth and income Britain had a thriving capital market, which mobilized capital readily at low cost.

While the Thirteen Colonies opposed certain aspects of British mercantilism, the United States did not hesitate to introduce similar economic policies to protect the domestic economy; the economic policies of the United States resembled what proceeded. The 'free spirit' of the colonists proclaimed individualism, accepting limited State intervention, including much State promotion, especially to aid the construction of roads and canals. The State continued to regulate entry, price, and quality; the market prevailed but the State never assumed that the market would suffice unaided.

Contrary to the economic policies of Britain and the United States, while pursuing mercantilist policies, the French under the absolutism of the *Ancien Régime* accepted a central role for the State in both the domestic and foreign economic sectors. From *Colbertisme* (mercantilism) in the seventeenth century through the French Revolution and Napoleon, the country that coined the term *laissez faire*, adopted *dirigisme*. Colbert sponsored monopolistic joint-stock companies to conduct extra-European trade, in contrast to the British model of private enterprise with State assistance. Especially in the use of armed force to exclude outsiders, the French companies were State enterprises with minimal private enterprise involvement. Furthermore, the State initiated and built large-scale roads and canals and, with State support French science became preeminent.

---

279 Peter Musgrave, a British economic historian, contends that one ought distinguish between the 'modern' and 'early modern' State. The modern State has been centralized, efficient, and organized for economic and political action. The early modern State fails this criterion since in most cases was inefficient and powerless to design and especially to implement economic and political action. Musgrave 1999, passim.

While Britain and France had been consolidated nations for centuries, and the Thirteen Colonies became the United States in 1776, one encounter difficulties in generalizing about Germany and Italy, which have not yet become integrated nation states. Yet, with a few notable exceptions, they adhered to the French statist approach to economic policy. France may well have been feared but it was also emulated in a world in which Britain constituted a deviant to absolutism and, after the American Revolution, the United States even more so. To be sure, not different from France, absolutist governments ruled most of the German and Italian states.

In the major German states by design or by habit the State became paramount and directly, as well as indirectly, performed various economic functions, especially in view of the low level of economic development and the weak private sector. 'Prussia epitomizes the absolutist bureaucratic state...while Britain exemplifies the parliamentary...state which was largely self-governing or self-regulating.'[280] The *Cameralists* and the monarchs whom they advised endeavored to develop industry through State policy, in particular, by owning profitable coalmines and iron foundries. The State acted when the private sector could not pursue activities which Prussia, Bavaria, and Hesse deemed critical. Policy makers concluded that the State had to interfere to improve foreign trade activity Prussia founded the *Seehandlung* (Overseas Trade Corporation) in 1772 since foreign trade was simply beyond the means of the Prussian economy.

Italian states were different from France but also from Germany because European rivals used Italy as a battleground. Among the Italian states, only Piedmont (fully), the Papal States (fully), Venice (to 1797) and the Kingdom of the Two Sicilies (partially) were independent. By the end the eighteenth century, in all the Italian territories the State, regulated, promoted, and augmented its economic policy making power, especially after the French invasion under Napoleon in 1796. Influenced by the French Physiocrats, many economists advised governments to adopt modified *laissez faire* but that ensued only in lively unresolved debates. Most of the Italian states attempted to liberalize trade, especially the grain trade, only to revert to controls; almost all of them protected domestic industries, even though they were rudimentary. As in France and Germany, the Italian states adopted mercantilist policies throughout the century.

Mercantilism was practiced everywhere in the eighteenth century. Nevertheless, Britain (after the *Wealth of Nations*) and, to a lesser extent, the United States (after independence) made a valiant effort to liberalize trade. Moreover, in contrast to Continental Europe, Britain and the United States proclaimed the minimal State and attempted economic liberalism by limiting interference in the domestic market as much as it attempted individual political liberalism.

The Anglo-Americans viewed *étatisme* and planning as anti-democratic, that is, coercive, vouched for private enterprise, limited government and economic

---

280   Brewer and Hellmuth 1999, p. 3.

individualism as a keystone of liberty.[281] On the Continent, France, Germany, and Italy rarely accepted economic liberalism with the State active in the market not only as promoter and regulator but also as direct participant. Absolutism reigned in France to 1789, while all German and Italian states had by far less individual political freedom than their Anglo-American counterparts.

---

281 Yet, in the nineteenth century United States, Hamilton and John Quincy Adams favored the 'elites' to formulate public policies.

Chapter 3

The Nineteenth Century

The nineteenth century can be defined literally from 1800 to 1900 or historically from 1815 Napoleon's defeat, to 1914, the outbreak of World War I. Victory at Waterloo allowed Britain to maintain its world economic hegemony. While Britain's economic leadership could be partially attributed to its domestic integrated market, the absolute control of the seas proved pivotal. Conventional wisdom asserts that the Industrial Revolution started first in Britain because, among other reasons, entrepreneurs could bet on the winners rather than the losers and therefore move more readily away from the Luddites (1811-1816) and the Chartists (1838-1848), who feared that the mechanization of industry would eliminate their jobs.

The countries of Continental Europe underwent the Industrial Revolution later than Britain, but experienced economic development during the nineteenth century.[1] Britain became *the* workshop of the world. As the first industrial nation, Britain operated in a largely unobstructed market; therefore British trade, shipping, and manufacturing responded readily to economic signals. Britain achieved market coordination without a coordinator in the sense that the State played an essentially passive role. *Laissez faire* thought helped to ignite the free trade movement. Other reasons include: searching for cheap food for low-wage factory workers, keeping the cost of exported manufactured goods down, assuming that free trade would bring peace, and political change after the Reform Act of 1832.[2]

This political upheaval corrected the existing system of representation that reflected gross inequities exaggerated by the population growth and rural-urban migration during the Industrial Revolution. The Reform Act redistributed parliamentary seats towards the emerging urban centers such as Birmingham and Manchester and extended the franchise to include more of the middle class. Although this Act shifted the balance of power to the industrial and commercial class, it still left the bulk of the population disfranchised; the number of voters increased only from about 500,000 to some 813,000.

The American political economy differed institutionally from that of Britain; federalism, based on written constitutions, created a polycentric political universe.[3] The public debate concerning economic policy and thought took place separately in the central government and the states, and, under concurrent jurisdiction, in

---

1   Mokyr 1990, pp. 256, 260; Findley 1992, pp. 158-161.
2   Taylor 1972, p. 39.
3   For instance, the United States Constitution mandates a population census each decade to determine representation in the House of Representatives.

both. The states shared sovereignty with the central government, which enabled them to pursue mercantilist state rivalries. Furthermore, the judicial branch exercised more power and influence in the United States than elsewhere, mediating between and among contending interests. The courts decided questions of constitutionality, and interpreted both the constitutions and the laws.

The State could readily and reasonably grant (or sell at nominal prices and on easy terms) vast amounts of public land for education, settlement, or transportation purposes to communities, enterprises, or individuals. In addition to political and social objectives, policymakers expected that the anticipated social benefits (based on the externalities of gain from rising land values and economic growth) would vastly exceed the present value of the otherwise unoccupied land.

With a relatively high per capita income, compared with other nations, optimism prevailed.[4] *Laissez faire*, as an abstract principle tenuously connected with the British, most notably Adam Smith, commanded the allegiance of some American economists. For the most part, State (local, state and/or federal governments) intervention generated enthusiasm rather than antagonism and found supporters among such Americans as Alexander Hamilton (1755-1804), Henry Clay (1797-1879), and Henry Charles Carey (1793-1879) who advocated trade protection.

From the outset, the federal government imposed a tariff with both protective and revenue features. As everywhere, consumers battled with producers in the political arena for their specific interests. Similarly, as the century advanced, policy tilted increasingly towards regulation rather than promotion. As individual enterprises grew larger and more powerful, the definition of competition changed from many buyers and sellers to only a few sellers. The tariff had little effect on economic development but a greater effect in transferring income from agriculture to manufacturing and from the South to the North.

By the beginning of the nineteenth century, individual states began to facilitate the incorporation process but this transition from unincorporated to incorporated enterprise did not end until circa 1875. Private incorporation bills were used earlier for all public services: roads, canals, banks, etc. but rarely for manufacturing.[5] Because railroads needed large long-term capital outlays, they were critical to the advent of the corporation. Even in Britain manufacturing enterprises used either the sole proprietorship or the partnership for the longest time. Atypically, by industrializing first, Britain succeeded in industrializing before the passage of a general incorporation law. British manufacturing enterprises generally were small and not vertically integrated and remained family enterprises until much later. Different from Britain and the United States, on the Continent, public utilities came under state scrutiny because of their natural monopoly condition. Prior to 1867, French State controls extended to all corporations and were not limited to public utilities alone. Gradually, the process

---

4   Americans believed in their *manifest destiny*, that is, the United States was destined to expand.

5   The Boston Manufacturing Company established in 1813, as a vertically integrated textile enterprise, constituted one such an exception.

of establishing corporations was liberalized over the entire Continent.[6] While there has been a certain amount of overlap, chartering and regulating have been conceptually separated and the former need not imply the later. All countries prohibited incorporation without State consent.

France supported and participated in the American Revolution before it had its own. On the Continent, the French Revolution of 1789 represents the great historical fracture. Not only did the remaining traces of feudalism and serfdom vanish but also a much larger number of mostly arbitrary administrative units supplanted the historic French provinces, each with special privileges. France emerged in the nineteenth century much more centralized than ever before. In sharp contrast to Britain, the State guided the economy through the industrialization process.[7] Following the Napoleonic Wars, French travelers once again flocked to Britain and realized the tremendous economic progress achieved there. Continental countries such as France, Germany, and Italy desperately tried to catch up with Britain. France and Germany industrialized relatively early, although still later than Britain, while Italy, the European economic center through the sixteenth century, lagged behind these nations even more.

The discovery of America as well as the all-water route to India shifted the trading center from the Mediterranean Sea to the Atlantic Ocean. By the eighteenth century, Italy had become peripheral and stayed that way through the better part of the nineteenth century. As latecomers, Continental countries needed, or so they thought, State intervention to accelerate the industrialization process. In each country, France, Germany, and Italy, strong State participation in the market during the eighteenth century carried over into the nineteenth century, and indeed well into the twentieth century.

The 1789 Revolution and the 'Declaration of the Rights of Man and Citizen' put an end to the *Ancien Régime*. True enough, the rights guaranteed by the Constituent Assembly limited suffrage to active citizens, that is, those who paid a certain amount of taxes; only fifty thousand individuals qualified under these conditions–some noble, a few peasants but mostly the bourgeoisie. Political power shifted from ancestry to wealth, which, in all its varied forms, brought in its wake considerable institutional instability and change but always with the State spearheading the economy.[8] France had a national economy, in which the State intervened, time and again, to preserve, protect, and defend the ostensible national interest. Different from the British, there has been a long tradition of French supporting State intervention.[9] France made strenuous efforts to increase its economic power through the State, aiming at a balanced economy with substantial self-sufficiency.

---

6   Kindleberger 1993, pp. 191-194.
7   Zysman 1979, p. 52.
8   Leveque 1989, p. 361
9   Hall 1986b, p. 230.

France emerged as a republic with nominal (that is, without ministerial responsibility) universal male suffrage after 1848, decades before its neighbors.[10] Although Britain preceded France on the way to political liberalism and parliamentary control of the executive, France tried to achieve the same in 1789, 1830, and 1848 only to make it definitive in 1875 when it combined manhood suffrage with ministerial responsibility.[11]

At the end of the nineteenth century, France remained far behind Britain and the unified Germany and Italy in implementing social legislation. Not wholly consistent with *laissez faire* philosophy, Britain instituted some State covered health insurance and unemployment assistance as well as an old–age pension program. Of course, in 1911, David Lloyd George (1863-1945), a British statesman, was premature in proclaiming that the State protected the individual from the cradle to the grave. *Au contraire*, in France, 'social progress remains constantly a philosophical problem – that of the nature of the French democracy – where irresolution paralysis action permanently'.[12]

To be sure, a short-lived government in 1896, led by the Prime Minister Felix Faure (1895-1899), attempted to legislate a *quasi-contrat social* to moderate the disparity between the wealthy and the poor. His populist program included a progressive income tax, tax returns for all income earners, social security, workers protection, and arbitration for labor management disputes. Lacking the votes in parliament, his government fell and France did not introduce these reforms before World War I.[13]

While Britain and France had been unitary states for centuries, Germany and Italy only consolidated the multiple independent entities into national states during the nineteenth century. With this transformation, nationalism triumphed as individuals begun to identify with an abstract and larger State rather than with their own narrow constituencies. Intellectuals and policy makers in both countries (Bismarck in Germany, Cavour in Italy, and numerous others) repeatedly responded to, and induced, a widespread desire for nation building. To accomplish this process, indeed, they used the resources of the State to institute and enforce economic policies as well as to correct ostensible market failures.

Even before unification, German idealists changed the orientation of ethical and spiritual values with the State replacing the Church as the ultimate moral authority. Different from other Western European countries where moral authority

---

10   However, universal male suffrage was all but meaningless under Napoleon III.

11   Owing to its subordination to the absolute monarch, before the 1789 Revolution, the nobility in France played a less important role than in Britain or Prussia-Germany although for quite different reasons. After Napoleon's fall, France restored a less absolutist monarchy. The Revolution of 1830 replaced this monarchy with the July monarchy that lasted until the Revolution of 1848, when the Second Republic was established, followed in 1852 by the Empire under Napoleon III. When the Emperor fled after the debacle of the Franco-Prussian War of 1870, the Third Republic succeeded the Empire.

12   Rosanvallon 1989, p. 533.

13   Mayeur 1973, pp. 215-216.

continued to reside in the established Church or natural law, in Germany the 'idealists' identified moral authority with the State.[14] Otto von Bismarck (1862-1890) believed that the State, like everything else, was part of a great Divine world plan. Different from Britain and the United States, Prussian philosophy and culture adopted idealistic historical analysis rather than natural laws.[15] Prussian idealists viewed German nationality as a common culture and not as a common citizenship.[16] Hegel defined the State as 'the world history proper' and those who obey the law feel free.[17]

During the eighteenth and most of the nineteenth century, Germany consisted of a multitude of mini-states and a few larger states such as Austria, Baden, Bavaria, Prussia, Saxony and Württemberg. After the defeat of Napoleon (who unintentionally precipitated German unification) about 50 German political units remained in 1815; by 1840 there were still 39 separate states. The forces of unification originated, among other things, with a common liberal and low tariff for all of Prussia in 1818 (which until then had internal tariffs) and the formation of the *Zollverein* (customs union) of all German states (except Austria) in 1834.[18]

Not every political German entity was enthusiastic about unification, before or after the fact. While Prussia aimed at unification as a means of absorbing the other German states, Bavaria and Saxony as well as some independent German city-states dreaded Prussian hegemony. Austria, especially, started to feel the weight of an expansionist Prussia. At the post-Napoleonic Congress of Vienna of 1815, a German-speaking majority dominated Austria, a polyglot State, even before 1789, politically.[19] Austria presided over the German Confederation, created as an outcome of the Congress of Vienna, but did not and could not belong to the *Zollverein*, the German customs union, among other things, a political and economic measure designed to strengthen Prussia at the expense of Austria.[20]

At the Congress of Vienna, the Veneto was added to the territories already held by Austria, (Austria controlled Lombardy before Napoleon), to Austrian control. Lombardy and the Veneto, among the advanced Italian territories, were in the forefront of social legislation before Italian unification. These regions with

---

14   Even though Immanuel Kant (1724-1804) preached human equality, the dignity of man, and popular sovereignty, his rigorous ethics of duty brought him to insist on the necessity of an authoritarian government. Pflanze 1963, pp. 23-25.

15   Georg Wilhelm Friedrich Hegel (1770-1831) legitimized power politics through his dialectic theory of history and distinguished between the State as it was and the State as it ought to be. According to Hegel, the State could find its stable equilibrium only through conflict between the pursuit of power and the rule of universal law and morality. For example, Hegel contended that the Holy Roman Empire (dissolved during his life time) was unsustainable because it lacked the power to enforce its governance and therefore the Empire could not be defined as a State.

16   Gagliardo 1980, pp. 256-259; Hegel 1954, pp. 527-539.

17   Hegel 1953, p. 53.

18   Pounds 1959, p. 190; Fremdling 1983, p. 122.

19   Austria included Germans, Hungarians, Czechs, Slovaks, Poles, Italians, and others.

20   Of all the major powers, Austria was the most threatened by nationalism, which eventually (1918) tore it asunder.

Austria's approval prohibited child labor in 1843; unified Italy in the 1870s adopted this policy.

During the 1830s Giuseppe Mazzini, a political philosopher and a revolutionary proponent of Italian unification, complained that the British had not advanced beyond Adam Smith. On the other hand, Camillo Cavour, the Prime Minister of Piedmont during the 1850s and the first prime minister of the unified Italy, greatly admired Smithian economic policy. Strongly influenced by the French example, Italy was neither a staunch supporter of *laissez faire* thought nor of policies based on *laissez faire* in the evolving British tradition. The 1750s physiocratic debate on agriculture vs. manufacturing in France reappeared in Italy a century later. This debate engaged mostly academia with little effect on policy makers such as Cavour in Piedmont or other Italian provinces that were still under foreign domination.[21] Like the German landed aristocracy (the East Prussian *Junkers*), after the unification of Italy, *la Destra Storica* (the Historic Right) was composed mainly of southern landowners, the *latifundisti*, and northern bourgeoisie; the *Destra Storica* governed Italy from 1861 to 1876.

Against the wishes of the southern *latifundisti*, towards the end of the nineteenth century the northern bourgeoisie and industrial interests captured the government and pursued a policy of industrialization in which the State played a primary role.[22] In the various Italian states before unification as well as in the Kingdom of Italy afterwards, the State was a predominant actor.[23] Some observers define the Italian model as 'precocious State capitalism', because the State at the end of the nineteenth century broke the rules of the market by inserting itself as the main economic actor in the market place.[24] However, others view the Italian success story more as a result of market forces than of often-counterproductive public policies.[25] Italian nationalists maintained that given the backwardness of the country 'only the State had the locative power needed to promote industrialization'.[26]

Britain

During the nineteenth century the British government refrained from economic intervention in a comprehensive, coherent, and deliberate sense. Nevertheless, the emergence of an industrial economy such as cotton textiles, iron, and steam power, first in factories and a generation later in railroads, resulted in a steady procession of specific regulatory legislation designed to rectify sectoral problems. While *laissez faire* prevailed as an abstract doctrine, circumstances altered cases on more than one occasion. The Industrial Revolution induced Britain to discard previous

---

21   Cafagna 1989, pp. 10-15.
22   Fenoaltea 1973, pp. 140-144.
23   De Cecco 2002, pp. 62-63.
24   Amatori 1997b, p. 255.
25   Federico 1996, pp. 779-781 .
26   Federico and Toniolo 1991, p. 210.

pre-industrial mercantilist legislation as no longer applicable. In addition, Adam Smith and the Classical School had an impact.[27]   When Smith castigated mercantilism in the late eighteenth century, an array of legislation on the statute books still prescribed and proscribed economic behavior.

In one of the most striking deviation from *laissez faire*, the opening of the Suez Canal in 1869 prompted the British government, for strategic reasons, to purchase a sizeable block of shares in the private enterprise that built the canal. This action can be seen as a military, political, and strategic move to maintain better connections with India and beyond. Similarly, Britain possessed the largest merchant fleet throughout the nineteenth century and also owned the largest colonial empire.[28]

The Great Reform Bill of 1832

In the half-century between the publication of the *Wealth of Nations* and the reform of the political process, new cities had sprouted while older towns had declined. Also, industrial entrepreneurs appeared who sought political participation because the Enlightenment had influenced them and even more because they had economic interests to defend. The Great Reform Bill broke the logjam in 1832 by extending the franchise to a greater segment of the middle class; after the Reform, twenty percent of the adult males could vote in Parliamentary elections. This Bill also redistricted the House of Commons to reflect the geographic redistribution of population so that, for example, Manchester acquired a seat while lesser populous places lost seats.

This political transformation profoundly impacted economic and social policy; one need merely mention the replacement of the old Elizabethan Poor Law of 1601 by the New Poor Law of 1834. The same factors blended with humanitarian impulses to bring about the enactment of protective legislation for workers in selected industries. Those least able to care for themselves, women and children, received the solicitous care of the State. The Health and Morals of Apprentices Act (1801) regulated the employment of pauper children. Furthermore, slavery was abolished in the British Empire in 1833. On balance, however, the State became less paternalistic.

Ambivalent feeling towards the government is exemplified by fears of social unrest after the French Revolution. Landlords fared well during the Napoleonic

---

27   Kitson Clark 1967, p. 13.
28   The British political process had been frozen since the Glorious Revolution of 1688-1689. At the end of the seventeenth century, James II (Catholic) fled and William and Mary (Protestants) replaced him, in a peaceful transition. Religion constituted only a fraction of the story; the other part was that James threatened property by attempting to reassert the power of the king over Parliament. Hence, in 1689 (after James II had escaped to France), Parliament prohibited the king from keeping a standing army in peacetime without its consent. The Revolution established the Parliament as the supreme kingmaker and controller of finances; while there has been a Royal Navy and a Royal Air Force, there has been no Royal army.

Wars and invested in British government bonds, not so much due to patriotism as to 'protection money' against the Jacobins.[29]   Some maintain that Britain Parliament was prompted to introduce legislation to help the poor between 1795 and 1834 as a response to increasing unrest, that is, food riots at home and the fear that the French Revolution might cross the Channel. When the food riots and the danger of Revolution dimmed, Parliament became less benevolent.[30]

It is difficult to reconcile the apparent absence of government intervention in the British economy, that is, *laissez faire*, with the simultaneous and ever-expanding role of the State in the very same economy. The policy makers never defined the State as any more than a watchman. What captured the imagination, then and since, was the repeal of two historic pieces of legislation. Britain repealed the Corn Laws in 1846. In addition, most of the Navigation Acts, which governed foreign commerce and shipping, were repealed in 1849, and foreign ships were admitted to the coasting trade (cabotage) in 1854.

Mercantilism Buried

The repeal of the Corn Laws and the Navigation Acts swept away the last vestiges of mercantilism. These antiquated trade laws had become outmoded; by mid-century Britain had become the preeminent shipbuilder and shipper and had shifted from the protection of domestic agricultural products to becoming a nation of shopkeepers and the workshop of the world. The extension of the suffrage ratified what had already occurred in the country at large. Political power had been transferred to those who had recently acquired economic power, that is, from agriculture to commerce and industry, or from the inherited landed aristocracy to the newly enriched commercial and manufacturing middle class. Free trade emerged in Britain owing to the desire to reduce government expenditures and to the distrust of corrupt government as well as to Smith's scathing critique of mercantilism.

In 1825, the British repealed the Bubble Act of 1720, enacted the Companies Act in 1844, and in 1856 passed a general incorporation law. The acceptance of the corporation as a way of conducting business accommodated both the railroad and, to a lesser extent, larger-scale capital-intensive manufacturing enterprises. It seems that by freeing the external economy and facilitating larger enterprises, *laissez faire* triumphed but not necessarily for ideological reasons. The first phase of industrialization had been completed well before corporations became common.

On the other hand, the State did play an important role in selected aspects of the economy. Althougfooh Britain did not initiate a national system of education until 1870, state grants supported elementary education between 1833 and 1869.[31] The

---

29   O'Brien 1959, pp. 255-267. The Jacobins, a French political partially revolutionary faction originated in the 1790s, advocated a republican system of government and *laissez faire* economic policies.

30   Lindert 1998, pp. 102-103, 128-129, 135.

31   Britain enacted laws for the regulation of railways in 1840, the inspection of mines in 1842, the inspection of steamships in 1846, the Ten Hours Act in 1847, and the Public

Factory Act of 1802 paved the way for the Factory Act of 1833; the Factory Acts required textile factory owners to provide primary school education for child employees. Add to the above, the Acts of 1866 and 1875, which conferred upon local governments the power to preserve and protect the housing stock and one can derive a sense of the range of the economic activity of the State.[32]

Public Utilities

The State decided whether to allow municipalities to provide public utility services (gas, water, tramways, and electricity) on pragmatic rather than on political or ideological grounds. This was in line with John Stuart Mill's (1806-1873) thinking. Probably one of the most influential British economists and thinkers of the nineteenth century, Mill differentiated between the sector of the economy in which the free play of individuals ought to prevail to maximize efficiency and the public service sector in which other values should become paramount. A liberal advocate therefore of public service, Mill rejected the public stand of Herbert Spencer (1820-1903), a contemporary social philosopher, political economist, and an opponent of any State intervention.[33]

Municipal gas distribution originated during the mid-nineteenth century; building gas lines interfered with existing property rights and therefore required acts of Parliament. Legislation conferred the power of eminent domain on private enterprises recognized as public utilities/natural monopolies. Nonetheless, Parliament never significantly affected the gas industry as to output, prices, or industrial structure. In this manner, Parliament protected the gas industry from consumers and from public scrutiny.[34]

Perhaps owing to the unsatisfactory nature of public utility regulation from 1845 to 1870, communities shifted from regulation to municipal ownership of gas distribution during 1870-1915. For example, in 1870, Parliament gave local authorities the right to purchase tramway companies at scrap value after the franchises expired in twenty-one years. In short, gas and waterworks socialism, that is, municipal public ownership, became meaningful in the late nineteenth century.[35]

In 1873, Joseph Chamberlain (1836-1914), mayor of Birmingham, a highly successful businessman, social reformer, and statesman, initiated a widely imitated social engineering policy. The Gas and Waterworks Acts of 1870 and 1871 enabled municipalities to act in this area without specific laws. As mayor of Birmingham (population 400,000) from 1853 to 1856, following the precedent established by Manchester in 1817, Chamberlain introduced 'gas and waterworks' socialism. Owing to Chamberlain's powers of persuasion, Birmingham purchased the local gas companies, which Parliament confirmed in 1875. Chamberlain

Health Act in 1848.
32 Parris 1960, p. 22; Court 1954, pp. 238, 260, 262; Tomlinson 1981, pp. 45-47.
33 Stone 1991, vii, xiii, 11, 14-15.
34 Matthews 1986, p. 263.
35 Grove 1962, pp. 7, 17, 26.

argued principally that the profitability of these companies rightfully belonged to the community and, furthermore, that local monopolies should be State owned. Thanks to the Public Health Act of 1872, and with the approval of Parliament in 1875, Birmingham bought the waterworks in 1876. In this instance, Chamberlain employed the sanitation or public health argument; consequently, he did not intend that the waterworks be profitable.[36]

Similarly, prior to electrification, Britain enacted the Tramway Act (1870), which enabled cities to finance and own but not operate tramways. Accordingly, Glasgow built and leased its mass transit facilities to the Glasgow Tram and Omnibus Company, with the lease expiring in 1894. Owing to a conflict between the city and the company over the lease renewal terms, Glasgow decided in 1889 in favor of municipal ownership. Thus, during the nineties, Glasgow, with a population of more than 600,000 people, owned and operated the electric trolleys. The European model (including Britain) used short-term concessions and franchises. In striking contrast, the United States followed its own course; the individual states, and not the central government commonly awarded long-term leases. Certainly compared with Europe, the United States valued franchises well above scrap value and therefore the franchise was worth more than 'a mere piece of paper'. During the late nineteenth century Britain replicated the example of Birmingham and Glasgow many fold in acquiring municipally owned services.[37]

The Telegraph Debate and Nationalization

Although nominally Britain epitomized *laissez faire*, in actuality deviations came thick and fast. Like other European countries, Britain embarked on a species of State enterprise, but with a twist. The Industrial Revolution not only increased the total British population, despite substantial emigration, but also accelerated urbanization and individual cities grew even larger, with concomitant problems. Charles I had founded the Royal Mail in 1635, and Parliament had created the Post Office and set a fixed rate for mailing letters in 1657. However, even in 1838, sending a letter across England cost two shillings (24 pence) and took two weeks. After the creation of the first prepaid postal service in 1840 via railway, mailing a letter cost a penny and took two days. This facilitated communication by the masses; the delivery of the mail possessed a social value regardless of the cost to society.[38]

The technological innovations of this era included developing the railway during the 1830s and patenting the telegraph in 1837. The railway quickly adopted the telegraph to control the movement of trains and thereby preventing accidents. Initially, this new form of communication originated and remained in the hands of private enterprise. Viewing the telegraph as an adjunct of the mails, however, by mid-century critics contended that what constituted in essence a private monopoly

---

36   Briggs 1965, pp. 221, 225, 227; Hennock 1973, pp. 117-125.
37   McKay 1976, pp. 19-20, 91-94, 169, 174-175.
38   Daunton 1985, pp. xv, 85.

provided the public with inadequate service. They therefore challenged rates, which deterred use, and profits inherent in a natural monopoly.

During the early 1860s, the British considered the alternatives: competition, privately owned but publicly regulated monopolies, or public enterprises. The Telegraph Act of 1863 regulated the telegraph system and the telegraph companies on behalf of competition and the public good. Maintaining universal telegraph service in little used rural areas proved expensive and generated little revenue. During the 1860s the Post Office shifted from financial to social considerations, which led to the nationalization of the telegraph.

The prevailing British *laissez faire* ideology customarily balked at nationalization as an interference with private enterprise, even if acceptable in specific instances of market and regulatory failure. The precise boundary line separating private from public enterprise evolved pragmatically. State intrusion was acceptable to economists and statesmen, apparently without doing violence to *laissez faire*. William Stanley Jevons (1835-1882), an economist and logician who did pioneering work in marginalist economics, in 1867 maintained that the telegraph, if nationalized under the terms proposed by the Government, would prove unprofitable. He found the financial analogy between the postal system and the telegraph fatally flawed because the postal network required little capital investment contrasted with the telegraph. Even the cogent argument of such a distinguished economist as Jevons failed to deter the nationalization of the telegraph. The Post Office added social considerations to financial considerations, that is, granting subsidies as a stimulus to increase communication.

The Telegraph Act of 1868 represented the first purchase of commercial assets by the State for the express purpose of nationalization; the transfer of the telegraph system from private enterprise to the State occurred in 1870. The nationalization of the telegraph certainly constituted a striking exception to the prevailing *laissez faire* orthodoxy. Even the failure of nationalization to live up to the expectations of its proponents had little or no effect. The Government woefully underestimated the cost of buying out the industry as well as the working expenses and, moreover, overestimated income.

In Britain the telegraph industry originated solely through private enterprise; the State then bought an existing industry. In at least some Continental countries, the State was the entrepreneur, that is, the State financed, organized, and operated an industry which private initiative either could not or would not bring into being. In those instances, the State's motivation was less ideological than practical, since the telegraph had political and military implications, not to mention national prestige.

Although infinitely faster than the mails, distances in Britain are so short that an ordinary non-commercial telegraph customer gained little time. The economies of scale and scope between the telegraph and the Post Office proved insufficient. Furthermore, the introduction of the telephone in the fourth quarter of the nineteenth century left the telegraph caught between the upper and the nether millstone. For those who valued price over time, the mail sufficed whereas for those who preferred time to price, the telephone served better.[39]

The State's Role in Ruling the Seas

Britain had been instrumental in constructing a railway across the Isthmus of Suez in 1858. Ferdinand de Lesseps formed the *Compagnie universelle du canal* (Universal Company for the Canal) in 1858 and the Suez Canal opened in 1869. As the leading maritime, commercial, and imperial power, Britain provided the overwhelming share of the ships that transited the Suez Canal and, consequently, British ships paid the majority of the tolls. The weakness of the Ottoman Empire, 'the sick man of Europe', French-British rivalry in Egypt, and the profligacy and heavy indebtedness of Egypt, constituted the background for a singular deviation from *laissez faire*.

In 1875, the British Government purchased almost half the shares in the Suez Canal Company from Egypt, thereby becoming a stockholder in one of the largest private enterprises of the day. Statecraft, certainly not economic policy, dictated this highly popular foreign policy and national defense decision, which helped insure the British lifeline to India.[40] Some 'critics claimed it was an unprecedented application of State resources and a mischievous anomaly'.[41] Others found diverse criticisms; nevertheless, no critic specifically ascribed dissatisfaction to *laissez faire*.[42]

The first ocean-going steamship burned wood; Britain mined coal in abundance and at relatively low cost, which soon supplanted wood, the much less efficient fuel, for steamships. However, every ton of coal carried as fuel meant fewer tons of revenue-producing freight that could be carried instead. Although petroleum had been used for illumination for a half a century, it quickly emerged as a source of energy. By the 1890s, petroleum became the fuel of choice, owing to its remarkably superior efficiency over all other energy sources. Therefore, the British Navy sought to convert from coal to oil but Britain lacked known oil reserves; before World War I, much of the world's oil production came from the United States and from the Russian Caspian Sea area wells.

---

39 Foreman-Peck 1989, pp. 81-85; Hochfelder 2000, pp. 741-742, n. 5, 744; Kieve 1973, pp. 46, 125, 147-159, 176-236; Daunton 1985, p. 318.
40 Chartered as a private enterprise in 1600, the East India Company defeated the rival French company as part of the almost century-long struggle between Britain and France for world domination, which began in 1689 and ended in 1763. The East India Company retained its trade monopoly and fulfilled the role of colonial administrator of India until 1833 when free trade with India became the rule. After proving incapable of dealing with the Sepoy Rebellion in which the native militia revolted against their British officers in 1857, the East India Company lost its administrative function. Public opinion forced the dissolution of the East India Company and a newly created government India Office assumed the governmental colonial function.
41 Farnie 1969, p. 235.
42 Marlow 1964, pp. 280-287, 304; Farnie 1969, pp. 234-235.

By the turn of the century entrepreneurs started to explore for oil in the Middle East.   Exploring, drilling, transporting, and refining oil, especially in the underdeveloped Middle East, required significant long-term capital investment in a high-risk venture with an uncertain time horizon. Circa 1900, Britain wanted an independent and wholly dependable oil supply, that is, one that could not be cut off during wartime, to fuel the British fleet. However, in 1903, Britain refused to advance money to William Knox d'Arcy based on his Persian oil companies, but in 1914, to be certain of its fuel supply, Britain invested in the Anglo-Persian Oil Company. In still another exception to the dominant *laissez faire* ideology, the British State thereby became a major stockholder. This decision suited the needs of capital-starved private enterprise, which needed fuel oil contracts in addition to capital, and also met the national defense interests of Britain. Scarcely in keeping with Britain's reputation as a minimalist State, the investment enabled Anglo-Persian to exploit the d'Arcy concession and gave Britain a sure and secure oil supply for the Navy. Since silence confers consent, the *laissez faire* ideology became totally subordinate in this instance to *haute politique.*[43]

Early in the nineteenth century Britain built wooden sailing ships using, if necessary, lumber imported from far and wide. The coming of first, the steam engine, and later the iron and steel hull, favored Britain, with superior iron and steel and engineering industries, in the effort to retain mastery of the seven seas. Britain's vast overseas empire mandated that the speediest means of communication and transportation be utilized, even if not necessarily the most cost effective.

Starting in the 1830s, to stimulate the ocean-going steamship during the infant stage and to justify the carriage of low bulk-high value products, that is, the mails, Britain subsidized steamship lines to the Mediterranean, India, and North America. The very survival of these steamship lines depended on the subsidized mail contracts; Cunard on the North Atlantic, Peninsular and Orient to India, and similar lines inherited the subsidies paid to carry the mail during the sailing ship era. Also, one must recall that until decades later merchant ships possessed auxiliary military use. Britain deemed the merchant marine too vital to entrust its fate to the winds of competition.

The Cunard Steamship Company inaugurated its trans-Atlantic steamship service in 1840 with a fleet of four steamships, which were obliged to use about 40 percent of their carrying capacity for fuel. Only the mails and passengers would pay such a premium for speed; in consequence, the heyday of the sailing ship lingered until the fourth quarter of the nineteenth century, especially on secondary routes, carrying high bulk-low value products such as wheat or coal where time hardly proved critical.[44]

After the turn of the nineteenth century, when Germany successfully challenged British supremacy by winning the 'Blue Ribbon' for the fastest crossing from Europe to New York, Britain loaned Cunard 2,600,000 pounds at a subsidized 2 3/4 percent interest rate. This subsidy permitted the building of the

43   Jones 1981, pp. 17, 160, 200, 248-249; Ferrier 1982, pp. 68-91, 113, 167, 195, 326.
44   Kirkaldy 1914, p. 135; Bowen 1930, pp. 285, 290.

Lusitania and the *Mauretania*, at that time the largest and fastest vessels in the North Atlantic passenger trade. A mix of commercial and imperial (strategic defense) motives muted *laissez faire*.[45]

Industrialization and Externalities

In yet another illustration of its response to industrialization, during the nineteenth century the State inaugurated the long and arduous process of coping with the negative externalities of burning coal, that is, air pollution. While segments of society impeded this regulatory control, they waged their controversy in terms of economic costs rather than *laissez faire* percepts. Coal mining in Britain began circa 1300 and restrictions on the use of coal appeared as early as 1307. Even during the pre-Industrial Revolution, burning coal with high sulfur content, and therefore generating noxious smoke, as well as the combination of industry and population density turned London into a smoky city. Nevertheless, Britain enacted no further smoke abatement legislation after 1641, perhaps owing to the emergence of economic individualism encapsulated in the Puritan Revolution (1642-1649).

Not until the classic Industrial Revolution did coal take off into the atmosphere, both literally and figuratively. Before James Watt the steam engine had pumped water out of coal mines and Watt's more efficient steam engine accomplished that task with considerable fuel saving. Watt later adapted the steam engine to factory use as a stationary engine. Consequently, the per capita consumption of coal tripled during 1775-1830 and boomed for decades thereafter. Britain mined ten million tons of coal in 1810, one hundred million tons in 1865, and two hundred million tons in 1875. Unfortunately, air pollution worsened commensurately.

While in cases of individual nuisance, the British resorted to the courts and the common law for protection; it gradually dawned on policy makers that State intervention had become mandatory because of the resulting health hazard stemming from the lack of clean air. Britain enacted its first smoke abatement law in 1821 and the Smoke Nuisance Abatement Act of 1853 supplemented the first, although leaving ample room for further improvement. To the best of our knowledge, there is no evidence whatsoever that opponents of this legislation-cited *laissez faire* in their defense of the *status quo*; instead, they based their opposition on alleged cost-benefit analysis.

It is perhaps worth noting that the British regulatory process starts from the premise of economic individualism and relies on the common law and case law to restrain the bad actor. On the Continent, however, with a different legal tradition, regulation has been comprehensive and has emanated from the top down. Therefore, one cannot speak about Napoleonic codes, which have no British or, for that matter, American equivalents.[46]

45   Court 1954, p. 333; Pollard and Robertson 1979, pp. 222, 226.
46   Clapham 1949, pp. 168, 228; Nef 1932, pp. 157, 157 n. 7; Ashby and Anderson 1981, pp. 1-2, 5, 8, 15, 18-19.

Farm Policies and the Irish Famine

Owing to its large scale, capital-intensive, and highly productive agriculture, coupled with dominance of the world's sea-lanes as well as its willingness to become a net importer of grain, Britain enjoyed low food prices. The relative decline of farming and the increased reliance of Britain on cheaper food imports facilitated the repeal of the Corn Laws; these factors helped to postpone imperial preference until the next century. Although Britain had intervened previously to prevent famines, British *laissez faire* agricultural policies, that is, minimal market intervention exacerbated the great Irish potato famine of the hungry forties, resulting in the death of a million people. An acre of potatoes fed more people than any other crop; owing to this high potato productivity, high fertility, and improved sanitation, the population of Ireland grew so much as to exceed the population of England and Wales in 1841.

When, as a result of a natural disaster, the potato blight, the potato crop failed repeatedly between 1845 and 1849, farm produce prices soared, with a decline in the quantity and quality of food, especially in Ireland. Economic policy makers assumed a natural substitution of grain for potatoes and made funds available for purchases of grain, more expensive than homegrown potatoes, on the international market. Britain spent a great deal to combat this Irish famine but obviously not nearly enough and the contemporary Irish wanted still more relief.[47] One might explain British handling the Irish famine with reference to the New Poor Law of 1834, which aimed to throw the poor more (not entirely) on their own resources and on the vagaries of the market.

Laissez faire economists drawing on Smith, (Nassau Senior, John Ramsay McCulloch, and John Stuart Mill) and policy makers, instead perceived government as the problem, not the solution, and did not consider relief from starvation and death to be one of the proper functions of government. 'The Irish famine relief effort was constrained less by poverty than by ideology and public opinion.'[48] This belief in the efficacy of *laissez faire* hobbled the State; in contrast, the Belgian, French, and Prussian governments mitigated the worst effects of the same crop catastrophe by timely grain purchases.[49]

What aspects of British history help to account for the failure of British to respond in accordance with what might be regarded as an ordinary humanitarian impulse? As early as 1587, England first regulated the grain market to relieve a dearth crisis. A quasi-free grains market prevailed in Britain from the mid-

---

47   Some assert that British insensitivity to the Irish famine stemmed in part from prejudice against Catholics. As a holdover from the Protestant Reformation of the seventeenth century, the British did not repeal the Test Act, granting Catholics the right to hold office until 1829. Britain governed Ireland as a colony and Ireland was therefore totally unlike England, Scotland, and Wales, even though the Act of Union (1801) created the United Kingdom of Great Britain and Ireland.

48   O'Grada 1999, p. 82.

49   O'Grada 1988, pp. 6, 9, 107-113, 122; O'Grada 1999, pp. 77, 82; Woodham-Smith 1989, p. 134; Mokyr 1983, pp. 278-295.

seventeenth century to the mid-nineteenth century.[50] When the sun shone and the rain fell in a timely fashion, the market performed in accustomed manner. However, during the late eighteenth century in response to bread uprisings, 'poor relief' expanded in Britain. In 1846, three-quarters of a century after the publication of *Wealth of Nations*, Britain repealed the Corn Laws,[51] that is, sliding scale tariffs on imported bread grains designed to protect the landed interest by sustaining grain prices and thereby keeping grain farming profitable.[52] In short, the landed interests had lost political power when the law ceased to provide a price floor; it seemed logical that the poor consumer (who did not vote) and the disfranchised poorest of the poor in Ireland should be left totally subject to the vagaries of the market without any State effort to furnish a price ceiling.

Social Policies

Not until late into the nineteenth century could the majority of the British male adult population vote or participate in policy-making, decades later than France and the United States.[53] Consistent with the general pattern of the time, economic and political liberalism and economic and political governance by the elite did not elicit a social compact between the governing class and the governed; the State did not include entitlements bestowed on the needy. Parliament did not respond to rising unemployment, claiming that it could not interfere in the labor markets.[54] It is not strange at all that between 1795 and 1824 the period of the Napoleonic Wars and its aftermath but not before 1795 or after 1824, Britain had the largest commitment to poor relief in Europe. As noted above, one can infer that the revolutionary mood across the Channel prompted this transitory change of heart.

'The English case... fits a pressure-group framework in which redistribution to the poor depends and on their self-interested perceptions of the likelihood that the poor might revolt or exit from labour supply.'[55] Social legislation attempting to protect individuals from life's adversities constitutes a somewhat inchoate category. This includes working conditions on the job, that is, occupational safety and health, in addition to income protection. Industrial accidents long antedated the coming of the factory but the use of mechanical power only aggravated both their frequency and their severity. Factory regulation began in 1802 and, once begun, Britain never faltered. Perhaps owing to the causal connection between the length of the workday and incidence of industrial accidents, in 1847 Britain enacted the ten-hour day.

Britain long had been concerned with the poor, as illustrated by the Poor Law of 1601, and spent heavily. The Poor Law of 1834 supplanted that archaic law and

---

50 Fogel 1991, pp. 38-39.
51 It should be noted that corn in British usage included all grains: wheat, oats, and barley and not only American maize.
52 Nielsen 1997, pp. 1-33.
53 Lindert 2003, p. 330.
54 Crouzet 1987, pp. 645-647.
55 Lindert 1998, p. 125.

all subsequent amendments. It reduced British relief expenditures by limiting the payment of charitable doles to the sick and aged paupers and established workhouses where able-bodied paupers were put to work. The relationship between the Reform Act of 1832, which brought more middle class voters into the fold and the new Poor Law was more than temporal. Since the new Poor Law was based on the work of Nassau Senior, one of the later classical economists, Britain sought a social policy that would not interfere unduly with the market system.[56] The British reformed the poor law in 1834 to reinforce the free operation of the market and adhered to many of its tenets until well into the twentieth century.

Mainly owing to the acute economic and social distress, the Luddite movement found a following during the early nineteenth century. Some economic historians contend that Ned Ludd was a revolutionary and that the Luddite movement represented a manifestation of a 'conflict of transition'. Others rebut that the Luddites did not constitute a labor movement but rather a conservative movement unhappy with technological progress.[57] Yet, the Luddites appealed to Parliament for minimum wages, unemployment benefits, and better working conditions. Parliament assumed that labor legislation would disturb the markets; instead, it preferred to help the financial market through Exchequer bills presuming that benefits would indirectly trickle down to the workers.[58]

Social progress surfaced during the first half of the nineteenth century; for example, the Factory Acts, which provided minimum industrial safeguards, appeared in the early 1800s. Pressured by the need to enlarge participation, in part, owing to economies of scale in production and distribution, the policy of inclusion gradually enfranchised a larger proportion of the population. As mentioned above, the Great Reform Bill of 1832 extended the suffrage to a wider segment of the middle class and Britain expanded the franchise again in 1867 and 1884. After this last Reform, Britain had virtual manhood suffrage excluding domestic servants, bachelors living with their families, and those with no fixed abode.[59]

Obviously, in the literal sense of the word *laissez faire* never existed in Britain, and State intervention surely became cumulative after 1832. The transition of Britain from an agricultural to an industrial society, in conjunction with the extension of the suffrage in 1867 and 1884 as well as other forces, resulted in a marked shift in the orientation of social policy during and after the Victorian Age. During the second half of the nineteenth century, social and political leaders became acutely aware of relevant legislation enacted in other countries, especially Germany; also, the Continental 1848 uprisings apparently exercised an influence.

---

56   Fraser 1973, p. 22; Mommsen 1981, pp. 24, 53.
57   Crouzet 1987, pp. xxxviii, ace.
58   Crouzet 1987, p. 783.
59   Social legislation included: the Factory Act (1833), the Mines Act (1842), the repeal of the Corn Laws (1846), and the Ten Hours Act (1847); thus, significant limitations on laissez faire existed. Also, during Benjamin Disraeli's tenure as Prime Minister (1874-1880), acts regulating public sanitation and working and safety conditions in mines and factories were extended and codified.

Although serious accidents to factory workers became more common during the Industrial Revolution, in keeping with the common law, most employers refused to pay medical costs to injured workers or to retain them any longer on their payrolls. In 1880, England enacted the Employer's Act, a weak form of workers' compensation law, but set no cost guidelines, leaving the employees only the option of expensive and difficult to win court suits.[60] The Worker's Compensation Act of 1897 corrected the weaknesses of the previous legislation. In 1908, Britain enacted an Old Age Pensions Law, and in 1911 the National Insurance Act that covered health and unemployment insurance.[61]

Especially after 1832, Britain partially democratized and political power passed from the landed aristocracy, with its tradition of *noblesse oblige*, to the market-oriented merchants and manufacturers. Perhaps giving the British middle class political participation relatively early (1832) and easily, as well as allowing them to enter the aristocracy, by being knighted or ennobled, made the disparity of wealth, income, and power more tolerable. For example, the Peels started as textile factory owners. Successful manufacturers, the Peel family, eventually became enlightened landed squires; Sir Robert Peel, the leading factory master of his day (1788-1850), pushed factory regulation (1819-1820). Peel served as prime minister in 1834-1835 and 1841-1846 and sponsored the repeal of the Corn Laws in 1846.

Smithian Market Forces at Work

Public policy in Britain was directed towards letting the market place operate in a Smithian fashion, that is, entire sectors had to sink or swim. Even the highly productive British agriculture could not compete with low cost imports from countries using extensive cultivation such as the United States. In the fourth quarter of the nineteenth century, when France, Germany, and Italy adopted agricultural protection, Britain declined to enact similar legislation; instead, Britain chose to buy cheap food products elsewhere and sacrificed agriculture.

Somehow Britain managed to industrialize without corporations except for roads and canals, which required incorporation by private acts as well as the power of eminent domain. Since Britain industrialized first (and early), sole proprietorships and partnerships sufficed except for capital-intensive transportation enterprises. Even the capital-intensive sectors, such as railroads, received little government support when economic liberalism peaked in Britain; railroad regulation (see Chapter 4) proved to be quite another matter.

Central government spending in Britain hardly reached ten percent of gross national product during the nineteenth century and that only during wartime. At

---

60 Such suits were not only expensive but the common law provided the employer with several lines of defense: assumption of risk – worker presumed to know that coal mining was dangerous; fellow servant contributory accident – another worker in which contributed to the accident; and the worker had to prove employer negligence. The same legal doctrine prevailed in the United States until reversed by legislation.

61 Fraser 1973, pp. 131, 142-151, 161; Mommsen 1981, pp. 84, 108.

other times the central government spent half as much; local governments hardly spent two to three percent of the national product. This is explained by the lack of support for public education at all levels until circa 1870; William Gladstone accepted the principle of state-supported public education during his tenure as Prime Minister (1868-1874). Britain lagged far behind France, Germany, and Italy with regard to public spending, but this holds true only when comparing central government expenditures. For instance, German local and regional government expenditures exceeded those of the central government while the ratio in Britain as well as in poorer countries such as Italy was higher.[62]

Conclusions

As the nineteenth century economy evolved towards the mature industrial state, economic thought itself changed, and *laissez faire*, not necessarily accepted by everyone before, lost adherents. For instance, Jevons could criticize the proposed nationalization of the telegraph on the practical financial grounds of prospective costs versus revenues without apparently invoking *laissez faire*. In order to make the 'sale' and committing without any fraud, the Postmaster, eager to expand the public sector and perhaps his own importance, underestimated costs and overestimated revenues. Jevons challenged this estimate and events vindicated him. Later, Parliament removed the Postmaster but cleared him of criminal intent.

Many factors contributed to the ever-growing role of the State in the British economy. One could mention: 1. The emergence of natural monopolies, such as the railways and the telegraph as well as gas and water supply in addition to urban transit; 2. The decline of competition in the Smithian sense of many buyers and sellers and therefore the presumed harmony of interests; 3. The increase in the size of the so-called representative firm and the appearance of very large capital-intensive enterprises; 4. The gradual expansion of the suffrage included virtually all-adult males; and 5. The *raison d'état*, that is, maintaining Britain's great power status in the face of foreign rivals.

Historically, Parliament succeeded in weakening the powers of the crown; the Glorious Revolution of 1688-1689 limited the power of the monarch and transferred control over taxing and spending to Parliament.[63] This held true in matters unrelated to the economy. Originally, and as construed by Smith, the term *police* included all government activity. In Britain, the protection of the people

---

62   Cameron 1997, p. 292.

63   In the aftermath of the Glorious Revolution, Parliament created the Bank of England in 1694. The financial revolution protected those who held bonds issued by the British State. The king could no longer delay interest payment, repudiate the 'national' or public debt in whole or in part, or in any form threaten the financial well being of the propertied. By diminishing risk, the British Government could borrow at a lower interest rate than the French. One need only recall that the French Revolution occurred in part because the crown had repudiated the debt several times during the eighteenth century; the consequent unwillingness of creditors to lend further without adequate protection precipitated the calling of the Assembly of Notables in 1787 and the Estates General in 1789.

had been entrusted to watchmen; towards 1810 criminality increased and the British suddenly realized that they had no police in the modern sense when Paris had had a police force since Louis XIV, more than a century earlier. In contrast, the British preferred to put up with crime as the price they paid for liberty; they opposed, for example, police spying because the British demanded that the State should have limits set on it. The Act of 1829 replaced the watchmen with a trained corps, thus limiting the arbitrary action of the police.[64]

Prompted by heightened humanitarian impulses and a desire to mitigate the chasm between rich and poor, a concern with social welfare came to the fore among the ranks of economists, embodied in Alfred Marshall (1842-1924), the leading neo-classical economist, as well as in society at large. Still, one cannot conclude that British government policies and actions signified the end of British *laissez faire*. Although a pure *laissez faire* never existed in Britain or elsewhere, it surely approximated a theoretical framework between 1840 and 1880. By 1882 Jevons could ask in *The State on Relation to Labour* why *laissez faire* prevailed generally although with numerous exceptions.[65]

Owing to a combination of the strictures of Smith and his followers as well as the transfer of political decision-making and leadership during the Industrial Revolution, Britain abandoned mercantilism and adopted a *laissez faire* policy. By mid-century the market, never unfettered, ruled the day at home as well as abroad. In Britain, *laissez faire*, that is, leaving things alone as much as possible, dominated more or less from the repeal of the Corn Laws in 1846 until circa 1914. Nevertheless, it would be hard to imagine a single significant instance in which Britain reversed either regulation and/or nationalization prior to World War I. The trend line, measuring State intervention in the economy, moved inexorably upwards.

This in no way implies that the State superseded the market in the allocation and distribution of resources and income. Instead, the State supervened selectively and sporadically, for example, expanding the percentage of the Government budget to monitor the economy and granting subsidies, such as promoting transoceanic shipping. Each and every instance of intervention of the Victorian regulatory State had to be justified on its own merits rather than rejected because it deviated from an idealized norm in the form of *laissez faire*. Nevertheless, the economic, ideological, intellectual, and political battle had ended at some indefinite and indeterminate time in the past.

---

64 Owing to Louis XIV, Paris had a professionalized constabulary about a century and a half before London; this speaks to the power of the State headed by an absolute monarch as against one in which even the monarch lived with constraints, however informal.

65 Court 1954, pp. 214, 253; Crouch 1967, pp. 199-201, 215; Taylor 1972, pp. 53-64; Holmes 1976, p. 688; Bartrip 1983, pp. 63-65, 80-83; Brebner 1948, pp. 59-73.

United States

After the American Revolution, Britain ceased governing the Thirteen Colonies but, for some time thereafter, the United States continued to have a colonial economy in the sense that the economic umbilical cord remained. Although the frontier characterized the United States, foreign commerce constituted the mainstay of the economy and foreign capital played a critical part in large-scale capital-intensive economic projects. Private British and other foreign investments were welcomed throughout the nineteenth century. The United States remained a debtor nation until World War I, although its total foreign indebtedness leveled off about 1900. As an early industrial country, the United States rejected free trade for pragmatic rather than ideological or theoretical reasons.

Infrastructure received State support and subsidies; until late in the nineteenth century, state and local governments paralleled the federal government either by owning enterprises, sharing in the ownership of mixed enterprises, investing in securities sold by private corporations, or using land grants to promote construction. Rare indeed was the transportation enterprise built only with private capital and then typically in well-settled markets. Constitutional limitations and practical considerations, including interstate and intrastate conflicts, instead of *laissez faire* ideology, dictated behavior.

As private enterprises became capable of tapping the domestic capital market, dependency on the British capital market diminished and public sentiment shifted from promotion to regulation, first at the state level, and by the end of the century, at the federal level. Large scale, capital-intensive enterprises seemed to both awe and alarm; with the passage of the Interstate Commerce Act of 1887 and the Sherman Antitrust Act of 1890, the tide turned and regulatory intervention ruled.

Laissez Faire and Slavery

Did the *laissez faire* encompass the ownership of one person by another and therefore the ownership of the product of that person's labor? The institution of slavery became contentious among the states starting with the Northwest Ordinance in 1784 as well as that of 1787 when the slave states outnumbered the free states. When the United States took the first Census in 1790, there were 700,000 slaves; in 1860, the United States had almost four million slaves. Emancipation gradually brought slavery to an end north of the Mason-Dixon line and north of the Ohio River, thanks in part to the Northwest Ordinance of 1787, which prohibited the extension of slavery into the Northwest Territory. Slavery spread south and west owing partly to the cotton gin invented in 1793.

The free states included Ohio, Indiana, Illinois, Michigan, and Wisconsin, although there were some slaves in the Northwest Territory. All slave states enacted Slave Codes to provide legal positive reinforcement for slavery. Slave codes originated during the mid-seventeenth century and spread to all slave territories and states. These slave codes provided that the status of the slave's mother determined that of the offspring. Further, the slave codes recognized slaves as property, the owner had the legal right to sell, and the slaves could be whipped because they had neither civil nor political rights. Interracial marriages were prohibited and the community was given the power to control slaves' movements. Without such legal sanctions, slavery could not exist. Furthermore Christianity did not affect the slaves' conditions.[66]

Slavery continued to be a sore point between the North and South until the Civil War. The South's economy was substantially based on slave labor – fit for plantation agriculture but not necessarily for manufacturing work. Much labor in the South was white, if only because there were not many slaves in proportion to the total population. In the South in 1860 there were seven million whites and four million slaves. Also, in 1860 only about one fourth of white southern families owned any slaves; some owned no slaves out of choice and others because the cost of a slave was beyond their means. Finally, if a family owned less than ten slaves, it had not yet reached the level of plantation owner; its slaves were likely to be domestic servants as well as field hands, especially if one considers the aged and the children. For instance, in Kansas, many whites did not want blacks, free or slave.

In 1860, about ten percent of the slaves were engaged in manufacturing, a contributing factor in keeping the South economically behind, because the output per man-hour was apparently lower for slaves. In 1820, when the number of free states equaled the number of slave states, the Missouri Compromise, while allowing slavery in the southern part of the Louisiana Purchase, that is, the vast territory acquired from France in 1803, prohibited the extension of slavery into the much larger northern part.

In 1850, once again the Federal Government acted to limit the extension of slavery into the territories. Though strengthening the 1793 Fugitive Slave Act, the Calhoun-Clay Compromise also banned the commercial slave trade in the District of Columbia and admitted California as a free state but left the status of slavery in the Mexican Cession to the free people of the territories. The Kansas-Nebraska Act of 1854 introduced the principle of popular sovereignty by repealing the Missouri Compromise's ban on slavery in the Kansas territory but had no effect on slavery's viability. All this time, the federal government treated slavery within an individual state as a domestic institution, subject only to the law of that state. Finally, the Civil War and the subsequent Thirteenth Amendment (1865) ended slavery everywhere.

Only twice in American history has a property interest been outlawed without compensation. The Thirteenth Amendment abolished billions of dollars invested in slaves while the Eighteenth Amendment (1919) did the same for the investment in the production of alcoholic beverages (the Prohibition Amendment). Within the parameters set by society or those in power, *laissez faire* precepts could go just so far and no further.[67]

---

66   Stampp 1956, pp. 22-23, 192-236.
67   Richards 2000, p. 47; Fehrenbacher 2001, pp. 88, 229-230, 254-255.

The Demise of the Second Bank of the United States

Despite the constitutional argument, the First Bank of the United States failed to be re-chartered in the House of Representatives 65-64 and in the Senate 18-17, with the Vice President casting a decisive vote. The bank was re-chartered in 1816 because the War of 1812 demonstrated the desirability of a central bank.

By far the largest financial institution, the Second Bank of the United States under the presidency of Nicholas Biddle, constituted a powerhouse that overextended its means. President Andrew Jackson disliked banks in general and, in particular, opposed the Bank on constitutional grounds and detested 'Czar Nicholas', as his enemies called Biddle. In 1832, Jackson vetoed the Bank's charter and Congress failed to override his veto. The demise of the Bank gave free rein to the expansion of state banking.

By the 1840s and 1850s, the 'free banking' system was adopted almost everywhere with the states strengthening their control. Bank notes varied in quality and bank services periodically published a listing with pictures of banknotes including counterfeited notes. In 1859, one of these services described fifty four hundred types of spurious notes. The banking system was indeed chaotic; financial crises and panics occurred during the free banking era (1832-1861). Conservative banking probably could not have achieved the rapid economic development of the United States; after all, the United States suffered crises and panics after the end of free banking.[68]

The State and the Transportation Revolution

The Initial State Role in Developing Transportation The spirit of improvement induced individuals to call upon the State to become a significant player. Where this did not hold true, interest rather than ideology motivated opposition to intrastate as well as interstate public works projects. Isolated examples though they may be, one could compile a short list of internal improvements projects that failed to attract majority political support only because there were too many ideas chasing too few dollars. In the wake of the panic of 1837, coupled with the strengthening of the national and international capital markets during the 1840s, economic liberalism had its day in court. *Laissez faire* 'rhetoric' flourished after the failure of some State ventures; especially after the Civil War, this tendency became particularly marked.

The principal cities and their wealthy merchants endeavored to expand their markets by building and improving roads, canals, and railroads. Improved roads, that is, turnpikes, used both public and private financing. Private enterprise could build turnpikes because the individual roads, being short, could be financed locally by those expected to benefit most directly. In 1792, private enterprise constructed a turnpike over the relatively short distance from Philadelphia west and south to Lancaster, Pennsylvania. Private capital provided financing but the state granted a

---

68   Larson 1990, p. 100; Larson 2000, pp. 23, 25, 55, 233-234; Studenski and Krooss
      1952, pp. 87-88, 104-107, 113-116, 120-121.

corporate charter, which enabled the first turnpike to be constructed through an already settled area. Although similar roads were built in various places, other methods had to be brought into play where the distances were vast and settlers with marketable products scarce.[69]

The United States came into existence in 1783 with the western boundary more or less at the Mississippi River. The power to build a national system of roads and canals had been deliberately omitted from the Constitution. Nevertheless, land had been granted to Ebenezer Zane in 1796 to aid in the construction of a road from Wheeling, Virginia, to Maysville, Kentucky, a link in the road from Cumberland, Maryland, to Zanesville, Ohio. The federal government authorized in 1806 the National Road, also known as the Cumberland Road or the Great National Pike, which reached Wheeling on the Ohio River in 1818 and Vandalia, Illinois, in 1838, before being discontinued when it became evident that railroads had superseded roads.[70]

The Transportation Revolution provides the key to understanding the economic policy of the United States during the nineteenth century. In the context of 'manifest destiny', several salient factors gain particular relevance. Land transportation in 1800 had not changed much for centuries; even in Britain, much less in the United States, the roads had not perceptibly improved since the days of the Roman Empire. The economy of the United States (as distinct from the government) had been in debt to foreigners before the American Revolution and the foreign indebtedness of the American economy grew throughout the nineteenth century before tapering off around the turn of the century. Much of this debt had been contracted to build capital-intensive roads, canals, and especially railroads.

Capital for transportation facilities could be obtained much more readily and at a lower cost if a project received State support in some form. Early in the century, and then again during the middle decades, the federal government led in State support for transportation projects. Afterwards, states and localities became much more important and consistent in support of transportation projects until late in the nineteenth century, by which time the railroad network had been completed. The State therefore played an active and significant, even if temporary, role in the promotion of the economy. Conversely, *laissez faire* thought, at least until mid-century, never developed into policy because no sector in society found *laissez faire* policies in accord with its interests.[71]

Albert Gallatin and the Canal Era

Albert Gallatin, Thomas Jefferson's Secretary of the Treasury, issued his *Report on Public Roads and Canals* in 1808. In view of the Jeffersonian belief that that government governs best which governs least, the origin as well as the contents of Gallatin's *Report* is in itself somewhat surprising. Gallatin revered Smith, yet he resorted to pragmatism rather than ideology because, some two decades after the

---

69   Nettels 1962, pp. 251-253.
70   Goodrich 1960, p. 19; Nettels 1962, p. 252.
71   Handlin 1943, p. 56.

1783 Treaty of Paris and the adoption of the Constitution in 1789, few settlers had migrated beyond the Appalachian Mountains. Still, there were still enough settlers to have Vermont admitted to the Union in 1791, Kentucky in 1792, Tennessee in 1796, and Ohio in 1803. Even though land in the trans-Appalachian West could be had more or less for the asking, and hard work could create farms, the high cost of transportation either by land or by water as well the tremendous risks left subsistence agriculture as a less than attractive option.

Not until transportation rates became low enough to justify the movement of high-bulk low-value agricultural products from the trans-Appalachian west to the states east of the mountains could one reasonably expect substantial westward expansion of the moving frontier. Thus Gallatin confronted a condition rather than a theory. His *Report* called upon the federal government to adopt a national plan of action. However, it did not happen that way: the War of 1812 intervened and, furthermore, the constitutionality of such federal government action surfaced as a political issue. Georgians could quite reasonably ask why they should be taxed to build a canal in New York, for example, which would primarily benefit New Yorkers at the expense of other states. *Laissez faire* thinking did not therefore determine economic policy.

In actuality, entrepreneurs had anticipated Gallatin's grand vision; for instance, during the 1790s individuals formed a private enterprise to take advantage of the natural break in the mountain barrier by building a canal in western New York. This, indeed, proved to be a case of premature enterprise; private enterprise could not possibly obtain sufficient capital for such a costly venture. Instead, the state of New York (1817-1825) could and did construct (through largely unsettled territory) the 300-mile Erie Canal, which connected New York City and the Atlantic Ocean with the Great Lakes via the Hudson River. New York State borrowed the necessary millions by selling bonds, especially in Europe, and the bonds attracted investors precisely because the taxing power of the state furnished a second line of defense. Thus, even if the Erie Canal had been a financial failure as an enterprise, the bondholders had another and ultimate recourse.

More than any other single event, the Erie Canal inaugurated the Transportation Revolution, opened the West, and triggered competitive reactions by the seaport rivals of New York City. Boston's response to New York was significant since the Berkshire Mountains prevented building a canal from Boston to the trans-Appalachian west. The Boston to Albany rail connection was designed to divert traffic from the Erie Canal and the Hudson River. The Commonwealth of Massachusetts advanced construction funds for the Boston and Albany and its predecessors (the Boston and Worcester and the Western railroads), completed by 1842. The port of Boston never recovered from its secondary status behind New York.[72]

The state constitutions adopted after the American Revolution reserved to the states the power to deal with intrastate economic matters. Thus, in 1843 Pennsylvania, regardless of the Allegheny Mountain barrier, built a technologically

---

72   Goodrich 1960, p. 128.

successful but economically unsuccessful canal-rail system over the mountains. In 1859, Pennsylvania sold the state canals to private investors.[73] Further to the south, having built the Chesapeake and Ohio Canal to advance the commercial interests of Baltimore, Maryland invested in the mixed or joint enterprise known as the Baltimore and Ohio Railroad, which became the first commercial railroad in the United States in 1830; this railroad reached its intended destination at Wheeling on the Ohio River only in 1851. Until quite late in the nineteenth century, by which time the Transportation Revolution had run its course, states (Virginia, Georgia, Ohio, Missouri, and New York among others) and numerous localities built canals and railroads or aided private enterprise in their construction. With the income from the Erie Canal as well as tax revenue at its disposal, New York used bounties, subsidies, grants, stock ownership, and loans.[74]

The federal government granted land to individual states for canal construction and as a result four canals received federal financial assistance during the 1820s.[75] However, during that decade strict constructionists challenged the direct and indirect road building and canal construction by the federal government. Finally, President Andrew Jackson's Maysville Road veto (1830) terminated this phase of federal promotion of the economy. This proved to be merely a hiatus, since in 1850 the federal government resumed its previous role, although with necessary modifications.

Following the introduction of the steamboat in 1807, the western rivers (the Mississippi River and its tributaries) became important arteries of commerce. In accordance with the interstate commerce clause of the Constitution and with its previous role in building lighthouses, the federal government dredged the rivers and removed stumps and other obstructions to keep commerce flowing. Safety regulation first appeared in 1828, followed by the Steamboat Act of 1852, designed to prevent accidents. Still, even after being admitted as states, such frontier states as Illinois, had considerable unsettled territory because most unoccupied land lay far removed from navigable rivers.

The State and Railroads

To accelerate the process of economic growth it was necessary to build low cost transportation, which could serve as a magnet for extensive settlement. In 1850, the Illinois Central Railroad became the first federal land grant railroad; this established the precedent for building the land grant transcontinental railroads during the 1860s and 1870s. Yet, by 1861 there was no American railroad network; eleven different railroad gauges existed; each of the four hundred railroads, with the advice and consent of the state granting the corporate charter and the power of eminent domain, could select its own gauge. In 1862, President Abraham Lincoln designated the so-called standard gauge (4'8½"), already the most widely used gauge, for the Union Pacific, the first so-called transcontinental

73   Hartz 1948, pp. 4, 161-162.
74   Gunn 1988, p. 100.
75   Goodrich 1960, pp. 40-41.

railroad. Even the adoption of the official standard gauge by the railroads in 1886 did not quite achieve national uniformity; the railroads did not fully accomplish this task until 1900. Similarly, in 1883 the American Railway Association instituted standard time, which divided the country into four time zones. Note that neither of these advances required a government mandate. The federal government did not enact standard time until 1918.[76]

Before the Mexican War, Asa Whitney (1797-1872), a merchant engaged in the China trade and a transcontinental railroad advocate, in 1844 proposed to build a railroad from Milwaukee, Wisconsin, to the Pacific, with federal government aid in the form of land at low cost. Following the Mexican War, the United States acquired a vast territory that brought its boundaries to the Pacific Ocean. The enormous expanse between the frontier and California was extremely sparsely settled. No one questioned that, for political as well as economic reasons, a railroad should be constructed to span the emptiness as soon as feasible. Were it not for the sectional impasse concerning the location of the eastern terminus, the federal government itself might have constructed such a railroad during the fifties. Instead, with the withdrawal of the southern representatives from Congress during the Civil War, the federal government chartered the Union Pacific-Central Pacific project as a land grant railroad, with additional financial support. Congress subsequently chartered three additional transcontinental land grant railroads with subsidies, which although substantial, were less generous than those granted the first.

Transatlantic Steamships

As steam transportation reached the rivers, so it also reached the ocean. In 1819, although with auxiliary sails, the first steamship crossed the Atlantic but not until the fifties had steam engines become so efficient and attained such a level of proficiency that sails could be replaced economically. As long as wooden ships and iron men dominated the high seas, the United States fared well as a shipping and shipbuilding nation because of its endless forests and therefore low cost lumber. With the change to iron ships and steam engines, the United States lost its competitive advantage to Britain, which had industrialized earlier and excelled in the manufacture of iron and the construction of marine engines.

In addition, Britain awarded Samuel Cunard a subsidy mail contract in 1838 to underwrite expected losses on Cunard's proposed trans-Atlantic steam line. To defend national honor, the United States responded with federal mail subsidies in 1845. Two years later the Collins Line, headed by Edward Knight Collins, officially the New York and Liverpool Mail Steamship Company, opened trans-Atlantic steamship service. However, the Collins Line lost two ships at sea owing to accidents and abandoned its routes after the reduction of the federal mail subsidies in 1857-1858, despite the superiority of Collins ships to their British counterpart. With the financial crisis of 1857, the Collins Line went bankrupt and

---

76   Stover 1997, pp. 143-146.

its ships were sold to British companies. Once again, ideological considerations, in the form of *laissez faire*, do not seem to have intruded either in initiating or terminating the federal government's subsidy to a private enterprise for a public purpose. As Hamilton had noted in his *Report on Manufactures*, since the international playing field was not level, practical considerations overrode principle. The Collins subsidy became caught up in the sectional controversy, reinforcing the long-standing Jacksonian antipathy towards federal government aid to business, which persisted into the 1850s.[77]

Infrastructure Development: Private versus Public

Private enterprise completed a handful of short and, for the most part, unsuccessful canals, such as the Middlesex Canal (1803), which linked Boston with the Merrimack River. This interregional local canal cost $440,000, a modest amount indeed, and a group of Boston financiers furnished the entire capital, since the State of Massachusetts could not be persuaded to help.[78] On the other hand, in 1791 New York State chartered a private enterprise, the Western Inland Lock Navigation Company, to connect the Hudson River with Lake Erie, more than 300 miles to the west; this venture had an inauspicious start since a private enterprise could not possibly raise the millions in needed capital locally.[79]

Since private enterprise could not and the federal government would not, New York State took the initiative. Once New York State built and owned the Erie Canal (1817-1825) at a cost of seven million dollars, other states followed suit. Pennsylvania, Ohio, Indiana, and Illinois built canals as public projects. Opponents raised objections based on cost, preference for railroads, and effect on parochial interests, but not because government investment represented an improper use of public funds. Pragmatism triumphed over *laissez faire* principle. While not necessarily constrained by traditional *laissez faire* ideology, New Jersey constituted an exception. 'New Jersey [did not] refrain from direct action in internal improvement because of any ideological scruples of a laissez faire nature; the moral right of the state to undertake such projects was never questioned.'[80]

The case of Massachusetts is instructive, if only to indicate that New Jersey was not unique. With a major though declining seaport in Boston, especially after the completion of the Erie Canal, Massachusetts possessed an economy divided in several sections, each with its own interests and agenda. While not necessarily precluding any single project, this conflict tended to set each proposal in opposition to all others. As a result, private rather than state enterprise not only built the Middlesex Canal, as noted above, but also the railroads. 'The Bay State men responded not to theories but pragmatically to each problem, taking the side of private, mixed or public enterprise as the specific situation warranted.'[81] In

---

77 Tyler 1939, p. 230, n. 52, and passim; Hutchins 1947, pp. 353-358.
78 Goodrich 1961, pp. 6-7.
79 Rubin 1961, pp. 19-24.
80 Cranmer 1961, pp. 116-117.
81 Salisbury 1967, p. 34.

1830, the Massachusetts legislature voted against state aid for a railroad from Boston west to Albany, New York. The opposition stemmed overwhelmingly from interest rather than a principled or ideological rejection of State or government participation in the economy. Only when the Massachusetts railroads failed to obtain public support did they become wholly private.[82]

Some states abandoned state-assisted projects when unsuccessful, others when they became profitable on their own, or when access to capital markets had been achieved.[83] Michigan had not been able to manage the Michigan Central Railroad, that is, to lavish the requisite attention on such an undertaking. Begun as a private enterprise in 1832 and purchased by Michigan in 1837, by the 1840s other railroads hemmed in this unprofitable railroad extending west from Detroit. Therefore sale to those with capital and experience seemed desirable to keep the railroad in operation. In 1846, the state of Michigan sold the Michigan Central to a coterie of Boston investors led by John Murray Forbes, former China trader and later a prominent railroad builder especially important in the growth of the Chicago, Burlington and Quincy Railroad; Forbes led in the transfer of eastern mercantile capital derived from trade (mostly foreign) to western railroad construction. The Michigan Central became a link in the Buffalo-Chicago route, expanding as a master trunk line. Practical considerations, including Michigan's indebtedness owing to the 1837 depression, rather than ideological considerations, explain the action of the state of Michigan.[84]

The Telegraph Debate

During the antebellum era the single greatest innovation in the technology information was undoubtedly the electromagnetic telegraph. A convincing demonstration of Samuel F. B. Morse's telegraph, developed between 1832 and 1844, required substantial financial backing from private sources but investors refused to risk their money on such a visionary scheme; therefore, Morse sought the aid of the federal government. In 1843, Congress appropriated $30,000 for the construction of a telegraph line between Washington, DC and Baltimore, Maryland; the first practical demonstration of the telegraph took place in 1844. This subsidy to the first telegraph line represented recognition of the social nature and utility of information and communication.

The federal government not only owned the first telegraph line but also proceeded to operate it through the Postmaster General. Morse now tried to sell his patent to the federal government for $100,000. The Postmaster General, who earlier had been skeptical, now urged that the telegraph, like the mails, should be financed and operated as a government monopoly. Divided by sectional ideological differences over internal improvement policy and becoming engrossed in other matters, Congress declined to develop the telegraph as a national public

---

82   Larson 2000, p. 229; Salsbury 1967, pp. 33-34, 75, 77.
83   Goodrich 1970, p. 298.
84   Goodrich 1960, p. 145; Overton 1965, pp. 6, 26, 28; Sears 1966, pp. 200-205, 210-
      217; Larson 1984, pp. 32-40.

utility. The profitability of the telegraph soon emerged and private capital took over. Although the telegraph remained a private enterprise, the states regulated the telegraph during 1845-1860 in various ways such as right of way and rates. Owing to consolidation, only six regional telegraph companies existed in 1857 but only three survived on the eve of the Civil War.

As a result of the Pacific Telegraph Act of 1860, Western Union received a federal government subsidy to construct the transcontinental line that was completed in 1861. The 1866 merger of Western Union with American Telegraph gave the Western Union an effective monopoly. This prompted the Telegraph Act of 1866, which provided that Congress could acquire telegraph assets under specified conditions if it so chose; however, Congress never acted. For years thereafter there were those who wanted a postal telegraph service to compete with Western Union or, alternatively, asked that the federal government buy Western Union. Congress decided to regulate the telegraph as a public utility; perhaps belatedly, the Mann-Elkins Act (1910) granted the Interstate Commerce Commission jurisdiction over the telegraph.[85]

Limited Government in Practice

Expanding on their experiences both before and after the American Revolution, the states, while constitutionally and philosophically committed to limited government, continued to promote and regulate their economies within the context of a mixed market-oriented economy. Consistent with the federal system and the localized nature of the economy, during most of the nineteenth century the federal government contributed relatively little to this process. Using the police power, in the Smithian sense, which had originated in seventeenth-century England, states enacted legislation regulating entry, quality, number, and consumer protection. The courts interpreted the police power to encompass much under the heading of general welfare regardless of *laissez faire* considerations.

State controls appeared at the opening of the nineteenth century. The states of Pennsylvania and Massachusetts, for instance, regulated quality. In addition, to government regulations, consumers relied on face-to-face dealing with small-scale local enterprises. However, as technology and transportation enlarged the quantity and variety of products, the consumer enlarged his choice and the state governments felt less compelled to regulate. As a prime example, in 1846, the state of New York abandoned its system of consumer protection.[86] Still, by the end of the nineteenth century the combination of *ad hoc* federal and state legislation incrementally produced a partially regulated economy. Nevertheless, private enterprise took the initiative as public policy helped the private sector maximize its opportunities.

---

85 Hochfelder 2000, pp. 747-748; Nonnenmacher 2001, pp. 20, 25, 33; John 1995, p. 88; John 2000, pp. 78-79; Thompson 1947, pp. vii, 3-34, 442; Hochfelder 2001, pp. 706-724.

86 Hughes 1976, pp. 132, 134; Gunn 1988, p. 188.

States created a category of licensed professions and state-licensing boards prevented individuals from entering specified occupations unless they met minimum standards. While by 1900 literacy in the United State was widespread, only five to ten percent of the population graduated from high school, and few graduates went on to college. Lawyers and medical doctors had to pass examinations, which had a bearing on the quality of their services. On the other hand, Abraham Lincoln became a highly successful lawyer with only minimal schooling; like many lawyers and medical doctors depending on place and time, he had essentially on the job training. Similarly, circa 1900 one could become a certified public accountant with only a high school diploma followed by an apprenticeship.

In varying degrees, states limited the number of banks in a community, not only benefiting the stockholders but also protecting depositors and note holders. Consumers were protected against fraudulent practices; for instance, skim milk often masqueraded as cream. The courts declared much of this legislation unconstitutional, especially after the adoption of the Fourteenth Amendment following the Civil War. Although enacted to protect the civil rights of newly emancipated slaves, this amendment restricted state regulatory powers concerning the economy; the courts introduced the concept of substantive due process. Some industries and occupations, such as banking and alcoholic beverages, were subjected to closer scrutiny than others. Before the Civil War, several states even prohibited banking and the production of alcoholic beverages. Rare indeed was the businessman who did not think that certain legislation—especially social legislation protecting workers—had become too intrusive and that the State (either local, state, or federal government) had exceeded its proper constitutional bounds. Some thought that legislation serving special interest groups should have been declared unconstitutional; frequently the common good was not served since legislation protected competitors rather than competition. Once again, *laissez faire* proponents remained mute in the face of the police power and constitutionalism.

Typically entrepreneurs attempted to go it alone when this proved to be impractical, businessmen sought partners.   Next, incorporation became the preferred means to mobilize capital, especially for capital-intensive enterprises such as roads, canals, and railroads, while simultaneously limiting liability. Corporate charters obtained in one state enabled an enterprise to do business in all states.   When, as, and if, private capital resources seemed inadequate or entrepreneurs too timid, enterprises asked the State to intervene. Thus, the states typically employed public funds in banks, fire insurance companies, roads, canals, and railroads, all of which required not only substantial amounts of capital but also corporate charters. Before the Civil War, several states did not flinch at owning and operating banks.[87] On the contrary, some states went so far in the opposite

87   The states included: South Carolina, Alabama, Indiana, Illinois, Kentucky, and Mississippi.

direction during the 1840s and 1850s as to prohibit all banks.[88] Recognizing that
the railroads had a public purpose, the states granted the railroads the power of
eminent domain.[89]

It is unlikely that any significant number or proportion of *laissez faire*
businessmen declined, on principle, to call on government for assistance.
Occasionally, some businessmen criticized opponents for invoking government but
the critics themselves were ready to accept privileges. Neither business nor
government was inhibited by *laissez faire* ideology. Instead, the relationship
between business and the State was pragmatic even when theoretically adhering to
a very amorphous *laissez faire* philosophy.[90]

Prior to mid-century, and particularly before 1840, one cannot speak about
laissez faire ideology at either the federal or state level. Inherited from the British
this ideology emerged only gradually in formal terms during the fourth quarter of
the nineteenth century when Herbert Spencer's Social Darwinism embraced Adam
Smith's strictures. *Laissez faire* became a convenient ideology for the controlling
merchant class in defending the amassing of wealth and political power. The
increase of income and wealth in the United States and abroad, combined with
improvements in capital markets, enabled private entrepreneurs, working through
the market, to mobilize capital unaided overtly by the State.[91]

The North-South Gap

The South (the most rural section) had a per capita income half the national
average between 1880 and 1930. The increased supply of cotton exceeded the
increase in demand, which depressed the price. The polemic as to whether the pre-
Civil War national economic policies were rigged against the South, and the
contention that the South had a colonial economy died out in the 1950s. To be
sure, only about ten percent of industries were located in the South in 1860 and the
leading financial intermediaries were located in the North. National policies, if
any, to close the North-South gap had no comparison with regional policies in
Germany and Italy. Nevertheless, southern states during the post-Civil War era
promoted the economy and lured northern industry, especially the textile
industry.[92]

The Federal System and the States

The complexity of federalism explains in part the interaction of the market with the
federal government and the legislative processes of individual states. A cursory

---

88   The states included: Illinois, Iowa (1846), Wisconsin, Florida, Arkansas, Texas
      (1845), and California as well as the territories of Minnesota and Oregon, Perkins
      1994, p. 355; Myers 1970, p. 124; Green 1980, p. 715.
89   Taylor 1951, p. 89.
90   Dobbin 1994, p. 34.
91   Dobbin 1994, p. 214.
92   See for instance: Engelbourg and Schachter 1986.

awareness of the federal system is critical to any understanding of United States economic policy in comparison with that of European unitary states.[93] Owing to written constitutions, the principle of limited government, and the concept of judicial review, one must consider selected landmark court decisions as well as the more customary political and administrative actions. While there has been only one federal constitutional convention (and therefore only one Constitution, as amended), individual state constitutions have been amended as well as rewritten at constitutional conventions from time to time. Only through the process of judicial review by the courts are the constitutions interpreted and applied to specific economic circumstances.

Owing in large measure to the federal system, economic policy making was quite decentralized throughout most of the nineteenth century. This conformed to the state of the economy because most commerce was intrastate rather than interstate, firm size tended to be small, and the national market was *becoming* rather than *being*.

Coping with Market Failures

The first railroad started operation in 1830; the first railroad regulatory commission was empowered in 1839, while the federal Interstate Commerce Commission did not enter the scene until 1887. Although not ideological, this gap was tied to economics and politics. As long as railroads were puny and intrastate, state regulation apparently sufficed. Weak or advisory regulatory commissions, as in the case of Massachusetts (1869), relied on the 'sunshine' principle (transparency in policies and their applications) to publicize deviant behavior and thereby foster reform. The typical state constitution before the Civil War usually accorded the state more power to promote than to regulate economic activity.

After the Civil War some states enacted new constitutions or amended existing ones, which conferred the power to regulate prices in a limited number of industries, and established strong regulatory commissions. This shift in policy stemmed from the greater power exercised by states during the Civil War. Significantly, by this time the relatively short intrastate local railroads had been transformed into large-scale interstate enterprises whose ratemaking powers affected farmers, manufacturers, and merchants from the Atlantic Coast to the Mississippi River and eventually beyond.

This induced the enactment of the so-called Granger laws in several mid-western agricultural states, particularly Minnesota, Iowa, Wisconsin, and Missouri, owing to pressure group campaigns. The Grange (officially, the Patrons of Husbandry) was founded in 1867. Northwestern farmers used the Grange as a means of attacking the railroads from the early 1870s on. States enacted Granger laws to regulate railroads and warehouses, that is, to limit their ability to exploit their monopoly power by charging what traffic will bear.

---

93   Perhaps post World War II Federal Germany with its *länder* (states), patterned on the
       United States model, provides the closest analogy.

The 1870 Illinois constitution designated private grain elevators as public warehouses and in 1871 the Illinois legislature passed a law that prescribed maximum rates for grain storage facilities. Munn and Scott, grain elevator owners, charged higher rates than permitted by law. In *Munn vs. Illinois* (1877) the Supreme Court ruled that the states could regulate those matters, that is, grain elevators, affecting the public interest. This constitutional decision, relying on a long series of precedents, upheld the rate setting power of the so-called strong state railroad commissions. Yet, in the *Wabash* case (1886) the Supreme Court vitiated the *Munn* decision by ruling that the Constitution accords only the federal government the power to regulate interstate commerce. The growth of individual railroads, especially into regional systems, during the intervening decades, also transferred railroad regulation from the states to the federal government.

The *Wabash* decision precipitated the Interstate Commerce Act (1887), which recognized the constitutional interpretation as well as the economic reality. This legislation created the Interstate Commerce Commission (ICC), the first of the federal regulatory commissions. Generally, governments act to correct perceived market failures or on behalf of special interests. The ICC, for instance, came into being as a result of political pressures exerted by an alliance of New York wholesale merchants and Midwestern farmers affiliated with the Grange or sympathetic to its objectives. These New York wholesale merchants, regardless of their belief in *laissez faire*, even financed the political ruckus raised by the farmers, since both had to contend with railroad freight rate discrimination, that is, charging higher freight rates for the short haul than for the long haul.

New York wholesale merchants gained at the expense of other wholesale merchants because they obtained preferential rates based on quantity shipped. However, they paid higher rates than high volume shippers such as Standard Oil. Rockefeller entered the oil refining industry in Cleveland, Ohio, where Standard Oil had a choice of the New York Central, the Erie, and the Pennsylvania railroads in addition to the Erie Canal. Standard Oil bargained to obtain the lowest possible rates; although Standard Oil did not originate this negotiating tactic, size enabled Standard Oil to extract minimum rates, whereas farmers typically had only one railroad available. The Grange wanted the State (state or federal government) to regulate railroads by ignoring other economic factors and levying charges based only on distance, therefore disregarding other commercial consideration such as scale or volume.

During the 1880s large-scale capital-intensive manufacturing enterprises became national in scope, taking advantage of economies of scale, vertical integration, and marketing innovation. The 1887 Act to Regulate Commerce applied to transportation only whereas the Sherman Antitrust Act of 1890 was the first regulatory federal law applicable across the entire economy. Small-scale local middlemen reacted to those giant enterprises by obtaining protective legislation from the state governments. As one illustration of this process, in 1873 the Singer Sewing Machine Company built a new factory with expanded capacity. Singer instituted a direct distribution marketing system thereby eliminating the middleman, that is, wholesalers and retailers. To preserve the livelihood of those adversely affected, certain states imposed punitive taxes, thus nullifying the advantage that accrued from Singer's marketing innovation. Ruling on behalf of a national market, the Supreme Court struck down those taxes as constituting an unconstitutional interference with interstate commerce.

Similarly, after the construction of the Union Stock Yards in Chicago in 1865, large-scale vertically integrated Chicago meat packers (Swift, Armour, and others) shipped meat products through their own branch houses to adjacent states. Small-scale local meat packers thereupon obtained ostensible health legislation in individual states which required local meat inspection; the Supreme Court concluded that this legislation constituted a considerable obstacle for the nationally-oriented meat packers and, perceiving the subterfuge, ruled it unconstitutional. In both the sewing and meatpacking cases, the consumer (public interest) benefited as did, of course, those few firms able to capitalize on their innovations.[94]

Post-Civil War Trade Policies

United States trade policy fluctuated considerably but seems to have been relatively unaffected by prevailing economic thought. The tariff rose between 1816 and 1832 and then declined thereafter so that the United States became an almost free trade nation circa 1860. Following the Civil War the United States embarked on a protectionist course until the end of the century. The tariff represented a form of profit protection or rent seeking in which non-industrial areas transferred income to the industrial areas. Although the tariff constituted a hotly contested political issue during the antebellum era, it is doubtful if the participants in the political debate understood or cared about the economic argument.

In 1824, by which time Britain had achieved virtually free trade, the proponents of protection in Congress employed the infant industry argument for all it was worth. The opponents did not claim that the protective tariff violated the well-known classical *laissez faire* argument; instead, they insisted that their pockets were being picked. Although the opponents of the protective tariff had much the better of the intellectual argument, especially since the proponents never developed a coherent counter argument, it made no difference in the outcome.[95]

Social Policies

The United States developed a positive social policy, in this instance, protective labor legislation, not only later than Britain but also intermittently and irregularly. This stemmed from the Constitution that delegated, both in the minds of men and as interpreted by the courts, responsibility for social policy to the individual states, which utilized the police power to regulate public health, public safety, and public welfare. On the other hand, the constitutions of both the states and the federal government limited the power of the government and regulation was subject to

---

94   McCurdy 1978, pp. 643-648.
95   Edwards 1970, p. 836.

judicial interpretation. Consequently, the opponents of such regulation appealed to the constitutional limitations and did not then invoke the more abstract principle of *laissez faire*.

Only a few states regulated the hours of work and prohibited child labor before 1860.[96] Such limited state regulation, a continuation of the colonial era, pervaded the industrial states after the Civil War. In fact, the 'ubiquity of state non-market control measures far exceeded anything known in the 1890s in Europe'.[97] For both constitutional and ideological reasons, the federal government had little to say about social legislation during the 1890s.[98]

Since the pace of industrialization was uneven across the nation, the laggard states also lagged in enacting such social legislation lest they increase cost and thereby retard industrialization. The consensus assumed that adult males could (or at least should) fend for themselves in the marketplace. Legislation aimed at the protection of those who presumably needed State intervention precisely because they could not be assumed to be able to take care of themselves, namely, children (who could not legally sign contracts and might even need protection from their parents) and women.

Regulation by the individual states was sporadic and none existed by the federal government except for the ten-hour day for its employees mandated in 1840. States, with a significant number of women and children working in factories, tended to legislate earlier, but with ineffective results owing to a lack of enforcement. By the end of the nineteenth century, half the states regulated child labor in whole or in part and many states regulated the labor of women. Also, half the states had factory acts modeled on the British factory acts.[99]

Conclusions

By the turn of the nineteenth century, the United States had attained a position of economic supremacy. In one industry after another, the United States had become the low cost producer as well as the nation with the largest gross national product and the highest per capita income. Economic policy and economic thought both burst beyond their *laissez faire* confines. Not only had British economic thinking changed but so had American, even though American academic economists continued to look with favor on Jevons and Marshall.

Organized in 1885 by men who had studied at German universities with their historical school of economics and its tradition of State economic policy, the founding of the American Economic Association (AEA) preceded that of the Royal Economic Society (RES). The AEA modeled itself on the comparable German Association, *Verein für Sozialpolitik*. The founders of the AEA believed in an interventionist State and therefore were twentieth century liberals. In contrast, their predecessors could be embodied in the philosophy of William Graham

---

96 Letwin 1989, p. 644.
97 Hughes 1991, pp. 119-120.
98 Higgs 1987, p. 104.
99 Taylor 1951, pp. 282-283, 379; Kirkland 1961, p. 386.

Sumner (1840-1910), author of *What Social Classes Owe to One Another* (1884), exponent of *laissez faire*, and opponent of any government intervention in the economy, including the protective tariff.[100]   Within the AEA there existed a 'persistent tension between the desire for scientific objectivity and non-partisanship and the urge to make an impact on public policy'.[101] The thinking of these younger economists influenced economic policymaking just as such policies affected their thinking as political economists.   During the first decade if its existence the AEA 'gradually lost some of its initial reformist tone'.[102] At the close of the century the large-scale enterprise, the national market, and the railroad coalesced to yield modified economic thought and policies with the State shifting its weight from that of promoter to that of regulator.

France

French economic thought and action originated in mercantilism, that is, long antedating the transfer of political power from the monarch and the aristocracy to the bourgeoisie. National economic policies only nominally related to national economic theory. 'While the English bourgeoisie saw the government as an external force, the French had come to view the state as a necessary agent for the protection of established positions and the creation of new wealth.'[103] Certainly the French during the nineteenth century had acquired a positive attitude toward the State, owing in part to the surge of nationalism and resulting from the French Revolutionary and Napoleonic eras.

France began the nineteenth century in the midst of the Revolution and had a war economy until 1814. The 1815 Congress of Vienna restored the monarchy, which although much less absolute than the *Ancien Régime*, lasted until 1830 when another Revolution brought about the so-called July Monarchy (1830-1848), centralized although far from being 'liberal' in economic policy.   The 1848 Revolution (that engulfed the Continent) installed a short-lived Second Republic. The newly elected president, Louis Napoleon Bonaparte, organized a *coup d'état* and proclaimed himself emperor Napoleon III. The State under him became autocratic; paternalistic towards the work force, he started with mercantilist policies, although towards the end of his reign he liberalized foreign trade. The 1870 Franco-Prussian war drove Napoleon III into exile and established the basis for the Third Republic. As everywhere in Continental Europe, the long depression, which began in 1873, triggered protectionist policies and further empowered the State to interfere in the market.

---

100   Coats 1960, pp. 555-574; Dorfman 1949, pp. 205-211.
101   Coats 1987, p. 87.
102   Coats 1987, p. 87.
103   Zysman 1979, p. 53.

Napoleon's Fall and the Bourbon Restoration

In the eyes of Europe, Napoleon embodied the Revolution, but as a despot Napoleon undermined the Revolution. Under his regime, women were put under legal tutelage and he affirmed class inequality by pronouncing that workers had no rights and that the employer was supreme; he even reintroduced slavery in the colonies. As an enlightened despot, he confirmed the right of the peasants to their land taken from the Church, defended the property rights of the bourgeoisie, and assured the clergy of his protection. The French gained security to compensate for the loss of liberty. Intellectuals became suspect and subject to harassment and therefore cultural life came to a standstill. Many people chose self-exile to escape the rigid constraints imposed by a regime that aimed at controlling everything.[104]

The Bourbon Restoration in 1815 did not entail a complete return of the *Ancien Régime* since the new government could hardly erase the Revolution and the accomplishments of the previous quarter century. The Charter of 1814 had to recognize the judicial and social accomplishments of the Revolution. The Charter established a constitutional monarchy, in theory similar to that advocated by Edmund Burke (1729-1797), a British political philosopher and statesman, who remarked that a constitution that does not give a State the means for change does not give the State the means to make policy.[105] Changing little from the *Ancien Régime*, the Bourbon Restoration excluded the overwhelming majority of the population from the political process.

Agricultural Policy

During the French Revolution, the State destroyed the political order of feudalism.[106] It ended vestigial serfdom and redistributed the land so that France became a country of peasant proprietors. Even though economically inefficient, French agriculture became a means of furthering social and political stability.[107] In contrast, especially after the Corn Laws were abolished in 1846, Britain imported agricultural products at the lowest possible price, which benefited the urban population by increasing their purchasing power. The State protected peasant property and thus, different from Britain, France encouraged peasants to stay on the farm. The limited French enclosure movement did not drive peasants to urban areas nor did France undergo an Agricultural Revolution comparable to Britain with large-scale capital-intensive farming.[108] French agricultural policy might have

---

104 Catherine and Gousset 1968 pp. 268-269.
105 Maurois 1948, p. 184.
106 Gueslin 1997, p. 25.
107 Still, there is much to be said for a country that produces several hundred kinds of wine and cheese.
108 Tulard 1985, pp. 352-354. No consensus exists on the role of the enclosures in pushing people off the land versus the view that the Industrial Revolution pulled peasants to industrial work.

5

retarded economic growth at the beginning of the nineteenth century because of the limited industrial labor supply.

When Britain repealed the Corn Laws, it allowed the free importation of food from the United States and other low cost producers. Like Germany and Italy, *au contraire*, France protected agriculture through tariffs that essentially denied the urban worker the full benefits of the agricultural and transportation (steamship and railroad) revolutions. French workers increased real income but not nearly as much as they would have if an alternative agricultural policy had been pursued. As a result of the 1789 Revolution, France practiced small-scale agriculture under various forms of tenancy and ownership, although with some large-scale managed holdings, which restricted the use of even rudimentary machinery. However socially and politically desirable, this agricultural policy surely hampered productivity to the detriment of the urban consumer.[109]

Industrial Policy

Observers maintain that as late as 1820 France 'had neither a national market nor a market economy'. The Restoration (1815-1830) empowered economic liberals who in practice did not hesitate to find an important role for the State in planning and financing canals. As in the previous century, it seems that there was a scarcity of private entrepreneurs because of unreasonably high economic risks and for the *haute bourgeoisie* alternative public employment. For instance, the French State, acted as a surrogate entrepreneur considering national strategic imperatives rather than strictly economic feasibility to maintain a strong presence through planning, financing, and managing the canals. This situation recurred twenty years later with the railroads.[110]

Some economic historians assert that it does not make a difference if the State helps in the process of industrialization by citing the examples of Britain and France. They maintain that the economic growth of France almost matched that of Britain. Their assertion that the State in France, compared to Britain, played an active role in the development of social institutions but a passive role in the process of industrialization is not sustained. They point to the history of *les manufactures royales* subsidized by the State, although hardly an economic success. Indeed, these enterprises were not intended to be an economic success; they primarily served the king and their contribution to economic development is debatable. The same might be said about infrastructure; it appears that the policies of the *Ancien Régime* continued into nineteenth century, as public investments seemed a political necessity. But infrastructure investments were potentially conducive to economic development since canals, roads, and railways might stimulate the economy through backward and forward linkages, even though these public investment decisions often resulted from political rather than economic criteria.[111]

---

109 Laurent 1976, pp. 637-639; Saboul 1976a, pp. 1-64.
110 Geiger 1994, p. 21.
111 Rosanvallon 1989, pp. 572-575; Trebilcock 1981, pp. 139-142; Saboul 1976b, pp.

At the beginning of the nineteenth century, France was plagued by market fragmentation and low agriculture productivity. Industry was only a step ahead of handicrafts and dependent on wood and water for power and fuel. During the 1830 Revolution labor asserted itself by organizing illegal strikes. After 1830, the factory system adversely affected handicrafts and homespun industry, which could not easily compete with the larger mechanized establishments. Under the July Monarchy, State encouragement, through protective tariffs and subsidies, induced a spectacular advance in the mechanization of industry and in industrial concentration.[112] While until 1848 the small manufacturing enterprises still predominated, big industry and big money concentrated in fewer families that under the monarchy controlled the State. With the coming of the railroads, access to markets and raw materials improved considerably, and the enlarged market increased national and international competition.

Protectionism

The State protected the emerging capitalism that had doubtful efficiency because of the lack of a parallel commercial revolution; trade was still not organized on the scale required by an industrial society. As long as the market had to rely on canals and rivers, which froze during the winter, business activity was seasonal and factories did not operate year round. Protectionism helped some industries in the short run but also benefited the State treasury; during the July Monarchy customs duties accounted for a large share of the government revenue. Throughout the nineteenth century the Customs Service employed ten thousand functionaries who formed a powerful interest group. A French economist has argued that protectionism took on a life of its own not only for economic protection but also because the State could not conceive that it could function without customs revenue.[113]

Frederic Bastiat (1801-1850), an economist, a staunch advocate of free trade, and a critic of broad protectionist policy, and Francois Guizot (1787-1874) a statesman and historian, as well as principal minister during the July Monarchy of Louis Philippe (1830-1848) represented the spirit and outlook of the *haute bourgeoisie*; both wanted France to emulate British free trade policy. On the contrary, Adolphe Thiers (1797-1877), a journalist, historian, and statesman as well as an opponent of Guizot, claimed that France could not be compared to Britain because of critical differences in the structure of the economy. For these reasons Thiers contended that the elimination of grain taxes, as suggested by the economic liberals, would be fiscally impossible.[114] Bastiat decried also State

---

105-107.

112 Tulard, 1985, pp. 362, 375-377; Leon 1976a, Vol. 1, pp. 273-304; Leon 1976b, Vol. 2., 1976b, pp. 581-618.

113 Jean Meyer, *Le poids de l'Etat*, 1983, Paris. Presse Universitaire de France, cited by Gueslin, 1997, pp. 71-72.

114 Rosanvallon 1989, pp. 566-571.

intervention in the domestic market and was respected by the liberal governments of the July Monarchy. Nevertheless, the State dominated a large part of economic activity all through the nineteenth century.[115]

The State Bureaucracy

As elsewhere, most ministers and senior civil servants were selected by necessity from the upper classes that had more schooling than the population at large.[116] The contemporary Jacksonian Revolution in the United Sates (1828-1848) had about the same results; the same better-educated social class continued to run the government as before. In France, the large landholders, the nobility, and the *haute bourgeoisie* retained political and economic control. Until 1830 only 80,000 people were eligible to vote; the franchise was based either on property or literacy or both. Afterwards, the number increased first to 160.000 and then to 241,000 but still constituted only a small fraction of the population.[117]

Until the end of the nineteenth century, parliament and the public administration remained in the hands of the landed and moneyed *haute bourgeoisie*; by 1900, only about ten percent of the top administrative hierarchy originated in the lower, middle, or popular classes. Elites generally controlled the State apparatus and therefore the State apparently acted to maintain order and continue the existing institutional arrangements with regard to social and economic relationships.[118] Guizot believed that only property gave people the right to vote and that property was not a privilege but a reward for hard work. According to him only the very rich could properly make policy decisions because they had proven their capabilities by their material accumulation; he did not see a place in public decision making for the proletariat and the poor—they were mere riffraff.[119]

---

115 Caron 1995, pp. 47-50.
116 Price 1987, pp. 44, 363.
117 Tulard 1985, pp. 366-369; Sée 1942, p. 67; Daumard 1976b, pp. 829-840.
118 Tulard 1985, pp. 334-356; Leon 1976c, pp. 479-482; Daumanrd 1976c, pp. 933-937.
119 Between 1815 and 1848 a sizeable migration took place from the rural areas to feed the almighty industrial machine. Under the monarchy, but not necessarily because of it, working conditions were similar to those in Dickens' Britain and living conditions were probably worse. A contemporary economist described the workers' living conditions in the borough of Saint-Sauver in Lille as a series of little islands of dugouts of cottages separated by narrow paths cramped and dark with little yards serving for storage of food and garbage. The so-called cottages, that hardly let light penetrate, were in front of a communal toilet that smelled to high heaven. In the yard, children were playing almost naked in good weather. Inside the cave all the family slept together usually directly on the earth and, the ones who could afford it, had some straw. None of these habitations had furniture. Three thousand people had this horrible existence in 1848 Lille. Adolphe Jérôme Blanqui (1849), *Les classes ouvrières en France pendant l'âne 1848*. Pagnerre, Paris, pp.74-75 ; Louis René Villerme (1840), *Tableau de l'état physique et moral des ouvriers employée dans la manufactures de coton, de laine et de soie*, J. Renouard, Paris, Vol. 1, pp. 74-75 cited by Sée 1942, pp. 183-184.

While relative poverty remained rampant in nineteenth century France, it was not much worse than in Britain. Apparently, the life of the very poor in France was better than in Germany and Italy since these two countries were poorer, that is, Italy and Germany had lower production per capita than France, at least before the unification of these countries.

Welfare Policy

Through the early nineteenth century the workday was 15 hours regardless of sex or age; since there were no rules or regulations, wages covered merely bare subsistence. This situation varied by region, skill, and industrial sector, with few shining spots. Poverty prevailed for most workers in all sectors, which meant also sickness; rachitic and tuberculosis diseases were widespread and during epidemics such as cholera in 1832, the poor were the ones hardest hit. Furthermore, alcoholism and prostitution were rampant among the women of the French working class, no different from Britain's Victorian era.[120]

During the 1789 Revolution the Church lost many of its assets and adherents. Under the Restoration the Church regained some assets and power only to lose it again less drastically after the 1830 Revolution when the anticlerical movement steadily flourished. The travail of the Church had serious consequences on policy making since, on and off, there has been antagonism and symbiosis between the Church and the State. For instance, under the *Ancien Régime*, the Church organized and controlled charitable institutions; the Revolution dissolved these charitable institutions, thereby creating chaos for the indigent.[121] Poor relief rested mainly with the towns all through the nineteenth century, since the State exercised the power of control but contributed only marginally with financial support; in 1885, the State was responsible for about three percent of all welfare costs in France. Also, since the beginning of eighteenth century large-scale enterprises, such as St. Gobain, a manufacturer of glass and crystal, organized assistance for the poor and indigent in conjunction with medical assistance for their workers and their families.

War, revolution, and instability left the lower income strata in destitution and misery. By 1847, one third of the people in Paris needed assistance. During the second half of the nineteenth century, while relative poverty was hardly wiped out, the situation improved. Food became more affordable for workers, partly due to increased agricultural productivity and reduced transportation costs as well as from the increased assertiveness of the labor movement. Real wages grew between 1852 and 1882 by 84 percent. While between 1850 and 1900 real industrial wages doubled, the cost of living (consumer prices) increased only by about 15 percent.[122]

---

120 Daumard 1976, pp. 139-141; a contemporary writer observed, 'Prostitution is the regular source of income of many young woman workers in Paris'. Eugène Buret, *De misère des classes laborieuses en France et en Angleterre*. Paris, Renouard 1840, Vol. 1, p. 408, cited by Sée 1942, p. 184.
121 Tulard 1989, pp. 356-358; Leveque 1989, pp. 390-403.
122 Mitchell 1998, pp. 186-187, 863-864.

After the 1850s, while poverty was still widespread, living conditions improved considerably.[123]

Labor Policy under the July Monarchy

After the Revolution of 1830, few workers succeeded in organizing; their power was minimal since the employers did not want to recognize labor unions. Nevertheless, workers succeeded in organizing small enterprises, where they found more understanding but less market power. Organized labor was not effective because it lacked finances backing and did not have any political influence since the majority of workers was not yet enfranchised. Small enterprises tended to produce for a local market; large-scale enterprises tended to produce for a wider market and faced competition from more distant competitors. The coming of the railroads destroyed local monopolies for both employer and employee.

Putting the wealthy in charge of the French government frustrated and troubled the masses since they remained disenfranchised.[124] Between 1815 and 1848, the beginning of the Industrial Revolution created a still relatively small industrial proletariat. The great transition to the industrial state, with subsistence wages and high unemployment together with the bad crops of 1847-1848, produced a sense of malaise. As Alexis de Tocqueville, one of the few analysts to be cognizant of the situation, observed, 'the government was blind to the needs of the society'.

When the French Government proposed a law to the National Assembly that would protect children a great debate took place concerning State intervention; the Government strongly favored intervention. A law was enacted in 1841 covering enterprises with more than 20 workers.[125] The industrialists obtained an important concession in not having salaried officials inspect the factories; instead, the law called for factories voluntary self-inspection. Obviously, it was a sham. Over the next decade attempts to amend the law by including protection for women, raising the minimum age to ten years, and having official inspection failed.[126]

The Revolution of 1848

The Revolution of 1848 succeeded when the government and the monarchy abdicated in favor of a republican State and universal suffrage was immediately instituted without resistance. The Second Republic lasted barely four years to

---

123 Price 1987, pp. 51-52.
124 In 1789, the masses were mainly composed of peasants and artisans with hardly any factory workers.
125 The 1841 law specified that employers were forbidden to employ children under the age of eight, children from eight to 12 years could work only eight hours a day, children between 12 and 16 could work only 12 hours a day; children under 12 could not work at night and under 16 could work at night in exceptional cases. Also, in accordance with the 1833 law, which expanded primary education, children under 12 had to attend elementary school.
126 Tulard 1985, pp. 418-420; Sée 1942, pp. 190-193.

1852. The economic consequences of the Revolution were disastrous in the short run. Capital fled the country, production declined by one third, and unemployment appeared everywhere.[127] With scarce understanding of economics, the new government attempted to establish *ateliers nationaux*, national shops of 'make work', to keep the unemployed content. In a few months these shops employed more than 100,000 workers. Since the State treasury was dry, it paid less than subsistence level wages because the cost to the State was immense. The project was abandoned within one year; the closing of these shops provoked riots.

By 1850, the rapid spread of industrialization due to improved transportation (the coming of the railroads), and the more efficient management of resources, attracted more workers to factories and increased labor productivity. Economic conditions improved rapidly in France; by the time of the 1851 International Exposition of London, France was still considered the second industrial power. As in most of the industrial world, the workers were impeded in their ability to organize and did not see substantial changes in the relationships with their employers. But the popular trust of the Second Republic influenced the French society for the next century.[128]

Promising not to change the gains of the 1848 Revolution, Louis Napoleon was elected President of the Republic, although he proclaimed that liberty is not a basis for a stable political process. Allegedly many who were afraid of the 'red peril' backed Napoleon, who received the overwhelming share of the votes.[129] While this peril was exaggerated, those who held power felt that stability and authority would perpetuate their control of the economy. By 1852, Louis Napoleon, crowned himself emperor as Napoleon III through a *coup d'état* and proclaimed France to be a constitutional empire. The hope of the majority of the public was that his government would bring bread at lower prices, large public works, and some relaxation of daily life. It might appear that Napoleon aspired to be a benevolent tyrant; unfortunately, there are no good tyrants.[130] During the first decade of his reign (1852-1860), he did not live up to his promises and instead instituted an authoritarian regime.[131]

Napoleon III

The 1848 Revolution had vented the workers discontent against the rising bourgeois State. In its aftermath, the workers felt betrayed, since their aspirations for better wages and living conditions did not result in much improvement. The workers' contact with their British counterparts made them aware of better conditions elsewhere and they felt short-changed by employers who repeatedly halted their efforts to organize. The workers contended: 'the Revolution of '89 has

---

127 These are hardly reliable statistics and are just estimates of the national income and unemployment; all figures cited here are, of necessity, approximate.
128 For instance see; Bruhat 1976, Vol. III, pp. 769-828.
129 'There is a specter over Europe, the specter of Communism.' Marx and Engels 1948.
130 Maurois 1948, p. 185.
131 Tulard 1985, pp. 439-440.

franchised the bourgeoisie and on this is based its power; we think that the working class has the same right to be franchised and that this new franchise will be stronger and greater'.[132]   While Napoleon gave lip service to the rights of the workers, obstacles and scare tactics were used to prevent them from organizing or striking.

Industrialization and the Agricultural and Transportation Revolutions increased output and reduced costs and therefore increased real per capita income. Napoleon sought popular support through paternalism and boasted that his government ameliorated working conditions. In 1853, Napoleon appointed Baron Georges Eugene Haussmann prefect of the Seine province, who carried out a huge urban renewal program, tearing down the worst slums in Paris. Simultaneously, as a social reformer, he introduced free home medical care.[133]   To no one's surprise, while Haussmann's reform benefited Paris, the rest of the country remained behind; usually, capital cities get the lion's share of the government's spending.

Although Napoleon preserved some of the gains of the 1848 Revolution such as nominal male universal suffrage, he maintained a symbiotic relationship with the small but powerful capitalist class. While a feeling of well being marked the beginning of the reign of Napoleon III, it took some time for the public to realize the absence of political liberty. However, the State established infant care centers and associations for mutual help, subsidized in part by the State; in many cities the State constructed functional public housing for the poor.[134]

Not particularly appreciated either by the capitalists or the clergy, Napoleon tried to mollify the popular classes of the workers and the peasants.[135]   For instance, in 1864, he allowed workers to organize and to strike.[136]   Economic conditions were better then ever before but the State did very little to ameliorate destitution. A few hundred families succeeded in accumulating enormous wealth; the bourgeoisie started to invest in the stock market that allowed the further development of corporations, which used these funds for the expansion of industry and commerce.[137]

---

132   Levasseur 1904, Vol. II, p. 620.
133   Rosanvallon 1989, pp. 513-522.
134   Leveque 1989. pp. 472-474; Sée 1942, pp. 245, 250-251; Gueslin 1997, pp. 100-101.
135   In 1864, Pope Pius IX condemned the spirit of the nineteenth century as monstrous.
      He declared that the Church is superior to the State, and demanded a monopoly in the
      education of children; on the other hand, he did not admit the freedom of non-
      Catholics or the freedom of the press. The Pope hoped to weaken Napoleon III;
      however, his condemnation backfired by weakening the liberal French Catholics.
136   But still the dismal conditions described by Emile Zola were not different from those
      depicted by Charles Dickens in Britain.
137   Culturally, France, mainly Paris, underwent a renaissance in arts and letters; Parisian
      'high life' attracted both scorn and praise. 'In Victorian England, where appearances
      were austere, the French novel with a yellow cover was scandalous. The English
      came to Paris to get emancipated, then blamed Paris for the pleasures that they came
      to seek.' Maurois 1948, p. 213.

The State and Private Enterprise

The laws from the *Ancien Régime*, modified during the 1789 Revolution and incorporated into the Napoleonic Commercial Code, required corporations, *société anonyme*, to be authorized by the highest level of government (the king, the emperor or the *Conseil d'Etat*). Formalities were very complicated and many would-be entrepreneurs could not and would not wait for months to have the State approve a stock corporation approve. After being chartered, the corporations were subject to more intensive regulation than unincorporated businesses because of the limited liability clause.

Private enterprise circumvented the law by relying on the first commercial code instituted by Colbert, that is, the 1673 Ordinance. The code defined two types of business organizations, the *société générale*, an unlimited liability partnership, and the *société en commandite*, a form of business organization that allowed stock distribution to some partners; it provided for the participation of full partners with unlimited benefits and unlimited responsibilities and limited partners who play the same role as stockholders in a corporation. After 1830, the *société en commandite par actions* was required to be registered but did not need to be authorized.[138]

This particular form of organization based on the Commercial Code was abrogated in 1867 at the same time when the *société anonymes* became free, that is, they could be established without previous State authorization. The Law of 1862 empowered the State to defend the rights of the shareholders; the 1867 Law, while liberalizing the formation of corporations, withdrew the State protection of shareholders. About the same time, most Continental European countries adopted corporate liberalization laws; Britain enacted the Joint Stock Company Act in 1856, refined in 1862. It is still debatable whether between 1815 and 1867, the State through the commercial code, retarded capital mobilization and, probably unintentionally, retarded economic growth.[139] Economic liberals objected to the limitations imposed in the 1867 Commercial Code as being more restrictive than British codes, and in an attempt to regulate everything, handicapped business. Yet, 191 *anonymes* were formed in France in1868 and 976 in 1881. The corporate form a business gained legitimacy after 1867 and the *commandite par actions* lost the appeal.[140]

Financial Policy

The development of the State regulated banking system has influenced the French political and economic culture. As we noted in Chapter 3, John Law established the *Banque Général* in 1715 and the *Banque Royale* in 1716 to assist the French State's treasury, which acted in consonance with the crown but were not truly national banks. The *Banque de France*, the central bank, has been considered from

138 Freedeman 1979, pp. 3-4, 13-14, 47.
139 Catherine and Gousset 1965, pp. 125-126; Kindleberger 1993, pp. 199-202; Cameron 1967, pp. 100-128; Daumard 1976a, Tome III, Vol. I, pp. 150-153.
140 Freedeman 1979, pp. 143-144.

its inception in 1800 an instrument for national policy. The bank's autonomy was more limited by the State than the Bank of England; for instance, during the nineteenth century, the State established monetary policies directing the *Banque de France* to take action benefiting various sections or interest groups.[141] A few economic historians argue that policy decisions were made according to economic rather than political concerns.[142]

As a central bank, the *Banque de France* has been keeping watch on private commercial and investment banks. *La Société du crédit industriel et commercial* (the Institute for Industrial and Commercial Credit), while meant to be private, had its statutes drawn up by the government; therefore, some argue that this institute was a quasi-State agency. In this way, the State was empowered to control investment and to interfere in the capital market. While objecting to the State's intrusion, industrialists wanted the State's backing in the financial markets.[143]

Some scholars argue that French lack of financial intermediaries until the innovation of the *Crédit Mobilier* hindered economic development. Yet, the *Crédit Mobilier*, established by the Saint-Simonist Periere brothers, invested in banks, ports, waterworks, gas works, and eventually railroads but not in manufacturing. In the1850s and 1860s another innovation was introduced, the deposit banks such as the *Crédit Industriel et Commercial* (1859), the *Crédit Lyonnais* (1863), and the *Société Générale pour Favoriser le Development du Commerce et l'Industrie en France,* The General Society to Promote Development of Commerce and Industry in France. (1864). After an initial involvement in investment in manufacturing, these banks switched to commercial short-term loans and speculation in foreign bonds.[144]

The State played an important role in the Panama financial debacle in 1892. Already in difficulty in 1888 the Panama Canal enterprise attempted to issue notes guaranteed by the State. A parliamentary inquiry found that members of Parliament were involved in covert financial actions with large State expenditures for a high-risk project. A major partner, the State stood to lose substantial amounts of money. This discovery triggered heated debate in Parliament on the State's

---

141 Partially to support the financing of the war economy, Napoleon I established the Banque de France in 1800. Thus, a close relationship developed between the government and finance. Napoleon appointed the official in charge of the bank. Because of this relationship, Napoleon's final campaign broke the bank. The Banque de France's lack of autonomy was an impediment in developing an efficient banking system. The Bank of England was established in 1694, after the Glorious Revolution; during the Nine Years War (1689-1697), the Bank of England funded the public debt and protected the public creditors. One should recall that the Medici Bank opened, in Florence in 1397; the banks of Venice, Amsterdam, and Hamburg were established, some by private investors, some by the State and some by a combination of these, between 1587 and 1619. The *Banque de France* was created with the investment of merchant bankers who had to respond to the stockholders but above all, until 1815 to the Emperor. Kindleberger 1993, pp. 102-104; Levy Leboyer 1976, pp. 391-430.

142 Parent and Rault 2004, pp. 328-354.

143 Sée 1942, pp. 272-274; Levy-Leboyer 1976, pp. 391-430.

144 Kindleberger 1993, pp. 110-115.

participation in dubious enterprises. Subsequently, a former minister of public works was condemned for accepting bribes from the Panama Company.[145]

An economic historian argues that economic development was impeded because: of an inadequate number and locations of banking offices, an insufficient number of specialized financial institutions, restrictions on the volume of credit, and an inelastic and expensive stock of money.[146] Another economic historian seconds this verdict, adding that France lagged Britain by one hundred years or so in financial institutions and experience.[147] Nonetheless, a French economist maintains that despite the State banking restrictions, during the first half of the nineteenth century the French economy grew three times as fast as that of Britain.[148]

Saint Simon

During the first part of the nineteenth century the entrepreneurial spirit originated with a group of individuals known as the Saint-Simonians.[149] The so-called utopian socialist, Claude Henri de Rouvroy, Comte de Saint Simon (1760-1825) condemned private property and the exploitation of man by man.[150] Saint-Simon introduced the socialist concept of *l'école industrialiste* (the industrialist school of thought), which maintained that social institutions have a duty to ameliorate the conditions of the lower classes, but the reform of the State had to be entrusted to industrialists because they had experience in big business.[151] Another socialist journalist and historian, Louis Blanc (1811-1882) advocated state socialism and played an important role during the Revolution of 1848.[152] In a sense, the Revolution of 1848 attempted to revive the so-called 'social contract' that seemingly had been implied in the Revolution of 1789 as well as that of 1830. Both Saint Simon and Louis Blanc followed in the footsteps of Rousseau regarding the relationship between the individual and the State and emphasized that the primary duty of the State is the welfare of the citizen.

While involved in many causes and financial enterprises, by his late middle age Saint Simon developed a philosophy based presumably on science and technology. He aimed to eliminate drudgery from day-to-day repetitive work. True, his ideas,

---

145 Mayeur 1973, pp. 203-205.
146 Cameron et al 1967, p. 107.
147 Kindleberger 1993, pp. 115-16.
148 Levy-Leboyer 1968, pp. 1-8.
149 This period witnessed many other utopian social reformers such as Sismondi (Jean Charles Leonard de Sismondi), Louis Blanc, Charles Fourier, and Pierre Joseph Proudhon. For an excellent presentation see: Tulard, 1985, pp. 383-385.
150 The revolutionary government confiscated real estate that sold to obtain revenue for the State's treasury; speculators traded these assets. Saint Simon descended from Charlemagne, fought in the American Revolution, and renounced his title during the French Revolution, only to speculate and get rich on *biens nationaux* (national assets).
151 Maurois 1948, p. 164.
152 Edouard Renard (1922) La vie et l'oeuvre de Louis Blanc. Dissertation, Paris, cited by Sée 1942, pp. 206-207.

to convert society in a scientific way, did not find a place during his lifetime but his disciples became captains of industry and finance. This entourage, as single individuals or as partners, established banks, railways (French capital dominated investment in railways from Spain to Russia), public utilities and mining and metallurgical enterprises on the Continent. To say the least, they shared in the power and prestige that France acquired up to 1914.[153]

Napoleon III considered himself a Saint Simonian-socialist. Nevertheless, his economic thought and policy were quite consistent with France's history. Napoleon assumed that as the leader of a strong State, he must justify his role as a successor of Louis XIV as well as his uncle. A student of both economic theory and practice, Napoleon III rejected the 'law of the markets' of Jean Baptiste Say (1767-1832), one of the founders of the classical school of economics, that is, supply creates its own demand, by asserting that the State has to direct the economy, the core of *dirigisme*. Napoleon preferred practitioners to theoreticians as policy advisers and succeeded in finally excluding the remaining cadres of previous regimes from political power. The transformation resulted in a reduction of the ossification of the State and the introduction of governance based on the philosophy of Saint-Simon.[154]

The 1860s Trade Liberalization

The French Classical School competed for influence with the dominant national school and harmonized liberal economic theory with the national interest. 'In contrast to Britain, the French State has been able and willing to influence forcefully in the private sector.'[155] An economic historian argues that a short-lived 'spurt' of economic growth in the 1850s stemmed from a liberal tariff policy and a favorable industrialization ideological climate. Another significant factor was the development of industrial banking.[156] This is hardly a universal view, since others maintain that this claim of spurts in growth and the impression of sluggish growth are not sustained by recent data reconstruction.[157]

The 1860s witnessed an extraordinary increase in trade and in capital accumulation, partially owing to the discovery of gold in California and Australia. Trade was not necessarily an outcome of the gold discovery, which definitely facilitated trade because of the doubling of the world monetary stock from 1848 to 1856; the production of gold alone represented one-sixth of the world's existing gold and silver. Monetarists maintain that the increased availability of money and the adoption of the gold standard in the fourth quarter of the nineteenth century induced the expansion of international trade. Their hypothesis remains debatable; while the gold standard allowed for international financial stability, it created new rigidities that would trigger protectionism starting in the 1870s.

---

153 Cameron 1961, pp. 60-61.
154 Sée 1942, pp. 249-253, 345-349.
155 Hall 1986b, p. 246.
156 Gerschenkron 1962, p. 12.
157 Levy-Leboyer and Lescure 1991, p. 153.

The leading international trade event took place in 1860 with the signing of the Cobden-Chevalier Treaty that signaled the end of the centuries long French-British trade war.[158] The treaty was signed by Napoleon in the form of a decree not ratified by the Chamber of Deputies. Parliament probably would have declared that the treaty was implemented against the will of the people and imposed by an authoritarian government. Also, this decree was issued without consultation and against the wishes of the industrial barons; some contend that the decree could be considered as a trade *coup d'état* although some call this period in history the 'liberal Empire'.[159] During the brief interlude between 1860-1873, and in keeping with the Cobden-Chevalier Treaty of Commerce, France adhered to a low tariff policy but never adopted absolute free trade. One recent scholar contends that Britain hardly constituted a bastion of free trade and that French tariffs were actually lower. Apparently, 'French average tariff levels were surprisingly below those of Britain throughout most of the nineteenth century, even after the abolition of the Corn Laws and before the 1860 Treaty of Commerce'.[160] Indeed, French foreign trade increased nine times over between 1820 and 1860. By the end of the century, France's economic growth and foreign trade was on an equal footing with that of Britain and the United States.[161]

The Beginning of the Third Republic

Napoleon's regime collapsed in 1870 in a catastrophic military defeat and France established the Third Republic (1871-1940). Some observers maintain that the Emperor's ideas, sometimes brilliant or even generous, often imprudent, often fantastic, contributed to delivering Central Europe to the Prussians. Posterity, including, for example, Tocqueville, condemned Napoleon for the repression following his *coup d'état*, the loss of political freedom, and the wars of prestige. Yet, some argue that the social reform pushed by Napoleon was ahead of his time and that the bickering among politicians also caused the demise of his Empire. For better or worse, the authoritarian Napoleon reinforced State intervention in the French economy.[162]

In the mid-nineteenth century, a skewed prosperity seemed to have spread all over the industrial world. The causes may be debated: economic growth, innovation, technology, the railroads, and the not easily identifiable or quantifiable capitalist spirit. Materialism was triumphant and this was an era of *parvenus* who wanted to get rich quickly; it was a fast moving society. While the conditions of the working class improved, they still faced high unemployment and terrible living conditions. The State attempted to remedy some of the negative consequences of

---

158 Sée 1942, pp. 280-281. The Eden Trade Treaty had been signed in 1786, a century earlier.
159 Maurois 1948, pp. 190-191.
160 Nye 1991, p. 23.
161 Broder 1976, p. 307; Caron 1984, pp. 314-318; Daumard 1976a, pp. 155-159; Granthan 1997, passim.
162 Maurois 1948, p. 209; Labracherie 1967, Ch. XXV.

this rapidly expanding capitalism. Among other activities, the State initiated action for public health, slum clearance, and established state owned or controlled credit institutions.[163] Fiscal policy was biased towards the urban areas while agriculture bore a disproportionate share of the tax burden. Monetary stability allowed more savings and enabled professionals such as medical doctors and engineers to receive pensions from the State at 50 years of age. By the end of the nineteenth century, some 100,000 people became *rentiers* living on savings and/or on State pensions that equaled their annual working income. Income distribution remained askew with probably ten percent of the population receiving 90 percent of the national income.[164]

The Labor Unions Ups and Downs

With the proclamation of the Third Republic, the workers' movement gained a new lease on life. Labor leaders advocated unionization in the quest for political influence since male universal suffrage and ministerial responsibility became the law of the land. *Les syndicats* (labor unions) and the Socialist political movement were closely connected. During the 1870s, *les syndicats* were reformers who argued against class war but for social legislation and for workers' cooperatives, although the left wing, under the influence of Marxist ideology, rejected all such proposals. At the 1879 Socialist Congress, those who advocated collectivization of the economy, class struggle, and opposed social legislation replaced the reformists.[165]

In 1895, labor unions were co-opted by the State to establish labor exchanges (*bourses de travail*) that facilitated the placement of workers; by being government subsidized, the State retained some control and lent an aura of legitimacy to labor unions.[166] It is remarkable that unionization brought a sense of stability through discipline with fewer work stoppages than before unionization. Yet, the Government did not hesitate to interfere when the unions seemed to abuse their recently gained power. In 1893, the army occupied labor exchanges offices after labor unions staged street demonstrations not permitted by the Labor Law of 1884.[167]

Labor Legislation

The French State appeared to be unwilling to regulate the conditions at the work place. Much later than Germany, France passed disability compensation legislation in 1898, after being debated for twenty years in the Chamber of Deputies. This legislation constituted a break with the conventional wisdom of the entire century. Contemporary *laissez faire* economists argued that the State should

---

163   Guerard 1969, pp. 312-313.
164   Mayeur 1973, pp. 86, 93.
165   As an outcome, the same labor leaders formed the Socialist Party.
166   Mayeur 1973, pp. 188-189.
167   Mayeur 1973, p. 208.

keep hands off and that industrial freedom should prevail. But, the exploitation of children could not be ignored, if only because French public opinion had been greatly influenced by the British Factory Act (1832) and subsequent similar legislation.

Economic growth was sustained by increased internal demand triggered by a more equal income distribution, which, in turn, was caused by higher real wages and salaries. In 1874, the 1841 Law prohibiting the employment of children below 12 years of age in factories was amended; the Law of 1892 included the protection of women by prohibiting both males and females below 16 years from working more than ten hours a day. In 1899, the government enacted partial control of the labor market and encouraged mediation of relationships of workers with employers. By 1904, the ten-hour day for every one became law and in 1906 the weekly holiday was mandated.[168]

Some labor unions and extreme left leaning factions opposed legislation regulating work rules such as disability compensation and provisions for pensions for workers. Mimicking Karl Marx who declared that 'the State is the executive committee of the ruling class', they maintained that the workers would lose their autonomy and would become puppets of the French bureaucracy responsible to industrial capitalism. The legislation regulating work rules did not contain an obligatory clause and remained toothless until changed in 1928.

Industrial Policy under the Third Republic

While until 1848 the small manufacturing enterprises predominated, large scale industry and big money concentrated in fewer families who controlled the State. With the coming of the railroad, access to markets and raw materials improved considerably and the enlarged market intensified national and international competition. Until the end of the nineteenth century, parliament and the public administration remained in the hands of the landed and moneyed *haute bourgeoisie*. By 1900, the lower, middle, or popular classes supplied only about ten percent of the top administrative hierarchies. Elites generally controlled the State apparatus and therefore the State acted to maintain order and continue existing institutional arrangements with regard to social and economic relationships.[169]

By World War I France was still not as industrialized as Britain, the United States, or Germany. It is possible that this stemmed from the lack of large carbon deposits and impure iron ore but also, as some contend, because the French bourgeoisie appeared less entrepreneurial, more conservative, and less ready for collective action. Furthermore, French markets were constrained by high tariffs to protect agricultural and manufacturing products; therefore, the cost of living was relatively high. French exports were limited and continued to be mainly luxury goods: wines, cheeses, and the tourist trade. An economic dualism occurred: on one hand, France remained a country of small artisans, shopkeepers, and small

---

168 Gueslin 1997, p. 104.
169 Tulard 1985, pp. 334-356; Leon 1976c, pp. 479-482.

farms; on the other hand, large enterprises, directly or indirectly, owned by the upper class families and/or the State, concentrated wealth and economic power.

Manufacturing giants, especially in metallurgical industries, while hardly on par with their German counterparts, were quite successful.[170] Schneider-Creusot became the leading iron and steel producer in France; the Schneider Freres & Company began operations as a foundry in 1832 and eventually expanded into coal mining, manufacturing locomotives, ships, bridges and other metal-based engineering projects. After 1880, the company became a major supplier of French military hardware and large electrical equipment throughout Europe. While the State was supportive in filling its procurement needs, it could not make France compete successfully first with Britain and later with Germany because of technological inferiority.[171]

Recent scholars portray France at the turn of the nineteenth century in a more favorable light. They contend that the various national income accounts are skewed against France and in favor of Britain because the accounts measure market transactions. For example, Britain urbanized more than France, which necessitated paved streets in cities rather than dirt roads in villages, water and sewer connections and security (police and firemen). The French State spent more that Britain on education. In fact, literacy spread rapidly after 1870; public elementary schools increased by about 15 percent by 1903. While currently all these are included in national accounts as 'non-marketable services', one cannot assess their inclusion at the time. One also could ask if there is a necessary correlation between economic welfare and the customary measurements of economic growth.[172]

Mélinisme

With the exception of Britain, protectionism triumphed at the onset of the worldwide long depression, which started in 1873. Following the high Méline Tariff of 1892, France entered the twentieth century with a controlled market economy, hardly showing the same reverence as the British for free trade. 'The Gallic forces of liberalism combined a certain reserve about competition with a protectionist state.'[173] Observers note 'the intervention of the State, contrary to the most elementary canons of economic liberalism aimed at social conservation. The objective was to protect society from susceptible disturbances and to modify the equilibrium'.[174] Neither the industrialists nor the population at large believed in

---

170 Maurois 1948, pp. 275-276.
171 France produced about 2 million tons of coal in 1830 and about 13 million in 1870; 26,000 tons of iron in 1830 and 1.2 million tons in 1870; 90,000 tons of steel in 1830 and 5.1 million tons in 1870. But, by 1870, Britain produced 8.5 million, Germany 20.5 million and United States 34.4 million while Italy lagged far behind with 160,000 tons of steel production,
172 O'Brien and Keyder 1978, passim; Caron 1984, p. 395.
173 Kuisel 1981, p. 295.
174 Rosanvallon 1989, p. 569.

free trade. Businessmen accorded lip service to free trade but pushed for protection.[175] Similar ambivalence prevailed in other places; in the United States, for instance, railroad builders wanted a low tariff on iron and steel rails while the manufacturers of iron and steel favored a high tariff even after they no longer needed protection.

In France for the short run, high tariffs helped the same heavy industries as in the United States. *Mélinisme* is derived from Jules Méline who held various high cabinet positions during the 1880s and 1890s. Nineteenth century *Mélinisme*, different from seventeenth century *Colbertisme*, did not aim to increase the State treasury through a favorable balance of trade. *Mélinisme* resulted from pressure from interest groups; the iron and steel and textile industries asked for protection and they were granted higher tariffs. Méline responded to the demands of the vocal peasantry with high import tariffs for agricultural products. Aimed mainly to benefit agriculture, Méline realized that the small farms were not capable of increasing efficiency and that agriculture had a generalized structural problem. He argued that tariffs would help but also he proposed that the State should support agricultural cooperatives and agricultural technical schools. Méline also instituted farm credits to eliminate the perennial farm problem of cash shortage between crops. To avoid a top-heavy bureaucracy, he installed regional credit offices that made financial decisions locally, which ameliorated but did not solve the agricultural development shortcomings.[176]

Low income from wages and salaries hindered internal demand and negatively affected the development of mass production. At least until circa 1870, export markets compensated for the lack of internal demand. With exports accounting for 41 percent of the gross national product, France ranked second in the world in the export of manufactured goods. However, France lost momentum afterwards initially because of internal upheaval and later because of protectionist policies as well as because of the increased competition from newly emerging countries such as the United States, Germany, and Italy. By 1913 with increased incomes and internal demand, stemming from cheaper transportation, French exports accounted only for 11.8 percent of gross national product.[177]

Conclusions

When one considers the role of the State in nineteenth century France, one must account for the contemporary vision of the economy. French nationalism originated and developed under authoritarian regimes, and Frenchmen sought guidance from the State for business ventures. Also, economics was viewed as a new unreliable discipline and economic laws were assumed by some to be natural and therefore unchangeable. *Laissez faire* economic liberals deplored the low level

---

175　As elsewhere, a majority in 1895 opposed the government's proposal to tax income and inheritance. Caron 1984, p. 439.

176　Gueslin 1997, pp. 86-88; Mayeur 1973, p. 123.

177　Price 1987, pp. 28-29.

of wages compared with the cost of living but believed that fixing a floor would be against natural economic laws.

During the first part of the nineteenth century, private banks issued money; furthermore, the State was adverse to emitting bank notes because of the terrible inflationary experience of the *assignats* (fiat paper money issued during the 1789 Revolution). The State reluctantly implemented monetary policy as against the 'natural order'. The new institutions, developed on the ashes of former regimes, required the State to take action and indeed strengthen French *étatisme*. Despite major upheavals, we argue that there is a notable continuity. France ended the nineteenth century, as it started, with a State bureaucracy substantially in charge of the national economy and impervious to the shifting sands of the popular majority.

Some label France in the nineteenth century as the century of revolutions. In this unstable century, regardless of the regime, the role of the State remained a dominant characteristic. With or without universal suffrage, *dirigiste* policies were accepted as the normal relationship between the electorate and the State. 'The French economy always required more informal and more active state policies than it received.'[178]

Germany

The eighteenth century witnessed the drive of Prussia to replace Austria as the major power in central Europe. Two expansionist monarchs, Wilhelm Frederick I and Frederick II, who ruled Prussia for almost the entire century, forged the Absolutist State as the ultimate arbiter in the economy. What would later become Germany was a product of the Prussian political and military system, characterized by Lutheran doctrine that subordinated the Church to the State.[179] This doctrine legitimized the Absolutist State, as Luther had 'made the Church a vital prop of princely authority'.[180] As Prussia evolved, the rulers were attracted to the concept that subjects cannot show legitimate resistance to the State, no matter what.

The German *Reich* with Prussia leading, evolved during the nineteenth century; the struggle between the monarchy and the *Junkers* continued even after the empire had been established. In most places land tenancy was still dominated by landlords even though serfdom had been officially abolished. The dominance of agricultural interests influenced the government to prefer agriculture to industry.

---

178   Trebilcock 1981, p. 185.
179   For the last one thousand years, religion molded the Germanic State and society; one
      cannot minimize the competition for control between the Catholic Church and the
      State in the northern Protestant and the southern Catholic Germany. Since Martin
      Luther the relation between the Catholic Church and some of the German States had
      been contested. After 1850 the Catholic Church, tolerated in Prussia and
      Württemberg, allied itself with those who opposed political liberalism, and making a
      common front with the State by warning its flocks about social upheaval.
180   Pflanze 1963, p. 19.

Yet, the State did not hesitate to subsidize industry overtly or covertly; neither business nor the State was comfortable with *laissez faire* policies.

Economic liberals (as well as the lingering *Cameralists*) were nationalists and therefore their policy prescriptions reflected their bias. They favored free trade among equals and most of them accepted an active role for the State in the market place. For instance, the Prussian-German State was among the first to enact social legislation that protected workers, even though it often harassed workers organizations. Also, the State encouraged and supported scientific research, which partially accounts for Germany becoming the world's third industrial power in by 1900.

Both before and after unification Germany pursued a mercantilist policy. The *Zollverein*, customs union, an internal affair of the German states was intended to expand the market and further consolidate the ties among the German territorial entities. However, the State offered protection from foreign competition for the expanding mining and manufacturing industries; furthermore, it condoned the industry-finance and the industry-State symbiosis and encouraged cartels. Moreover, the State participated in business ventures as a majority or minority partner, and subsidized industrial undertakings.

German Unification

After the Napoleonic wars, the Congress of Vienna (1815) consolidated the multitudinous German 'states' into thirty-six states. These states by and large had an inner-looking culture, each dynasty seeking to protect its own independence. Since Germany had its own nationalist and absolutist traditions, in practice the implementation of economic and political ideas took their own course. The spreading English free trade philosophy influenced a limited aristocratic political liberalism. More common were the still ultra conservative Prussian *Junkers* as well as the Württemberg landowners. The lower classes, the peasants and the *Bürgertum*,[181] townspeople, were as conservative as the nobility; for them, stability was more important than social change. The masses cared little about anything other than economic security; short run uprisings were aberrations led by some elites, which believed in strong leaders with the *Volk* (people) obeying the decisions of the leadership.[182]

At the turn of the eighteenth century, German intellectual development paralleled the French enlightenment of the previous fifty years but with a stronger nationalistic tone. Two Prussian statesmen, Karl Freiherr vom und zum Stein (1757-1831) and Karl August Fürst von Hardenberg (1750-1827) were instrumental in initiating structural reforms. The reforms included peasant emancipation freeing them from bondage to the landlords and introducing

---

181 In Germany a *Burg* is a town and a *Burger* is a townsperson; *Bürgertum* has had different connotation at various time and places. For example, 'the Prussian legal code of 1794 defined Burgerstand negatively as "all the inhabitants of the state not born into aristocracy or the peasantry"'. Sheehan 1989, p. 132.

182 Sheehan 1989, p. 598.

'occupational freedom', *Gewerbefreiheit* that ended the power of the guilds to restrict entry.[183]

The reformers were not completely victorious in surmounting the *Junker* reaction but initiated a new intellectual foundation for the power of the State. The German bourgeoisie embraced political liberalism derived from the English parliamentary system and the French Enlightenment. However, in all actions and policies from the relatively small states to Prussia to a powerful national State, it has been a continuity of the 'cultural' environment based on nationalism and a strong role for the State. Napoleon's defeat of Prussia at the battle of Jena (1806) ignited a strong impetus for national affirmation. The 1808 *Reden and die deutsche Nation* (Addresses to the German People) by Johann Gottlieb Fichte (1762-1814) became the corner stone of German liberal nationalism; he insisted that to gain liberties one needed to have a united forceful German State.[184]

The liberal bourgeoisie became comfortable with Adam Smith's ideas regarding individual economic freedom and effective proprietorship to maximize material welfare and thus the welfare of the State. German economic liberals acknowledged that some groups would be marginalized because industrial progress, following the English example, would necessarily leave some individuals behind. At the beginning of the nineteenth century, noted German followers of Adam Smith deviated from the Smithian system, observing that the sum of the material welfare of individuals did not necessarily equate with the welfare of society as a whole. German academicians had other reservations regarding Smith's theories; they questioned the universality of classical economic laws, arguing that policy should be empirical, thus refuting economic 'laws'.[185]

Agricultural Policy

The Prussian political system was based on an uneasy alliance between the monarchy and the *Junker* aristocracy. Under the influence of the French Revolution, the peasant-serfs were emancipated in Western Prussia, while in the East the *Junkers* and other landlords still exercised a strong hold over the peasantry. In 1808, Prussia decreed peasant emancipation; when serfdom ended, the peasants still did not have any means of redress against the former feudal lords. The secularization of Church lands, especially after 1806 when Napoleon defeated Prussia at Jena, turned the German states themselves into major landlords. The post Jena states also gained control over property, organization, and social

183 Tipton 2003, p. 113.
184 Huber 1957, pp. 97-99, 122-125, 412-413.
185 For instance, Georg Sartorius, professor of history and political economy at the University of Göttingen, introduced Smith at German universities. Georg von Waltershausen Sartorius (1806) *Abhandlungen, die Elemente des National-Reichtums und dies Staatswirtschaft betreffend*, Göttingen, p. 24, and *Von den Elementen des National-Reichtums und der Staatswirtschaft nach Adam Smith*, Göttingen. pp. 120 ff, cited by Tribe 1988, pp. 166-167.

relationships, but the southern German states found it difficult to control cultural life, because of the antagonism between the State and the Catholic Church.[186]

In Prussia between 1816 and 1850 most of former tenants-at-will became wage laborers; the landlords succeeded in appropriating the uncultivated land that accounted for about half the farmland before the 1850s. Large estates were eligible for credit from *Landschaften* (credit banks) and therefore had access to a cheap source of capital and could consolidate their holdings. While credit availability was expanded to include smaller holdings, it was only in 1890 that similar credit institutions were founded to help small peasant holdings. Some economic historians conclude that the course of the peasant emancipation in the southern states probably retarded development. For example, in 1820 Baden enacted a law favorable to the peasants but with no financial provisions; therefore, this law was meaningless for most peasants. Similarly, in Württemberg and Bavaria the peasants had to wait until the revolution of 1848 for emancipation.[187]

Before unification, the Prussian government did not look favorably upon introducing a capitalist organization framework in agriculture or agro industries. It did not encourage the 'factory'-type farm management with wageworkers. Also, it did not allow joint stock companies of agro industries such as sugar beet refining in Prussian Saxony, while other states, especially Braunschweig, did not impede such organizations. These conditions changed somewhat after 1870, when state banks were created to facilitate agrarian reform.[188]

The continuation of land tenancy in Württemberg and Brandenburg-Prussia remained unchanged and the landlords retained feudal rights to govern, as 'kings in miniature' peasants and burghers. Even in the more 'liberal' German south and west, including Bavaria, Baden, and Hesse-Darmstadt, the landed aristocracy could control parliament by maintaining an unrepresentative electoral system. Generally, in the individual German states suffrage was based on income tax qualifications, therefore guaranteeing the dominance of the wealthy landowners.[189]

Most German states were faced with the necessity of implementing capitalist agriculture and the Stein-Hardenberg reforms while still adjusting to the grain trade after the 1870. This particular trade could not operate under complete free trade conditions and still benefit agricultural workers because of low agricultural productivity. In general, liberal economists believed that abolishing the servitude of the peasants would increase wellbeing, because individuals work best when they work voluntarily on their own property.[190]

Industry versus Agriculture

The reforms introduced after the 1848 Revolution were not meant to protect the lower classes but to further industrial capitalism; some economic liberals (those

---

186   Sheehan 1989, p. 245; Huber 1957, pp. 186-187.
187   Tipton 1976, pp. 24-25, 37-38, 60; Blackbourn 1997, p. 78; Huber 1957, pp. 186-191.
188   Tipton 1976, p. 62; Tilly 1991, pp. 190-191.
189   Berghahn 1994, p. 198.
190   Gagliardo 1969, pp. 132-133. 189-191, 290-291.

who preached *laissez faire*) fought hard to exclude industrial workers and others from political participation. Also, the rural population did not perceive any immediate change from absolutism to a parliamentary system; the peasantry lived on the verge of poverty under either system. During the 1850s the landowners, found a willing ally in the conservative peasantry in resisting the encroachment of economic and political liberalism.

At least through the middle of the nineteenth century, the Prussian government relied on the large landowners and 'preferred agriculture to industry and aristocrats to commoners'. Also, Prussian economic policies favored the eastern over the western provinces. The *Rhinelanders* believed that the 1834 *Zollverein* (customs union) policies harmed their economy because of trade agreements that did not include adequate protection for infant industries. A conflict arose between the eastern *Junkers* and the Rhenish merchants and manufacturers. Yet, both economic interests sought to increase the power of the State, the former to preserve their prerogatives, the latter to allow unhampered industrialization. Most businessmen liked the protection they received from the bureaucratic State but despised the associated controls and taxes; of course, the *Junkers* remained wary of industrial development. Indeed, 'the needs of the industrial society that had begun to emerge in the German Empire in the 1880s were, simply, not compatible with the continuing dominance of a purely agrarian elite'.[191]

Regional Differences

Regional peculiarities have a historical basis connected with their past geopolitical association and institutional framework. Quite different from most countries in Europe, the single regions pursued substantially independent policies. For example, during World War I, Bavaria, a German state second only to Prussia, retained a somewhat autonomous status for its military units. Even though the role of the State was ingrained, it varied considerably from one region to another.[192] The process of industrialization did not trigger an immediate political shift of vested interests. In the United States, where the agricultural sector shrank at an even faster rate than in Germany, the farmer's political clout persisted even through the twentieth century, in part owing to equal state representation in the Senate.

Under revolutionary French influence the southwestern states Baden, Bavaria, and Württemberg went through a period of political liberalism after Napoleon's defeat at Waterloo in 1815. The German rulers of these states decreed (the *Volk* was not involved) constitutions that nominally (more in Baden than in the other two) included a role for an elected parliament and a council of ministers. At a minimum the new institutions constituted a watchdog over finances. In Bavaria and Württemberg the constitution protected only freedom of property while in Baden civil rights were extended to most citizens. In each case, while the ruler preserved monopoly on policy decisions, his actions were limited by the

191   Mommsen 1995, p. 48.
192   Lee 1988, pp. 346-367.

constitution that he promulgated. Ultimately, the above constitutions gave legitimacy to relatively absolutist regimes.

A vivid debate took place in Prussia whether to adopt some sort of representative or corporate constitution based on regional *Stande* interest groups easier controllable by the monarch than the *Volk*. Prussian rulers did not follow in the footsteps of the southwestern states and chose *Verwaltung*, a bureaucratic State rather than *Verfassung*. A representative constitution as a more efficient form of government. Prussia-Germany remained by and large a bureaucratic State for most of the nineteenth century despite the emerging of a parliamentary democracy. The Constitution did not limit the aristocratic-monarchical order.[193] Nonetheless, throughout the second half of the nineteenth century, the State played an important role in fostering conditions of innovation and development. The conflict between agricultural and industrial interests continued until the close of the century. The territory east of the Elbe River, like the *Mezzogiorno* in Italy, felt slighted by the central would-be policy decision-making, the German government decided that the State would have to intervene to ameliorate regional disparities.

The Expanding Role of the State in Saxony

Saxony let slip away the position of German leadership gained before the eighteenth century. Vacillating by changing sides in 1806 from being an ally of Prussia to one of Napoleon proved fatal for Saxony. For siding with Napoleon for too long, Saxony was penalized; at the Congress of Vienna, in 1815, Prussia demanded the right to incorporate the entire state of Saxony and instead was granted two-fifths of the Kingdom. In the aftermath of the Napoleonic wars and under the influence of the Physiocrats, the Leipzig, Saxony, commercial community, different from Prussia, argued for industrialization. The merchants envisioned a bureaucratic State to benefit the majority of the population; they also opposed monopoly grants, urban privileges, and guild control of industry. The guilds retained power in Saxony, and in Germany generally, long after they had lost it in Britain, France, and Italy; of course, the United States never had guilds. The dissolution of the guilds encountered strong resistance from the old guard, afraid of losing its privileges.

Saxony's economic development during the first decades of the nineteenth century differed from Prussia's or other German states. Here the struggle was between the central government and individual communities. Saxony tried to eliminate the guilds' power and to require greater loyalty to the kingdom than to localities. In order to extend the power of the State, the central government encouraged entrepreneurs in the industrialization process even though they opposed local community interests. In Saxony (and Prussia, especially east of the Elbe) the landlords undermined the policies of the central government and retarded development.[194]

---

193   Sheehan 1989, pp. 417-426; Craig 1978, pp. 39; 'The Reichstag's assent was required for all legislation but it had few powers of initiative'. Craig 1978, p. 45.
194   Tipton 1976, pp. 31-35, 132, 145.

When the shift occurred in textiles from wool to cotton, the State encouraged this transition and established schools to retrain workers. A 1715 Ordinance made the installation of weaving machines illegal; yet, in 1816, the Saxon kingdom rejected the hand weavers demand to prohibit the installation of one hundred weaving machines. The impetus of growth came from the textile industry until the 1830s when railways became the leading industrial sector. The Saxon State was more willing than that Prussian State to invest in potentially unprofitable railways to promote economic development. The Saxon metallurgical and mechanical industries developed subsequently as prime suppliers to the railroads, which needed rolling stock, such as passenger and freight cars as well as more sophisticated locomotives.

In 1832, Saxony was the first German state to introduce early and effective peasant emancipation and it also established the first credit institution to serve the peasants, so successful that by 1839 it was dissolved as no longer needed. Therefore, Saxony was well prepared in the agricultural sector needed for rapid industrialization. The signing, with other German states, of the *Zollverein* the customs union, in 1834 slowed Saxony's industrial growth; the *Zollverein* protective tariff induced the Saxon manufacturers to limit technological change and thus played a role in retarding Saxony. Socially, Saxony did not do better than other German states in considering the needs of industrial workers.

Industrial Capitalism

Before unification and the founding of the Empire, in Prussian Silesia, south of Brandenburg on the Oder River, such basic industries as mining and iron works had been government owned and operated. Gradually, Germany became an economic power, owing in part the overt support of the State for science and technology during the push for industrialization; military strength accompanied industrial power.[195]

The growing pains of German industrial capitalism associated with rising nationalism, led not only to the Revolution of 1848 but also to economic integration and political unification. The ideas of the 1789 Revolution as propagated by Napoleon were popular in the Rhineland and Westphalia; a consensus among historian exists that the population of these regions was not happy when in 1814 the Prussians replaced the French. The western German states sought to retain the French revolutionary institutions and the 'Declaration of the Rights of Man' that appealed to the emerging bourgeoisie in the pursuit of economic development. The Prussians recognized the advance of the Rhineland economy and grudgingly accepted the Napoleonic codes; Prussia retained the French commercial courts, which ensured equality before the law and facilitated resolution of trade disputes.[196]

195   Hallgarten 1974, pp. 30-53.
196   Tipton 1976, p. 67; Brophy 1998, p. 28.

Corporate Social Welfare

Both before and after unification, neither the State nor businessmen were wedded to *laissez faire*. Bureaucrats and others were concerned by the misery, presumably created by the earlier British industrialization. Since businessmen benefited from government intervention, they willingly supported the role of the State in the economy. The close association between banks and industry reinforced the State-business symbiosis. Business also aimed to co-opt workers by building company houses and exclusive company stores, thus creating company towns similar to those in the United States; Lowell, Massachusetts, textile mills adopted this model in the 1820s. Krupp pioneered in placing these settlements under supervision with strict disciplinary rules emulated by many companies. By 1914, the Ruhr mining companies rented 82,000 company-owned apartments at below market rents.[197]

Most enlightened policy makers believed that economic growth entails social emancipation. Major free cities before 1870, such as Bremen, Frankfurt, Hamburg, Hanover, and Lübeck underwent profound structural changes. During the nineteenth century, some of the consolidated states granted citizenship only to owners of enterprises or property; others were considered *Schutzverwandter* (strangers enjoying limited citizen's rights) without civic rights. Eventually, the *Rhenish Gemeinderordnung* (Rhineland Community Ordinance) divided citizens into three classes according to their tax bracket. Some observers call these developments 'corporate conceptions of community'.[198]

'Seehandlung', The Overseas Trading Corporation

State participation in the market was a continuation of the eighteenth century policy. The most obvious State action was the *Seehandlung* (Overseas Trading Corporation) created by Frederick II in 1772. The *Seehandlung* was a privileged State trading corporation operating as a mixed public-private enterprise, where both the State and private individuals owned shares; initially, the *Kurmarkische Landschaft*—a State credit institutions guaranteed ten percent interest on shares held by the public. The *Seehandlung* benefited from a host of privileges such as a monopoly on trade in salt in East Prussia, the wax trade, no import duties on Polish timber, landing rights on the Baltic ports; by 1794 it fulfilled certain banking functions and by 1820 participated in trade and finances. Indeed in the early nineteenth century this institution was more active in raising funds for the State than in trade.

During the post-Waterloo period among the bureaucrats who tried to rehabilitate the Prussian State was Christian von Rother, a Silesian, appointed to head the *Seehandlung*. Rother engaged in expanding the institution to shipping and industry. The *Seehandlung* built its own ships, and established textile as well as metal and engineering factories. All these State activities were not without critics, who argued that manufacturing and trading should be limited to private enterprise.

---

197 Berghahn 1994, p. 64.
198 Tipton 1976, pp. 69-71, 115-117; Sheehan 1989, pp. 102-103, 490-491.

Rother replied that the *Seehandlung* was performing a vital public service by providing capital to firms in difficulty and by establishing efficient factories in a country short of capital.

By 1853, in the midst of a financial crisis both *Seehandlung* shipping and manufacturing were experiencing heavy losses while some establishments were retained; the State sold most of the assets on the open market. But the *Seehandlung* continued to give aid to private firms; in 1866 a substantial loan was given to Krupp of Essen. Rother argued that the State should own or control public utilities and should assist struggling industrial firms to become efficient so that these firms could face international competition. Rother's experiment of cooperation between the State and private business was repeated during the nineteenth and twentieth centuries in Germany and other countries.[199]

The Zollverein and 'Libertaet'

Beginning with the post Napoleonic Congress of Vienna in 1815 when the German Confederation was established, German economic integration developed quickly. Dominated by Prussia and Austria, as the largest and most powerful members, the Confederation included thirty-eight independent states and constituted a purely consultative body with no legislative powers.[200] Another step towards German unification was the 1834 *Zollverein*, the customs union, which stemmed more from political than economic considerations. The *Zollverein* achieved its peak in 1868 with the adherence of two states that previously had not joined, Mecklenburg and Lübeck.

While it is true that the *Zollverein* adopted common rules of commerce within a single market, confusion prevailed in measurements because of the lack of uniform standards even though the metric system has been adopted in 1799 in many places. By veering to free trade in 1818 and joining in the *Zollverein* in 1834, Prussia could give the impression of accepting *economic* liberalism. Nevertheless, trade liberalization among the German states did not translate into freer trade outside the customs union. *Political* liberalism in Germany (*Libertaet*) constituted contested grounds; some define it as the common rights of landlords and local power interests against the power of the active State while others focused on the natural rights for everyone.[201]

---

199 Henderson 1958, pp. 121-146. Heckscher probably had in mind Rother's school of thought when he wrote that in Germany, 'mercantilism has never entirely disappeared, there having persisted a continuous thread between and the far more recent tendencies of, for example, "Socialism of the Chair" (*Kathedersozialismus*), the new protectionism, and the authoritarian notions of the century'. Eli F. Heckscher, 'A Survey of Economic Thought in Sweden 1875-1950', *The Scandinavian Economic History Review*, Vol. 1, 1953, p. 107, quoted by Henderson 1958, p. 147.

200 Denmark was a member of the German Confederation representing Holstein and Lauenburg; Holland represented Limbourg and Luxembourg.

201 Pflanze 1963, pp. 22, 81-83, 117; Nipperdey 1993, pp. 594-595; Borchardt 1991, p. 1-15.

The Bureaucracy, Culture and Education

Statistics vary but, a decade after the birth of 'Germany' in 1871, government employment, excluding the armed forces, approximated 648,000 and 815,000 and reached between 1.5 million and 2 million.[202] The aristocracy distinguished between the protective State and the bureaucracy that tended to eradicate class distinction because it relied on merit. Hegel had described the civil service as the 'universal estate', *Algemeiner Stand*, that is, an institution not tied with particular interests.[203] Some economic historians maintain that the links of business with the Prussian-German State '...explain how an aristocratic, land holding political elite retained power in Germany until 1918 in spite of shrinking economic influence of agriculture'.[204]

In the early nineteenth century Goethe, Schiller, Fichte, Kant, Herder, and Hegel dominated 'German' intellectual life. Yet these idealists were not identified with the middle class but rather with the bureaucracy since most of them were on the State payroll as university professors as well as in various consulting capacities. While hardly homogeneous, this German cohort valued individual freedom as a 'freedom of the spirit' not a 'social and political freedom of the citizen'.[205] To expand intellectual pursuits, Wilhelm Freiherr von Humboldt (1767-1835), Prussian Minister of Education (1809-1810) and a disciple of Pestalozzi, a famous Swiss educator, introduced reforms in the education system and sent teachers to study in Switzerland; he also persuaded the king to establish the University of Berlin in 1811. A new *gymnasium* (secondary school) was dedicated to classical studies. 'As a result he presided over a marriage of *Staat* (State) and *Bildung* (education) that would have lasting consequences for German politics, culture, and society.'[206]

So successful were the German schools (especially Prussia and Saxony) that during the Common School Revival (1837-1848), American educators such as Horace Mann visited Germany to observe the schools and learn from the German example. In both nations, although for different reasons, nation building was seen as one of the principal purposes of education. As a reaction to the catastrophic defeat at Jena, the Prussian cultural renaissance awakened a new nationalistic spirit throughout Germany and patriots looked toward Prussia for leadership. As we shall see, the same process unfolded for Italian unification where Piedmont emerged as the catalyst.[207]

202 Nipperdey 1993, pp. 128-129.
203 Blackbourn 1997, pp. 102-103; Mommsen 1995, p. 46.
204 Brophy 1998, p. 2.
205 Pflanze 1963, p. 23.
206 Sheehan 1989, p. 365.
207 After the 1848 Revolution, Prussia overtly or covertly exerted pressure on the lesser German states and cajoled without success the larger states, like Bavaria and Saxony, to form a unitary nation. Prussia's success in excluding Austria from the *Zollverein*, together with Prussia's victory over Austria in the war of 1866, was decisive for the future of Germany. Prussia-Germany succeeded in replacing Austria in dominating Central Europe.

The State, Banks, and Industry Symbiosis

The 1870s witnessed advances in corporations and banking and restrictions on joint-stock corporations were eliminated.   Also, in 1870 the *Deutsche Bank* (German Bank, a private universal bank) and, in 1875, the *Reichsbank* (the Imperial Bank, a State Central Bank) were established as symbols of the new German *Reich*. Immediately afterwards, a tug of war over financial control arose between Ludwig Bamberger, the director of the *Reichsbank*, and the Treasury, resulting in the State according quasi independence to the Central Bank.   Still, there remained 32 note-issuing *Zeitelbanken* limited to their specific state; these petered out by 1905.[208]

During the process of rapid industrial expansion, the German banking system played a pivotal role. The symbiosis between the State and industry was further strengthened by the intimate relationship between banks and industry. Bankers sat on the boards of directors of industrial enterprises and leaders of industry sat on the boards of directors of banks. This supports Gerschenkron's contention that in laggard countries (compared to Britain), the State and the banks substituted for private entrepreneurs. No consensus exists regarding this hypothesis in the case of Germany since there were many private enterprises flourished in Prussia-Germany, especially in the Rhineland.   Yet the close industry-finance as well as State-industry ties, especially in heavy industry, continued into the twentieth century.[209]

Theoretical Debate on Economic Policy

After the 1848 Revolution and before German unification, that is, between 1848-1866, the free trade mystique attracted disparate interests such as the *Junkers*, industrialists, and merchants as a basis for future Prussian hegemony.[210] The defenders of free trade were torn between a philosophical belief in economic liberal policies and self interest that required protection.

Two social scientists exercised a great influence in shaping the academic but not necessarily the public policy orientation of Germany during the nineteenth century: List and Weber. A German economist, Friedrich List (1789-1846), especially with *The National System of Political Economy* (1840), contrasted a proposed 'national economy' with Smithian *laissez faire* philosophy built around the concept of the 'economic man'. He contended that controlling and directing the internal national market could help to accelerate economic development. Returning to the core of mercantilism List preached economic nationalism and the protection of infant industries.

---

208   Hamerow 1958, p. 253; Kindleberger 1993, p. 127.
209   Kindleberger 1993, pp. 129-130.
210   Bohme 1966, pp. 16, 60.

List refuted Jean Baptiste Say's (1767-1832) theory, 'that the State can and ought to do nothing; that the individual is everything and the State nothing at all. The opinion of M. Say as to the omnipotence of individual and the impotence of the State verges on ridiculous.'[211] He accused Smith of advancing untenable assumptions by ignoring the very nature of nationalities, excluding 'politics and the power of the State', perpetual peace, ignoring the national level of manufacturing, and absolute freedom of trade.[212]

List favored free trade only among equals whereas the economy of Germany lagged far behind Britain's. Since the two nations were at different levels of economic development, List argued that they must apply different policies. Therefore, laggard vis-à-vis Britain, Germany had to protect its nascent manufacturing industries. In Britain, industrial development resulted from a combination of private entrepreneurial initiatives and market expanding policies mainly through freeing the flow of goods. He argued that Britain's free trade policies were a way of dominating world markets because of British industrial superiority. List contended that Germany should not succumb to British free traders and be kept behind forever while strongly advocating abolishing all trade impediments among the numerous German states.[213]

Max Weber (1864-1920), an influential social scientist, argued in *The Protestant Ethic and the Spirit of Capitalism*, published first in 1904-1905, that the northern Protestant population of Germany was achieving faster economic development than the southern Catholic population because there was a positive relationship between the rise of capitalism and the Protestant ethic.[214] Weber discarded the Hegelian idealistic dialectic analysis in favor of materialism but he did not accept Karl Marx's dialectical materialism that envisions economic development through class struggle. Like List, Weber envisioned an important role for the State in the process of development, but unlike List, fearing the political power of interest groups, he perceived the State more as a moderator than as an active participant.[215]

---

211 List 1991, p. 157.
212 List 1991, p. 347.
213 Sheehan 1989, pp. 500-501; List, 1991, pp. 163-173.
214 A tug of war developed between the Catholic Church and the nascent German State over the control of public policies. In the 1870s Bismarck considered the Prussian Catholic minority as an enemy within in the new *Reich*. After the expulsion of the Jesuits in 1872, Bismarck instituted a *Kulturkampf*, cultural war against the Catholic Church; he feared a great challenge in the Pope's declaration of infallibility in 1870. By 1878, the *Kulturkampf* came to a conclusion with the death of Pope Pius IX and Bismarck shifted from his dependency on the liberals to a more conservative stance. The German Catholics, accused of double loyalty, felt a sense of inferiority within the Reich, but remained influential in Catholic southern Germany. Blackbourn 1997, pp. 223-230, 261-263, 281-283, pp. 282-283; Carr 1991, pp. 134-135, 138; Dawson 1912, pp. 177-189, 199-200.
215 Bendix 1977, pp. 44-48, 86.

Post-1848 Revolution Social Legislation

The social gains from the 1848 Revolution were soon to be dissipated with the Prussia's reinterpretation of legislation introduced as a response to demands during the Revolution. This was not a proletarian revolution as Marx had predicted (the expansion of the proletariat occurred during the following decades) but rather an uprising of distressed artisans and peasants. During the 1850s and 1860s, German governments gradually dismantled restrictions on economic activity. In the post-revolutionary period, liberal economists preached *Handelfreiheit* and *Gewerbefreiheit* (free trade and freedom of enterprise).[216]

During the 1850s, the Prussian government made amends by introducing agrarian reform (intended to finalize the end of the manorial system), limited child labor, abolished the barter (goods for good exchange) system, and subsidized welfare associations. At the same time, under Chancellor Otto von Bismarck's leadership (1862-1890), Prussia-Germany continued to harass trade unions. When the Silesian weavers in 1864, appealed to Bismarck for help against their employers, he replied the State could not make a general practice of alleviating social distress created by labor-management disputes. His approach was consistent with the defenders of *laissez faire* who asserted that an interference with the 'natural law' of supply and demand of labor would destroy the economy.

Bismarck had long talks with Ferdinand Lassalle (1825-1864), a leading socialist, from whom he probably borrowed the ideas of social legislation and introduced them to forestall dissent or revolution. Lassalle was convinced that the liberal movement would not help the workers; in 1863 he founded the *Allgemeine deutscher Arbeiterverein* (German General Labor Society) that advocated the democratization of State and society. While Lassalle did not live to see any of his programs implemented, and his society dwindled at his demise, he succeeded in dividing the liberals from the workers as antagonists rather than partners and influenced Bismarck in his social policies.[217]

In 1865, Bismarck introduced a large-scale program of State funding for artisan cooperatives in Prussia and intervened on behalf of producers associations and cooperative banks. He also backed a plan for building homes for industrial invalids and attempted to change the tax code to shift some of the tax burden from the workingman.[218] Bismarck is attributed as saying 'The kings of Prussia have never been exclusively the kings of the rich'. On the other hand, when the Socialist newspaper *Der Sozialdemokrat* criticized his policies of repression, he did not hesitate to confiscate the paper and send the main Socialist leaders into exile.

Bismarck has been accorded the distinction of initiating the 'Interventionist State', while following a pre-established German paternalistic tradition. In this

---

216   Tribe 1987, pp. 216-218; Sheehan 1989, pp. 501, 734-735; Koselleck 1967, passim.
217   Shortly afterwards, Lassalle was mortally wounded in a duel with the fiancé of his paramour. Sheehan 1989, pp. 887-888.
218   After the fall of Bismarck in 1890, the government of Georg Leo Count von Caprivi (1890-1894) for the first time introduced a graduated income tax in an overall finance bill.

context, influential economists and university professors founded the *Verein für Sozialpolitik* (Association for Social Policy) in 1872 and derided the *Kathedersozialisten* (Academic Socialists) who exerted pressure on legislators for a half a century. This Association popularized the Hegelian belief that the State is morally bound to attend to the well being of its citizens.[219]

The utterance *Der Staat kann* (the State can) was heard but not liked by liberals. While Lassalle fought for unionization, soon after his death in 1869, the *Reichstag* passed a bill granting the right to unionize. The defenders of *laissez faire*, the liberals, regarded the freedom to organize as a fundamental right of industrial freedom. As long as unionization was prohibited, the workers could feel that wages were kept low by the State legislators who sided with the employers rather than because of the natural law of supply and demand in a free labor market.[220]

Starting with Bismarck during the 1870s, European nations gradually shifted from policies of poor relief to the modern welfare state. Germany mandated national health insurance for all its citizens in 1883, a form of retirement benefits in 1889 and extended overall social insurance coverage in 1911. 'Industry generally supported the welfare state measures of the 1880s...sectors oriented towards the domestic market tended to be more supportive of social insurance.'[221] Bismarck persuaded industrialists that it was necessary to have a dose of 'state socialism' to avoid that workers be enticed by 'international poison of socialism', and secure loyalty to the *Reich*. His strategy failed; by 1890 the Social Democratic Party, SPD, became the largest in he country. Moreover, some economic historians point out that while the social measures set the standard for other to emulate, their social and political impact and the benefits were modest and excluded many categories of workers.[222]

The German State deliberately did not adopt a *laissez faire* policy of the British type. While Bismarck often boasted of his economic liberalism, he argued that the economic doctrines of liberalism were the product of English clergymen, Jewish bankers, and French merchants and jurists and was meant to protect private interests while ignoring the public needs and ultimately the objectives of the State.[223]

Prussia-Germany was in the forefront in the protection of the young, regulating child labor, prohibiting the employment of children under 12, and limiting the employment of children between12 and 14 to six hours a day compared with a minimum age of eight in England and in France, nine in Bavaria, and 11 in Baden. By 1891, the *Reichstag* regulated working conditions; the employment of children under 13 and Sunday work were forbidden. Children under 16 and women could

219 Pflanze 1963, p. 282; Carr 1991, pp. 136, 164.
220 Richter, Adolph (1935) *Bismarck und die Arbeiterfrage im preußischen Verfassungskonflikt.* Stuttgart, pp. 252-257, cited by Pflanze 1963, pp. 118-119, 222-3, 228, 278-281.
221 Steinmetz 1996, p. 297.
222 Stachura 2003, pp. 228-230.
223 Pounds 1959, p. 191; Pflanze 1963, p. 8.

work no more than 11 hours; labor courts were established to arbitrate labor disputes. Finally, the Child Protection Act came into force in 1904, which under strong agrarian opposition excluded rural families.[224]   Similarly, in the United States economic and social legislation either has exempted agriculture or treated it differently; for instance, the National Labor Relations Act (1935) regulating labor-management relations exempted farm workers.

German Empire: 1871-1918

As a pragmatic leader, Bismarck did not care for those who believed in the automatic market mechanism; instead, he perceived a significant social role for the State. As an ardent nationalist, Bismarck's primary goal was to achieve a strong Germany.[225] Prussia's victory over France in 1870 gave rise to German hegemony in Continental Europe.   The constitution of the German Empire was an authoritarian society burdened by its militaristic and bureaucratic inheritance. The Empire removed from legislative control those institutions that constituted the preserve of the conservative elite: the army, the bureaucracy, and foreign policy. Germany lacked ministerial responsibility; the chancellor was appointed by and responsible to the emperor and not to the *Reichstag*.[226]

Industrialization German Style

Continental Europe took a different path from Britain and the United States in the industrialization process. On the Continent there were much closer links between the State and business.   The *laissez faire* advocates called for less State interference in the economic sphere but also 'could not bring [themselves] to

---

224 Hamerow 1958, pp. 172, 219, 235-236; Heffter 1950, pp. 246-267; Carr 1991, p. 164; Berghahn 1994, p. 82.

225 Prussia won the 1866 war against Austria giving him a free hand against France whom he vanquished and humiliated in 1870. These wars had two preponderant objectives. The wars would cause the reluctant south German states to align themselves with Prussia and the rest of the German states and thus permit the formation of the German empire. Also, the defeat of France would enable Germany to replace France as the dominant power in Continental Europe. Bismarck fulfilled his objectives entirely and more by gaining territory for Germany. Important additions were Alsace, conquered from the Holy Roman Empire by Louis XIV, as a result of the Thirty Year War (1618-1648), and Lorraine, annexed by France in 1739.

226 Hamerow 1958, pp. 57-62, 70; Pflanze 1963, pp. 8-9, 20-21, 45-46, 57; Heffter 1950, pp. 92-103; Nipperdey 1993, pp. 878-894; Mommsen 1995, p. 42; Berghahn 1982, p. 23; Carr 1991, p. 120.   It is not strange that Wilhelm Liebknecht (1825-1900), cofounder of the Social Democratic Workers Party in 1871, defined the Prussian-German system as 'a princely insurance company against democracy, managed by an efficient bureaucracy'. Wilhelm Liebknecht's son, Karl, (1871-1919), also a leader of the extreme left, described the Reichstag (the Imperial Parliament) as a 'fig leaf covering the nakedness of absolutism'.

abandon fully...the benefits and privileges that stemmed from state's long established as the promoter and director of economic growth'.[227]

Not different from Britain, the early phase of industrialization was based on the ease of capital accumulation triggered by the concentration of property and property income; the recipients of unearned income were potentially high savers. Market forces that allowed this situation were based on favoring owners of capital rather than labor by '...the rules governing conversion of feudal claims and obligations upon peasant land and labor into private property; the law weakened the guilds, the regressive taxes and the defenses against labor organizations'.[228]

By 1879, Bismarck had been converted to protectionism, apparently through a political *quid pro quo* between Rhineland industrialists and East Prussian *Junkers*. Bismarck was ready and willing to use the power of the State to achieve industrialization. Businessmen complained bitterly of interference and the restraints of the State in the market. Nevertheless, the same entrepreneurs and businessmen asked the State to regulate relations among them and between them and the State and also to provide institutional instruments and rules of behavior for orderly trade.

Technical Training and the Bureaucracy

German policy to propel the process of industrialization emphasized scientific technical education and research. In imperial Germany vital links connected scientific innovation, technology, the State, and industry. Towards the end of the nineteenth century, the State established and funded research and development institutes. On the contrary, Britain failed to adequately fund its universities and allocate public investment for research in steel, electric machinery, and the chemical industries. Before World War I, Germany had the best-educated population in the world and the best universities and therefore attracted students from many countries.[229]

The German Chambers of Commerce were public-private institutions backed by the State. These Chambers constituted officially sanctioned effective pressure and lobbying groups; by 1914 Germany accounted for some three thousand business associations, a united front against labor unions.[230] In addition to encouraging business association, legislation favored industrial and commercial development by taxing consumption and encouraging greater mobility of capital and labor. In Germany (as in France) the State civil service was well educated, even after 1850 university-trained officials became one of the key instruments of State building. Also as in France, the largest segment of highly educated people

---

227 Brophy 1998, p. 90.
228 Tilly 1991, p. 187.
229 Between 1885 and 1915 some 50,000 students from the United States attended German universities. Following the release of the Flexner Report on medical education in 1910, the United States modeled medical education in accordance with the German stress on research.
230 Berghahn 1994, pp. 222-224.

was composed of State functionaries, regional and provincial administrators, judges, professors, grammar school teachers, senior foresters, and medical health personnel.[231]

Business Organization and the State

While technical education progressed and the civil service was strengthened, business organization lacked the required management skills thus restricting economic expansion. An institutional problem was the State's limited chartering of corporations. As a remedy, entrepreneurs introduced the comandite organization that limited the liability of silent partners; this was a way to obtain capital funds for business ventures. Since this form of organization was not a corporation, it did not need to be chartered by the State.[232]

During the 1870s, the German empire aimed to copy the French *Conseil supérieur de commerce de l'industrie et de l'agriculture*, the Superior Council for Commerce, Industry and Agriculture, to foster momentum in the process of industrialization. The German State played a critical role such as promoting engineering education for the development of manufacturing. 'Not only was there a well established mercantilist tradition, but many leading industrialists in the early stages of German development ascribed a major role to the state'.[233] For instance, the Prussian government had supervised coal mining as early as 1737; legislation of 1865 encouraged private capital in coal mining. In Prussia-Germany, even before unification, as soon as the State stepped aside, coalmines proliferated rendering investment less and less profitable. With the encouragement of the government, a cartel, the Rhenish-Westphalia Coal Syndicate was organized in 1893 to avoid cutthroat competition. This cartel had an avowed purpose to abolish 'unhealthy competition' in the coal trade, that is, to deny entry and to maintain high prices and profits.[234] With the government's blessing, the cartel also practiced price discrimination, charging customers at home more than those abroad. In the wake of the formation of the coal cartel, the small collieries all but disappeared. After 1870, the State owned (operated or leased) a large share of the collieries and succeeded in having a virtual monopoly in the Saar, a coal-rich western territory.[235]

The German State chose joint partnership with private investors in electric power enterprises. As in all mixed state-private enterprises, even when a minority stockholder, the State could dominate the enterprise's policies and appointments by selecting directors on the board and controlling credit through State-owned banks. When private electric power companies did not provide electricity to sparsely populated rural areas, the State stepped in ordering enterprises to supply electricity to 'economically weaker areas'. In part to play the same role, during the 1930s

---

231 Blackbourn 1997, pp. 185-186, 209-210; see also Bohme 1978, passim.
232 Mommsen 1972, p. 363; Bohme 1966, p. 187; Hallgarten 1974, pp. 54-68; Brophy 1998, p. 90; Carr 1991, p. 134; Mommsen 1995, p. 117.
233 Kellenbenz 1976, p. 216.
234 Feldman 1977, pp. 21, 29-30.
235 Bohme 1972, p. 338; Dawson 1912, pp. 96-101, 118-121.

depression, the United States established, the Tennessee Valley Authority (TVA), a wholly State-owned enterprise.[236]

During the nineteenth century, Germany (and also France) had government-owned pig iron smelters. In Germany, the cartelized iron and steel industry, practiced price discrimination. Between 1870 and 1914 a symbiotic relationship developed between industry and the State; the State aimed at curtailing competition, even going so far as to make the *Kartell* legally enforceable. Bismarck was intrigued by the corporate State and the possibility of an integrated enterprise controlled by the State seemed quite attractive.[237]

The Ever Present 'Kartell'

Between 1880 and 1914 the *Kartell* movement flourished. The cartels became common in the heavy industries such as coal, iron and steel, chemicals, and continued well into twentieth century. With the overt or covert approval of the State, their objectives were to maintain high prices and limit competition. Imposing tariffs on chemical and steel products also encouraged the *Kartell* practices. This restraint of trade made imports prohibitive; it allowed arbitrary price setting since no consideration of supplies from abroad was required. By World War I, the *Kartell* groups were formed in almost all German trades and forced domestic consumers to pay prices above the international markets. Contrary to the United States, German public opinion favored cartels for eliminating waste, promoting trade, and enhancing German prestige. While in the United States consolidations have taken place, the law (Sherman Antitrust and Clayton Acts) has forbidden monopolies and restraint of trade; in Germany the law has encouraged cartels.[238]

While there is no consensus, contemporary analysts contended that the cartels achieved great results in the efficient organization of industry, in the regulation of prices and employment, and in promoting exports. But, of course, the consumers suffered most from these monopolistic practices. While the German *Reichstag* debated ways to control monopolies, the German government tacitly continued to support them. For example, it was active in the establishment of the Potash Syndicate and encouraged the Westphalia Coal Syndicate by selling all the output of State-owned collieries in western Germany to this Syndicate.

At the close of nineteenth century, public opinion was divided between those who pushed for control of the syndicates and those who advocated outright nationalization; nothing resulted from the debate before World War I. The State condoned and encouraged cartels as a more readily controllable organization form. Since there was no competition and the members of the cartels were allocated sales quotas, prices for the consumers for domestic and imported consumer goods were

---

236 In 1935 in the United States, the Rural Electrification Administration lent money at a low interest rate to utilities and farmer cooperatives to bring electricity to rural areas.

237 Dawson 1912, p. 135; Carr 1991, p. 139; Berghahn 1994, p. 245.

238 Wengenroth 1997, pp. 139-175; Clapham 1968, pp. 309-319; Berghahn 1994, p. 30; Carr 1991, p. 169.

kept high and, unwittingly or perhaps not, impeded mass consumption. Yet higher profitability allowed for larger business savings and capital accumulation permitted Germany to achieve a more rapid rate of growth than either Britain or France between 1870 and 1913.[239]

Labor Policy

In spite of the social legislation he initiated, Bismarck opposed State intervention to improve on the job working conditions, siding with those who argued that employers should not be hampered by rules and regulations. Before 1869, most often German workers did not have the right to choose their occupation or place of work. Worker combinations were therefore hard to bring about; unionization came to Germany only after unification, and as a surrogate, the Socialists succeeded in organizing workers for political action. When unions were established, they differed from the British trade union movement by being centralized and discouraging independent local organizations. While the State encouraged business combinations, cartels, it restricted unions. Also, the employers' federation used successfully collective lockouts and blacklisting to fight strikes and boycotts; despite this, union membership expanded and at the close of the century became sufficiently powerful to constitute a model for unions in other countries.[240] Even after the 1870s the German *Reich* always favored business and looked with suspicion on any labor organization; working class recreation areas were policed in the name of safety and health.

Contradictory as it may seem, German political liberals, that is, those who wanted more popular control of the political process, opposed universal suffrage. Also, based on broad *laissez faire* fundamentals, they were unwilling to confront social issues. In contrast, a growing segment of the proletariat was convinced of the validity of class struggle.[241] In the 1860s the government policy of benign neglect of workers conditions left business to act unhampered. By 1888, the reaction, if not swift, was brewing and reached a climax with a strike involving most of the Ruhr, the core of coal and steel manufacturing at France's border. As a response, after 1890, the State regulated working conditions and adjusted complaints before they exploded. The Labor Code of 1908 fixed the maximum work for women at 60 hours a week. In 1900, the French legislated the workday at ten hours for men when working in the same place with women. Germany still legislated 65 hours a week for men, not different from 1848. In the United States, the ten-hour a day six day week was the norm (not federally legislated) and some steel workers and hospital nurses worked 12 hours a day as late as the 1920s.[242]

---

239 Dawson 1912, pp. 137-141. By 1913, German per capita income was still lower than that of Great Britain and France. Crouzet 2001, p. 148.
240 German unions allied with the Social Democratic Party, which by 1914 became the largest political party in the Reichstag.
241 Pflanze 1963, p. 336.
242 Tipton 1976, pp. 128-129; Clapham 1968, pp. 404-405.

Conclusions

State policy towards the end of the nineteenth century, was based on the premise that a successful great power needs modern, efficient industry. The State was increasing its stake in the economy; between 1890 and 1913, the public share of the GNP increased from 13 to 18 percent, owing in part to publicly owned enterprises such as railroads and utilities, as well as the expansion of the educational system and the social welfare coverage. Under Bismarck, Germany pioneered in State provision for social insurance as well as an array of regulatory initiatives. By 1890s the working hours of youth and women factory workers were limited, labor exchanges were established, and arbitration procedures were instituted. While remaining anti labor union, industrialists and the State competed for the loyalty of the labor force in the rapid economic expansion of the turn of the century German economy. Also, the historical Interventionist State was expected to be a benevolent umpire.[243] Some economic historians would argue that 'Bismarck's heritage was a nation without political education and accustomed to submit'.[244]

With the help of the State, supporting coal, iron, steel, electric and weapons industries as well as other sectors, German economic policy achieved in a very short time an economic success not to be equaled until the opening of Japan.[245] Yet, by 1914 'the failure of the German society to liberalize, led to the growth of an overweening, strident, aggressive, integrative brand of nationalism, with all its fateful consequence'.[246] This economic success convinced many contemporaries to disavow *laissez faire*. The State was perceived as the 'ultimate guarantor of domestic stability, important at a time when the "social question" impinged powerfully on middle class minds'.[247] A new era based on the heavy hand of the State in the market place seemed to be on the horizon.

Italy

At the beginning of the nineteenth century, Italy remained 'a geographic expression'. For the first fifteen years of the century most of the Italian states were dependencies of France, which imposed the Napoleonic civil and commercial codes, but retained limited autonomy in policy decision-making. After Napoleon's fall, the victors restored the pre-1789 *status quo antebellum*; the Italian states had some new geographic configurations. The 1815 Congress of Vienna made some minor border changes; Austria acquired the Veneto in addition to Lombardy and also, by proxy, governed the Grand Duchy of Tuscany.[248] The major restored Italian independent or quasi-independent states continued to be the Kingdom of

---

243 Blackbourn 1997, pp. 345-350, 414-416.
244 Carr 1991, p. 145.
245 Perry opened Japan in 1853, the Meiji Restoration followed during 1868-1912.
246 Mommsen 1995, p. 206.
247 Blackbourn 1997, p. 368.
248 Woolf 1973, pp. 251-252.

Sardinia (Piedmont, Sardinia, and Liguria), the Papal States (central Italy, that is, the Romagna, Marche, Umbria, and Latium) while the Kingdom of the Two Sicilies (Italy south of Rome and Sicily) was restored to the Bourbon dynasty. Increasingly nationalism slowly emerged in all Italian states. Before unification the twelve component states fared differently economically; in Lombardy, the State secured control of the economy, and succeeded in raising incomes to the highest level of all the Italian states. Also, the State enacted labor protection legislation. Lombardy remained, both before and after unification, the most economically advanced state-region.

The *Carbonari* associated themselves with discontent and dissident groups, which affected Lombardy relatively little. Giuseppe Mazzini (1805-1872), a member of the *Carbonari*, was a lifelong Italian political revolutionary who advocated a unified republican Italy. He clashed with Camillo Cavour, the Piedmont premier on the form of government—republican versus monarchic—and on the State-Church relationship. Even though both were convinced political liberals, they favored State action to correct market failures; they advocated having the State invest not only in infrastructure and education but also in industry directly or through subsidies.

Italy remained economically backward compared with Britain, the United States, France, and Germany throughout the nineteenth century. Moreover, Italy with a high illiteracy rate lacked a professionally trained civil service comparable to that of Britain, France, or Germany. In most of the Italian states agriculture continued to be backward and with low productivity, industry lagged behind other leading European countries, and financial markets were, particularly before the unification, rudimentary. Regional differentiation of the natural and human made endowment, persistence of a post-feudal land management system, lack of an adequate (road and later railroad) transportation system, a tariff policy that favored the North, as well the not quantifiable 'cultural environment' kept the southern state-regions even more backward during the entire century and beyond.[249]

While no consensus exists, it is doubtful whether Italy could have accomplished industrialization faster without State participation. Even in the northern part of the country, the major drawback was the lack of coal and iron ore deposits needed for the iron and steel and metallurgical industries. The State imposed tariffs to protect the iron and steel and steel product sectors, offered subsidies and/or tax exemptions to entrepreneurs, and also relied on State procurement mainly for the military and the railroads. A triangular relationship was established among the State, the banks, and heavy industry, which fostered industrial development but also proved prone to financial crises. Italian style economic liberalism meant that the State was not only a referee but also intervened in the economy. Furthermore, the prevailing economic liberal philosophy did not prevent Italy from joining the chorus of beggar thy neighbor protectionism prevalent at the end of the century throughout the Continent.

---

249   Merigi 1994, pp. 119-128.

Economic Progress in Lombardy under Austrian Control

Lombardy remained under Austrian control until 1859 but exercised some autonomy in local economic policies although not for those that would negatively affect Austria. With the most advanced economy in Italy even before unification, Lombardy introduced social legislation for the benefit of the working people. The State regulated child labor but, as elsewhere, opposed labor organizations as interfering with the principle of *laissez faire*, thus disturbing the process of industrial expansion. It encouraged private mutual aid societies for the relief of the sick, the indigent, and the aged members of society. On the other hand, in 1841, when Lombard industrialists wanted to establish training for arts and crafts, the government contended that this was a State prerogative. Also, the State, (Lombardy with Austrian backing) did not have any sympathy for chartering limited liability corporations; instead, the State preferred the *societa in accomandita*, a stock company, in which some shareholders had unlimited liability while other investors had limited liability.[250]

The Carbonari

Riots and revolution occurred in Naples in 1820 and in Piedmont in 1821 connected with a social reform movement, the *Carbonari*; as a result of this unrest, the King of Piedmont conceded a constitution. The 1830 French Revolution found an echo in the Italian states, with riots in Bologna, Modena, and Parma, major cities in the Papal States. As the major Continental power, Austria intervened diplomatically and militarily in Naples to quell these uprisings. In Lombardy and the Veneto, Austria liberalized intra-empire trade, but instituted protective tariffs against France and Piedmont in order to direct trade towards the Austrian imperial market.[251]

The *Carbonari* movement had more of a romantic than a practical influence on what would become Italy. In part, this society originated with the secret Masonic orders that began as an association for mutual welfare and then split into sects, each one with a particular agenda. Many of these sects were considered politically suspect and did not survive government police scrutiny. In the wake of Napoleon's conquest, the French sect known as the *charboniers*, colliers or charcoal burners, moved to Naples in 1806.[252] In Italy, the *charboniers* and the *Carbonari* spread rapidly in all the Italian states. They were famous for their

---

250 Greenfield 1965, pp. 122-127, 131.

251 Woolf 1979, pp. 235-238; Montanelli 2001, pp. 283, 503; Campolieti 2001, pp. 307-308; Salvatorelli 1970, pp. 77, 90-91.

252 Briot, a French political commissary, came with Napoleon's brother Joseph to rule Naples. A charbonier, Briot came from a traditionally sectarian area of Franche-Comté, organized groups of crafts in sects of the 'cousin' type. Montanelli 2001, p. 290.

flexibility by associating with the discontent or dissident groups, preceding by a century the adage that 'all politics are local'.[253]

Mazzini and the Republican Movement

Mazzini joined the *Carbonari* movement in 1827; he was jailed in Piedmont and subsequently exiled to France. When, in his view, the *Carbonari* adopted clientelistic and corrupt behavior, Mazzini established the *Giovane Italia*, Young Italy, to oppose them. Since he advocated a republican Italy, Mazzini proposed a series of guidelines with a visible role for the State. These included universal suffrage, abolition of privileges held by people of property, freedom of trade, and justice made available to everyone regardless of wealth.

A great believer in cooperative enterprises, Mazzini argued that the State should grant credits to worker associations from funds obtained from confiscated ecclesiastic property, from unused lands, and from profits of State enterprises. Mazzini rejected 'Socialism' and instead proposed populism where the less privileged were under the protection of the State. During the mid-1800s, Mazzini maintained that there should be a connection between a republican State and the Church; he contended that the Church implanted morality in the politics of the State. His reform proposals included inheritance limitation to avoid wealth (land) concentration, progressive taxes, and public works.[254]

Mazzini opposed Camillo Cavour, the Piedmont Prime Minister (1852-1861) during the unification process and briefly of United Italy. Cavour argued that the State had an obligation to correct the market in favor of the workers since the employers constituted a privileged class. Later, as the key policy maker, Cavour fought for basic political liberties; a convinced royalist, Cavour aimed at the separation of Church and State but failed in his goal of an all-laic school system. His policies provoked frequent clashes with Mazzini and later with Giuseppe Garibaldi (1807-1882), a professional revolutionary and a key protagonist in Italian unification.

Piedmont's Hegemony during Unification

Located in the northwestern part of the Italian peninsula and the only truly independent state by 1822, Piedmont attempted to play the same role in the unification of Italy as Prussia in Germany.[255] Similarities stop there because

---

253 In the South, under Murat, the Carbonari defended the Catholics persecuted by the French regime. In the Romagna where the movement appeared much later, the Carbonari defended republican and democratic causes. By the 1830s, following the French July Revolution the Carbonari took over the city of Bologna briefly. On the other hand, after the Restoration, in Piedmont, they supported the monarchy. Montanelli 2001, pp. 290-293; Hales 1960, pp. 265-266.
254 Salvemini 1915, pp. 163-177; De Francesco 1994, pp. 286-287; Woolf 1973, p. 324; Montanelli 2001, p. 293.
255 The Kingdom of the Two Sicilies was also independent but so backward in every

Piedmont was much less powerful than Prussia and the single Italian entities were more backward than the individual German states; also, at unification, there were 36 German territorial entities compared with the 12 Italian. Nationalism surfaced when Mazzini and others (mainly Garibaldi and Cavour)[256] attempted to raise the metaphoric rabble but without success. Mazzini tried to imbue others with his fervent belief in Italian unification but few cared.[257]

A renaissance man who acted as impresario of Italian unification, Cavour also founded the Piedmont Agricultural Society, promoted railroads and steamships in Italy, established the newspaper *Il Risorgimento*, the Revival, and was Minister of Agriculture in 1851. Cavour's travels to Britain in the decades preceding unification put him in contact with the free trade proponents and he remained influenced by *laissez faire* philosophy thereafter. The king of Piedmont-Italy and the Cavour government were inclined towards the liberal philosophy. During his years in office, Cavour remained convinced that every tariff cut was beneficial even without reciprocity. He visualized a role for the State in public services and in natural monopolies; for instance, he did not hesitate to defend the *Banca Nazionale*, the National Bank, against those who maintained that this institution constituted a monopoly, which infringed upon the freedom of private banks. Cavour could not enjoy the liberal unified Italian State; he died in 1861 with the unification almost completed.[258]

An Italian economic historian argues that during the pre-unification decade a clear distinction between private enterprise and the State was lacking in Piedmont's financial markets and industry. It proved difficult to separate the individuals as representing the private sector or the State, since the economic oligarchy was superimposed on the political oligarchy. While Piedmont experienced rapid economic growth before unification, the liberal vision of Cavour seem to have failed institutionally in the midst of the industrial, transportation, and political revolutions because special interests distorted the market.[259]

Partially responding to the German *Zollverein* (customs union), the unification process began in 1847, with uniform tariffs for Piedmont, Tuscany, and the Papal States while the Kingdom of the Two Sicilies declined to join. Austria, of course, did not permit Lombardy and the Veneto to participate. On the other hand, there

---

sense compared with Piedmont, that it had no claim to being a force in Italian unification, even if it had had that aspiration.

256 Garibaldi had vague socialist ideas but, after being instrumental in creating Italy, withdrew from the political process. In most places, Lombardy constituting an exception, the majority of the population at large did not participate in the Risorgimento that was carried on by a handful of armed men, idealists, students, and mostly professional revolutionaries and politicians. Even in Lombardy there is no evidence that the bourgeoisie was the driving force of the *Risorgimento*. Greenfield 1965, p. 4.

257 More Italians fought for Austria at the naval battle of Lissa (1866) than for Italy. Also, nothing occurred in Germany comparable to the need for troops in southern Italy to suppress 'brigands'.

258 Romeo 1984, pp. 33-34, 134, 191, 239-240, 363.

259 Coppini 1994, p. 367.

were numerous currencies circulating in all the Italian states. Even after unification, Italy did not immediately adopt Piedmont's currency, the *lira*, as the national monetary unit. The *Banca Nazionale degli Stati Sardi* (National Bank of the Sardinian States) was transformed into a central bank as the *Banca Nazionale del Regno d'Italia* (National Bank of the Italian Kingdom) and, it was renamed in 1893 the *Banca d'Italia*, which absorbed the two Tuscan banks of issue and the *Banca Romana*.[260]

The marginalized masses benefited very little economically from the *Risorgimento*. Joseph Alois Schumpeter (1883-1950), an American-Austrian economist, contended that, regardless of the country, the poor owed more to the entrepreneur than to the reformer; this closely follows the classical economic idea that an economy must first produce before distributing. It required a generation of industrialization for social legislation to be accepted and to improve living standards, especially in the North.[261]

Economic Backwardness at Unification

Both before and after unification, the Italian states lagged Britain, France, and Germany. Probably, Italy lagged further behind Britain even more by 1900 than in the 1800s owing to the British lead in industrialization.[262] Italian agriculture was inefficient (low output per acre) compared with that of other European countries; there is a close relationship between agricultural productivity and industrialization since an agricultural surplus is needed to feed the urban areas and also for capital formation. As a whole, Italy underwent no meaningful agricultural reforms during the nineteenth century resulting in low productivity and low income; for most of the century it remained somewhat dependent on imports for bread grains.

Low agricultural income meant that there was a limited domestic market for industrial products. Moreover, the inferior and high cost of roads and the railway system handicapped both agriculture and industry. Also, no adequate financial market existed; stock exchanges were founded in Turin and Genoa between 1850 and 1855. In the South, there were only a few private banks and two public banks, the *Banco di Napoli* and the *Banco di Sicilia* with branches only in Bari and Messina. In addition, there were about 1200 grain-banks that lent to peasant farmers to enable them to obtain seed on a barter basis.[263]

---

260 Barone 1999, pp. 250-252; Kindleberger 1993, pp. 137-139; De Grand 2001, pp. 20-23, 60-62; Romano 1991b, Vol. 3, pp. 363-375. The Banco di Napoli and the Banco di Sicilia retained the privilege of issuing privileges until 1926.

261 De Ruggiero 1961, p. 371; Geremia 1961, pp. 618-620, 629.

262 The economic backwardness of Italy at unification is self-evident from selected salient data. While Italy had half a million spindles, Britain had 30 million, France had 5.5 million, and Germany two million; also, while Italy produced 30,000 tons of pig iron, Britain produced 3.8 million tons, France one million, and Germany 600,000.

263 Zamagni 1993, pp. 21-25.

Regional Economic Differences at Unification

Even before unification, the South was handicapped by the lack of physical, cultural, and psychological communication with the North; for the longest time, there had been no reciprocal exchange between the North and the South. The lack of roads and railroads impeded the development of trade; at unification there were only 99 kilometers of railroad track in the South, in the Campania region, and there were few all weather roads. Indeed, the southern regions were at markedly different levels of economic development.[264]

The Italian peninsula south of Rome, and the islands of Sicily and Sardinia, that is, the South, known as the *Mezzogiorno* or the 'Land of the Midday Sun', was especially poor, disappointed, and frustrated. The local variant form of feudalism in the Kingdom of the Two Sicilies ended in 1796 in the continental provinces, and in 1812 in the islands. Even by the 1850s, the South experienced a sharply skewed income distribution; if one accounts for rents and other property income, 650 baronial families and the clergy received 60 percent of the southern regional income. Sicily has been the primary Italian grain producer but yielded its primacy to Lombardy during the nineteenth century. Agriculture in Sicily was dominated by *latifundia*, that is, extensive farming with ensuing low yields; cereal yields were one third that of Lombardy. With low productivity, there was a very little surplus for exports owing to local food needs.[265]

Agriculture hardly constituted the only sector with problems in the *Mezzogiorno*. As early as 1813 the Kingdom of the Two Sicilies attempted to industrialize with State support. In 1822, the King assigned a Neapolitan worker to copy the French Jacquard loom so that the kingdom could improve its textile industry.[266] During the 1820s, the Kingdom of the Two Sicilies stimulated a process of industrialization by adopting tariffs to protect local industry, public procurement, and public management of iron works in Mongiana and engineering works at Pietrarsa, both near Naples. The southern textile industry was concentrated between Naples and Salerno but did not compare in size with the industry in the northern regions. Different from Lombardy or Piedmont-Liguria, almost all southern entrepreneurs and technicians were foreigners. Southern landed aristocrats preferred to retain their established modes and privileges and resisted change. The newly rich or quasi rich became this way just by being commercial intermediaries or *gabelotti*, mediating between absentee landlords and peasants.

No different from most northern policy makers, while having traveled to Britain and France, Cavour never visited the South. Yet, notwithstanding his economic liberalism, he argued that the State had to intervene by building

---

264 The regions were not unified in terms of language. French was the language of the Savoy court and most of the Italian localities used their own dialect. It is estimated that at time of the unification only two percent of the population spoke Italian as a first language.

265 Capone 1989, pp. 134-139.

266 Campolieti 1999, pp. 423-424.

institutions and infrastructure in the *Mezzogiorno* to avoid the perpetuation of two societies within the same nation. The common assumption was that the Italian South was rich in resources and that the Bourbon regime had mismanaged the socio-economy. As Giustino Fortunato, a southern political luminary, deputy, historian, and social reformer, remarked that policies for the South were based on false hopes and illusions '...all of Italy believed in mirages based on the superiority of southern natural resources without counting on the damage inflicted by the people in charge of those resources'.[267]

The State built the first Italian railroad, a princely road, from Naples to the royal palace in Caserta and then extended to Capua, more for the convenience and prestige of the King of the Two Sicilies than for economic development.[268] While Lombardy and other northern and central areas were nearer the central European markets, lack of adequate transportation put the South at a competitive disadvantage. The immediate impact of unification was an economic slowdown similar to that witnessed in East Prussia a decade later after German unification in 1871, and the pre-Civil War dualism between the agricultural South and the industrial North in the United States.[269] While in the north, Piedmont and Lombardy expanded industry and commerce, the southern latifundia absentee owners mostly used extensive farming and lacked any interest in industrial enterprise.

Most scholars observe that the *latifondo* literally a large tenure of land, practiced essentially a feudal system with tenants deprived of permanent rights to the land they cultivated. The peasants depended on the good will of the *campieri* overseers, in a labor abundant market, which kept wages low for agricultural laborers, most oppressed group in Italy. Large landlords rarely directed back profits into farming for modernization while the southern Italy standard of living remained lower that its northern counterpart.[270]

After, unification, national fiscal policies were sharply skewed against the South; land taxes inhibited agricultural development. The few southern infant industrial enterprises were annihilated by a relatively liberal tariff policy, which consisted of protecting northern manufacturing and charging low tariffs for agricultural products. Therefore, the South, which had little industry, had to pay high prices for manufactured goods, and sell agricultural products competitively.

267 Giustino Fortunato (1926) *Il Mezzogiorno e lo stato italiano*, Bari, Laterza, as quoted by Castronuovo 1997, p. 37.
268 Before the Naples-Caserta line, the State built a railroad from Naples to Portici, a suburb of Naples without a major road, and then extended it a few miles to Torre Annunziata, Castellmare, and later to Nocera. Hearder 1983, pp. 151-152.
269 Since the collection of statistics was considered subversive in the Kingdom of the Two Sicilies, we really do not have good data on the economic situation in the pre-unification South. Schram 1998, p. 81. True enough, the United States did not begin the collection of economic data until the Census of 1840 based on 1839 data.
270 Gilbert and Nilsson 1999, pp. 196-197; see also, Schachter 1965. A minority of scholars claims that: 'the latifondo economy...was geared to optimal and rational resource use...and by avoiding investments in fixed assets, the enterprise was able to convert capital rapidly from one to another'. Petrusewitz 1996, pp. 217-218.

But the South lacked a competitive edge; southern agriculture was inefficient before and after unification not only within Italy but also in the world market.[271]

Culturally, the northern bourgeoisie developed in the cities around commerce and was well educated. In 1871, 57 percent of the population in the North was illiterate and 84 percent in the South; by 1901, illiteracy diminished to 32 percent in the North and 70 percent in the South.[272] In addition, lacking opportunities in the private sector, the southern bourgeoisie gravitated to the public sector searching for secure public employment.

The State's Failure to Solve Regional Dualism

After unification, the State became the major non-agricultural employer in the *Mezzogiorno* encouraging a bloated inefficient bureaucracy. Through benign neglect or otherwise, the Italian State furthered this cultural environment inherited from the Bourbon era. This non-policy hampered the consolidation of the nation until the end of the nineteenth century and beyond.[273] The State might have become the great equalizer by building the railroad system in the North and in the South, but the financing of the infrastructure (rails, ports, and land reclamation) was proportionate to existing assets in the regions, based not only the size of the area and its population but also on existing economic activity. For instance, when the port of Genoa needed sizeable infrastructure work because of high demand, caused by manufacturing expansion in Turin, Milan, and Genoa, the State complied. On the other hand, since industrial activity in the South was at a minimum, the State offered little infrastructure financing. For the next century the State perpetuated through benign neglect, or worse, the steadfast North-South dualism.[274]

It appears that the newly unified State played a major role in perpetuating and re-enforcing the North-South dualism; the North-South divide was probably greater in 1914 than in 1860. The tariff policies, very liberal at the outset, changed to protectionist late in the century and created havoc in southern agriculture and, moreover, did not encourage pre-infant manufacturing. For a decade, southern leaders argued with at least some justification that the North exploited the South. Francesco Saverio Nitti (1868-1953), lawyer, professor of economics and public finance, and Prime Minister in 1919, lamented these alleged politics of victimization; he argued that the *meridionalisti* (southern interest groups) when advocating financial dole from the State were applying extortion; perhaps national

---

271 Engelbourg and Schachter 1986, p. 579; see also Capone 1981, pp. 134-139, 426.
272 Gaeta 1982, p. 3.
273 See, for instance, Schachter 1965, passim; Caracciolo 1973, pp. 686-689; Gaeta 1982, p. 181.
274 Pescosolido 1995, pp. 237-238, 293-295; Cohen and Federico 2001, pp. 26-27; Schachter and Engelbourg 1988, passim.

solidarity but more likely political trade-offs maintained special laws for aiding the South for the entire twentieth century.[275]

The Role of the State in Industrialization

The State enticed local financiers and entrepreneurs to open factories competitive with those abroad; substantial subsidies were offered but with meager results. The newly enlarged domestic market remained limited because of low incomes, inadequate transportation, and foreign markets that were difficult to penetrate. Plants in important northern cities such as Turin, Milan, Genoa, Venice, and Brescia as well as in Naples continued to have a higher unit cost than the foreign competition.

During European industrialization, Italy had many disadvantages compared to Britain, France, and Germany. A significant handicap was the lack of coal (that had to be imported from Britain) and iron ore, both needed for the development of the iron and steel and metallurgical industries. State intervention in the market helped sectors in pre-infancy; for instance, when in mid-century, railroad building started, and the mechanical industry survived mainly through State subsidized purchases. Railroads had important backward linkages, especially with the metallurgical industry, but linkages were not entirely effective primarily because of the lack of intermediate inputs that had to be imported. State spending on infrastructure projects had a great impact in the economy not only by creating short-term employment but also by encouraging further investment in the private sector.[276]

A latecomer, Italy lagged behind the early industrialized countries and, if anything, the gap widened so that Italy was further behind in 1914 than in 1861; in 1913, Italy's national income was only half that of France. Also, as a latecomer, Italy was too poor to have many choices; in its quest of becoming a world power and facing scarce domestic resources, policy makers concluded that the State had to take direct action. To encourage economic development, the State initiated large infrastructure projects, protected various interest groups, and granted subsidies to heavy industry. The State served as a moderator between the banks and industrial investors and as a reorganizer of an entire sector in trouble.[277] The State became a dominant actor in the market place; indeed, 'it would probably have been impossible for Italy to acquire a modern industrial apparatus without strong government intervention'.[278]

In the late nineteenth century and continuing into the beginning of the twentieth century, the State and the banks became the main protagonists of industrialization. The banks supplied the initial capital and participated in the investment decisions while the State protected private investments ex-post, directly or indirectly from

---

275   Cafagna 1989, pp. 208-210; Castronovo 1997, pp. 165-166. See also Schachter 1965, passim.
276   Crepax 2002, pp. 113-116.
277   Cafagna 1989, pp. 164, 377.
278   Amatori 1997b, p. 274.

the public purse. It is still controversial whether the banks had the support of the State to invest in industrial initiatives, that is, to copy the German industry-banking symbiosis. There was a three-way interaction among the State, the banks, and the real sector of the economy; this arrangement might have been beneficial to all but for the world wide financial crisis at the beginning of the twentieth century. The failure of a bank, of necessity, affected its industrial clientele and the State had to come to the rescue.[279]

State-Industry Relationship

The State has long had monopolies of salt, tobacco, and matches, and has owned the Elba iron mines believed to be an important supply source for the emerging iron and steel industry. The Ansaldo Steel Works, a mechanical engineering enterprise, began operations in Genoa in 1852 and the Terni Blast-Furnace Steelworks and Foundry Company was formed in 1884 with public financing through the merger of smaller companies; ILVA and the Elba Mining and Blast-Furnace Joint-Stock Company followed in 1887. The Falck family consolidated many small ironworks and by 1908 opened a modern steelworks in Sesto San Giovanni (Milan). By World War I, Italy produced one million tons of steel compared with Britain's nine, United States' 30, France's five, and Germany's 20. Italy's steel production depended on the fortunes of the domestic mechanical industries and indirectly on the armaments industry. The State often had to come to the rescue of steel and mechanical enterprises with financial support not only because of poor management but also because of non-competitive production; indeed, the first State intervention took place through financial salvage of these enterprises by the Bank of Italy in 1911.

Towards the end of nineteenth century the mechanical and engineering industry made strides; yet, the number of workers in the mechanical industry did not exceed sixteen thousand. While Ansaldo, opened in 1853, until 1881 Italy produced railroad cars but not sophisticated locomotives. Afterwards, the State or State-backed railroad procurement and naval construction provided the initial stimulus. The Breda mechanical enterprise was founded in 1886 and by 1890 the Breda ironworks was the largest heavily subsidized industrial complex in Italy. In addition to procurement, the State supported the steel and mechanical industries through high tariffs and tax easements, but tariffs made imports of inputs for mechanical industries more expensive. By 1910, the surge in industrial growth stemmed in part from the metallurgical and engineering enterprises that exported much of their output. By 1911, these industries employed two hundred fifty thousand workers, mostly located in the industrial triangle of Milan, Turin, and Genoa.[280]

FIAT, *Fabbrica Italiana Automobili Torino* (the Italian Automobile Factory Turin), founded in 1899 by a consortium of entrepreneurs led by Giovanni Agnelli,

---

279 Bonelli 1979, pp. 1231, 1236; Barbagallo 1999, pp. 9-10; Zamagni 1993, pp. 144-156; De Rosa 1982, Vol. I, pp. 34-48; De Rosa 1982, Vol.1, pp. 34-48.
280 Pescosolido 1995, pp. 287-288; Zamagni 1993, pp. 96-97; Barone 1999, pp. 306-397.

emerged from a multitude of small companies, to become the leader of the Italian auto industry after the financial crisis of 1907. Even FIAT had to be rescued by the State through the *Banca Commerciale Italiana*. Between 1860 and 1914, the weakness of the Italian financial markets forced the State, regardless of the ideology of the governing party, to intervene repeatedly to avoid the collapse of economically strategic sectors such as steel, and mechanical and electrical engineering.[281]

Italian Style Economic Liberalism

Influenced by Smith and British success, at unification Italian academia was a stronghold of economic liberalism that preached free trade and limited State action. Indeed, after unification in 1861, Italy adopted liberal policies; one need only recall that Cavour was an economic liberal and that between 1852 and 1859 the Piedmont government had pursued liberal economic policies. Italian economic liberals of the 1860s and 1870s proclaimed that only private enterprise should operate in the market with the State taking care of law, order, and defense.[282]

During 1860-1882, the State operated a quasi-private concern, the *Società anonima per la vendita dei beni del regno d'Italia* (Corporation for the Sale of Assets of the Italian Kingdom) to realize revenue.[283] The State sold much of the public domain to private interests, a policy that permitted further concentration of land holding by the already wealthy, usually absentee landowners, leaving the small landholder impoverished.[284] This in part might explain the necessity of public agricultural subsidies for the next century.

The Italian State inherited and adopted the 1851 Piedmont low tariff policy, but the component states had incipient industries that were not efficient enough to compete in the international market. As a result, the liberal trade policy was changed in 1878, under pressure from northern industrialists; protection was further expanded in 1887. It is debatable whether the protectionist policies adopted at the end of the nineteenth century helped or hindered Italian economic expansion. The consensus is that the policy damaged the southern economic expansion because the South had a very weak industrial base and inefficient agriculture.[285]

While economic liberalism was preached, and occasionally implemented, the Italian State was omnipresent in the domestic market. Not different from many continental countries, 'the government elite of united Italy adopted dirigisme and an active role of the State in the economy under the pressure of events rather than for theoretical reasons'.[286] Many policy makers argued that the State had to be concerned with the welfare of society and not limit itself only to defense and

---

281 Gaeta 1982, pp. 124-126; Zamagni 1993, pp. 95-98.
282 Remond 1997, pp. 35-36, 103-104.
283 Kindleberger 1993, p. 140; Clough 1964, p. 49.
284 Both the American and French revolutionary governments auctioned confiscated land
     to maximize revenue. Fiscal considerations overrode any and all other considerations.
285 Bottiglieri 1991, pp. 280-282.
286 De Cecco 2002, pp. 65-66.

security. In practice, the dilemma remained between protecting infant industry, and thus encouraging inefficiency, or following intellectually fashionable *laissez faire* ideas imported especially from Britain. Italian economic liberalism during the 1860s was affected by the nationalism of an insecure recently unified country. A very strong current flowed in favor of economic liberalism; however, after the panic of 1873 and particularly after 1878, State intervention in the economy increased in quantity and quality assuming a dirigiste mode.[287]

Italian style economic liberalism centered on the State, meaning that the State was not only a referee but supposedly constituted the engine of the economy. While German economic liberalism was similar, the German State was more effective due to a solid bureaucracy as well as a more advanced economy.[288] A nineteenth century Italian political scientist alleged that in Italy economic liberalism failed the test. The so-called Italian liberals included a middle class that was not independent since the members were mainly state and local functionaries, lazy absentee landlords, industrialists who asked for tariff protection, speculators spending public money, and politicos in control of the State.[289]

After unification political power continued to reside in Piedmont with the inheritors of Cavour's liberalism, *La Destra Storica*, the 'Historic Right' retaining power. The main items of contention with *La Sinistra Storica*, the 'Historic Left' included the influence of Piedmont, taxation and the role of the Church in the State. But the issue on which the government lost parliamentary confidence was the private versus public ownership of the railroads. In 1876, when Silvio Spaventa (1822-1893), a champion of a strong State, proposed nationalizing the railroads, the government of *La Destra Storica* fell. *La Sinistra Storica* promised to lower taxes on lower income groups but on assuming power encountered difficulties in executing its program because of the sad state of the economy.[290]

However, under *La Sinistra Storica* government, in 1881 the electoral suffrage was extended substantially, expanding the right to vote to the literate tax paying males over 21 year, and increasing the number of voters from about two percent to almost seven percent of the population. The law again favored more literate working class in the industrial north rather than illiterate peasants in the agricultural south.[291]

287 Cammarano 1995, p. 24; Pescosolido 1995, p. 245.
288 Barbagallo 1999, pp. 4-5.
289 G. Ferrero (1895) *La reazione*, Olivetti, Turin, pp. 10, 37-38, 42, cited by Mangoni 1999, p. 471.
290 *La Sinistra Storica* pushed for a secular State while *La Destra Storica* government supported the Church fearing diplomatic repercussions from such powerful Catholic countries as France and Austria. When *La Sinistra Storica* came to power in 1876, the dominion of the Church was confined to the Vatican City; as a compromise, the government allowed the teaching of religion in public schools and maintained the ban on civil marriages.
291 Di Scala 1998, pp. 131-132.

Labor and Liberalism

Francesco Crispi (1819-1901), a statesman who fought for unification and twice served as minister and Prime Minister between 1887 and 1896, was a leading exponent of political liberalism. Under his government, liberals attempted to emulate their British counterparts. As such, Italian economic liberals did not cater to labor, since they did not consider the workers worthy partners in policymaking.[292] Nevertheless, a serious attempt was made in Italy to mitigate conditions among the working poor similar to those that had resulted during the early British industrialization. For instance, in 1883 the National Fund for Insurance against Accidents was established. Giovanni Giolitti (1842-1928), Prime Minister 1892-1893, 1903-1905, and 1906-1909, was in the vanguard in proposing legislation that regulated working conditions; he had to cope with legislation enacted by his predecessors limiting the right of employers and workers to form associations. What seemed fair to industrialists hardly seemed so to labor unions since that meant the prohibition of collective bargaining. Since the State declared them illegal the strikes that followed were not successful.[293]

Giolitti accepted workers' cooperatives bidding on public works despite the opposition of business contractors.[294] Also, at the turn of the century, the Giolitti governments enacted social legislation such as the regulation of women and child labor, insurance for sickness, old age, unemployment, and relief for the poor as well as for the depressed South. Finally, in 1912, the State founded the National Institute for Insurance because the private sector could not or would not enter this sector.[295]

Liberals considered skirmishes between workers and employers a private affair that did not require State intervention.[296] Slowly, these views started to change but still a lively debate continued until the 1870s, when it became accepted that the State can and must intervene selectively in labor disputes. This went hand in hand with a shift in the academic world that became less attracted to the classical school.

Drive for Protectionism

Liberal economists such as Vilfredo Pareto (1848-1932) believed that the State's assistance in the industrialization process came at a price: handouts to rich

---

292 Castronovo 1999, pp. 36, 41. In an interlude, between 1898 and 1900, a period of oppression and loss of civil liberties occurred. The State suppressed recurrent bread riots mercilessly. Oliva 1998, pp. 428-431. In 1890, the factions opposing to Crispi's government met at a Congress and formulated the Pact of Rome, a manifesto for social reform, adopted in part by governments after 1900. Saladino 1970, pp. 64-66.
293 Gaeta 1982, pp. 149-150; Barbagallo 1999, Vol. 3, pp. 3-134.
294 Mack Smith 1997, p. 206; Saladino 1970, pp. 104-105.
295 De Grand 2001, pp. 20-21.
296 Salomone 1960, p. 86. Note that President Theodore Roosevelt intervened in the 1902 anthracite coal strike; in an unprecedented action he appointed a mediation panel and the findings of this panel resulted in the United Mine Workers labor union gaining recognition.

industrialists were paid from the State's general revenue and through tariffs which kept prices high for poorly paid consumers. Policy makers debated *laissez faire* versus protectionism; in 1863, during the debate over the adoption of a commercial treaty with France, one deputy, Carlo De Cesare, declared that the climate, the air, the sun, and the landscape, would never permit Italy to be industrialized like Britain and France. Therefore, in addition to a liberal policy, he claimed that one had to realize that Italian economic development should be based on agriculture.[297]

With the impact of the Agricultural and Transportation Revolutions, Italian agriculture, for instance, wheat, required tariff protection from low cost imports. Nevertheless, Pareto argued that protection damages the development of the national economy and favors the limited number of industrialists and financiers and through taxation drains investments towards parasitic ventures.[298] During the 1880s, a Western European agrarian crisis, resulting from cheap imports from the United States and Russia, among other countries, induced the Italian government to shift decisively from liberalism to protectionism. International trade was affected by a beggar thy neighbor policy, limiting gains, if any, from protection. At first, there was a strange partnership between northern farmers' associations, and, above all, southern absentee landlords; later, an alliance between northern industrialists and southern landowners favored increased tariffs. In pushing protective measures, policy makers cited the higher tariffs in Germany in 1879 and in France in 1881.

The new and increased tariffs introduced in Italy in 1887 were meant to protect the steel industry but impeded the development of the mechanical industries that depended on steel; furthermore, the high cost of steel badly hurt the railroads.[299] Although adhering to free trade during 1860-1878, thereafter the State resorted to high protective tariffs, especially after 1887, to foster a modern industrialized economy. Some tariffs were intended to be a source of government revenue as well as protection, as was the case in the United States, France, and Germany.[300] Earlier, Cavour had favored lower tariffs for consumer goods to encourage lower prices through competition in order to improve the real income of workers. Business people feared lower tariffs because competitive forces and diminishing treasury revenue might induce replacement of the tariffs with internal taxes.[301]

In 1882, Carlo Cigliano, editor of the Neapolitan journal, *Gli Operai* (The Workers), often ridiculed the idea of free trade, since every other country, except Britain, had high tariffs; he argued that a free trade policy is an anti union policy. Cigliano viewed free trade as the dominance of the stronger over the weaker.[302] One should note that Friedrich List had articulated the same critique of the British domination of the market through free trade.

297 De Rosa 1974, p. 15; Castronovo 1999, pp. 158-159.
298 Rosa 1975, pp. 1002-1003.
299 Zamagni 1993, pp. 60-64, 113; Pescosolido 1995, pp. 480-484; Bonelli 1978, p. 1218.
300 Federico and Tena 1998, pp. 73-74, 86-90.
301 Cafagna 1989, pp. 229-232.
302 De Rosa 1974, pp. 77-9.

Certain economic historians contend that the protective measures fostered industrialization and succeeded in integrating the Italian economy.[303] Others assert that it is dubious that the high level of protection at the end of nineteenth century accelerated the Italian industrialization process.[304] Some industries benefited from protection but 'the price paid by the whole economy in terms of misallocation of resources was probably high. It is difficult, however, to judge how high that price was.'[305] An effective national market did not exist during liberal period but coincided with the introduction of industrial protectionism and, above all, with the coming of the railroads. While free markets are supposed to be more efficient than protected markets, *laissez faire* policies tended to suffocate the technologically primitive family-owned handicraft-industrial enterprises.

Conclusions

United Italy aspired to great power status; many but by all means not all Italian industrialists supported policy makers who wanted to enhance Italian economic and military prestige. Both the private sector and the State displayed ambivalence towards *laissez faire* as well as nationalism that drove the nation into foreign adventures. Like other industrialized continental countries, during the nineteenth century Italy witnessed a symbiosis between the State and the private sector. Italian industrialists founded trade associations aimed at common action in dealing with the State and the workers. Some industrialists not only wanted to maximize profits but also to promote the glory of the State. Navy and merchant shipyards and metallurgy plants born with the assistance of the State, mostly around Genoa, became productive centers depending in part on the procurement needs of the State.[306]

Neither politicians nor academicians saw any contradiction between State intervention and/or participation and *laissez faire* when particular interest groups needed to be defended. Indeed, Quintino Sella, an industrialist as well as a deputy in the Italian parliament and Finance Minister 1862, 1865, and 1868-1873, argued that 'the industrialists have, as all other classes of citizens, the right to government protection'.[307] The newspaper *L'industria italiana* editorialized in 13 July 1864 in an attempt to clarify the dichotomy between freedom and role of the State. 'An economic structure can be perfectly liberal and at the same time the government can respond when it is necessary by its very nature of representing the general interests of the country.'[308] When he issued the encyclical *Rerum Novarum* in 1891, Pope Leo XIII (1878-1903) held the same position.[309]

---

303 Castronovo 1997, pp. 55, 63-64.
304 Gerschenkron 1965, pp. 98-127.
305 Federico and Toniolo 1991, p. 207.
306 Zamagni 1993, pp. 106-107; Crepax 2002, pp. 120-124; Bonelli 1978, pp. 1211-1212.
307 Cafagna 1989, p. 227.
308 De Rosa 1974, p. 63;
309 Wallace 1966, pp. 254-276; Kelikian 2002, p. 48; De Francesco 1994, p. 290. While Pope Pius IX condemned secularism and liberalism, as a follower of Thomas Aquinas,

As a consequence of unification, Italy inherited debts from the component states; it also confiscated church properties as well as private estates. During the 1870s a debate on State intervention raged; by 1874, the outcome of this debate under the influence of a leading Italian economist, Luigi Luzzatti, insured the State's interventionist policies. Ultimately, the State furnished social overhead capital to help overcome the understandable reluctance of would-be investors.[310] Some historians note that until 1900, public expenditures rose rapidly, taking an increasing share of national income; thus they claim that these expenditures were crowding out private investments.[311] Others note that while it is true that the State received a large part of the national income, the State not only subsidized firms but also instituted a policy of procurement from domestic business.[312]

Massive and guaranteed State purchases, subsidies, and bounties sustained the metallurgical industry, shipbuilding, and the merchant marine. A prime example was the State financing of the Terni steel mill during the 1880s to discourage steel imports needed by the railroads. Owing to subsidies, in one form or another, enterprises seldom made decisions solely for economic reasons; rather, they acted to obtain a better bargaining position with the government. In short, the State became a catalytic agent for the 1896-1913 spurts. Because of the State's role in the market, through protectionism, financial support to enterprises, and industrial rescue, private firms lost an important market freedom, that of declaring bankruptcy.[313]

The Nineteenth Century: Concluding Remarks

British nineteenth century constituted an economic liberalism and prosperity achieved largely through the market. In line with *laissez faire* ideology but also resulting from the full range of economic and political circumstances, in Britain the private sector built and operated roads, canals, and railroads; nevertheless, limited regulation appeared subsequently.[314] Telegraph nationalization represented an aberration not repeated during the nineteenth century. The British system of regulation derived from the premise that the State was and should be considered exogenous. Certain regulatory legislation stemmed from the common law, which

---

Pope Leo XIII participated in the Italian social and market question debate; his famous encyclical *Rerum Novarum* anticipated twentieth century progressive policies. He outlined labor management relations, upheld collective bargaining, just wages (defined centuries before by Thomas Aquinas), and private property as a natural right. But *Rerum Novarum* condemned both *laissez faire* capitalism and socialism.

310 Zamagni 1993, p. 112.
311 Toniolo 1990, pp. 78-80.
312 Bonelli 1978, p. 1236.
313 Amatori 1997b, pp. 246, 256-258.
314 What distinguished Britain from its counterparts on the Continent philosophically was an individualistic culture similar to the United States, and institutionally, a legislature with periodic elections, ministerial responsibility, and fiscal control as well as a legitimate opposition.

safeguarded the community from transgressors. Britain adopted some poor relief in 1795, which lasted until the Poor Law of 1834. During those forty years the poor received just enough to relieve absolute destitution in the hope that this would impel them to work. This reflects the rise and fall of the market economy or the tension between society and the economy in nineteenth century 'liberal' world.[315]

British education at the primary level became a State responsibility circa 1870. At the secondary level, the so-called British public school was hardly public. Also, the State allocated resources sparingly for higher education, which, among other things, limited the number of institutions. Science education became the target of much criticism because the commitment of the State proved so miserly as to constitute an all too easy explanation for the relative decline of the British economy in the face of German competition. British policy makers hardly perceived a relationship between State investment in science and technology and economic progress. While aberrations were abundant, British adopted economic liberal policies more often than not.

A similar process took place in the United States.[316] When several State ventures failed after the panic of 1837, revulsion at State investment took place because the failure of State enterprises (mainly canals) causing increases in the tax burden and the perception that some State investments were unwise. Again, after the Civil War, social Darwinism led *laissez faire* proponents to become strident. Nineteenth century American economic liberalism coupled with the limited government principle embodied in the various constitutions, shielded entrepreneurs from those who sought a general welfare state. Businessmen criticized those who sought government support but this did not stop them from seeking privileges for themselves and opposing any forms of government regulation. Overall the relationship between business and the State was pragmatic rather than ideological even though both adhered to a mythical *laissez faire*.

The United States substantially left the market to its own devices. Nevertheless, economic liberalism went just so far and no further; owing to the sectional conflict, the protective tariff declined as a result of the 1832-1833 crisis and thereafter the United States had almost free trade by the Civil War. Immediately after and until the end of the century, while praising *laissez faire*, the United States resorted to protectionism in response to interest group pressures.

As a departure from liberalism, the United States pursued a three-pronged development policy during the nineteenth century. First, the State enthusiastically supported internal improvements; second, the State financed public education, considerably more than Britain, because policy makers realized that, due to externalities, the benefits would far exceed the costs; third, as with education, the State funded scientific exploration to locate valuable natural resources; the land grant colleges and State sponsored research brought vast improvement to agriculture, the sector with the largest share of the labor force.

---

315 Polanyi 1944.

316 The United States has been different from Britain, having judicial review, as well as federal and state governments, which conflict and compete and sometimes have concurrent jurisdiction, and, above all the principle of limited government.

   Much more than in Britain or the United States, the French bureaucracy, aimed at self-perpetuation. In the process the bureaucrats made themselves indispensable and created a culture of economic policy from above, thus encouraging *dirigisme* as the accepted norm. The French State assumed a leading role in industrialization and railroad construction, but markedly less than Germany in providing social welfare. Critics proposed laws to correct market failures, but by the end of the nineteenth century hardly any legislation had been passed.

   Often dictated by political rather than economic considerations, by investing in infrastructure, the French State stimulated the economy through backward and forward linkages. On the other hand, not fully developed financial markets impeded the full-fledged economic transformation. Yet, the State did not hesitate to help industries in need through tariffs, subsidies, government procurement, and direct State participation.

   Regardless of political institutions, all through the century (including the Third Republic), France practiced mercantilist policies for much longer periods and more consistently than economic liberalism.[317] However, enamored by the British free trade example, Napoleon III imposed trade liberalization through the Cobden-Chevalier Treaty of 1860. France maintained a low tariff policy until 1873 when the worldwide long depression set in. During the 1890s '*Mélinisme*' capped the tendency of two decades of protectionism by increasing tariffs still further.

   Not that different from France, Prussia-Germany was mercantilist almost throughout the entire century and developed a powerful State bureaucracy.[318] The German *laissez faire* liberals, while praising Smith, contended that the welfare of society is not the summation of the welfare of individuals. They agreed with List that free trade could be maintained only among equals and advocated a protective tariff. This tariff policy not only shielded, probably unwisely, German agriculture from the vicissitudes of the world market but also fostered the industrial sector's challenge to foreign competition.

   In the same vein, the *Reich* not only allowed but also promoted cartelization, which encouraged large-scale enterprises with consequent scale economies. The State-business like the industry-bank symbiosis made it difficult to distinguish the interests of the actors. Yet, Bismarck's Germany was the first industrialized country to legislate significant social welfare programs; also, the State became owner of railroads and utilities. In the process of nation building, the State could be singled out for investing heavily in education at all levels and especially in

---

317 During the nineteenth century France had had a different kind of political turmoil than the United States, with a succession of more or less absolutist governments, the Empire to 1815, monarchy between 1815 and 1848, and again the Empire between 1852 and 1870.

318 While Germany had universal male suffrage, it lacked ministerial responsibility, that is, the executive (cabinet) was not responsible to the majority in the *Reichstag*. In contrast, in 1911, Italy, like France, had an approximation of universal male suffrage, based substantially on literacy and military service. Also, the executive was responsible to parliament.

scientific research, which in part accounts for Germany becoming the third industrial nation by 1900.

As in Germany, Italy witnessed a high degree of State participation in the market. This is why some observers assert that the Italian process of industrialization was not 'natural' (i.e., through market forces) but instead induced through State policies. While this remains speculative, these observers doubt whether Italy could have industrialized that rapidly at the end of the century without substantial State assistance. Although there are similarities between German and Italian style economic liberalism, Germany was by far more successful owing to a professional bureaucracy and a stronger economy.

Italian public policies directed the transfer of the agrarian accumulation to industry but capital markets were thin with narrow participation. For these reasons, Italian capitalism can be viewed as State capitalism even before the State took a direct role in the market place.[319] Italian style capitalism had the State as a willing player in the economy although businessmen claimed to be adherents of *laissez faire* philosophy.

The perception has been that the unification of Italy was politically but not culturally successful. Northern socio-economic culture favored free enterprise while the South, even more backward, expected State intervention. Admittedly, this constitutes an over simplification, especially since the North wanted the State to support industry with high tariffs, State procurement, and overt and covert subsidies. Thus, one should not maintain the illusion of a northern Smithian free market economy, either before or after unification.[320] Both the North and the South sought State support but the better organized north profited much more than the South.

Many of the individualistic principles adopted by the United States were borrowed or inherited from Britain. One cannot conclude that the rapid economic progress of the United States at the end of the century was due to *laissez faire*. Perhaps individualism played a role, but the matter is beyond quantification. Hardly a *laissez faire* nation, Germany progressed economically at the same pace. In 1914, with apparently far less State intervention in the economy than in Continental Europe, mainly as a result of being the first industrial nation the British workers enjoyed a higher standard of living and a much higher per capita income than the Continental counterparts but not that of the United States. The invisible earnings derived from investments abroad even if not accruing directly to the workers, seem to also have had an impact. In addition, British workers also benefited from an array of social legislation, which may well have equaled if not exceeded those available in France and Italy, but not in Germany.

---

319   Bonelli 1978, p. 1204.
320   Cafagna 1989, pp. 183-4.

Chapter 4

The Railroads and the State During the Nineteenth Century

The coming of the railroad represents the transcendent economic event of the nineteenth century.[1] With vital backward and forward linkages and thus a widely diffused impact on industrialization as well as a huge initial capital investment, the railroad proved to be by far the most important innovation of the century.[2] All this held true for Britain but with a unique twist; as the first industrial nation, the Railroad Age arrived in Britain after the first phase of industrialization and capital accumulation had been completed. Perhaps for this reason, the State, hardly absent (nor could it be), played a distinctive but a lesser role in railroad growth and development, they were regulated early and often.

While the Anglo-Americans and the Continentals have had different approaches to building, operating, financing, and regulating railroads, there were critical differences between Britain and the United States. Britain was the world's exporter of both manufactured goods and capital while the United States imported both manufactured goods and capital. Britain had ample domestic capital readily available, enough so that it exported capital, while the United States depended substantially on foreign investors for constructing railroads. British railroads connected existing cities, that is, essentially Britain did not build exploitative railroad whereas the United States built both exploitative and developmental railroads. This is why in the United States, especially before the Civil War, railway entrepreneurs relied on State aid such as financing and grants of unoccupied public land.

During the first decade or two of the railroad era, most people underestimated the economic potential of the railroad. Like most innovations, the railroad underwent critical improvements, which had profound economic impact. Locomotives became more and more powerful and switched from wood to coal and, by the end of the century, to electric power. By 1880 steel replaced iron rails,

---

1   For an overview of railroads during the nineteenth century see Huneke 2003, pp. 329-338.

2   Railroads eased the movement of people to such an extent that increased communication among places and cultures became possible. Since Roman times a trip from Paris to Marseilles took about one week under the best conditions. By the end of the nineteenth century the railroad shortened the journey to one day. Mass migration, but also mass tourism, became available anywhere railroads were built. While until the middle of the century only the well to do could afford a vacation away from home, the mass tourism era can be placed in the mid-nineteenth century.

increasing traction and durability. All these innovations incurred a tremendous sunken cost that investors and/or the State had to bear. The choices were not that clear, and all countries toyed with private, public, and a mix of private and public scenarios.

The ascension of the railroad starkly illustrates the dichotomy between Britain and the United States and Continental Europe regarding the role of the State. National traditions have influenced economic policymaking, and path dependence has endured. For instance, in France the State built roads and canals and therefore played a key role in railroad building. In the United States, while not in the national tradition, the State had a hand in roads and a central role in canals but, at most, provided assistance in varied form (finance and land grants) to railroads.

In contrast with their British and American counterparts, French policy makers never viewed the railroad as a wholly private undertaking. One can easily observe the contrast between British and American ingrained economic liberalism and Continental European public-private partnership in implementing transportation policies. In Britain and the United States, the State rarely considered ownership or construction of railroads, but always regulated them once the railroad demonstrated its economic power.

Continental Europe considered the railroad as a public service and railroad fees and rates were often connected with the tax system rather than a payment for a service rendered; occasionally, the State treasury administered railroad finances. Different from Britain, where private enterprise built railroads without significant State aid, in France, Germany, and Italy, the State helped to build railroads and other forms of infrastructure and thus established a claim to State regulation. During the 1800s, regardless of the institutional framework, ideology, and means, Britain, the United States, and Continental Europe achieved comparatively similar railroad efficiency.[3]

During the nineteenth century, the United States and Britain regulated railroad rates. In the United States the railways, like all other businesses, and until regulation intervened, charged what the traffic would bear. However, individual states acted to protect shippers and the public well before the federal government. In 1839, Rhode Island was the first American state to have a railroad regulatory commission and forty years later, in 1877, the Supreme Court sustained the strong Illinois railroad regulatory law. Britain and the United States assumed that if a railroad project were financially viable, it would attract investors. In France, Germany, and Italy, the viability of a railway was based on national objectives for the use of national resources. The Continentals viewed the State as the source of the public service; the railroad by providing a public service fulfilled this criterion.

Different from Continental Europe, both Britain and the United States, because of their institutional framework had achieved government stability and therefore have sustained long term policies more than their Continental counterparts. To be sure, in France and to a certain extent in Germany the upper level civil servants

---

3   Dobbin 1994, pp. 2, 114-115; Schram 1997, p. 17.

provided continuity regardless of who held political power. Railroads constitute an infrastructure that requires long-term investment and delayed expected returns. American policy makers sought means of financing railroads without interfering in the market process. The British stayed aloof from the financial travails of railroad companies while the French, Germans, and Italians attempted to mobilize domestic and foreign private capital with State control. In France, Germany, and Italy with more limited capital at their disposal, the State tried to use the railroad to stimulate industrialization, exactly the opposite of the British experience; Britain was already an industrial power when the railroad age begun. The overt and covert political rather than economic goals of the United States were to master the continent; the railroads helped to achieve this.

France, Germany, and Italy observed Britain increasing its wealth and power and therefore Britain constituted the model to emulate. By 1815, after the Napoleonic wars, Europeans resumed visiting Britain and were startled by the economic advance and attempted to copy the British, but they lacked the means, having limited markets and weak financial intermediaries. France had a larger continental territory, rather than a spatially limited island as Britain, as well as the legacy of a stronger State. Along with Germany and Italy, France had a smaller economy and less developed financial intermediaries.

Perhaps Adam Smith's most widely quoted sentence is 'the division of labor is limited by the extent of the market'; however, the State in part defines the extent of the market. To reap the full benefit of the railroad required gauge standardization; this could be achieved by the State or by voluntary action. Britain led in standardization by prohibiting in 1846 the expansion of other than standard gauge; France, Germany, and Italy adopted the same gauge to conform to British locomotives.[4] The United States accomplished gauge standardization through the voluntary association of the railroads although decades later.[5]

France led in technical and scientific education; during the eighteenth century, the French State established several advanced schools to prepare people for engineering careers. Therefore, France could employ the graduates of these institutions for the construction and maintenance of railroads. Britain excelled when railroads as well as industry relied on skilled workers rather than highly trained engineers.[6] For instance, Thomas Telford (1757-1834) and John McAdam (1757-1836), noted road builders, relied on trial and error and both were self-taught rather than professionally trained engineers.

Continental Europe pragmatically relied on private entrepreneurs for public works when they needed technical expertise and/or financial resources not

---

4   Puffert 2002, p. 287. At the beginning of the railroad era Britain supplied locomotives
     to everyone.

5   Kindleberger 1983, p. 388.

6   Britain underwent relative economic decline after the 1870s because, among other
     factors, it lacked professionally prepared engineers and scientists. Germany's success
     in the late nineteenth century is frequently explained as the result of public investment
     in all levels of education, from primary schools to scientific institutes.

available in the public sector.[7] However, the weak private capital market could not and did not mobilize the needed funds for such long-term massive capital-intensive ventures, since few Continental entrepreneurs were ready to assume such high risks, with industrialization barely under way. Therefore, France especially, but also the various German and Italian states, before and after unification, invested to accelerate the railroad construction lest they not have railroads at all at that time. On the Continent there were early railroad experiments as well as those used for princely pleasure, with no intended economic value.[8] After the 1880s throughout continental Europe the tendency was to secure public control of the railroads. Excluding Britain, European public policy makers argued that railroads were too important for the well being of the economy and the nation for the State not to get involved.[9]

Britain and the United States and Continental Europe differed sharply in railway construction, management, and the State's role. During the seventeenth and eighteenth centuries, France had used the State to build roads and canals while Britain employed private enterprise; the United States used private enterprise in addition to considerable State promotion or financial support. On the Continent, while granting railway charters to private interests, the State intervened, at times arbitrarily, by controlling routes, timetables, financing, profits, and rates; the State considered railway transport a public service.[10] Ultimately, as an economic historian argues, government ownership did not have an ideological content as during the twentieth century. 'In the nineteenth century, state ownership was not based on any distrust of capitalism but rather on more pragmatic [economic, social and political objectives] like…speeding up construction work and ensuring social and political unification.'[11]

Britain

Bounded by the seas and with neither substantial territory nor contiguous enemies prompting military considerations, private enterprise built British railroad lines considering solely market profitability. Thus, the first commercial railroad, the

---

7   Not accounting for the respective size of each country, in 1860, the approximate railroad mileage was: Britain 10,000, United States 30,000, France 5,000, Germany 8000, and Italy 1300 miles.
8   In Britain, an early colliery line, not a common carrier, operated in 1825 linking Stockton to Darlington. France opened a railway from St. Etienne to Roanne on the Loire in 1832, and a princely railroad from Paris to Versailles in 1837; in Germany, the Nuremberg to Fürth railway opened in 1835; and in Italy the Turin to Moncalieri opened in 1848.
9   Milward and Saul 1977, p. 42.
10   Schram 1997, p. 17.
11   Millward 2004, p. 22.

Liverpool to Manchester line opened in 1830.[12] Parliament enacted private bills chartering joint-stock companies as public utilities with the power of eminent domain. The State's role in the promotion of British railways turned out to be essentially passive, that is, limiting dividends and relating them somehow to rates, never acquiring rights-of-way for railways, but rather responding to entrepreneurial initiatives.

Laissez Faire Approach to Railway Construction

Railway policy in Britain evolved essentially by leaving all critical functions to the private sector. Nevertheless, by 1890, the government reluctantly outlawed rate discrimination and played a role in forthcoming mergers. British railroad operations, rates, and fares were closely regulated at a time when the rest of the economy remained substantially unregulated. Regardless of the ascendant *laissez faire* ideology, the State hardly left the railroad sector entirely to its own devices. If only as an exception, which proves the rule, railroad regulation was quite consistent with *laissez faire* economics; the later nationalization of the telegraph surely exceeded railroad regulation. Finally, path dependence certainly affected policy actions since the canals and turnpikes had been regulated already for the public benefit.

The richest nation during the Railway Age, Britain possessed a dense market and the most developed financial intermediaries, which lessened the need for State support. To no one's surprise by 1838, the four largest cities in Britain, a small and compact country, were connected by rail. Britain industrialized significantly before the railroad era, which reduced risks by assuring entrepreneurs returns from adequate freight traffic despite significant competition from coastal shipping. The mature capital market and the high per capita income facilitated mobilizing funds, with only rare State aid, for long-term but short distance risky capital intensive ventures such as railroad construction; also, turnpike and canal financing paved the way for railroad financing.

In most western countries, except for Britain, industrialization either preceded or else accompanied railway building. Since by the Railway Age, the monarch no longer exercised much political influence, railway legislation emanated from Parliament. The city of Bath, on the southwest side of England but within London's orbit, became a popular resort. Bath became a meeting point of the wealthy and the influential.[13] The railway enabled more people to get to Bath, thus driving away the gentry; the railway changed not only the type and the quantity of people who traveled but also the associated services.

---

12   This line linked Manchester, with only 10,000 inhabitants in 1700, but a booming
cotton textile center with 84,000 people in 1800, with the nearby sea at Liverpool with
6,000 people in 1700 and 78,000 in 1800.

13   In part because the monarch patronized Bath before the railway (Queen Anne visited
in 1702).

As the richest and most economically advanced country, Britain generated its own capital domestically, and, in addition, manufactured its own iron and steel rails as well as locomotives and railroad cars and also exported these products to the United States and Continental Europe. High bulk-low value products such as coal and cotton were still shipped by water. Owing to these and other factors, the State did not plan, construct, operate or financed railroads.

Since private enterprise first built turnpikes and canals, Britain adopted the same model for the railroads. The railroads acquired State charters and developed essentially uncoordinated and fragmented small units operated mainly by private unregulated individuals and/or enterprises. Planning railway routes was left entirely to private investors and the market. Although the private sector was able to build British railroads substantially unaided directly by the State, it has been estimated, ex post, that a more interventionist regulatory policy or public ownership would have yielded a lower capital construction cost and therefore a more optimal economic result.[14] Parliament debated accepting the railroad as an unregulated private enterprise or as a public utility, that is, a regulated natural monopoly. It decided that railroads might become State owned after twenty-one years but a Royal Commission of 1865-1867, citing British *laissez faire* market standards, disallowed this extreme proposition.[15]

Over a thousand enterprises constructed British railways with private domestic capital, which did not need public aid to prompt private investment because profitability seemed likely. The rate of economic growth as well as both the private and the social rate of return fostered rapid capital formation. On the other hand, the authority of the State asserted itself from the very beginning. Parliament granted railway charters in private bills, building on the precedent established with turnpikes and canals. The long term, intensive capital sunk in railroad enterprises, made it difficult for returns over the short term. Small private railroad construction companies were born with a high mortality rate. By 1843 seventy-one lines averaged 30 miles each, and only four years later, 647 railroad companies had been chartered. Yet by 1872, the total British railroad mileage reached 13,000 and the large number of railroad companies was amalgamated into twelve.[16]

Since railroads put every other means of transportation on the defensive, the government straddled the fence between competition and regulation. William E. Gladstone (1809-1898), President of the Board of Trade, and in and out of government from 1868 to 1894, advocated much tighter control over the railways than embodied in the Railway Act of 1844. Gladstone favored government ownership, if necessary, as did the editor of *The Economist*, Walter Bagehot (1826-1877), to achieve effective control. The railway acts of 1854, 1873, and 1888 assumed competition; however, the laws of 1893 and 1913 ceased making this

14   Foreman-Peck 1987, pp. 699-718.
15   Hawke and Higgins 1983, p. 184; Dobbin 1994, p. 25.
16   Splawn 1928, p. 191.

assumption. As a consequence of the change in public sentiment, the State took a stand by fixing maximum rates.[17]

Despite the dominance of the *laissez faire* ideology, circumstances altered cases and therefore justified regulation. To facilitate railway construction in the face of prevailing property rights, Parliament conferred the power of eminent domain on railways. Some entrepreneurs took advantage of the relative freedom to speculate; the British financier, George Hudson (1800-1871), gained the nickname of the 'railway king', managing many lines between 1844-1847 and during 1847-1848 Hudson was found guilty of financial irregularities. At its peak, Hudson controlled over 1,000 miles of track centered in York in northern England. Perhaps it is not surprising that between 1845 and 1849 Hudson was a member of the British Parliament (MP).

Railroad Regulation

British regulation of canal tolls furnished a precedent for the regulation of commodity railway rates. Even during the building phase, contemporaries criticized the *laissez faire* state policy towards the railroads. Opposing *laissez faire*, William Stanley Jevons, a leading economist concerned with policy problems, in 1867 and again in 1874, argued for more effective regulation. However haltingly, the State intervened on behalf of shippers, workers, and that always-elusive public interest.

Loosely responsive to the popular will, the State did not remain silent for long. The development of the British railway network was controlled only by the actions of the Special Parliamentary Committees, primarily concerned with the protection of investors. This was accomplished by a careful study of the likelihood of securing a volume of traffic sufficient to cover the costs of the outlay and the viability of a particular railroad. The Railway Act of 1844, establishing specific rules and regulations, constituted the first important general declaration of public policy and consequently deviated significantly from *laissez faire*. Among other provisions, this Act called for the purchase of railways, which generated a not well-defined excessive rate of return after 21 years as well as limiting profits and regulating rates.

Once substantial railway mileage had been constructed, that is, circa 1850, and the principal cities and commercial and industrial centers linked, technical and managerial problems surfaced. To coordinate operations, gauge, scheduling, and time, Parliament passed the Railway Gauge Act in 1846 and in 1850 chartered the Railway Clearing House to arrange through rates and, incidentally, facilitate consolidation. The increase in the number of trains as well as their speed resulted in numerous accidents and a commensurate loss of life and limb, which agitated the public. Regulation grew imperceptibly at first but finally, the Railway

---

17   Court 1954, pp. 167-9, 172; Cain 1972, p. 624.

Regulation Act in 1899, mandated that the railways utilize the best available safety technology, that is, signaling and braking devices, for accident prevention.

Railways constituted a natural monopoly and a network industry as well as a capital-intensive infrastructure. Since the public expressed objections to the railways charging what the traffic would bear, the State furnished a political response to ineffectiveness and market failure with regard to competition, safety, and rates. Until the 1860s competition prevailed with little State interference. Ultimately, Britain outlawed rate discrimination, blocked mergers, and upheld cartel treaties. Although in an ad hoc fashion, after 1867, the State asserted its sovereign power over railways. For instance, the Railway and Traffic Act (1873) granted the State quasi-judicial authority over rates and the Act of 1894 established a system of statutory maximum rates, never effectively enforced, to prevent arbitrary increases.

Call for Public Ownership

Certainly, by World War I, if not before, voices were heard alleging inefficiency and espousing public ownership. In accordance with the original railway charters, the State had reserved rights; the 1869 Act enabled the State to buy out all railways charters issued since 1844. Recognizing that railroads were different from other sectors of the economy, Britain accepted the principle of railway monopoly, in 1921, merging 120 railways into four regional lines. Nonetheless, the vision of public ownership, the absolute antithesis of *laissez faire*, did not come to fruition until after World War II, although under quite different economic circumstances. For one, it was a political move (the Labor Party won the post-World War II election), and for another, the motorways took over much of the rail traffic.[18]

United States

Constructing the railroad network during the nineteenth century in the United States constituted an extraordinary achievement. Both the amount of capital invested and the mileage built dwarfed railroad building in other countries, prompted in part by the vast unsettled territory, especially west of the Appalachian mountain barrier. For instance, although Illinois entered the Union as a state in 1818, for the next several decades, settlers flocked to the territory adjacent to the Great Lakes and the rivers, leaving a more or less unoccupied broad swath from north to south and removed from the waterways.

---

18   Dobbin 1994, pp. 158, 167-187, 195-197, 210; Gourvish 1980, pp. 49-54; Foreman-Peck and Millward 1994, pp. 4, 20-23, 81, 242; Brown 1991, pp. 238, 242-243; Bagwell 1974, pp. 169-194; Dyos and Aldcroft 1969, pp. 156-165; Paris 1965, pp. 1, 24, 202; Cain 1980, pp. 13, 22-23; Channon 2001, pp. 128, 230, 297, 301.

Eastern cities built railroads while western railroads built cities. Except for the first short lines, radiating outward from cities, which met the construction costs by selling stock to local investors, railroads added much mileage in sparsely settled areas or to transcend the Appalachians. For instance, the Baltimore and Ohio achieved its Ohio River goal in 1851, 20 years after opening and then only with the participation and support of the city of Baltimore and the state of Maryland. However, the state of Maryland, never more than a minority stockholder, left the management of this railroad in private hands.

State's Provisions for Railway Construction

The United States had unsettled land, which could be used to foster construction and, in addition, access to virtually unlimited foreign capital. In the short run, the availability of land did not aid railroad construction since it could be sold only after construction and not before; still, land grants helped entrepreneurs issue bonds more readily with the land as collateral. Railroad construction, in a place and at a time when neither the anticipated private rate of return nor the expected social rate of return seemed promising, needed encouragement. The federal government provided massive land grants and other subsidies to the so-called transcontinental lines, from west of the Mississippi River to the Pacific Ocean. These and other developmental lines frequently required decades of economic growth to generate adequate traffic to cover operating costs, much less the payment of interest on the bonded debt and especially the repayment of the principal. Before the Civil War, the State provided one third of railroad investment and between 1865-1890, ten to 15 percent.

Private Entrepreneurs and Foreign Investors

Private enterprise built the first railroads in Minnesota during the 1850s with the government of Minnesota using state land grants to stimulate construction by luring private investors. However, not until the late seventies did profitability ensue for the Minnesota railroads. Owing to the immensity of the task and the competing demands for capital, much of the investment for American railroad building came from abroad, mostly Britain and to a lesser extent the Netherlands, typically obtained by selling thirty-year bonds; foreign capital was mostly passive, but became active during financial crises. The United States supplied its own entrepreneurs, managers, and technicians but despite the high tariff until 1866, only 40 percent of American rail iron came from domestic sources, with the rest imported from Britain.

Foreign investment enabled United States railroads to be built a generation or so sooner than otherwise would have been the case. Only the exploitive dowager railroads in New England could be built with local capital. All larger developmental railroads needed help, initially from the domestic capital market (Boston, New York, and Philadelphia) and then from abroad. British financiers in the 1870s founded the equivalent of mutual funds to sell United States railroad bonds to British financial institutions as well as individuals.

Transcontinental Railroads

Inside construction companies siphoned off profits at the expense of other investors. The Credit Mobilier of America (Union Pacific) is but the most famous (or infamous) of the inside construction companies; this type of manipulation was used widely before John Murray Forbes drove away the offending insiders from the Chicago, Burlington & Quincy Railroad in 1875. Insiders could use their names, assets, and reputation for the good of the railroad, which as a new corporation with limited liability might have trouble borrowing. However, investors generally were wary of railroads with inside construction companies because the insiders could abuse their position. For instance, Oakes Ames, a shovel manufacturer and a director of the Credit Mobilier, amassed a fortune by selling shovels to the Union Pacific.

The Union Pacific Railroad, together with the Central Pacific, went through an extraordinary saga. Eastern financiers who started it, like virtually everyone else, decided to make use of a construction company. When they were refused a charter in Connecticut, they chose a Pennsylvania corporation, the Pennsylvania Fiscal Agency, chartered to build railroads south and west. Later this enterprise changed its name to Credit Mobilier, a limited liability stock company. By having limited liability, it could sell shares more easily on the open market, financing the Union Pacific Railroad in this way. A scandal of potential bribery fermented and burst open when it was reported that congressmen, who owned Credit Mobilier stock, attempted to legislate some favorable terms for that corporation. In addition, the financial markets were in tumult because of stock manipulation of the two interconnected corporations, the Union Pacific and the Credit Mobilier. By inflating construction costs, insiders loaded the railroad with bonded indebtedness. The federal government turned a blind eye to such proceedings, assuming that inaction was the expected norm. While the disturbance died out once the building contract was completed, this scandal remained the most infamous episode of the American Railroad Age.[19]

Railroad building constituted only the latest in the succession of other investments for internal improvement. For the most part, roads could be financed locally and steamboats cost little enough so that a mere handful of investors could place a steamboat on navigable rivers. However, canals and roads were quite different from railroads in their construction requirements like the Erie Canal cost millions, quite a large sum for that era.[20] Finally, owing to the level of development of the American economy, including the financial intermediaries, the

19   White 1973, pp. 21, 22, 77-80; Fogel 1960, pp. 17, 53, 79.
20   Note that the Second Bank of the United States (1816-1836) had a capital of $35,000,000.

State, that is, local, state, and federal governments, played a much larger proportionate role in the provision of capital earlier (roads and canals) than later (railroads). The depression of 1837-1843 led many states to withdraw from public ventures in railroad ownership; some state constitutions even prohibited such public investment.[21]

Land Grants

By the mid-1870s, with tens of thousands of miles of line in operation, the State gradually withdrew from railroad financing while the capital market surged to the fore. As always during a depression, failure discouraged public investment; entrepreneurs and investors customarily preferred, if possible, to go it alone but resorted to the State as the next best alternative. The vast open land was a great resource, enabling the federal government and the individual states to back railroad construction. When the policy makers realized that railroads could serve as a strategic tool to economically and politically consolidate the nation, local, state, and federal governments did not hesitate to grant land to would-be entrepreneurs to encourage railroad construction. Since this raw unsettled and untilled land possessed little market value, railroads competed with the free or almost free land available from the State as well as with each other.[22]

Land grant railroads maintained land departments to sell land as quickly as possible. Railroads used advertising as well as other means of promotion to entice settlers, such as selling farm sites at low prices and lending on easy terms and at low interest rates; if farmers prospered, railroads prospered. Railroads had to decide whether they were in the railroad transportation business or in the real estate business; after indecision, they opted invariably to become transportation companies.

In 1850, the Illinois Central became the first railroad to receive a federal land grant. The Illinois Central land grant owed much to the political power of Stephen Douglas, senator from Illinois and Chairman of the Senate Committee on Territories. To secure the necessary political support for the measure, similar grants had to be made available for a railroad from the Ohio River to Mobile, Alabama. Thereafter, the federal government allotted land to any railway project in a region where the federal government still owned land. Representatives from western and Gulf states could not, by themselves, muster enough votes, but with considerable eastern support, the bill became law. Douglas and others made large investments, in land in the outskirts of Chicago, in the hope that the land would appreciate in value when it became part of metropolitan Chicago, and this eventually happened.

---

21   Goodrich 1968, pp. 365-383; Goodrich 1950b, pp. 145-169.
22   The Homestead Act (1862) granted land to settlers. For the short run, this law did not have a great impact because the incentive of free land versus $1.25 an acre was not really as important as location in relation to towns, water, land fertility, and security.

Up to the 1870s, the State partly financed railroads with land grants. These railroads used some of the land for construction but mostly for would-be town sites. Since the supply of cheaply available land was overwhelming throughout the nineteenth century, the railway companies benefited little financially from the sale of land. During this period, the railroads indirectly received 49 million acres through land grants to the states. Another 155 million acres were granted directly to the railroads, 75 percent of which helped to build the transcontinental lines. Usually the amount of government aid tended to vary inversely with the anticipated profitability and risk of the routes. In some instances, states had several potential entrepreneurial suitors and could strike a good bargain, while in other cases states faced great difficulty finding anyone who would undertake the task. Giving away the public domain wound down during the 1870s after the completion of the transcontinental railroads, even though the Northern Pacific Railway was completed in 1883 and the 'frontier' was declared closed in 1890; the Northern Pacific had received a land grant earlier but land was transferred only after construction. The State (at all levels of government) became less important in providing railroad capital than it had been with canals earlier.

More railway mileage was constructed during the 1880s than in any other decade.[23] By 1890, the American railroad network was virtually complete although still more mileage was added before peaking around World War I. Railroad consolidation in various forms reduced the number of separate railroad enterprises substantially, which facilitated railroad financing. Only somewhat related to railroad financing, consolidation frequently took place between completed or substantially completed railroads. For example, the New York Central (1853) merged half a dozen or so short lines between Albany and Buffalo. Consolidation occurred between end-to-end railroads or parallel railroads or competing railroads whether parallel or not. This consolidation process altered the role of the State, which began to shift from promotion to regulation with the passing of the heroic age of railroad building.

The Lack of Common Railway Policy

Since the multitude of disparate political entities vied with each other in economic and political prowess, a common railway policy could hardly be said to have evolved. While some of the growing number of states managed, through shrewd manipulation or subsidies or other forms of aid, to retain a firm grip on the money spigot, and therefore to formulate a significantly railroad policy, others conceded to the force of the market. For example, before the Civil War, Georgia adhered to the 'chosen instrument' principle, subsidizing a single strategic railroad. In contrast, Virginia appeased the political pressures within the State by supporting several railroads. In any event, few states or localities actually performed the

---

23   Railroad mileage constructed in the United States totaled: 30,000 by 1860, 35,000 by
      1870, 93,000 by 1880, and 166,000 by 1890.

entrepreneurial function and then only partially or temporarily. The last settled of the original Thirteen Colonies, Georgia owned and managed the Western and Atlantic Railroad from the Atlantic Ocean to Chattanooga, Tennessee, before the Civil War.

By the mid 1830s, the Michigan territory had enough people to apply for admission to the Union. Michigan was admitted in 1837 and by the 1850s, except for the northern sections, had passed from the frontier stage. During the 1830s Michigan initiated the construction of the Michigan Central and the Michigan Southern, private enterprise proved unequal to the task of building developmental railroads in such a sparsely populated state. Owing to its financial difficulties, the state of Michigan in 1846 sold the Michigan Central, a profitable railroad, to John Murray Forbes and other Boston investors. They infused eastern capital as well as excellent management into the Michigan Central and absorbed this local line into what later became the Chicago, Burlington & Quincy. The Michigan Southern became the first railroad to connect Chicago with the East Coast; but, the state of Michigan decided to quit the railway business and sold Michigan Southern to a Detroit financier, Elisha Litchfield, and New York investors.[24]

Barring the exceptional such as the railroad in the Panama Canal Zone, built and operated by the federal government, the State left the initiative to promoters, local or otherwise. Only with regard to the limited number of federal land grant railroads, did the federal government exercise an influence on railroad routes. Here, too, the federal government had to woo entrepreneurs and investors by making the terms sufficiently attractive, compared with alternative investment opportunities. In these cases, management made innumerable mid-level decisions that cumulatively represented policy.

A railway plan, that is, a single plan or even a constellation of documents or maps, never existed. The United States gave the market control of the railroad sector during the expansion phase. The State assumed that competition would induce efficiency in all sectors including transportation; thus, the market system provided coordination without a coordinator. Local and state, that is, sub national governments as well as the federal government exercised no more than a subsidiary role. The same held true for railroad finance; the more highly developed the capital market and the more the railroads passed through the pioneering stage, the smaller the public share of the capital supplied.

The State, in particular the federal government, did not take any action concerning pricing and competition during the first phase of the railroad era, assuming that railroads operated in a competitive market. Until the late nineteenth century policy makers did not recognize that railroads constituted natural monopolies. Yet, an oligopolistic rather than a competitive market held sway. Some routes had only a single railroad, and even the Chicago to the Atlantic coast route had only four main lines.

---

24   Taylor 1951, pp. 91, 100; Goodrich 1960, p. 145.

Railroad Regulation

Many United States railroads failed after the panics of 1873, 1884, and 1893. During the 1873-1896 long depression, a period of falling prices and profitless prosperity, firms in all industries struggled to survive and failure became endemic.[25] Railroads, like the earlier iron and steel and oil industries, promised increasing returns to scale and thus, regardless of antitrust legislation, witnessed concentration.[26] First, the state governments (1839 and after) and then later the federal government, in the desire to reinforce the market mechanism, interceded with regard to both pricing and competition. The *Munn vs. Illinois* (1877) and the *Wabash* (1886) cases, although the issues differed, induced the United States, in 1887, to pass the Act to Regulate Commerce that established the Interstate Commerce Commission (ICC). The Hepburn Act (1906) raised questions concerning the implementation and the interpretation of the law.

The Hepburn Act reflected popular dissatisfaction with the judicial interpretation of freight rate discrimination just as the Clayton Act (1914) reflected popular dissatisfaction with the judicial interpretation of the 1890 Sherman Antitrust Act. The Hepburn Act stated that rates must be 'just and reasonable'. To clarify certain powers delegated by Congress, in 1887 both the ICC and the railroads took the points in dispute to court and sought new legislation, especially regarding the issue of price discrimination. In the disagreements between shippers and railroads the law used an adversarial system with no assumed public interest. (In the United States and Britain juries decide matter of fact whereas in France, Germany, and Italy judges render this decision). The 'public utility' principle had been well established in the United States, certainly from *Munn vs. Illinois* (1877). The key phrase in that ruling 'affected with a public interest', proved decisive until the mid-1930s.

The long haul-short haul controversy, as much as or more than any other factor, prompted federal government regulation in a vain effort by the South to establish a rate making principle based on distance, thus disregarding the significance of overhead cost for railroad pricing. In short, the State established and enforced the game's rules. Parenthetically, even after regulation, the Chicago-East Coast route represented the standard; points in the South equidistant from Chicago, but with much less freight traffic, continued to confront a cost-based rate differential, hence this was not judged to be illustrations of unjust discrimination.[27]

---

25   For instance, small-scale oil and iron and steel enterprises proved helpless in their attempts to compete with the Rockefellers and the Carnegies. Similar and later consolidation occurred in the United States auto industry. Between the late 1890s and 1929, hundred of companies were organized to produce autos; in 1929, six auto companies survived, of which three were responsible for 90 percent of the output.
26   Of course, railroads had a unique problem; if route selection proved incorrect, the railroad company was stuck with an inferior route.
27   Poole and Rosenthal 1993, pp. 837, 851.

Conclusions

With hundreds of individual railroads, each managed independently for the benefit of its managers, stockholders, and creditors, the railroads effectively set technical managerial standards. The demand for civil and mechanical engineers was overwhelming; for a while Britain supplied railroad technicians to everyone, and later France and Germany furnished them to Italy. Some civil engineers in the United States, as elsewhere, were self-educated or learned on the job, augmented by a supply of engineers graduated from the public institutions of higher education including the United States Military Academy established in 1802, and the United States Naval Academy (1845), as well as from the private ones such as Norwich University (1819), and Rensselaer Polytechnic Institute (1824). Many West Point graduates resigned their commissions owing to the limited opportunities for a military career, became civilians, and built careers as engineers and managers of canals and railroads, both before and after the Civil War.

The army shrank after the Civil War just as railroad building revived during 1865-1873. The Morrill Land Grant Act (1862) provided grants of land to aid the establishment of agricultural and mining colleges, which resulted in a vast expansion of agricultural and engineering schools, with the Massachusetts Institute of Technology among them. It appears that governments everywhere (although not in Britain until the twentieth century) used the power of the State in various ways to generate a trained corps of engineers. In the United States there has been and still is a public and a private system of higher education, whereas generally, Britain and Continental Europe have no tradition of private higher education.

In the United States, coordination between and among railroads remained private not public. Thus, track gauge, time zones, signals, and safety continued, to be by and large, in the hands of railroad managers. One notable exception occurred regarding track gauge but only because the federal government had to decide the appropriate gauge for the Union Pacific, a federal land grant railroad. In so deciding, the Government helped tip the scale for gauge uniformity, not achieved until almost three decades later, and then cooperatively and voluntarily.[28]

France

The French 'public versus private' railroad debate stretched from the inception of the Railway Era until nationalization in 1937. Contending that the State was better equipped to build this new infrastructure, the State bureaucracy argued for the public construction of railroads. As elsewhere, the State had the power of eminent

---

28   Dobbin 1994, pp. 3, 24, 29-40, 59, 90; Engelbourg and Bushkoff 1996, Chapter 4 and
       passim; Dawson 1991, pp. 144, 151, 157; Goodrich 1960, p. 127; Taylor 1951, Ch V,
       pp. 78-91; Parks 1972, pp. 8, 106, 213; Kennedy 1991, pp. 138-141; Puffert 2000, pp.
       933-960; Puffert 2002, pp. 282-314.

domain but France had also an expert corps of technocrats educated at public civil engineering schools; these bureaucrats claimed that by subsidizing private construction, the State would bear some part of the cost anyway. The supporters of private construction rebutted that private enterprises were better motivated to operate lines profitably and efficiently. However, one of the main reasons for not having the State construct the entire system was the inability to finance it.

Great State public works were hardly an innovation for France, rather a continuation of policies adopted during the previous centuries. The construction of roads, bridges, and canals, as applied to railroads, merely continued French *étatisme*. Pierre Joseph Proudhon (1809-1864), a noted French utopian socialist, argued that railway companies were essentially aristocratic and 'an aberrant alienation of the public domain'.[29] A prominent deputy argued: 'The State has the right and duty to execute all the major railway lines, just as it executed the royal roads, and I don't think it can delegate this right of sovereignty'.[30]

State Concessions for Building Railroads

At the beginning of the railway age, two models evolved, one run by the State and the other by private concessionaires, that is, contractual permits granted to private enterprises to operate a railroad (or any other business that the State deems necessary under public control).[31] The State was prevented from undertaking the huge financial responsibility needed for such a task because the State's finances were in poor shape. As a consequence, the railways developed as a mixed system of supervised concessionaires that presumably safeguarded the public interest without discouraging private investors.

Concessionaires were granted an exclusive charter under which private enterprises operated a railroad line or system for a determinate period of time and shared the net earnings with the State. The State-concessionaire system evolved as a mixture of the by and large uncoordinated railroad construction prevalent in Britain and the United States and the *étatisme* prevalent on the Continent. The laws of 1842, 1845, and 1846 stipulated that the State would build the track while private investors would supply the rolling stock and operate the railroad lines.[32]

The individual state legislatures alone in the United States could grant a railroad a franchise based on ad hoc policy decisions that considered the anticipated state benefits of a line. Everywhere the investors were ultimately at

29 Dobbin 1994, p. 127.
30 Adam 1972, p. 31.
31 'A concession is a contract or convention whereby a state grants the management of a public service to a private company.' Piquet 2004, p. 108. For instance, vendors of tobacco products but also some ice cream vendors in public parks are granted a 'concession' for which they pay a fee. United States national parks have facilities owned by private enterprises, which receive a monopoly; in exchange, these concessionaires pay a flat fee, a percentage of net revenue or both.
32 Clapham 1968, p. 145; Splawn 1928, p. 33.

risk but in France the State was more willing to salvage failing railroads. Concessions were granted based on the criteria of the nation's needs, determined by policy makers and government bureaucrats. Since these were not responsive to the preset master plan devised by government technocrats unsolicited applications were not accepted. The 'concession' of eminent domain has been needed everywhere for railroads therefore, becoming a societal issue.[33]

French liberal economists and political leaders opposed government ownership, yet the 1830s debate on railway financing presumed a dominant role for the State with little reference to private initiative. As elsewhere, it seems that few realized the economic importance of railroads; many believed that the railroad was a passing fad, perhaps useful to transport people but not freight. Followers of Henri de Saint-Simon (1760-1825), one of the founders of modern industrial socialism, anticipated the great potential of the new transportation mode although Saint Simon himself never had the opportunity to ride a train, dying before 1832. In that year, the first train ran from Lyons 33 miles south to St. Etienne; this Rhone valley area was rich in iron fields and coalmines as well as in raw silk supplies and as such commercially viable. Afterwards, the French Parliament initiated a study to determine the routing of new railroad lines and, in order to maintain financial control, decided that railroad concessions, henceforth, would be the prerogative of Parliament and not of the crown.[34]

State Financing of Railroads Construction

The model proposed by government technocrats called for the State to construct the track and to grant the right to operate railroads to private concessionaires through competitive bids. The works financed by the State were consistent with prevailing public policies. Constructing railways, the State responded to: 1. The needs of national defense. Although Germany was not yet unified by the 1850s, France viewed some the German states, notably Prussia, as potential rivals and enemies; therefore, some lines had terminals at France's border with German states, 2. Social order. During the eighteenth century, Physiocratic economists had insisted that the periodic grain crises were caused by poor land transportation, 3. Unification of the national market. Owing to the construction of railroads, an improved national interregional integration took place during the 1860s, 4. Public expenditure on railroads created jobs. This infrastructure expenditure solved some short-run cyclical unemployment problems long before John Maynard Keynes (1883-1946) proposed such policies.[35] Before railroad lines consolidation, when

---

33   Dobbin 1994, pp. 107-109.
34   M. Wallon (1908) 'Les saint-simoniens et les chemins de fer', *Annales de l'écoles des sciences politique'*, cited by Henri Sée 1942, p. 212; see also: Clapham 1968, p. 143.
35   As commonly realized, the perennial problem was that *long-term* State infrastructure expenditures were a *short-term* contra-cyclical tool.

struggling private railroads were in danger of ceasing operations, the State came to their assistance to maintain a public service.[36]

Different from Britain and the United States, in France the State organized the railways to achieve a coherent network. Public policy makers assumed that private enterprise could not achieve this goal since it would only pursue business goals, that is, the private rate of return, rather than consider the social rate of return. By 1842, the State's principles (not always implemented) included: control of the geographical plan of the system, supervision of rates, representation in the council of railway companies, and, if and when necessary, railway ownership.

To be sure, before 1875, the federal and state governments in the United States, granted to private railroad entrepreneurs ten percent of the unoccupied public land, in addition to financial subsidies, as an incentive to construct railroads but without anything resembling an overall plan. These State actions were justified politically, conquering the frontier and unifying the country. Economically, not that different from France, the social rate of return exceeded the private rate; the key difference remained that France implemented a plan while the United State did not. The State promoted railroads by attempting to keep fares within the reach of the citizens and of commerce.[37]

The Role of Technocrats

French policy makers claimed that expert technocrats, that is, trained administrators and engineers, could efficiently direct the economy rather than leaving it to whimsical market forces. The best examples are the Corps of Mines and the Corps of Bridges and Roads, initiated in the mid eighteenth century, who were charged with the establishment of a railway network. It is significant that these Corps (*Ponts et Chaussées*) charged for rail service 'rights of passage' (*droits*) rather than fees since they viewed railroads as within the public domain. During the nineteenth century, in France, the State, in consultation with the railway enterprises, controlled rate setting based on economic returns; in contrast, the Americans and British viewed rates as a prerogative of the market through demand and supply.[38]

After 1842, the *Corps de Ponts et Chaussées* had practical control of the railroads and symbolized the propulsive role of the State in the industrial sector. This was not regulatory intervention but rather the continual actions of discrete persuasion. Decisions between the State and the market were resolved through networks based upon the personal relationships of the members of the corps. In 1840, political observers argued that the State is the capitalist that has more credit, the engineer has more talent, and the entrepreneur has more resources and know

---

36   Doukas 1945, p. 13; Dobbin 1994, p. 4, 24-25; Clapham 1968, p. 146.
37   Passenger/kilometer fares declined from 11-16 *centime* in 1840 to 3.4 *centime* in 1913 while freight/kilometer declined from 23-28 *centimes* to six *centimes* between 1840 and 1870. Caron 1995, pp. 72-74.
38   Dobbin 1994, pp. 134-135, 142-143.

how. A combination of the three sources, they maintained further, would optimize the railroad system.[39]

Emile Legrand, director of the Corps of Bridges and Roads in 1837, and Charles de Freycinet (1828-1923), a mining engineer,[40] were instrumental in building the railroad system.[41] Technological efficiency accomplished the objectives of the State through compromise between the technocrats and the political faction in power. It made it easy when the technocrats were able to set public policies.[42] Legrand argued that, '...the great railway lines...are among the great reins of government; the state must be able to keep them in its hands...', private industry could operate railways only as concessions so that the State could retrieve them.[43]

French Tradition of Technocrats Training

Different from Britain, at least since Louis XIV and Colbert in the seventeenth century, in France high quality rather than productivity had been stressed. French engineers were placed at the helm of railway planning and they intended that France should have a superior quality railroad system. These engineering graduates of Les Grand Ecoles were well trained and experienced in executing public works such as ports, canals, dams, and highways.[44] Without State supervision and control, these engineers claimed that they could not guarantee a viable system regardless of cost; while they aimed at the optimum technical outcome, they paid less attention to the economic outcome.

As permanent civil servants, the technicians were little affected by political change.[45] As Alexis de Tocqueville (1805-1859) put it in 1846, 'the administrative system has always stood firm amid the debacles of political systems...the course of day to day affairs has neither interrupted nor deflected'.[46] The French public held and still hold technocrats in high esteem and capable of managing the private economy. The State bureaucracy attracted talent and skill for the perceived rewards and security. 'The state later took charge of the railways more by habit

---

39 Gueslin 1997, p. 77.

40 Freycinet later became a statesman and served as Premier in 1879-1880, 1882, 1886, 1890-1892.

41 Legrand and Freycinet were enthusiastic about railroads; they felt like religious missionaries and worked hard for the community.

42 Rosanvallon 1989, pp. 575-579; Milward and Saul 1977, pp. 119-120; Trebilcock 1981, p. 166.

43 Armand Audiganne, *Les chemins de fer aujourd'hui et dans cent ans,* Capelle Librairie, Paris, 1858, Vol.1, p. 461, quoted by Dobbin 1994, p. 124.

44 Kaufman 1900, p. 6.

45 Since 1789 several revolutions have changed the government but most of the population remained unaffected or hardly aware that a revolution had occurred.

46 Tocqueville 1955, p. 202.

than by design.'[47] To some extent the British benefited from the French canal and
road building experience and vice versa.

Railroad Regulation

Early on, the French State took a hand in promoting and regulating railroads;
particularly, the State planned lines radiating outward from Paris, France's
undisputed center for centuries, like the spokes of a wheel, similar to the political
hierarchy that had Paris at the center of authority and from which power radiated to
the provinces. France debated public versus private ownership and, while private
ownership continued, regulation increased; the State even assumed ownership of
bankrupt railroads to keep them operating as a public service.[48]

Parliamentary wrangling over the question of State versus private enterprise
and sectional disputes over the location of the main lines may have delayed the
railroad era in France until the coming of the Second Empire in 1852.[49] In that
year alone the State granted concessions for more than 1500 miles. The State
continued to grant concessions of more than a thousand miles each year and by the
end of the Empire in 1870, these concessions constituted half of the entire French
network of 27,000 miles. The construction of the railway network probably was
the greatest economic achievement of the Second Empire. The impact of the
railroad on the French economy is still debated by economic historians.[50]

The Role of Railroads in Industrialization

While admitting that railroads were a primary factor, Robert Fogel, an outstanding
economic historian, challenged the indispensability of the railroad in the process of
economic growth in nineteenth century United States. During the second half of
the nineteenth century French railroad construction certainly represented a prime
factor in the process of economic growth. As in the United States, French railroad
construction was accompanied by the first phase of industrialization, contrary to
Britain where industrialization preceded railroad construction.

In the 1840s, French railroad construction was a dynamic force for the
economy, initiating a great expansion of the iron industry. With the help of the
State, railroad investment, peaked at 20 to 29 percent as a share of total investment,
in periods when rapid economic growth occurred, and 16 percent in the downswing
of 1867-1874, and 12 percent in 1894-1897. On the other hand, France could not
produce quality iron rails (or other iron products) at a competitive cost; therefore
British rule of thumb reigned supreme. Protection of the iron industry did not help;

47   Dobbin 1994, p. 224.
48   Even in the United States railroads were rarely allowed to physically disappear; when
       a railroad was in financial difficulty, the most directly affected were the stockholders
       and the bondholders.
49   Smith 1990, pp. 657-659; Caron 1983, p. 28.
50   Cameron 1961, p. 69.

only with steel and the coming of metallurgical science in the fourth quarter of the nineteenth century did France become a steel rail producer at competitive prices.[51]

The Limits of Market Forces in French Railroad Development

Contrary to the United States, where apparent competition among independent railroad systems prevailed, the French State encouraged railroad combinations. Ironically, the French, the country that coined *laissez faire*, had a deep-seated mistrust of free market forces. In sharp contrast, the United States aimed at limited government; first, the state regulatory commissions and, later, the Interstate Commerce Commission were challenged on constitutional grounds in their treatment of railroad rate inequities. On the contrary, the French State early in the railroad age set rates.[52] When in 1875 ten local rail lines were on the brink of bankruptcy, the French State vowed not to allow the nation's well-planned network to be destroyed by market forces.[53]

The worldwide depression between 1873 and 1878 increased French unemployment and slowed down railroad construction. Freycinet, then Minister of Public Works, planned to spend one billion francs to add 5,000 kilometers of new rail lines that would create jobs. His reasoning was based on a social cost-benefit analysis taking into account externalities.[54] The French believed that it would be irrational to allow market forces to decide railroad policies or to abandon a railroad project based on business profitability alone.[55] Business people observed that Freycinet's planned railroads would traverse poor areas and therefore would not be profitable. He retorted that the State should not reason as a private business; the State should initiate public works that would attract capital that otherwise would go abroad.[56]

The French State consistently pushed the expansion of the railway network. Different from the United States and Britain, State incentives guaranteed a return to investors; when this was found to be insufficient, the State offered various subsidies.[57] The Law of 1878 committed the State to actual railroad operations, even though the French government asserted vigorously that the State repurchase

---

51   Levy-Leboyer and Lescure 1991, p. 156; Milward and Saul 1977, p. 87; Trebilcock 1981, p. 144.
52   Luthy 1955, p. 455; Dobbin 1994, pp. 152-153.
53   Peyret 1949, p. 243; Dobbin 1994, pp. 108, 120-121, 129-130, 148; Catherine and Gousset 1965, pp. 123-124.
54   Any public project analysis, different from a business analysis, must consider secondary returns, cost and benefits to society, in addition to the direct income from the railway operations.
55   Dobbin 1994, pp. 149-153.
56   Mayeur 1973, pp. 119-120.
57   Similarly, in the United States the Pacific Railroad Bill of 1862 essentially brought no takers; therefore, the State increased incentives in the 1864 law. Any number of investors declined to invest in the transcontinental lines because of the risk-reward ratio and the alternative rate of return.

provisionally and temporarily railway lines to prevent the cessation of service. After 1879, extraordinary budget resources financed the railroad program. Those who favored public ownership of railways maintained in 1883 that the State treasury contributed to the initial construction and even shared the operational costs whenever private railway companies experienced a deficit.[58] To sum up, French railway policy encompassed all major functions: planning, finance, coordination, pricing, and competition.

The Path to Nationalization

France promulgated a national railway plan in 1842, amended in 1852, 1859, and 1883; in 1878, the State reacquired the unprofitable short lines. France thus created a State railway network that was completed with the reacquisition of the *Compagnie de l'Ouest* operating in western France. Aiming to strike a balance, France offered a compromise of private construction with partial State financing; the State provided more than half of the funds, the remainder furnished by private capital. Nationalization merely awaited the charter expirations.

Indeed, in 1908-1909, France introduced permanent public ownership of railroads to salvage unprofitable lines and to control militarily strategic lines near the German border.[59] At the Socialist Congress of 1910, some leaders such as Jules Guesde, the caretaker of Marxist orthodoxy, opposed the idea of nationalization saying that the State is the enemy and that the State is the arsenal and fortress of the enemy class, whom the proletariat will have to remove. One would add the 'State Boss' to the 'State Gendarme'.

This debate paralleled the railway workers' strike of 1910. The Socialist Prime Minister, Aristide Briand (1862-1932), called out troops to break the strike. The National Union of Railway Workers and Employees thereupon called a general strike but, when it became clear that the movement was collapsing, the strike committee ordered the resumption of work. Since the railways were vital to the functioning of the French economy, Briand defended the use of force to maintain the functioning of the railroads as essential to the life of the nation and its defense.[60] This is the same Briand who earlier in his career had advocated the revolutionary general strike as the means of transforming society. Finally, with a Popular Front government and a Socialist premier, France nationalized the railroads during the 1930s depression, in part as a necessity for a failing industry and in part fulfilling a political promise.

---

58   Caron 1970, pp. 320-322; Caron 1973, passim; Doukas 1945, pp. 40-41, 51.
59   R. Godfernaux 'Les grands réseaux français depuis la guerre', *Revue politique et parlementaire*, June 10, 1931, p. 356, cited by Doukas 1945, p. 39.
60   Rosanvallon 1989, pp. 588-9.

Germany

Owing to extreme political fragmentation, Germany benefited relatively little from the canal era. As the railway superseded the canal and the railway fever spread, construction policy varied from one German independent state to another. During the pioneering stage of the railway era, in the late 1820s and early 1830s, private entrepreneurs hesitated to invest in railway construction, with only potential long-term returns. The seemingly high risks owing to the low level of the economy as well as the prevailing the State mercantilist role in the market deterred private investors. For instance, the 1838 Prussian Railway Law did not offer significant incentives to would-be investors; however, the 1842 Law offered easy charters, dividend guarantees, and subsidies, which private investors wanted. It appears that the State became a significant partner in forging the Prussian and later the German railway system.

The Initial German States Involvement in Railroad Construction

As early as 1833, Friedrich List, a well-known nineteenth century economist and railroad entrepreneur, proposed an integrated rail system to unify Germany. In 1837, List assisted in developing the Leipzig-Dresden (Saxony, one of the most economically advanced German states) railroad, one of the first on the continent. Previously, while in the United States, his building of the Little Schuylkill Railroad in Pennsylvania in 1831, made List wealthy. Between 1830 and 1848, there was a seemingly uneasy alliance between the eastern Junkers and the western capitalists. These railroad investors relied on the State for subsidies, subscription to capital stock, and expediting land acquisition for railroad construction through eminent domain. Indeed by 1850, the governments of the German states contributed half of all railroad investment.

On the other hand, *Rhenish* private investors, in one of the most economically advanced Prussian provinces, were in the forefront of railroad construction, so much so that by 1845, they built half the railroads of the German Confederation.[61] The special status of the Rhineland originated in its particular political and economic institutions, that is, the French 1789 Revolution and Napoleon's short-lived governance. Richer and more economically developed, the Rhineland remained strongly influenced by French laws and institutions.

With the blessing of the Congress of Vienna, in 1815 Prussia extended its pre-Revolutionary holdings in western Germany by acquiring the rest of the Rhineland.[62] Aside from the State's backing, the Rhineland had strong private banking facilities along with a concentration of population, income, and industry,

---

61 Brophy 1998, pp. 8, 25.
62 This addition represented a plum for Prussia in its struggle with Austria for German hegemony.

which made railroads potentially more economically viable than elsewhere. No wonder that railway construction developed there first.

Private versus Public Railroad Construction

Some German states vehemently opposed private railways. In Bavaria, the second largest German state after Prussia, a high government official in 1843 'announced that he would never allow such an important institution as the railway to fall into private hands'.[63] During the early stages, the private sector built all the railroads in Prussia and Saxony; on the contrary, in Hanover in the northwest, in Württemberg south west of Prussia, the State built and operated railways. In some states, the State greatly influenced the privately owned companies.

In some cases the State was a minority or a majority shareholder whereas in other instances the government guaranteed minimum returns on capital. Occasionally, State functionaries operated privately owned railroads when they could not perform efficiently. An economic historian argues that the State did not necessarily play a positive role in the railway development process in the 1830s. The states reluctantly granted concessions to private companies when they crossed borders and retarded the construction of lines by making it difficult for private companies to operate through regulations, rate setting and controls.[64] Private railway operation was based on regalia, a royal privilege in Prussia; the sovereign could milk the enterprise or arbitrarily withdraw the privilege.[65]

To achieve an efficient transportation network, railway construction needed coordination among the numerous members of the German Confederation, created in 1815 as a political precursor of the *Zollverein*, the customs union, two decades later. Contrary to *laissez faire* advocates, 'commercial leaders in both the western and eastern provinces perceived the state…not as an impediment to development but, rather as an institution to promote economic change'.[66] The symbiosis between the State and private investors was complemented with many government civilian cadres, on temporary leave, taking positions with private railroad firms while some private railway executives held government assignments or were government consultants.

By 1860, in Prussia the situation reversed itself, the State owned half the railway lines. Owing to State support, in western Prussia, which experienced a higher level of economic activity and greater population density than East Prussia, private railroads showed profits. Mainly due to the worldwide depression of the 1870s, private railroad deficits coincided with the completion of German

---

63   Kitchen 1978, p. 50.
64   Fremdling 1983, p. 122.
65   Millward 2004, p. 7.
66   Brophy 1998, p. 26. No wonder that Cologne businessmen chose the young Karl Marx
      as editor for their *Rheinische Zeitung* in 1841.

unification. Prussian-German policy makers considered railroad investment within the national economic strategic framework.[67]

The State Take Over of Private Railroads

After 1840, based on the perceived success of the State operated Belgian rail system, the government in such states as Hanover (1842), Baden (1843), Bavaria (1844), and Brunswick, and Württemberg (1845), aimed to replicate the Belgian experience by taking over partial or complete railroad control. To be sure, Bavaria, Saxony and Hesse-Kassel opted for a mix of private and public railroads. Finally, in the largest state, Prussia, as well as in Hesse-Darmstadt, and Mecklenburg-Schwerin private control prevailed until after the Revolution of 1848.

Public or private ownership need not necessarily affect the operations of the railroads. At the beginning of the railroad era, this diversity created many problems for shippers and passengers alike since there was no uniformity in gauges, rates, standards, and contracts. Some diversity stemmed from the multiplicity of jurisdictions; the south German states, especially Baden and Bavaria, resisted the forces of nationalism as long as possible. A railroad congress in 1847 suggested the creation of a central railroad authority; nonetheless, the Confederation of the German States rejected this proposal because of the implied criticism of the current policies and also because it potentially could have hurt various interests.[68]

As an outcome of the Revolution of 1848, August von der Heydt was appointed Prussian trade minister. Heydt was known as a Westphalian political liberal reformer who advocated a constitution for Westphalia and subsequently for Prussia, the right of petition, and civil equality for minorities. As a means of promoting rapid industrialization, Heydt backed State ownership of railroads while pursuing the commercial and military goals of the State. Aiming to take over railway companies, he was determined to use the political, legal, and financial powers of the State. To implement this policy, in 1852 Heydt nationalized the profitable Berlin-Frankfurt am Oder line, despite the objections and unsuccessful court suit of the stockholders and management.[69]

The Push for State Control of Railroad in Prussia-Germany

During the 1850s, the German states controlled and/or regulated private railroads. For instance, Prussia increased the sinking fund requirements, thus decreasing the railroad short-term profitability, returns to stockholders, and therefore the market value of railroad stocks; however, it exempted some of the state-owned railways

---

67   Hoffman et al 1965, pp. 809-810.
68   Fischer 1972, pp. 68, 76; Hamerow 1958, pp. 8-9.
69   Brophy 1998, pp. 43-60.

from this stipulation. The State increased the supervision of private railroads and limited their freedom to issue bonds and stocks or to declare dividends and refused to grant new charters to private companies in favor of extending the State lines. Between 1849 and 1862, Prussia chartered only two railway companies, owing to Heydt's preference for State-owned lines. Private businessmen rationalized that the State involvement in the railroads could help them because it guaranteed stability in freight rates and scheduling.

To support the railroad expansion, and to increase the State railway holdings, Heydt used the Railway Fund, created in 1838. To enlarge his power base, Heydt expanded the bureaucratic apparatus of the Trade Ministry. Liberal political analysts criticized the reformed Commercial Code for granting the State too much control over the management of private railroads. Although policy makers feared that railroad stocks would collapse and take down the entire industrial corporate structure, the State did not have the financial resources to take over the private lines. When the Liberal Party, which defended free trade, was victorious in the 1858 election, the advocates of private railroads believed that they had found an ally by having business interests represented in the government, yet railroad policies hardly changed.[70]

Railways and the Economy West and East

The eastern agricultural elite, the Junkers, the industrial and commercial leaders in Berlin and in Rhineland-Westphalia, and the Prussian government clashed regarding railway connections, traffic, rates, and profitability, and not necessarily on the derived externalities in the regions they served. Agricultural East Prussia was marginalized because of the low population density, low per capita income, and limited markets. Finally, by the 1850s, eastern, mainly Junkers, land owners, to gain a market share for high bulk-low level agricultural products, western industrialists to ease the transport of raw materials and industrial products, and government bureaucrats agreed to have the State finance important railway links.

The State in Prussia-Germany used railroads to promote national (aside from political and military) economic and social goals. Commuter railways were used for settlement policies and to encourage workers to move to the suburbs; policy-makers believed that moving the workers from the city center lessened the dangers of Socialism. The unification wars of the 1860s and the depressions of the 1870s and the 1880s retarded the construction of new lines. By the end of nineteenth century, the German East-West dualism was still as significant as at the beginning of the century with the east increasingly lagging partly because of the inadequacy of the transportation system.[71]

---

70   Brophy 1998, pp. 61-67, 107-134, 143-144.
71   Tipton 1976, pp. 105-106, 149-150.

Nationalization

Led by Bismarck, the push for railroad nationalization moved ahead unabated during the 1860s and following unification unsuccessfully in 1876, and successfully in 1879. An observer maintained that nationalization of German railroads was driven by policy makers to capture railway profits as non-tax revenue for the State out of the reach of the *Reichstag* and the State's desire to have control of the railway system the same way it had control over the post and telegraph.[72] Private railroad entrepreneurs had only lukewarm objections after the stock market crash of 1873, since they were compensated for their losses. Bismarck advocated a universal state-owned system that would encourage German economic and political integration.[73] There were misgivings from Bavaria that was jealous of its railroads and its autonomy after unification (as the second largest state after Prussia) and objected to the inclusion of Bavarian railroads into the imperial system.

Following unification, Bismarck established the Imperial Railway Office, using routes and subsidies as instruments of economic policy. The German railroad nationalization of 1879 was not accomplished without a struggle between the federated states and the unified German Empire. Individual states, led by Bavaria, Saxony, and Württemberg, larger and more important economically, were reluctant to begin 'national' unification in order to avoid having their railroads fall in the hands of the Prussian-dominated imperial government. They attempted to purchase the railroads within their borders but, lacking the financial means to compensate shareholders for such a vast undertaking, their attempts failed.[74] Between 1879 and 1909 State-owned railroads increased from 5300 km to 37,400 km and privately owned ones decreased from 9400 km to 2900 km.

At the beginning of the railroad era, it was not apparent that towns that remained without rail service would stagnate, the towns that were not within the narrow band of the railway would lose both politically and materially. Most policy-makers assumed that the State should not aim to earn profits like an ordinary private corporations; ideally, in profitable years, the State would decrease the fares or vice versa. While this did not happen, the system's efficiency quieted critics.

---

72   Fremdling 1980, p. 21.
73   'Bismarck established the Imperial Railway Office, whose function was to...use the railways consciously as instruments of economic policy, for example, by giving favorable rates on goods destined for exports.' Cameron 2003, p. 289.
74   Clapham 1968, p. 346; Tipton 1976, pp. 53-54, 113, 139-140; Brophy 1998, pp. 167-169; Splawn 1928, pp. 65-66.

Conclusions

There is no doubt that railroad construction influenced the process of industrialization in Germany.[75] Yet, the debate continues whether railroad construction acted as a primer for economic growth through the demand for iron and steel products and thus the expansion of the steel industry.[76] In the early phases of railway construction, such inputs as iron ore had to be imported, but within a decade import substitution by domestic production replaced some of the imported inputs; also, at first imported, by the 1840s locomotives were increasingly produced domestically. The *Zollverein* freed inter-German trade but Germany erected a tariff wall on all processed iron products in 1884, thus encouraging domestic production. Still, up to World War I British coal remained competitive; while the domestic share of coal used by Germany increased, imports of British coal rose from 1840 to 1913.[77]

While in 1870 Bismarck pushed for rail integration, Prussia advocated cooperation through a coordination council headquartered in Berlin. By that time, there were seven state railroads in Germany. Before World War I, both private and public railroads were efficient and profitable. The war destroyed much of the infrastructure and some of the rolling stock not destroyed was claimed as reparations by the victors. Most of the states with Bavaria in the lead were reluctant to sell their state railroads to the *Reich*.

After World War I, the private and quasi-private railroads, threatened by bankruptcy, were sold to the *Reich*. A unified German rail system was in place by 1920.[78] Wilhelm Groener (1867-1938), Quarter Master General during World War I, and the Transportation Minister, believed that the *Reichsbahn*, the Imperial Railroad, represented a unifying factor in Germany, replacing the former army as the strongest institution holding Germany together. Groener contended that an integrated *Reich* rail system would benefit the depressed and defeated German population. He placed himself in the Prussian and German tradition of charging the State with being responsible for the welfare of its citizens, *Fuhrsorglicher Staat*, literally, 'the State that takes care of their own'.[79]

---

75   Referring to Germany, one economic historian argued that '...the relevance of the railway sector as a source as spreader effects for industries such as metal-processing and machine building is clearly established'. Trebilcock 1981, p. 56.
76   Clapham 1968, pp. 347-349; Fischer 1972, p. 185. Sheehan 1989, pp. 469-470, 733, 740-741.
77   Fremdling 1983, pp. 130,136.
78   Milward and Saul 1977, pp. 43. By 1912, railways became the biggest single public employer with 697,000 people on the payroll.
79   Mierzejewski 1999, Vol. I, Chapters 1 and 2.

Italy

'The dominant ideological influence of economic liberalism...made many of the Italian ruling class reluctant to allow the State a major role in the construction and management of railways.'[80]   Yet, like Germany, Italy was among the first European countries to have a major share of the railroads State-owned and operated. The State played an important role since Italian railway construction lagged, mainly owing to shortage of domestic capital. The low and uneven regional level of the economy signaled private investors to expect that railroads would not generate much revenue compared with costs in the reasonable future.

The development of Italian railroads underwent four phases from 1830 to 1913. Between 1839 and 1860, private investors and the State established local short lines, while during 1861-1880 a national network was initiated. Between 1880 and 1895, *La Sinistra Storica*, the Historical Left, instituted a large program of public spending on railroads and the Italian railroad mileage increased by 75 percent. Railway construction slowed down from 1895 to1913 and the railroads were nationalized in 1905. By World War I, Italy trailed Britain, France, and Germany, in railroad mileage per capita and per square kilometer.[81]

The first Italian regional railroad networks were built in the most economically advanced states, the independent Piedmont and Austrian controlled Tuscany. In the Austrian Veneto, between 1835 and 1852, as elsewhere in the empire, the Austrian government provided needed capital for railroads. Similar to France, most of the Italian state(s) adopted a system of concessionaires and relied on foreign capital more than any other western continental country. From the outset, the State in Piedmont operated most of the railroads. Overall, Italy was much poorer than France or Germany and, moreover, had only a rudimentary capital market. Therefore, Italy had little choice but to rely quite heavily on foreign capital for railway construction.

Increasing Role of the State in Railroad Construction

Inadequate commercial codes encouraged various financial schemes, not always beneficial to the railways. Between unification and World War I the State provided about two-thirds of the infrastructure budget for the railroads. The railroads played a less important role in Italian industrialization than in the United States, France, and Germany. At the beginning of the railroad era, the iron and steel industry was not developed; therefore Italy could not benefit from backward linkages. Perhaps this explains why Italy had a late start in the mechanical and engineering industry and did not produce locomotives until the 1880s.[82] Around the 1850s, the State had to rescue the stagnating small iron and mechanical plants

---

80   Schram 1997, p. 23.
81   Fenoaltea 1983, pp. 51-52.
82   Zamagni 1993, pp. 163-165; Schram 1997, p. 15.

in the Kingdom of the Two Sicilies with protection and subsidies. The situation in Tuscany and the northern Italian states was somewhat better but, in order to survive, the northern plants still needed the State's assistance.[83]

Before and after unification, Italy did not come to grips with the role of the State in building a railroad system. As in Germany, before unification, regional differences dictated different approaches and different political philosophies. The three Italian states that could independently decide railway policies, were Piedmont, the Papal States, and the Kingdom of the Two Sicilies. Prior to entering politics (as Minister of Agriculture in 1851) Cavour had been a successful railroad promoter in Piedmont; after he entered the government he was a partisan of rapid construction of railroads to induce economic development and his liberal economic philosophy did not alter his view that the State needed to support railroad construction.

Piedmont's Experience

From the beginning of the Railroad Era, the State in Piedmont had a hand in railway construction. After analyzing railway operations abroad, Carlo Illarione Pettiti di Roreto (1790-1850), a Piedmontese aristocrat and a government adviser, argued in 1846, for a State-owned railway system. Petitti feared that speculation on railway stocks would bring financial chaos to the country and contended that when the State is short of funds, it may grant concessions but with strict control of stock issues, management, and operations. Sharing a long border with France, linguistically, culturally, and economically, France heavily influenced Piedmont/Savoy. Hence, Piedmont followed the French model in which the State constructed the main lines and granted concessions to private investors for secondary lines with State subsidies.[84]

Italian Railroads under Austrian Dominion

Before Italian unification, Austria constituted the main power broker in Italy. As such, Austria pursued a policy of building a railroad system that connected with the vassal Italian states, whether or not administered directly from Vienna. Since Trieste was the main outlet to the sea for the Austro-Hungarian Empire, Austria in 1854 backed the construction of a rail line linking the port of Trieste with Vienna. Soon after, it supported the construction of railroads in Lombardy and the Veneto (at that time both Austrian provinces) and, to a lesser degree, in Tuscany. With the blessing of Austria, Lombardy expanded its network, which facilitated industrialization. In Tuscany, the State granted railway concessions but did not interfere with private investors. As elsewhere during the railroad boom, this

---

83   Pescosolido 1994, pp. 89-90; Coppini 1994, pp. 360-361.
84   Carlo Ilarione Petitti di Roreto, *Delle strade ferrate italiane e del miglior ordinamento di esse. Cinque discorsi*, Capologo, 1845, cited by Schram 1997, pp. 29-31, 64.

brought about a wave of speculation that destabilized the narrow capital markets, and even affected foreign financial markets.[85]

Southern Railroads

A direct line joined Venice with Milan as well as Turin by 1860, but there were no rail connections with the southern part of the peninsula, that is, the Papal States and the Kingdom of the Two Sicilies, accounting for about one half of Italy.[86] One can hypothesize that the Continental process of industrialization is linked to the development of a rail network. The honest intention of policy makers of the new Italian State (1861) was that incorporating the less advanced Mezzogiorno in the national rail system would serve as a propeller for change. This did not happen, not because the hypothesis was necessarily false, but because intentions alone cannot accomplish policies. The State neglected the commitment of the unitary State; the southern railroad endowment remained behind the North all through the nineteenth and into the twentieth centuries.

Railroad Consolidation

By 1864 there were 22 railway companies in Italy, 14 in the North. The Railway Act of 1865 consolidated the railroads into five nominally independent regional systems.[87] Obviously, since profit maximization was the objective of private entrepreneurs, the South did not look attractive; potential merchandise and passenger traffic did not call for railroads since industrial activity was minimal and the majority of the population lived in abject poverty in rural settings. Therefore, governments of any stripe realized that to unify the country, a unified railroad network was needed. To accomplish this, the State offered import protection to non-competitive suppliers of railroad equipment (for instance, Ansaldo and Breda), which increased the cost of procurement by 20-25 percent.[88]

The chaotic status of financing, constructing, operating, and servicing the railroads brought about the 1865 Railroad Act, which, however, could not solve many of the problems. The relation between the private railway companies and the

---

85   Schram 1997, pp. 26-30, 34-37; Falasca 1997, pp. 501-504.
86   By 1860, some scattered lines have been built in Tuscany (Siena-Florence-Lucca-Pisa-Livorno) as well in the Papal States (Civitavecchia-Rome-Frascati). While in the Kingdom of the Two Sicilies, the Caserta-Naples line was the first Italian railway, followed by Naples-Castellamare, these were not of any economic value since they were short princely lines serving the king's travel. By unification, the rest of the South had not started constructing any other rail line. Kalla-Bishop 1971, p. 10.
87   The railways were grouped as: The Upper Italy Railway Company (all North of Florence), the Meridionali Railway Company (Tuscany and the Adriatic South), the Romane Railway Company (Central Italy), the Reale Sarda Railway Company (Sardinia), and the Victor Emmanuel Railway Company (Sicily). Schram 1997, p. 42.
88   Papa 1973, pp. 92-93.

State became more stressful because each private company had, by contract, a different set of rules, subsidies, and organization. Owing to the State's budgetary difficulties, in that year the Upper Italian Railway Company purchased the State-owned Piedmont Railway Company when the State discontinued financial support. In addition, by 1870 the State revoked the promised subsidies to domestic and foreign private investors; this proved counterproductive because the unified Italian State overtly encouraged private enterprise and ownership by furnishing half the construction costs while still controlling and regulating the railways through continuous subsidies. Between 1865 and the worldwide economic crisis of 1873 most of the private railway companies endured financial difficulties. The State came to their rescue, on and off, and burdened itself with a public debt increasingly difficult to manage.

The Drive for Nationalization

In 1876, Silvio Spaventa, Minister of Public Works, proposed that since the State subsidized the railroads, it should take them over. Reasoning that railroads should not operate as a private industry in a competitive system, he invoked the public service argument. The monopolistic nature of the railroads implied a privileged position that is not necessarily related to economic freedom. Therefore, the profit motive of the private enterprise should be replaced with the public interest represented by the State. Spaventa rejected the Anglo-American model because it led to monopolistic conditions and unfair practices; he favored the Belgian and German mixed state-private model. The majority in the Parliament rejected Spaventa's analysis, arguing that in Britain and in the United States the free market had created an efficient railroad system. The bottom line was that interest groups, such as construction companies and the Tuscan banks that had invested in these railroad companies, derailed Spaventa's proposal.[89]

Those who argued for *laissez faire* expected private entrepreneurs to build the railroad system but in the end the State was heavily involved in the construction of the railway network. Free markets were supposed to attract foreign investment for this infrastructure. But, as expected, in the newly unified State, strong nationalism developed that was antagonistic to foreign investment. The main rationale for State ownership of railroads in Italy was to cement political unification.[90]

After unification, the main private railway, the Upper Italian Company, was negatively affected by the devaluation of the lira, but also because the subsidies were not forthcoming since the Italian treasury asked the railway to pay the *ricchezza mobile* (net fixed assets wealth) tax. Matters became more complicated because the Rothschild bank owned a majority of the stock in the Upper Italian Railway Company and at the same time constituted a principal source of credit

---

89   Cammarano 1995, p. 68; Papa 1973, pp. 11-12, 37-38; Mack Smith 1997, p. 96.
90   The State had to buy the Lombardy and Venetian railroads from Austrian interests to free them from foreign control.

first, for Piedmont and then for the Italy. Unexpectedly (the Italian State's finances were still troubled), to the consternation of many Italians and some West Europeans, the State in 1875 purchased the Upper Italian Railway Company from the Rothschilds. With this purchase, the Italian State became the owner and operator of the most profitable portion of railway in the country.

The steel and mechanical and engineering industries were favorable to the State takeover of railroads since they expected an increasing procurement flow. The State compensated stockholders directly (payments) or indirectly (bonds) from the treasury. Substantial funds were made available for entrepreneurs in search of lucrative alternative investments. The public invested in fast growing electric and mechanical enterprises that enabled Italy to participate in the process of industrialization of Western Europe. Railroads replaced waterways in determining industrial location and centers of economic activity. Cities like Siena in Tuscany and Perugia in Umbria, bypassed by the main rail axis, constitute excellent examples of urban stagnation.

Railroads in the Process of Industrialization

While there is no consensus, undoubtedly the railroad played a major role in Italian industrialization. However, before 1861, the direct effects of railroads, that is, backward linkages were limited owing to a lack of coordination among the single Italian states. As in the United States, France, and Germany, but not Britain, in Italy the railroad construction industry propelled the economy with the State being instrumental. In the 1860s and 1880s the State subsidized the construction industry contributing 25 percent of the Italian value added.[91]

Until 1880, most railroads supplies, that is, track, locomotives, and freight and passenger cars were manufactured abroad because of a delayed start in the mechanical and engineering industry. The State attempted to persuade or even force the railway companies to purchase in the domestic market but since the domestic costs of equipment was five to ten percent higher, railways preferred to place their orders abroad. Locomotives started being produced by Ansaldo in Genoa in 1880, but only after 1900, and as a result of railroad nationalization and State procurement, did a locomotive industry develop. While not as keen about planning as the French, the Italian State followed industrial policies that encouraged investment in railroads as well as in iron and steel, mechanical and engineering, and electrical industries.[92]

---

91   Zamagni 1993, p. 116, 164-165.
92   Papa 1973, pp. 116-118, 154-155; Schram 1997, pp. 12-18, 118, 159-160, 152, 156; Trebilcock 1981, p. 350; Zamagni 1993, p. 163.

222 Cultural Continuity in Advanced Economies

The Railway Act of 1885

In 1885, the government entrusted two private companies with the operation of the mainland railroads; this move was not ideological but occurred because of the State's short-run need for cash. The State policy supported, in a limited market, a high-risk but regulated railway system before nationalization in 1905. Furthermore, in Italy the railroads served as a means of promoting economic, political, and cultural unification.

One could argue that giving preference to the State's railroad expenditure over other public needs such as land reclamation, education, and health, as well as making available funds for southern development, was ex post rather the wrong policy. It is true that the pre-1885 Railway Act rate setting was flexible, and at times discriminatory, favoring the poorer southern regions. This railway act eliminated such arbitrary rate setting and standardized the rates for the country to the disadvantage of the *Mezzogiorno*, which lost its privileged status.[93]

By the end of the nineteenth century, the South was poorly endowed with a rail network. Consequently, southern political leaders complained that the railroad network was magnificent in the North but lacking in the South. The State was reluctant to grant railway charters in the South because of the high cost and the low traffic. Because of mountains, cost per square kilometer was high but not higher than in the North; the limited traffic has its origin in the low level of economic activity that is less freight and the high level of passenger fairs. True, built in the less mountainous than the western peninsula Bologna-Bari railway line was profitable but the western side of the *Mezzogiorno* did not participate in the benefits because the needed investment from the State were not forthcoming.[94]

Piedmont became the Italian State after unification but with greater responsibilities and more pressure by interest groups than before unification. The State just did not have the funds to adequately finance railways or for that matter other public services. Also, Piedmont-Italy spent a large share of the government budget on wars, past, present, and future, which surely cramped Italy's ability to spend on much else. In contrast, even as late as 1914, the United States spent a trivial share of the federal budget on the military. Consequently, as was done in the United States and Germany, the government welcomed foreign capital for railroads. An economic historian observed that, 'foreign capital contributed usefully to Italian infrastructure growth and operated as a genuine subsidy to economic modernization'.[95]

The 1885 Railway Act reshaped the national system into three networks, the Mediterranean, Adriatic, and Sicily, but also contained more stringent regulations for railway operations. The State had to approve freight rates and timetable

---

93   Schram 1997, pp. 115, 122.
94   Gaetano Salvemini, *Movimento socialista e questione meridionale*. Milan, 1963, p. 72. cited by Papa 1973, pp. 74-75.
95   Trebilcock 1981, p. 365.

changes before implementation. This law created a mongrel organization by having the State decide when and where new lines should be built and how to pay for them, but leaving the technical execution to the various companies. Rather than clarifying responsibilities and benefits between the State and private companies, it appears that this law generated more confusion and the State hardly received its share of the revenue while providing subsidies.[96]

The State vs. Private in Financing Railroad Construction and Operation

At the end of the nineteenth century, the financial situation of and the service offered by the private railroad companies were deteriorating. Bickering between the State and private companies concerning profit sharing and arbitrary rate setting induced a loss of consumer confidence in railroad management, regardless of either public or private ownership and operation. Italian per capita income lower than in France or in Germany, meant low rail travel demand; passenger fares were set so high that rail travel became a luxury for many and for some traveling by train became cost prohibitive; this might explain why Italy had one of the lowest rate of travelers per capita in Europe. On the other hand, after the nationalization of railroads in 1905, when the bureaucracy assumed control, a large number of people (especially public employees) were allowed to travel free or at preferential rates.[97]

The public policy of maintaining high freight and passenger railroad rates had negative consequences on market integration. An economic historian agues that 'the Italian railways' ability to unify the domestic market thus seems to have been limited by the high price of their services, and not...by the comparatively [with France and Germany] small size of their market'.[98] It appears that railroad subsidies could not replace poor management; in a vicious cycle, railroad rates were kept high limiting demand, with little demand, fares were high to cover costs that limited railroad demand. Therefore passengers and freight did not travel among the regions thus leaving regional integration for a later time.

After unification by using domestic intermediate (not primary) inputs (steel) especially in the mechanical and electrical industries, railroad construction created important backward linkages; it is debatable whether railroads siphoned funds that could have been used in manufacturing. During the 1880s when the era of railroad construction era approached completion, funds were freed somehow for use in industry. It appears that while Italians were eager to invest in railroad securities, they preferred to direct their available funds to local savings banks, to be used for municipal infrastructure or to purchase foreign securities. Possibly, because of

---

96   Cammarano 1995, p. 64.
97   Fenoaltea 1983, pp. 87-88; Papa 1973, pp. 92-93, 113; Schram 1997, pp. 44-52; 55-63; Splawn 1928, pp. 93, 94-95.
98   Fenoaltea 1983, pp. 78. 82.

limited investment in industries in the 1880s, and little guidance or support from the State, Italy might have postponed the industrial transformation by a decade.[99]

Nationalization Completed

The 1902 railroad union strike had a sobering effect on the unions, when the first Giolitti government militarized the railroads. The public versus private ownership debate included ambivalence on the status of railroad workers, the rights of public workers to unionize or to have the right to strike. Yet, 25 years after Germany in 1905, partially in response to national labor strikes of 1902 and 1904 but also because of military considerations, Italy became the second European country to nationalize most of the railroads. The 1905 railway Nationalization Act was not ideological but practical; subsidies and regulations could not establish an efficient system to serve business and public at large. All through the nineteenth century, and especially after national unification, policy makers were torn between ideology and pragmatism. Leasing lines to private companies have not been entirely successful since these companies wanted less State control and regulation while demanding large subsidies.[100]

The Railroads and the State during the Nineteenth Century:
Concluding Remarks

Railroad construction had a slow start, by 1840 with Britain in the lead and Italy far behind. Throughout the nineteenth century both the Anglo-American and Continental countries played a role in the construction and control of railroads; that role must be qualified in terms of scope and degree of State intervention in the market place. Within each institutional/political framework, railway construction, operation, and public control evolved differently in Anglo-American countries and Continental Europe. In the former, the State did not intervene directly in railway operation but both Britain and the United States regulated entry, service, coordination, safety, and rates to varying degree. In Continental Europe railways were considered a public service and the fare corresponded to principles of taxation, so that one could define payment for the service as a user tax.

Britain was a special case since it was industrialized when the railroad era set in, which meant a potential demand of moving freight existed. Therefore, private investors initiated railroad construction without coordination or a master plan. The State chartered private enterprises to which it granted eminent domain and imposed some rules and regulations by the 1840s; the State coordinated gauge and scheduling as well as facilitating consolidation of multiple short lines. By the end of the nineteenth century, the State controlled rates, safety, and could block

---

99   Gerschenkron 1968, p. 19.
100   Barbagallo 1999, p. 96; De Grand 2001, pp. 95, 116.

mergers.   While preaching *laissez faire*, the State felt compelled to act pragmatically to protect investors and consumers.

The United States did not regulate railroad rates, but after 1839, individual state railroad commissions did influence rates; these commissions had the right to approve or reject rates. After 1887, the Interstate Commerce Commission was empowered to approve railroads rates in most cases were limited in their freedom to establish rates. In Britain and the United States railroad rates were set, subject to regulation, on the basis of what the traffic could bear and other considerations. The United States did not 'plan' routes nationally but the State in the United States subsidized the construction of transcontinental railroads.

France offers the best example of how perennial government technocrats planned the railway network. On the Continent, some of the reasons for the State's role in planning and coordination of the railway system were: needs of national defense, unification of the national market, and a short- run fiscal stimulus for the domestic economy. Also, in the long-run railroads were instrumental in speeding up the process of industrialization on the Continent. Not necessarily ideological, but as a choice of public policy, France, Germany, and Italy encouraged private investment, offered easy terms for concessions, used public procurement, and subsidized the construction of railroads.

In Continental Europe more often than not, the State controlled and regulated railway companies and participated in management. Since on the Continent railways crossed national borders, the State regulated border crossing, rates, and often consideration was given to defense strategy.[101] In Britain, railways bought land; in the United States western developmental railways were frequently given unoccupied public land to stimulate construction. In Britain railways purchased the land while on the Continent the land frequently was leased from the State for a specific period. Finally, the Anglo-American railways had few subsidies while in Continental Europe, heavy subsidies were granted especially through the construction period; once the railroad company was in full operation, whenever possible the State reclaimed a fraction of the company's profits through taxation.[102]

---

101   Railroads were important for military purposes for France, Germany, and Italy, they were intended to move troops for both offensive and defensive reasons. Moreover, the United States Civil War convinced all and sundry of the military importance of railroads. Since Britain had no potential land enemies, no military railroads surfaced.
102   Schram 1997, pp. 12-18.

Chapter 5

The Twentieth Century

One could date the beginning of the twentieth century somewhat arbitrarily with 1900, or some similar date, or with the outbreak of World War I in 1914. The dating employed here views the decade or so between 1900 and 1914 as a bridge between the nineteenth and twentieth centuries. While the characteristics of Britain, the United States, and the Continental countries varied in degree during the last two centuries, the cultural core did not alter appreciably, irrespective of the changing economic and political circumstances.

During the twentieth century, the dichotomy between the Anglo-American and the Continental approaches to the role of the State in the economy remained, by and large, stable even though cataclysms plagued the first half of the twentieth century. World War I, the Great Depression, and World War II, wrought havoc. These events mandated short-run policy solutions for economic and often physical survival and forged today's world. The century experienced two destructive global wars as well as the temporary collapse of the economies of the capitalist system during the great depression.[1]

In defending a seemingly failed capitalist system, perhaps Fascism and Nazism constituted aberrations in the European Continent. Surely they gave a marked impetus to the State's role in the economies of the Continental countries. During the 1920s, some French defenders of the democratic State were confused by the political success of Mussolini in Italy. For the doubter, there appeared to be a choice between freedom and property or perhaps both freedom and property.

As the foremost capitalist countries, Britain, the U.S., and the Continentals were concerned with the apparent demise of capitalism and the spread of Communism. The capitalists lost faith in the capitalist ideology and believed that Marxist ideology was becoming all-powerful (wherein they were proven wrong). With the rise to power of Adolf Hitler in Germany, some thought or even hoped that a barrier had been erected against the Bolshevik threat. Unwittingly, in the vain hope of saving themselves, the capitalist countries practised benign neglect or appeasement for Nazi Germany that almost destroyed the entire capitalist system.[2]

---

1   Also, the century experienced a brutal period of German hegemony in Europe, as well as the rise and fall of the Soviet Union.

2   When Germany started rearming openly, instead of opposing her, Britain secretly granted Germany the right to build a navy superior to that of France. When a military insurgent ignited a rebellion in Spain in 1936, the French premier, Leon Blum, wanted to assert France's right to sell arms to the legitimate government under international law. Britain warned Blum that if this were to lead to a conflict with Germany or Italy,

The resurgence of nationalism as a consequence of World War I and the dissolution of the Austro-Hungarian, Russian, and Ottoman empires coupled with the Great Depression, increased both tariff and non-tariff barriers such as quotas, subsidies, and foreign exchange controls. World foreign trade collapsed much more dramatically than world gross product between 1929 and 1932. In an effort to restore the flourishing international economy that had prevailed prior to World War I, after World War II, the major world trading partners in 1947 signed the General Agreement on Tariffs and Trade, GATT, known later as the World Trade Organization, WTO.

To avoid future wars and increase economic efficiency, six West European countries, Belgium, France, Italy, Luxembourg, the Netherlands, and West Germany but notably not Britain, formed the Common Market in 1957, culminating the process of European economic integration under way since 1815. Membership in the Common Market increased gradually to include Britain and most other European nations, which reduced the ability of the member countries to protect their domestic industries.

During the breakdown of the 1930s governments everywhere intervened in the economy to mitigate market failures. The United States under the New Deal emulated other countries, especially Britain, by enacting social legislation, which provided for old age pensions and unemployment insurance.[3] Immediately after World War II, Britain and the Continental countries underwent a period during which the nationalization of enterprises and control of the economy attained a peak. Since the 1970s, however, a strong reversal has taken place in Britain through a process of privatization and the limitation of State interference in the economy. In the Continental countries, by the 1990s the European Union also opted for privatization and attempted to cap social welfare expenditures.[4]

By the mid-twentieth century the Continent attained rates of economic growth and levels of per capita income comparable to Britain's, and by the end of the century comparable to that of the United States.[5] While in 1960, Britain had the highest public sector employment as a share of total employment, peaking at 21 percent by the late 1970s and by 1995 the share of government employment declined to 14 percent. By comparison, in France public sector employment

---

he could not count on British support. Unfortunately, the sacrifice of Spain encouraged the German and Italian dictators and precipitated the conflagration that followed. Guerard 1969, p. 414.

3   Also, in the United States, Medicare (health insurance for the elderly) and Medicaid (health insurance for the poor) were introduced aspects of the 'Great Society' of the 1960s. However, the U.S. remained the only industrialized country not to mandate universal single payer health insurance.

4   By 2000, in addition to the initial Common Market, the European Union included Austria, Britain, Denmark, Finland, Greece, Ireland, Portugal, Spain and Sweden.

5   During the heyday of the 1960s, the economies of the Continental countries grew at rates between 4.4 and 5.6 percent, Britain by 2.9 percent and the United States by 4.2 percent. In the 1990s the economies of the Continent and of Britain grew at about 2.2-2.7 and of the United States by 3.2 percent. Crepax 2002, p. 215; ISTAT 2000.

increased from 13 percent in 1960 to 25 percent in 1995. The United States, Italy, and Germany experienced about the same percentages of public employment as Britain.[6]

The statistics on public expenditures are even more revealing. In 1900, the British central government spent ten percent of the national income, the United States four, and France 14 percent. Between 1961 and 1996 public expenditures, including administration, transfer payments, public education and defense as a share of GNP, increased in all western European countries but in Britain rose to forty-two percent while in France, Germany, and Italy attained fifty or more percent. While the United States saw substantial increases, these still represent 30 percent or much less than 50 percent of the gross national product prevalent in France, Germany, and Italy. It appears that on the Continent the State shared equally with the private sector in spending. Given the historic desire by the British to minimize the public sector, it seems a bit strange that public expenditures in Britain reached 42 percent.[7]

One must be careful to disaggregate the public expenditure statistics as best one can. In the United States, education expenditures take the greatest share of the budget at all levels, federal, state, and especially local, where they account for 50 to 70 percent of the budget. Even though a significant share of higher education is private/independent (50 percent in 1940 and 25 percent in 2000), a larger percentage of Americans are enrolled in colleges and universities and remain in school longer than in the European counterparts. All European countries, including Britain, have had just a token private education system at all levels.[8]

To clarify the statistics further, while in the United States, since World War II, the State has spent a larger proportion of its budget on research and development than has France, Germany, and Italy; much of these expenditures have been connected to defense and space, although it is true that defense research and development expenditures has filtered down to the civilian economy, as a hidden subsidy. The interstate highway system as well as certain education expenditures nominally related to defense has gathered political support. Therefore, in the foremost *laissez faire* economy, the State has remained only somewhat neutral.

Economic theory went though contortions in an attempt to explain events and counsel policy makers. During the twenties, Alfred Marshall's (1843-1924) moderate neo-classical economics were in vogue with expectations that the markets clear goods and services at a competitive price. Austrian economists

---

6   Ackley 1987; OECD 1981,1990a, 1990b, 1997; United States Department of Commerce 1975, 2001.

7   In 1961 public expenditures as a percentage of gross national product were: Britain 33 percent, the United States 23, France 34, Germany 34, and Italy 29 percent. Ackley 1987; Somers 1998; United States Council of Economic Advisers to the President 1997. Unfortunately, the data are not all consistent among countries or over time. We use the statistics here only to indicate broad tendencies and trends.

8   Towards the end of the twentieth century approximate outlays on education as a percentage of total public expenditures were: 22 for Britain, 21 for the United States, 22 for France, 20 for Germany, and 29 for Italy.

Ludwig von Mises (1881-1973) and Friedrich August von Hayek (1899-1992) for whom any government intervention meant disaster followed in Marshall's footsteps. Even in the free market United States Mises and Hayek found few adherents. Grudgingly Britain and the U.S. adopted short run interventionist policies promoted by John Maynard Keynes, while France hesitated but by the end joined the interventionist political liberal group; Germany for a decade and Italy for two decades were taken over by believers in the corporate State.

By mid-century, monetarists led by Milton Freedman rejected the Interventionist State generally accepted by Keynesian economists. Their limited government theory discarded the discretionary policies of the central bank and government fiscal policies. By the 1970s Sargent further revived neoclassical economics by advancing a 'rational expectations' theory. Consistent with Mises and Hayek a half a century earlier, the rational expectation theory assumed perfect market clearing and called for a non-interventionist State, greatly influencing policy makers in both the United States and Britain.[9]

Recently, an American observer claimed that in the United States freedom has been associated with autonomy of propriety, that is, wealth grants independence and security. The role of the State has been to guarantee individual propriety rights. In Western Europe freedom has been associated with interdependence that in a way has created more empathy for those who have not been successful. For example, at the end of the twentieth century, public transfer payments as a share of government expenditures amounted to 11 percent in the United States and 26 percent in France. This might explain why in the United States, 17 percent of the population was poor, while France classified 8.1 percent of the population as poor, Germany 7.5, and Italy 14.1 percent.[10]

Culturally Continentals have preferred 'better to more'; ultimately, with a shorter workweek the Continentals have chosen more leisure and consequently lower average family income. Immediately after World War II, Continental Europe boomed with high productivity levels and by 1980s Italy, the poorest of the five countries, overcame Britain in per capita income. However, in the aftermath by the end of the twentieth century, productivity rates declined, while unemployment increased in France, Germany, and Italy at a rate twice as high as in Britain and the United States.[11] Yet, European have had longer vacations, the welfare State has been stronger and reached further than in the Anglo-American countries. The European Commissioner for Economic Affairs asserted that 'for Europeans, growth is a tool, not an end in itself...we need to protect our economic and social model'.[12]

9   Schachter 1973, p. 332; see also Sargent 1993, passim.
10 Rifkin 2004, pp. 13-14, 40, 46, 49.
11 Ball 1994, pp. 16-129.
12 Katryn Bennhold in *The New York Times*, 29 July 2004.

230 *Cultural Continuity in Advanced Economies*

Britain

The rate of economic growth in Britain slowed perceptibly between the 1870s and 1914. Concomitantly rival countries dominated in the so-called 'new industries', such as steel, chemicals, and electrical machinery. To illustrate, in 1914 none of the four largest electrical machinery firms in Britain were British-owned; two were American and two were German multinationals. During the late 1890s, public sentiment or at least a highly vocal minority in Britain, clamored for protection in the form of imperial preference, but the *laissez faire* ideology, among other factors, delayed gratification of this demand until the depression of the thirties.

The extension of the suffrage combined with Bismarck's German precedents resulted in the extension of social programs. Industrial accidents, health, and unemployment received the attention of the State, partly on the grounds that individuals could not (and presumably should not have to) cope with the vicissitudes of modern economic and social life. Certainly the heyday of *laissez faire* had passed well before the end of the nineteenth century. The State intervened intermittently, and inconsistently, presumably to right alleged wrongs. Thereafter, intervention seemed to come in waves, frequently occasioned by a specific crisis.

The decade or so between the turn of the century and the outbreak of the World War I witnessed new departures in myriad directions as well as the extension of old public policy ventures. Britain established the Port of London Authority (1909) under the Port of London Act (which followed the pattern of the Mersey Docks and Harbor Board set-up in 1858). In turn, this can be traced back to the precedent of the turnpike trusts during the eighteenth century and, more specifically, Liverpool's policy starting in 1715, of constructing its own docks. Not surprisingly, when it came time for the State to decide regarding the Port of London, principled controversy did not exist; State action needed only a reconciliation of private interests.[13]

The heritage of Adam Smith and those classical economists who followed in his wake, some of whom favored at least limited intervention, influenced British economic policies. The Industrial Revolution, the extension of the suffrage, and the establishment of health insurance and old age pensions in Germany in 1883, markedly augmented the British State's regulatory activity at home. The long train of domestic regulatory policies initiated during the nineteenth century culminated in a vast expansion of the State's role during the twentieth century. What began as Tory socialism, from the top down, became a reform movement surging to bring workmen's compensation in 1906 and the National Insurance Act (providing national compulsory coverage for accidents and sickness) in 1911.[14]

---

13 Gordon 1938, pp. 7-10, 18-25.
14 Thomasson 2002, p. 233 n. 2. The Unemployment Workingmen Act (1905) coped with cyclical unemployment through municipal public works. Also, the Development and Road Fund Act (1909) was instituted without the benefit of countercyclical spending theory. Similarly, the National Insurance Act (1911) provided national

World War I mandated intervention on an unheralded scale. The recovery of the twenties proved weak and the exchange rate crisis of 1925, which furthered the interests of the City, London's financial district, at the expense of the country, exacerbated conditions. Declining or sick industries, for instance, coal, which depended heavily on exports, received the care of the State; even the nationalization of the coal industry received consideration. World War II exacted such a toll that people could not help asking: How much better will the new world be? In the immediate aftermath of that war, nationalization burst previous bounds and included not only the predictable coal industry but also numerous others. Furthermore, social welfare programs expanded to protect the population from the cradle to the grave. In short, by about 1950 the British economy had adopted policies that seemingly were aberrant to its historic culture.

Before World War I Britain enacted social legislation; for instance, the working poor received special treatment but their families did not receive medical services. Also, Britain manifested special concern for the most important and hazardous mining industry. Safety regulations first appeared in 1902; more than a half century later, owing to the adverse consequences of asbestos, Britain passed the Health and Safety of Work Act of 1974. Workmen's compensation legislation was enacted in 1897 and 1905, and the Eight Hour Act (1909) established the eight-hour day. The large number of coalmines coupled with excess capacity and the reliance on exports tended to depress wages in the industry. As a response, the Minimum Wage Act (1912) was passed. Furthermore, the Trade Boards Act (1909) reversed the 1824 Spitalfields Act and fixed minimum wages for specified trades.[15]

Public Utilities and Natural Monopolies

Public rather than private ownership tended to occur in network technology industries with high fixed costs. These infrastructure industries became public pragmatically rather than ideologically.[16] The introduction and expansion of the telephone imposed a choice between private and public ownership.[17] Many viewed the telephone as a natural monopoly network in which the value of each telephone instrument increased geometrically as the number of users expanded. Constructing a telephone network required considerable capital investment as well as the technical ability to transmit over ever-longer distances. In 1880 the courts decided that the postal service could take control of the development of the telephone system. *The Economist*, the dominant business/economic weekly, advocated a government rather than a private monopoly and vigorously supported

---

insurance against sickness, accidents, invalidity, and old age; the last supplemented the Pension Act (1908).

15   Court 1954, pp. 279, 282-283, 285-286; Kirby 1977, pp. 15, 20, 31; Winch 1970, p. 55.

16   Foreman-Peck and Millward 1994, pp. 1, 2, 7.

17   Alexander Graham Bell invented the telephone in 1876; other critical improvements such as the switchboard (1878) and the loading coil (1899) followed.

nationalization. While half a dozen towns operated their own municipal telephone enterprises, the National Telephone Company shared a virtual monopoly with the Post Office by 1890, which deployed its power to protect the State's investment in the telegraph.

The Telephone The nationalization of the telephone resulted from a bureaucratic imperative. The Post Office had the right (derived from the nationalization of the telegraph) to license all means used to transmit messages through electricity. The nationalization of the telegraph in 1868 had been challenged on the ground of expediency and practicality, that is, on a cost benefit analysis, rather than on the basis of *laissez faire* ideology. The sequence of events in Britain commenced with the cheap postal service instituted in the 1840s; from thence the nationalization of both the telegraph and the telephone seemed to follow inexorably. General dissatisfaction with the retarded development of the telephone system resulted in a gradual takeover by the Post Office, completed in 1911.[18]

Electricity and Gas Electricity supply constituted another illustration of a network or natural monopoly, which was seen as a public utility industry. When electric lighting became technologically feasible by the early 1880s, economies of scale dictated increasingly larger scale power plants. The desire to avoid constant street reconstruction mandated a single power source while the variability in the demand for electricity necessitated the transmission of electricity from one area to another. In 1882, the Electric Lighting Act not only regulated maximum pricing but also limited the duration of company franchises and fostered local government electric supply ownership. Municipalization enabled local governments to defray their expenses from profits rather than taxes.[19]

During the nineteen twenties the use of electricity for both residential and industrial purposes expanded tremendously; in addition, the technology of generating and distributing electricity improved greatly. The Electricity (Supply) Act, non-interventionist, established the Electricity Commission to encourage enterprises to voluntarily accomplish economies of scale by achieving optimum size. In 1926 the Electricity Act created the Central Electricity Board to implement a national grid. Predictably, the critics of the Board's mission contended that such interventionist legislation presumed eventual nationalization and thus socialism.[20]

Britain regulated the local network gas industry even before electricity; this policy, sometimes known as 'gas and waterworks socialism', widely accepted across the spectrum of political opinion, certainly indicates the porosity of *laissez faire* by State intervention. During the polemical debate, the opponents expressed concern about municipal ownership and invoked the 'specter' of socialism.

---

18   Kieve 1973, pp. 199-215.
19   Foreman-Peck and Millward 1994, p. 142.
20   Hannah 1977, pp. 208, 210, 218; Hannah 1979, pp. 75, 88, 101, 108, 330, 349.

Limited scale economies and geographic scope favored private enterprise before World War I.[21]

The Radio Guglielmo Marconi invented wireless telegraphy (radio) in 1895; the Post Office succeeded in gaining control by 1904. Public radio broadcasting appeared only after World War I, and became a regulated activity from the start. When a House of Commons committee opposed radio advertising in 1922, entrepreneurs organized the British Broadcasting Company as a virtual private monopoly and obtained a license, which stipulated that income should not be derived from advertising. The British Broadcasting Corporation (BBC) was founded in 1926, with only one minor dissent, as a public corporation to furnish non-commercial radio broadcasts with the owners of radio-paying a user fee. The British Broadcasting Corporation had been founded with a monopoly of programming defined by its progenitors; the avowed mission was to uplift the masses. To this end, BBC inaugurated the 'Third Program' in 1946, which attracted only two percent of its listeners. Perhaps in recognition of this reality, private television appeared on the scene in 1954. The public service argument proved persuasive, especially since the BBC obligated itself to ignore market considerations and pursued an elitist highbrow programming.[22]

Government Intervention in Industries

World War I, the first such widespread conflict since the Napoleonic Wars a century earlier, exerted profound pressure on the British economy. During the more or less prosperous twenties when *laissez faire* still constituted nominal official policy, Britain embarked on public policies such as subsidies for coal mining and shipbuilding. Britain emerged from World War I as a wounded victor, no longer occupying the same relative position in the world economy that it had enjoyed prior to 1914. Much to the consternation of the 'nineteenth century liberals', some people favored protection, nevertheless, 'imperial preference', that is, protection, had to wait until 1931. Based on historical experience, a primary post-war depression was expected at the cessation of hostilities. The Unemployment Insurance Act of 1920 extended the coverage originally adopted in 1909.[23] Another counter cyclical measure, the Trade Facilities Act of 1921, enabled the British government to guarantee loans extended by private lenders to private enterprises.[24]

Coal Workers as well as businessmen can pursue rent-seeking behavior with equal alacrity; neither theory nor ideology offers a convincing explanation in such

---

21   Hannah 1977, p. 207; Hannah 1979, pp. 5, 23-24, 329.
22   Taylor 1965, pp. 232-233; Youngson 1960, p. 62; Mowat 1955, pp. 242-244; Coase 1950, pp. 4, 10, 17, 23, 60, 63.
23   Another piece of legislation, the 1925 Widows, Orphans and Old Age Contributory Pension Act, derived from prewar efforts. Gilbert 1970, p. 235.
24   Winch 1970, p. 100; Grove 1962, p. 46.

instances. World War I not only resulted in government intervention in the economy on a hitherto unprecedented scale but also left a marked residue. A so-called 'sick industry', coal mining had such fundamental problems that many pragmatically advocated nationalization even though ideologically this solution seemed repugnant. At least since 1912, Britain had regulated coal mining in what was otherwise overwhelmingly a free enterprise economy. So troubled was this industry, so beset with problems beyond resolution through the market, that in 1919 nationalization was seriously discussed although blocked; however, nationalization took place in 1946 with the opposition all but silent.

The aftermath of World War I only exacerbated already existing conditions in coal mining. Partly because the Versailles Treaty called for Germany to export coal as part of the reparations in kind, in 1921, and again in 1925, Britain briefly subsidized coal miners wages to maintain existing miners income over the short run. When Britain returned to the gold standard in 1925 at the unrealistic prewar parity, it exerted downward pressure on export industries, especially coal mining. The immediate effect of this ill-advised monetary policy handicapped the coal export trade. The consequent fall in coal prices depressed wages, which provoked a coal miners' strike, and a general sympathy strike in 1926.

If coal mining had possessed all the attributes of a classic sick industry for years, the 1930s severe and prolonged depression virtually killed the patient. Demand collapsed leading to depressed prices and wages and increased unemployment. Britain curbed the excessive competition brought about by an excessive number of mines and miners. This atypical industry, in which the supposedly self-adjusting market could not balance demand and supply at a socially defined acceptable level, received extraordinary State intervention. The Coal Mines Act of 1930, augmented in 1938, established the Coal Mining Reorganization Commission, which cartelized selling and regulated marketing; it also mandated the amalgamation of coalmines and reduced competition. Unfortunately, such a policy could in no way benefit the coal miners, once the aristocracy of labor who became the victims of permanent unemployment.[25]

Cotton Before World War I cotton goods constituted Britain's major export and Britain dominated the world cotton textile industry. Exports declined substantially by 1930 and then further still during the 1930s owing, among other factors, to the competition of several nations. The British cotton textile industry remained trapped with a large number of relatively technological backward and small-scale not integrated enterprises, that is, a long outmoded industry structure. A classic sick industry, the cotton textile industry could not extricate itself from its plight unaided. The industry voluntarily destroyed six million spindles but with meager results. To rescue the cotton textile industry, the State responded with the Cotton Industry (Reorganization) Act of 1936, which created the Spindles Board; financed by a mandatory fee on spindles. The Board fixed minimum prices and scrapped the oversupply of spindles and thereby reduced excess capacity.

---

25   Kirby 1977, pp. 2, 73, 137-138, 166, 197; Kirby 1973, pp. 160, 172-173.

The Cotton Industry (Reorganization) Act of 1939 authorized the industry to fix prices with the State monitoring the process; this legislation replaced the invisible hand of the market with compulsory 'cartelization'. Furthermore, since the industry and therefore mass unemployment remained unevenly distributed spatially, the Special (Depressed) Areas Act of 1934 aimed to affect the location of industry.[26] As a result of this and similar legislation, it would appear that during the depression, collectivism triumphed over individualism.[27] 'By 1939 the industrial landscape in Britain was a peculiar mixture of free competition, voluntary restrictions, and (occasionally) compulsory cartelization.'[28]

The Chemical Industry In several instances Britain intervened in particular industries or companies for reasons of state. Imperial Chemical Industries (ICI) was formed in 1926 to create a large-scale British counterpart to I. G. Farben (1925) of Germany and the giant American chemical firms. Prior to World War I, Germany had dominated the world chemical industry. The State's concern with ICI was military and an intimate relationship developed between the ICI and the British government, despite the absence of State shareholding or board representation. While one can readily assume that *laissez faire* exercised an influence on British thinking and action, the State-enterprise relationship went beyond enterprise profit.[29] It appears that ICI constituted a private enterprise vested with certain attributes of a public corporation and illustrated the military-industrial complex.

A less interventionist example is that of Courtauld, a long-established textile company that became the major British rayon producer during the early 1900s. By the sixties Courtauld constituted a vertically integrated fiber-textile firm. The acts of the thirties, intended to affect the location of British industry, had little effect on Courtauld. But the Board of Trade under the Monopolies and Mergers Act of 1965, which granted the power to control acquisitions, exercised a considerable weight on enterprise decision-making.[30]

Trade Policies

For approximately half a century, that is, from circa 1880 to 1934, Britain had an export-based economy. Britain exported cotton textiles, iron and steel, ships, locomotives, and all manner of manufactured goods, which paid for the imported food and fiber. At the outset, the trade balance fostered capital exports; later, the invisible earnings from capital exports enabled the British to live better than current output warranted. All this changed after World War I, especially with the onset of the depression of the thirties. The center of the international capital market shifted from London to New York; new areas of manufacturing emerged,

26   Taylor 1965, p. 340; Youngson 1960, p. 162.
27   Greaves 2002, pp. 58, 60-61, 68, 72, 75.
28   Greaves 2002, p. 75.
29   Reader 1977, pp. 227, 229-231, 241-242.
30   Knight 1974, pp. 17-18, 68, 174, 192.

both within and outside the Empire. The low tariff era ended abruptly; for example, the United States, historically a high tariff country, increased its tariffs in 1922 and markedly so in 1930, which necessitated the British response.

By mid-nineteenth century, Britain had become more or less a free trade country but the great contraction (1929-1932) precipitated an abrupt course correction. In 1931, Britain abandoned the gold standard and in 1932 replaced free trade with 'imperial preference' that protected British domestic industry, and urged the public to 'buy British'. In all likelihood, the most dramatic revolution in British economic thought and policy occurred in foreign trade. For a century or more Britain had been the workshop of the world, manufacturing not only for itself but also for all corners of the world, both within and outside the Empire.

In 1932, Britain enacted a ten percent general tariff, especially on manufacturing, with the exception of food and raw materials. In 1914, Britain, still the world's preeminent exporter, lacked tariff protection so industry had to swim or sink. A tariff had been imposed in 1921 (and earlier) on a narrow range of luxury goods, through the Safeguarding of Industries Act. The mass unemployment during the thirties cast free trade into the dustbin of history. While the tariff reform movement circa 1900 favored protection, the pressure, coming only from the industries besieged by latecomers, proved insufficient to overcome the forces of tradition as well as the intellectual argument. Now, however, suffering stalked the land in the form of idle men and idle machines. Consequently, Britain inaugurated a protectionist policy and annulled decades of, by and large, free trade.[31]

The severity and the duration of the 1930s depression wrought havoc in the British economy (as in most economies of the world) and compelled profound changes in policy making. The State addressed both cyclical and structural problems in ways that would not have been contemplated earlier. For the third time within a century, Britain came to the assistance of its shipping and shipbuilding industries. Both suffered acutely from the depression although with a somewhat differential impact. In 1930, Cunard started constructing the liner *Queen Mary*, intended to be equal or superior to any other trans-Atlantic luxury liner. Building was halted in 1931 because of the Cunard Line's financial difficulties, only to be resumed in 1934, in part because popular feelings was aroused to the extent that people, including children, all over Britain sent humble contributions in an effort to assist. Cunard received a subsidized interest loan of 8 million pounds to help build the *Queen Mary* and the sister ship *Queen Elizabeth*.[32]

During the 1930s, Britain broke with its free trade tradition and formed marketing boards for several commodities. In many instances, ideological considerations seemed to prevail, at least in retrospect. The most recent turning of the wheel has introduced an element of the pragmatic, asking what place efficiency plays in such policymaking. After World War II, Britain found it inexpedient to end agricultural support; the United States demanded hard currency during the post-war dollar shortage decade. The Agricultural Act (1947) has protected

31   Feinstein 1983, pp. 11, 11n, 52, 93, 95.
32   Aldcroft 1970, pp. 226, 346.

agriculture ever since; British consumers have paid about 50 percent above world market price; and, therefore, they have supported the subsidy to agriculture. After joining the Common Market in 1973, (now the European Union) agricultural protection was strengthened within the scope of the Common Agricultural Policy (CAP). The policy in the various industrial sectors followed the same pragmatic approach.

Industrial Policy

All nations have areas in which industry and income are concentrated owing either to the location of resources or other factors. During the immediate postwar period, Britain's policies aimed to correct market failures. In 1945, that is, immediately after World War II, Britain passed the Distribution of Industry Act, similar to the legislation of the thirties, and then the Town and Country Planning Act in 1947 to regulate the growth of communities. With the word 'planning', the State supplemented the free market in the sense the State did not accept the 'invisible hand' on its own to optimize the use of resources and maximize welfare.[33]

Of necessity, World War II enormously expanded the role of the State in the British economy. During the austerity of World War II, the principle of fair shares for all or equality of sacrifice, impacted social policy.[34] Shortly thereafter, the State instituted national health insurance, completing a comprehensive social insurance program, and nationalized several key industries.[35] Prior to 1945, ideology played little part and decisions were primarily pragmatic; after that date the reverse is true. Air transport nationalization before World War II, that is, the British Overseas Airways Corporation (1940), paved the way for the Transport Act of 1947.[36]

Both coal and rail nationalization were based on the need for public investment. In a typical case of rent seeking, perhaps British rail workers and their unions supported nationalization hoping that the political pressure would bring higher wages. Coal had long been recognized as a sick industry with excess capacity; the 800 private coal companies had come close to nationalization after World War I. Similarly, railways had been regulated intensively almost from the outset and nationalization had been seriously considered during the late nineteenth century. Increasingly debates focused on expediency rather than on *laissez faire* ideology. Changes of government brought about ups and downs of economic and social policies. For example, in its heyday prior to World War I, the Bank of England had been quite autonomous of the government and this contributed to later

---

33 Court 1954, p. 227; see also Hayek 1944.
34 Zweiniger-Bargielowska 2000, pp. 1, 256, 264.
35 More or less immediately following World War II, Britain nationalized the Bank of England (1946) and Cable and Wireless (1947); also, it established the National Coal Board (1947), the British Transport Commission (rail and road) (1948), the British Electrical Authority (1948), the British Gas Council (1949), and the Iron and Steel Corporation (1951).
36 Aldcroft 1975, p. 71.

nationalization. Now neither independent nor private, the Bank of England could
no longer interpose its judgment against that of Her Majesty's Government.[37]
Nationalized industry (circa 1978 and therefore before privatization) in France,
Germany, and Italy was more broadly distributed, for instance, chemicals, tobacco,
and glass than in Britain.[38]

If one wished to engage in hyperbole, one might contend that since the end of
World War II Britain has undergone a revolution in economic policy and thought
followed by a counterrevolution. If one pursued this line of reasoning, one would
inevitably focus on the nationalization of selected companies and industries and
then on the subsequent privatization of many of these same companies and
industries. On balance, however, there definitely has been an extension of the
boundaries of State action.[39]

The motives for nationalization were, in each instance, quite varied. After
World War II, Britain depended upon a continuation of its wartime economy,
which during the war had subordinated the market to the overriding goal of victory
on the battlefield. At times, industry had been so thoroughly regulated, perhaps as
a natural monopoly or network industry or capital-intensive industry, that moving
from regulation to a public corporation merely constituted the next natural step and
therefore was barely perceptible to anyone. In other instances, the industry had
been sick and therefore dependent upon the State for continued survival. In still
other cases, new or infant industries prompted State ownership. Finally, defense
considerations must never be ignored as an aspect of statecraft.

As a particular variant of State intervention or for that matter any form of State
intervention since World War II, nationalization must be viewed against the
backdrop of the relative decline of the British economy, especially marked since
1945. Neither in Britain's old industries, for example, coal, cotton, and
shipbuilding, nor in the new, for instance, automobiles, could Britain hold its own
against foreign competition. Not only did competitors edge Britain out of foreign
markets but also Britain could not retain its domestic market. In a cruel jest some
years ago, when Britain seemed particularly afflicted with so-called 'British
disease', there were those who suggested that, owing to deindustrialization, Britain
be converted into a giant Disneyland.

The consensus accepted the necessity of having the State intervene increasingly
to correct specific market and managerial failures and therefore regulate such
matters as minimum wages, maximum hours, and child labor as well as working
conditions.[40] During the 1920s the Bank of England covertly acted as the lender of
last resort for the steel and textile industries and in 1929 salvaged the *Banca Italo-
Britannica*, a British bank located in Italy with some Italian participation.[41]

---

37 While not adhering to the European Monetary Union (by not adopting a common
    currency, with the introduction of the Euro in 1999), Britain could not help but be
    affected by common policies adopted by the European Union.
38 Foreman-Peck and Millward 1994, p. 7.
39 Cairncross 1992, p. 293.
40 In 1998, Britain finally initiated a national minimum wage policy.
41 Checkland 1983, pp. 315, 318; Kindleberger 1995, pp. 351-352.

During the 1930s Britain minimally accepted public works programs to strengthen an unemployment policy dependent on the self-adjusting market mechanism to revive the economy; the railroads were not nationalized as an instrument to combat the depression.[42] Government contra cyclical intervention in the United States economy exceeded Britain's action but the United States economy showed about the same outcome as Britain's before World War II.

The State became more involved in the economy during the immediate post-war period. The theories of John Maynard Keynes permeated British professional and public opinion; no longer did either accept mass unemployment as inevitable, especially when Keynesian contra cyclical policy seemed at hand. Although such beliefs continued to influence the thrust of the British economy, Britain proved to be a most reluctant planner; the immediate post World War II triumph of the loosely defined socialist ideology proved fleeting indeed.

Nationalization and Privatization

When the interventionist Labor Party came to power in 1945, mostly for ideological reasons, the State pursued the nationalization of selected industries; afterwards, an up and down game with changing governments ensued. The State nationalized coal (a sick industry), steel, iron, railroads, civil aviation, electricity, gas, and the Bank of England. Coal would have been nationalized regardless of which party won in 1945; Britain had a desperate need for coal to heat houses and run factories although there was a shortage of people willing to work in the mines. Such direct State intervention in the economy was essentially novel for Britain, which historically had stressed that individual welfare would more or less automatically lead to collective welfare. For instance, whereas before 1914 Britain had been the world's largest shipbuilder, after World War II its seemingly impregnable position proved vulnerable to foreign competition. Consequently, the State intervened to bolster this lame duck industry before nationalization in 1977. Also, in the 1970s the State became a partner of France in the consortia that build the economically unsuccessful now defunct supersonic passenger plane, the *Concorde*.[43]

Only in the instance the nationalization of iron and steel serious opposition surfaced. Iron and steel in no way constituted a classic sick, inefficient, or unprofitable industry. Moreover, the oligopolistic iron and steel industry had not been micro managed through a regulatory authority, which controlled prices, products, and rates of return. Rationalization had been fostered during the thirties to correct alleged inefficiency and market failure. The resistance to nationalization never invoked the battle cry of the nineteenth century, that is, *laissez faire*. The opposition, pragmatic rather than ideological, rallied around a much more circumscribed defense, namely, efficiency.

The British government essentially advanced an *a priori* rather than an economic argument for steel nationalization and the opposition defending private

---

42   Hall 1986a, pp. 269-270.
43   Lorenz and Wilkinson 1986, p. 124.

ownership replied in kind. Some perceived the nationalization of steel as a prelude to more widespread nationalization (socialization) and favored it for that very reason while others opposed nationalization for precisely the same reason. These policies illustrate the controversy; the Iron and Steel Act of 1949, as revised in 1951, nationalized the industry only to be reversed in 1953 and then re-nationalized. The Iron and Steel Act (1967) was based on inefficiency and applied only to the largest companies; the private sector produced specialized products and bought from and competed with British Steel. Finally, the British Steel Corporation was privatized in 1988.[44] Ideology hardly furnished a consistent government policy for the British steel industry.

Another wave of nationalization swept over Britain during the 1970s, this time frequently motivated by job maintenance rather than ideological considerations that had loomed vital earlier. Nationalization embraced aircraft, automobiles, and shipbuilding, among other industries and represented signs of the weakness of the British economy. In each instance, Britain deemed it imperative, despite a substantial protective tariff, to rescue the industry, either as a matter of national prestige or to preserve employment in depressed areas.

Circa the 1950s Britain possessed a significant automobile industry characterized, however, by too many British-owned firms fragmenting too small a market, resulting in low productivity and high unit costs. The sixties wrought havoc in the British automobile industry, with a declining share of both world production and exports. By the mid seventies the British-owned sector of the automobile industry withered on the vine while imports and the US multinationals thrived. These conditions prompted an illustration of 'lemon socialism'.

Rolls Royce collapsed as a private enterprise as a consequence of government failure. Following bankruptcy in 1971, Britain nationalized Rolls Royce, a preeminent but lame duck manufacturer of luxury motorcars as well as the major supplier of airplane engines for the British air force. The State could hardly disengage and national defense considerations proved decisive. The State, the big customer, owned the engine sector of the aircraft industry by 1977. Rolls Royce was privatized in 1987 but remained heavily reliant on public markets and State aid. Then again, aerospace is not and never has been anywhere a run of the mill industry.[45] Reconstituting Rolls Royce as a limited liability company with the British government as the sole shareholder, Britain privatized the motorcar division (the diesel engine division) as the Rolls-Royce Motor Cars Limited.

Two other British automobile companies, BMH and Leyland, merged in 1968 to form British Leyland. The Act of 1975 gave the State the power to rescue solvent companies in anticipation of trouble. Britain rescued British Leyland (1974-1975), the last British-owned motorcar company, and, in effect, nationalized

44   Ross 1965, pp. 54, 99-100; Bryer 1990, pp. 84, 100; Vaizey 1974, passim; Tolliday 1986, pp. 100-104; Abromeit 1986, pp. 4, 47, 111, 118-120.
45   Hayward 1983, pp. 99, 116-117, 187; Hayward 1989, pp. 187-188.

this company (privatized more than a decade later).[46] With regard to the U.S. company Chrysler, the cause (social accounting) was the same but the remedy differed, since the American multinational firm was subsidized but without nationalization.[47]

During the nineteenth century, for diverse reasons, including low cost iron and steel as well as marine engines, Britain had been the world's leading shipbuilder and, despite the emergence of challengers, this superiority persisted down to World War I. However, after World War II, the British shipbuilding industry engaged in a valiant and desperate struggle for survival. Between 1959 and 1977 shipbuilding moved toward nationalization, a policy that had been advocated for an industry in decline. Shipbuilding had been subsidized before nationalization. When the British shipbuilding industry, using British steel, as well as labor and other inputs, defeated all comers, the State intervened little; ultimately, when these inputs became high cost, State owned-shipbuilding required huge and open-ended subsidies.[48]

Despite the nationalization of many key sectors, about 80 percent of the British economy remained private. There had been only minor opposition to nationalization, except for steel and long distance road haulage. The Transport Act of 1953 reversed part of the Transport Act of 1947 in the belief that competition would be superior to government ownership. In turn, the opposition to privatization stood mute when privatization occurred, except for public utilities. Ideology drowned out other and more pragmatic analysis. Perhaps the conviction of the efficacy of privatization only replaced a prior naïve trust in the efficiency of nationalization.[49] Britain privatized gas, electricity, water, and telecommunication in addition to British Steel, British Airways, and others.[50] Nonetheless, by 2002, new thinking emerged after the railroads and electric energy debacle, when privatized rail systems went bankrupt and the energy companies were on the verge of bankruptcy. Some argue that 'we've learned that not everything is right for privatization', and even free market advocates accept that the State must interfere to avoid bankruptcy in the energy sector just as in the case of the railroads.[51]

Until sometime following World War II family rather than managerial enterprise characterized the British economy. Britain tolerated agreements among competitors to allocate markets and maintain profitability; the British perceived

---

46 'A less interventionist policy...would have cost the taxpayer, and therefore the economy less, the history of the industry would gave been the same.' Foreman-Peck, Boden and Mckinley 1995, p. 216.

47 Whisler 1999, pp. 121, 124, 264-269; Lewchuk 1986, pp. 135-137; Dunnet 1980, pp. 117-118, 133, 135; Hayward 1971, pp. 133-140, 161-163.

48 Hogwood 1979, pp. 178, 193, 197, 206, 263.

49 Aldcroft 1975, pp. 85, 184-185; Cairncross 1992, pp. 268- 270, 293.

50: Major privatizations included: British Petroleum (1979), British Aerospace and Cable and Wireless (1981), Associated British Ports (1983), Jaguar and British Telecom (1984), British Gas (1986), Rolls-Royce and British Airways (1987), British Steel (1987), The Water Companies (1989) Twelve Regional Electricity Companies (1990), and British Rail (1993).

51 New York Times, 29 August 2002.

such restraint of trade as consistent with *laissez faire* and freedom of contract. Consequently, before World War I, Britain had no antitrust law and relied on the Smithian invisible hand. However, Britain adopted the Monopolies Act (1948) and the Restrictive Trade Practices Act (1956); this legislation reflected an evolving market structure to which *laissez faire* could no longer be applied.[52]

Social Services

The same public policy process occurred in housing and health. Since at least the eighteenth century, Britain's land ownership has been extremely concentrated, especially before 1925; Britain never had a revolution that redistributed land or a law, which accomplished this purpose. Consequently, throughout history, Britain has been a nation of tenants rather than owners. Prior to World War II, Britain regulated housing with regard to health and safety, renovated existing housing, and built public housing, for those whose housing needs could not be met appropriately through the market. This policy did not find general approval. Bombing during the World War II reduced the stock of housing and, of course, housing construction; the supply-demand imbalance became acute. A Rent Control Act became law in 1946, reformed in 1949, when a Housing Act was also passed. Partially owing to rent control, only half as much housing was built in the decade following World War II, as during the depressed decade of the thirties. During 1979-1982, and in 1989, housing underwent privatization, which diminished the role of the State in the housing market in accordance with *laissez faire* theory. To promote private rented accommodations, Britain lifted rent controls, made eviction much easier, reduced the minimum tenancy length to six months, and sold public housing units to tenants.

The combination of the 1930s depression in conjunction with World War II resulted in the adoption of a broad array of special policies. Some merely continued or extended longstanding policies while others departed from the past in response either to new conditions or new perceptions of existing conditions. The Unemployment Insurance Act of 1920 simply could not cope with persistent mass unemployment. Consequently, the Unemployment Act of 1934 replaced the Poor Law of 1834. British public social policy continued to evolve with the National Heath Insurance and Contributory Pensions Act of 1932 and the Old Age and Widow's Pension Act of 1940.[53]

After decades of special purpose legislation, Britain more than flirted with the 'welfare state'; as of 1930 France and the United States spent less than Britain on social transfers.[54] In the midst of World War II in 1942, the social reformer William Henry Beveridge (1879-1963) authored the 'Social Insurance and Allied Services' Report, which advocated cradle-to-grave social security legislation. This report stressed individual responsibility, hence the subsequent legislation, derived from the Beveridge Report, relied on contributory insurance rather than taxes. In a

---

52   Freyer 1992, pp. 1-4, 8, 13, 327.
53   Gilbert 1970, pp. 235, 253, 299, 308.
54   Lindert 1994, p. 26.

burst of enthusiasm and the consensus that ensued immediately after World War II, Britain enacted a succession of measures, which broadened the scope of social services, all of which, however, can be traced to narrower laws enacted before World War I. Consequently, social spending doubled from ten percent of GNP in 1950 to 20 percent in 1990.[55]

The National Health Insurance Act (1946) provided compulsory free medical and hospital care and also nationalized most hospitals. The National Insurance Act (1946) covered unemployment, sickness and disability, maternity and death, payments to retirees, widows and orphans. It, too, depended on the contributory principle supplemented by grants from taxes. Finally, the National Assistance Act (1948) repealed the Poor Law but mandated a means test. All of these sweeping changes gained more or less unanimous support with dissent concerning details rather than principle. In 1948, the National Health Service Act supplied universal and comprehensive medical care.[56] It seems that the British have been divided and have felt uncomfortable with this 'social' legislation.

While various alterations have been introduced, the structure of the British welfare system remained basically unchanged by the end of the twentieth century; there has been a rising threshold concept of poverty. Modifications that occurred over the last two decades of the twentieth century were less inclusive for benefits and groups of the population. For instance, the Social Security Act of 1986 has made the welfare system less inclusive. Similarly, the National Health Service reform of 1987 enabled the affluent to opt out in their quest for better medical care and therefore the health care system became less 'all inclusive' and more burdensome to the less affluent. After years of special laws for specific occupations and segments of the population, Britain enacted a Minimum Wage Law in 1998.

Conclusions

Britain has remained a market economy in most aspects and according to most criteria. With prosperity, the mood changed rapidly; the philosophy of the 1980s minimized the role of the State in the economy. One observer best epitomized this philosophy, which assumes that by reducing the role of the State in the economy the market forces would be liberate from interventionist constraints. This '...would trigger an unleashing of capitalist creative animal spirits and usher in a renaissance of British entrepreneurial talent and risk taking'.[57]

During the 1980s government policies included: the virtual elimination of regional grants, financial deregulation, the reduction of the share of public expenditures in the economy, privatization,[58] and labor market reform aimed at

55   Johnson 1994, pp. 284-285.
56   Taylor 1984, p. 104.
57   Wells 1991, p. 174.
58   Not many British citizens were satisfied with the privatization of British railways in the 1980s. Rather than improving, British railways experienced deterioration of service, frequent derailments, and have been on the verge of bankruptcy, probably

weakening labor unions.[59] It appears that some of the goals of the eighteenth-century British institutional pattern have been accomplished largely in the twentieth-century. Yet, the economy has been regulated much more comprehensively in this century than in the previous two centuries. As then, market and government failures in the form of frictions and incongruities have remained apparent.[60]

Britain reluctantly maintained national health insurance as well as other entitlements to assure minimal protection for individuals. Also, unions weakened and lost membership and collective bargaining power; while public policies facilitated the decline in union membership, one should account for other causes. Unions have been traditionally strongest in the sick industries such as coal and cotton textiles; the steel and auto industries had high wages and restrictive work rules without substantial increases in productivity, which caused a loss of international competitiveness and therefore loss of employment. In addition, technological change enabled Britain to produce steel with fewer workers, which impacted union membership.

The years since World War II have been interesting indeed, filled with both fresh initiatives and abrupt course reversals. Not only did the depression of the thirties leave an angry scar on the body politic but also a recurrence of depressed conditions was widely predicted after the war. Britain has seen its relative position in the world, economic as well political, decline for some decades, dated variously with the 1870s or 1914. Finally, certain sectors of the economy have been so closely regulated for so long that the nationalization of invalid industries hardly seemed worthy of notice; one such instance, the Electricity Act (1947) ended more than half a century of government scrutiny regarding virtually all aspects of the industry.[61] Rather different was the evolution of agricultural policy. During the mid-nineteenth century, Britain opened its markets to low cost agricultural products, available as a consequence of the Agricultural cum Transportation Revolutions; by 1914 food prices in Britain had become the lowest anywhere. Since World War II British policy has abandoned the consumer in favor of domestic producers.

Between the death of Queen Victoria in 1901 and the assassination of Archduke Ferdinand in 1914, Britain ruled the roost and British economic policy and thought reflected this ascendancy. During that golden age Britain achieved the world's second highest per capita income, by far the biggest colonial empire, and the largest foreign trade as well as the greatest foreign investment. Also, Britain dominated traditional industries such as cotton textiles and shipbuilding. Only in the technologies of the Second Industrial Revolution (chemical and electrical machinery) or in those sectors dependent on large-scale capital-intensive industries

---

becoming one of the worst managed railroad systems in Western Europe or the publicly owned Amtrak in the United States.

59 OECD 1991.

60 Deregulation, as well as poor internal management and supervision made possible the downfall of the Barings Bank through the fraudulent action of a single individual.

61 Hannah 1979, p. 256.

such as iron and steel, did Britain fare poorly compared to its rivals. Britain could not compete with low cost resources in the United States or newer and science-based plants in Germany.

British economic policy seemed appropriate to its standing in the world economy as well as to its inherited thought. While Britain considered modifying its historic policies, it rejected such ostensibly outlandish notions as tariffs. Alfred Marshall the transcendent British economist of the Edwardian era turned to economics as a practical means for implementing ethics and social welfare. Exemplar of neo-classical economic thought as well as a liberal social reformer, Marshall accepted the efficacy of government intervention. Marshall's ideas conformed by and large to the flourishing British economy at the beginning of the twentieth century.

Before World War I, Britain adhered with tenacity to a policy of minimum State intervention, free trade, and the international division of labor. Rather than nationalizing, it regulated selected economic sectors, mainly natural monopolies. In this way, Britain rejected the idea that the government should own productive enterprises. It seemed that the public accepted market failure as part of the price for economic, and perhaps, political freedom.

By comparison, at the end of the twentieth century, two world wars had decimated British foreign investments and consequently invisible earnings; foreign competition wrought havoc in industry after industry. The depression of the thirties, followed by the Keynesian Revolution, and much more, including market failure, resulted in the temporary nationalization of numerous sectors of the British economy. Even after denationalization (prompted perhaps by government failure), the State has occupied a far more central place in the British economy than in 1939, and much more than in 1914. Still, there has been an uncertainty as to the proper place of the State within the economy. While *laissez faire* in any recognizable form has been quiescent these many years, pragmatism rather than *étatisme* has prevailed. The State has intervened frequently on a stopgap basis as a consequence of market failure rather than from any implicit or explicit grand design.

United States

American uniqueness has been both affirmed and denied since the settlement of Virginia in the early seventeenth century. During the twentieth century the United States has been unique with private (though subsidized) airlines and telecommunications, but with no state enterprises in oil, gas, and steel. Public expenditures in the United States have represented a smaller share of GNP than in Britain, France, Germany, and Italy. The State at all levels (federal, state, and local) has promoted and has regulated business, even if at times arbitrarily. Until the late nineteenth century, the United States lacked an extensive professional civil service. Although the Army Corp of Engineers furnished, directly or indirectly, engineering services for railroad construction and management, the limited number of such engineers circumscribed the scope of this aid. Moreover, having a significant navy but an insignificant army as late as 1914, America did not have a military tradition comparable to France, Germany, or Italy.[62] One can only echo the words of a noted historian, 'the past determines the future'.[63]

It is appropriate in treating the United States to divide the twentieth century into three unequal chronological segments. The first began more or less with the turn of the century and ended with the coming of World War I. The second followed the Great Depression and lasted until sometime after World War II. The third started in the 1960s and has continued. In a parallel fashion, the expansion of the State's role in the economy has come in spurts: the Progressive Era (1900-1917), the New Deal (1933-1938), and the second half of the twentieth century.[64] While the regulatory and promotional pace has varied, the trend has been constant and upward.[65]

The federal government rarely undertook a process of nationalization or a policy of state enterprises. The federal government since 1887 has regulated the railroads. However, two public corporations came into existence in 1971: the National Passenger Railway (Amtrak) and the Consolidated Rail Corporation (Conrail) for freight; the latter was privatized in the 1990s after beginning to show profits. Also, during the 1930s the federal government undertook a significant enterprise the Tennessee Valley Authority, a large energy and multi-purpose public corporation operating in seven southern states.

Regulatory agencies have proliferated at the local, state, and federal levels. The traditional regulatory agency has focused on such economic criteria as entry, exit, service, price, and rate of return. A newer category of regulatory agency has concentrated on non-economic issues, especially health, safety, and the environment. While lagging in the provision of publicly funded social services, the United States has been the world regulatory leader in the securities industry. The investor has been protected, albeit imperfectly, against misfeasance and malfeasance committed by an investment banker, a large-scale enterprise whose securities are publicly traded, or a broker. The New York Stock Exchange, regarded as a private club as late as 1912, and other exchanges have been regulated since 1933-1934. Public regulation has been grafted on to the self-regulation of the securities and commodities exchanges and the professional and trade associations to ensure a well-functioning capital market.

With the Federal Reserve Act (1913), the United States embarked upon an implicit role for the semi-autonomous central bank in the management of the economy. This was accomplished much more consciously with the Banking Act of 1935 that transferred the locus of power in the banking system from Wall Street to

---

62 McCraw 1984, p. 35.
63 Chandler 1980, p. 11.
64 An excellent discussion of this topic can be found in an article by Richard H. K. Vietor in the Cambridge Economic History of the United States; Vietor 2000, pp. 969-1012.
65 Solomon Fabricant estimated that circa 1900 the State represented five percent of GNP. Fabricant 1950, pp. 4-18.

the Treasury. The organization of the Federal Deposit Insurance Corporation (FDIC) and the Securities and Exchange Act, both in 1934, added to the ability of the State to affect the allocation and mobilization of capital. The Employment Act of 1946 and the formation of the Council of Economic Advisers, while hardly initiating a command economy, incorporated Keynesian theory into economic policy.

If the United States ever had an essentially *laissez faire* economy, that surely evaporated with the coming of the new century. The State continued to engage in the promotion of economic activity, ranging from the federal government's ownership of a barge line on the Mississippi and Missouri rivers and the protection of American shipbuilding by requiring that American-built and manned vessels carry all sea borne cargo between American ports. Other examples include the Tennessee Valley Authority and the St. Lawrence River Seaway. In addition, the Export-Import Bank was created to facilitate exports through subsidies so as to surmount impediments imposed by foreign governments such as exchange controls and tariffs.

Government and Business

Business Ethics Some highly regulated financial institutions failed or needed to be rescued during the 1980s, perhaps in some measure because of the failure of the regulators; examples can be cited of fraud, mismanagement and/or unwise investments such as the Western Savings and Loan Associations' debacle that cost the American tax payer billions of dollars. At the end of the century regulatory oversight proved inadequate. Such a giant energy company as Enron, and companies such as Tyco, World Com and Vivendi, allegedly defrauded their stockholders by more than one hundred billion dollars through accounting manipulations. The accounting firm, Arthur Andersen, was itself found guilty of misdemeanors. Many of the respected brokerage houses were fined for cheating the public. It proved that regulatory legislation is only as good as its enforcement; otherwise *caveat emptor* prevails.

Regulation and the Public Interest The emphasis definitely shifted towards the regulation of economic activity on behalf of an elusive and changing 'public interest'. Shortly after a community had succeeded in promoting a railroad through its domain during the late nineteenth century, the same community became dissatisfied either with the general level of railroad freight rates or the specific rates charged. In an effort to level the playing field for diverse, and at times contradictory reasons, government regulation encompassed such business practices as: conflict of interest, restraint of trade, competitive tactics, stock watering, and financial reporting.

Expanding the broad base already firmly established, whether as a vestige of mercantilism or as a response to industrialization, the State augmented and refined existing regulatory legislation affecting both single economic sectors and the overall economy. Individual localities and states regulated the electric utilities. Since the Interstate Commerce Commission lost fifteen out of the first sixteen cases taken to the courts, the first two decades of the twentieth century witnessed a succession of legislation, which ultimately bound the railroads hand and foot. Similarly, for more than a decade the courts interpreted the Sherman Antitrust Act so narrowly as to leave much of the public dissatisfied.

The Northern Securities (1904), the Standard Oil, and the American Tobacco decisions (1911) definitely initiated not only new law but also a new antitrust policy, which attempted to regulate the relation of a limited number of large-scale enterprises to their competitors as well as their customers and the public interest. After all, in the eyes of many, the Sherman Act had targeted, Standard Oil above all. New laws and new regulatory agencies produced administrative as well as judicial decisions, which beyond all possible doubt reduced the scope for individual initiative.

The new century brought new men and new interests to the fore but the questions hardly qualified as new. Arguments surfaced in opposition to government intervention but the efficiency or fairness of the intervention rather than some vague and inherently ill-defined concept such as economic individualism ruled the day. Despite occasional flights of rhetoric, *laissez faire* did not constitute the dominant and recurring defense of the old order against the new. Frequently invoking the Constitution, some businessmen opposed any and all interference while others favored supervision and regulation. Practical considerations, such as enhancing consumer confidence or repugnance to adulterated products or, furthermore, the promotion of foreign trade, dictated a positive attitude to regulation by businessmen. Shippers and railroads rarely shared the same views regarding railroad regulation and, similarly, exporters and importers divided; neither challenged the principle of regulation itself.[66]

The Progressive Era (1900-1917) encompassed a burst of legislative activity.[67] Comprehensive government regulation, especially regarding railroad discriminatory rates, and ultimately of abandonment, discontinuance, and revocation, as well as much more, replaced market failure in an inherently oligopolistic industry. Historically *caveat emptor* had been the principle, with salient exceptions, which only seemed to prove the rule. *Caveat emptor* assumed knowledgeable and wary consumers fully able to protect themselves in the marketplace against vendors of metaphorical wooden nutmegs without needing government intervention.

The blend of large-scale enterprises impersonally selling nationally in conjunction with the evolution of chemistry lessened the ability of reasonably sophisticated consumers to act on their own behalf. This resulted in continued efforts to pass laws against food contamination during the late nineteenth century. During the fourth quarter of the nineteenth century, Swift, Armour, Morris, and other enterprises became large-scale vertically integrated meatpackers. By the late 1890s oligopolistic meat packing companies controlled regional, national, and international markets, despite a multitude of small-scale slaughter houses selling

---

66   Wiebe 1962, pp. 48-49, 56-57.
67   As regards the railroads, one need mention only the Elkins Act (1903), the Hepburn Act (1906), and the Mann-Elkins Act (1910).

fresh meat locally. The Meat Inspection Acts (1890 and 1891) had been enacted at the behest of local butchers and their trade associations who claimed that dressed meat shipped to distant markets by refrigerator car was unsanitary. Occasioned by a special interest rent-seeking group, these laws constituted the federal government's first quality guarantees nominally on behalf of the consumer or the general interest.[68] A muckraking journalist, Upton Sinclair, evoked a storm of protest in 1906, as a result of his expose of the unsanitary conditions in the meat packing industries. Owing to his book, *The Jungle*, Congress regulated the meat, food and drug industries through the Meat Inspection Act (1906) and the broader initiative, the Pure Food and Drug Act of that same year.[69]

Public Control of Business By the turn of the century relatively little had been accomplished under the rubric of the public control of business. Starting in the mid-nineteenth century the city of Chicago through a public authority had engaged in resource allocation, to cope with such conflicting objectives as water supply, sewage disposal, and drainage.[70] The Interstate Commerce Act (1887) had governed the railroads, but only in a rudimentary fashion. Also, the Sherman Antitrust Act (1890) had been applied only in a limited number of instances; the meaning of each of these laws had just begun to be interpreted by the courts. During the Progressive Era (1900-1917), the federal government enacted legislation covering particular industries as well as the economy as whole. While the State rarely operated businesses, it interfered on behalf of the ostensible public interest through commissions, such as the Federal Trade Commission, and the courts.

During the New Deal, the State refined existing legislation and ventured new methods, most notably the Tennessee Valley Authority (1933). Since then, the railroads have gone from being minutely regulated on the grounds that excessive power led to discriminate and inordinate rates and profits to having freight and passenger rail service subsidized to keep the trains operating. Nonetheless, while the federal government has regulated the airlines in various ways, the United States has not owned or operated an airline, but has subsidized the airlines in many forms. As in most countries, government at all levels, federal, state, and local, has been constrained in some way or other and in varying degrees in backing all transportation modes.

Like the Reconstruction Finance Corporation during the 1930s depression and after, since World War II the federal government has intervened selectively in the market. It has bailed out large-scale enterprises judged either too big to fail (job preservation) or in some other way too vital to the economy to be allowed to go under. In 1971 to avert bankruptcy, the federal government arranged a rescue for Lockheed Aircraft, the largest defense contractor. Similarly, in 1972 Chrysler, the

---

68   Kujovich 1970, pp. 460-464, 481-482; Libecap 1992, pp. 242-244, 258-260.
69   Sinclair 1946, passim.
70   Cain 1978, pp. ix-xii.

smallest United States automobile manufacturer received a huge loan guarantee to prevent bankruptcy.

Business Concentration Francis B. Thurber (1842-1907), a New York wholesale grocer, self appointed spokesman for New York shippers/merchants, and an advocate of railroad and consumer protection legislation, rejected nineteenth century *laissez faire* in favor of twentieth century liberalism, that is, limitations on *laissez faire* through regulation. Many self-interested competitors of adulterers allied themselves with Thurber; after all, the 1890s laws applied to meat intended for export to remove restrictions imposed on American meat products by certain European governments.[71]

Whether government should interpose its will against monopoly and/or big business had been decided during the 1890s. Regardless of their interpretations, the courts never questioned this with reference to first principles; common law strictures against monopolistic practices long antedated state and federal laws and furnished abundant and often misleading guidelines. Each of the four presidential candidates in 1912 offered a particular remedy for the restraint of trade wrought by the emergence of the managerial enterprise. None doubted the government's responsibility to preserve competition, however defined, and thereby protect both competitors and consumers. The Clayton Act (1914) amended the Sherman Act and constituted a nominal victory for organized labor.[72] The new act specified that labor is not a 'commodity of commerce', exempting labor unions and agricultural organizations from antitrust laws and curtailing the use of injunctions in labor disputes. In addition, the Federal Trade Commission Act (1914) created a watchdog regulatory agency to cope with unfair competitive tactics.

Telephone service existed by 1900 wherever the density of population and commercialization justified the investment of private capital; gaps lingered, especially in rural and low-income areas, where the expected cost exceeded the anticipated revenue. From an engineering standpoint, the telephone serves the public best as a natural monopoly at the local level but this does not hold true nationally. In 1907, American Telephone & Telegraph (AT&T) owned half of the nation's phones and controlled long lines service. Under these circumstances, *laissez faire* never constituted a viable option. State regulation of telephone service preceded federal; half a dozen states instituted telephone regulation by 1907.[73] Although primarily concerned with railroad regulation, the Mann-Elkins Act (1910) bestowed upon the Interstate Commerce Commission the authority to regulate the telephone industry.

Theodore N. Vail (1845-1920), president of AT&T from 1907 to 1920 and initiator of the national telephone system, realized that a universal monopoly required public control if only to forestall municipal ownership of local telephone

---

71   Okun 1986, pp. 104-105, 291-292.
72   The president of the American Federation of Labor, Samuel Gompers, called the Clayton Act, the 'Magna Carta' of Labor.
73   Garnet 1985, p. 191, note 4.

service. In 1909, AT&T acquired control of Western Union, its main rival; in 1913, the Justice Department initiated an antitrust suit against AT&T and, in addition, the postmaster general called for federal ownership. As a consequence of the Kingsbury Commitment (1913), AT&T accepted the universality of service and became a publicly regulated monopoly. The possibility of public ownership died and AT&T retained dominance in long distance telephone service but obligated itself to connect with independent telephone companies. In 1914 AT&T had to be concerned with a potential antitrust suit and possible nationalization of the telephone and telegraph. Ultimately, this resulted in the public regulation of a private enterprise, which owned and operated a nationwide telephone network.[74]

The New Deal

Owing to the most massive market failure in American history, the next wave of regulation occurred during the New Deal (1933-1938). The State's visible hand increasingly replaced the market's metaphorical invisible hand.[75] The roster of new laws and agencies almost defies comprehension, ranging from the National Industrial Recovery Act (1933) and the Fair Labor Standards Act (1938), both of which applied to the entire economy, to the Securities Exchange Act (1934), the Motor Carrier Act (1935), and the Civil Aeronautics Act (1938), which governed only a single sector of the economy.

In *Schechter versus United States*, the Supreme Court in 1935 declared unconstitutional the National Industrial Recovery Act, which mandated cartelization and consequently suspension of the anti trust laws. This split decision left a void in two industries, which suffered acutely from the depression, bituminous (soft) coal mining and agriculture, or at least certain crops. The number of producers of bituminous coal or wheat, corn, cotton, and tobacco was too large to enable them either individually or collectively to affect either total output or pricing without government intervention.

The Guffey-Snyder Bituminous Coal Stabilization Act (1935) created the National Bituminous Coal Commission to administer production quotas, fix prices, and establish labor regulations (including minimum wages) based on the National Industrial Recovery Act. The Supreme Court ruled this law unconstitutional. The Guffey-Vinson Bituminous Coal Act (1937) reenacted all the chief provisions of the outlawed Guffey-Snyder Act with the exception of the wages and hours clause. This act placed the output of soft coal under federal regulation and aimed to achieve fairness rather than the historic condition of a 'sick' industry characterized by excessive competition and low profits.[76]

---

74 Garnet 1985, pp. 130-131, 153-154; Lipartito 1989, p. 203; Mueller 1997, pp. 129-130; Hochfelder 2002, pp. 706-724.
75 Hovenkamp 1991, p. 362.
76 Graebner 1974, pp. 49-72.

Agricultural and Farm Policies

Since the years immediately before World War I constituted a golden age for farmers, they neither sought nor received aid from the State. While during the late nineteenth century, farmers targeted oligopolistic manufacturers, the railroads, and the money standard, after World War I the farmers recognized that the law of supply and demand was the new devil. During the 1920s farmers futilely clamored to be heard and farm relief bills made their way through the legislative process only to be thwarted by presidential vetoes based on both the Constitution and a conviction in the virtues of *laissez faire* competition. Since agriculture represented one of the weak sectors during the otherwise 'seven fat years', farm protest via the farm bloc culminated with the Agricultural Marketing Act (1929), which formed the Federal Farm Board. Lacking production controls, the Federal Farm Board's attempt to support farm prices by buying farm products failed abysmally.

The failure of the voluntary Agricultural Marketing Act, followed by the disastrous collapse of farm prices during 1929-1933, prompted farm relief legislation on a hitherto unimagined scale. Ever since, agriculture has been a closely regulated sector of the economy; the State has concerned itself with supply, demand, price, and income for basic crops, that is, those nonperishable products grown by a multitude of farmers. In short, agricultural policy has evolved in response to market failure. Whereas market failure justified the regulation of the railroads, an oligopolistic industry, market failure occurred in agriculture for diametrically opposite reasons. The prices for wheat, cotton, corn, and tobacco had been set in a competitive world market with an untold number of buyers and sellers. These commodities have suffered from inelastic demand, which has responded relatively little to changes in either price or income.

Setting the stage for a new agricultural policy, based on the preservation on the so-called family farm, the federal government replaced ineffective voluntarism with the control of supply, through the Agricultural Adjustment Act (1933). After the Supreme Court declared unconstitutional this innovative law, the New Deal enacted the Soil Conservation and Domestic Allotment Act (1936), designed to accomplish the same tasks through constitutionally acceptable means. This law mandated the State to take action whenever it appeared that demand exceeded supply or vice versa by a sufficiently wide margin aiming at forestalling havoc among producers and consumers; this, too, received an adverse Supreme Court constitutional decision. The Agricultural Adjustment Act (1938) followed; this and all subsequent farm legislation depended upon a combination of acreage and production restrictions and subsidies to growers of the so-called basic or staple crops.

The worldwide collapse of agricultural prices during the early thirties dwarfed the supply-demand imbalance of the twenties. No mere rhetoric could stand in the way of the outcry for farm relief, that is, price and income supports by and on behalf of the poor downtrodden farmer. What originally had been initiated as an emergency measure to cope with a presumably temporary condition has been extended and expanded in a myriad of ways. If ever the *laissez faire* should have been equal to the task, agriculture should have constituted the model.

Government to the Rescue

So devastating was the economic catastrophe of the early thirties that large-scale managerial enterprises themselves needed rescue because they could influence supply but neither demand nor price. With this in mind, in 1932 the federal government formed the Reconstruction Finance Corporation, (RFC) which lent rather than granted, money secured by collateral, to such victims of market failure as banks, railroads, and insurance companies. Although not financed by government appropriations the RFC represented an important extension of State authority.[77]

While during the late nineteenth century small business had attempted to invoke the State to retard the growth of large-scale vertically integrated enterprises, these efforts had been largely without success. Individual state resale price maintenance preceded national policy; during the 1930s depression small retailers achieved a modicum of success with two separate but ideologically related federal laws. The Robinson-Patman Anti Price Discrimination Act (1936) amended the Clayton Act by limiting quantity discounts to protect small-scale retailers, especially of cosmetics and liquors, from the mass marketers, specifically, the chain stores.[78]

Even more telling as a negation of *laissez faire*, the Miller-Tydings Fair Trade Act (1937), supported by regular price independents and wholesalers, authorized resale price maintenance. During the period 1937 to 1976, federal legislation permitted resale price agreements in those states, which also enacted enabling statutes. In effect, these so-called fair trade laws exempted from Sherman Act prosecution agreements that otherwise might have been challenged as a form of vertical price fixing. Despite widespread nominal acceptance of *laissez faire* and competition, under the pressure of massive bankruptcies, people discarded principle. Owing to early 1970s inflation, competition ultimately became equated with the public interest. The federal government enacted the Consumer Goods Pricing Act (1975), which repealed resale price maintenance.[79]

The Spread Effect of State's Activities

Since World War I the State's sponsorship of research and development as well as procurement policies have had a significant spread effect in the United States economy. Due to exigencies of the New Deal programs, especially Social Security, during the 1930s the federal government was the largest user of punched card equipment. During World War II American engineers supported the war effort by building an electronic digital computer using vacuum tubes, eventually used in the Manhattan Project to produce the atomic bomb. After the war the knowledge gained therein, generated both nuclear energy and nuclear medicine.

---

77   Mason 2003, pp. 101-102.
78   Hollander 1966, p. 68.
79   McCraw 1996, pp. 187, 207, 209, 215, 227, 229.

As in the nineteenth century when the State fostered and accelerated the Transportation Revolution, during the twentieth century the State induced and helped the Computer Revolution. Further computer innovation during the mid-1950 to the mid-1960s owed much to federal government finance, which supplied research funding and, in addition, constituted the prime customer [80] Similarly, the United States employed radar to direct artillery fire and to detect enemy submarine and aircraft. Later radar revolutionized travel by enhancing the transportation of people and goods.

Since World War II the federal government has furnished more than half the funds for research and development.[81] Virtually all government intrusions into the economy could be included under the rubric 'economic'. Both proponents and opponents played by the same set of rules, that is, loosely defined models in which gains or losses derived from efficiency or fairness could be calculated, according to the economic criteria, in however arbitrary a fashion. Government sponsored research and development as well as procurement, even though relatively modest compared with the totality of the economy, has served to supply spin-offs and act as a benchmark for other buyers. Unwittingly, and not by design, the role of the State in the economy has penetrated regardless of policy makers who profess a modified *laissez faire* with limited intervention.

Electric Power Policy

The Tennessee Valley Act (1933) represented a marked departure from the past and precipitated a fight between private and public power advocates. The electric power industry has constituted a so-called natural monopoly. For this reason, a public power movement emerged as an alternative to private monopoly, and a number of communities and states have engaged in the production and/or distribution of electric power. Moreover, the federal government built hydro dams early in the century; many local and state governments have regulated the electric power industry.

There were several reasons why the TVA, a producer as well as a distributor of electric power in seven southern states, received the green light: 1. The government owned a hydro plant at Muscle Shoals, Alabama, erected to aid the World War I defense program, 2. The colossal market failure (1929-1933), 3. The pyramiding of public utility companies, and, 4. The financial shenanigans of a distinct minority of public utility holding companies and executives. The broad appeal of the TVA affirmed the possibilities of regional planning in an economically depressed area, especially in flood control, low cost water transportation, and recreation.

Once again, the opposition, the private electric power companies, argued constitutionality and practicality rather than an abstract *laissez faire*. Admittedly,

---

80   Flamm 1988, pp. vii, 12, 29, 41, 80, 86, 253.
81   During the 1960s '...some 15 percent of...defense outlays were for research and development, and somewhere between 50 and 60 percent of total research and development were financed by defense agencies'. Clayton 1970, p. 22.

some detractors contended that if the government could compete with an electric power company, it could equally compete with a shoe manufacturer. Such reasoning evoked little response, if only owing to the quite disparate circumstances. Nevertheless, the precedent of the TVA yielded no replication.[82] Circa 2000 the private sector accounted for two-thirds of electric generating; the public sector, cooperatives and other sources, accounted for the rest.[83]

Controversial from the start, the TVA has remained so thereafter; advocates of *laissez faire* or at least of traditional limited government, challenged the TVA as socialistic and monopolistic. They asserted that since TVA is a tax-exempt government agency, whose original capital derived from the federal government's appropriation process, the 'yardstick' concept has been unfair; furthermore, the allocation of joint costs (hydroelectric power compared with other purposes) only exacerbated the complexity. The TVA originated as a regional planning authority; reconciling planning with grass roots democracy has proved impossible. While economic growth within the seven states in the TVA area pleased the advocates, the critics rebutted that the rate of growth in that bounded territory did not exceed that of the non-TVA South.

Attempts to replicate the TVA precedent elsewhere in the United States generally have failed to come to fruition. A Missouri Valley Authority (MVA) based on the TVA example was suggested in 1934; nothing happened then but the concept, controversial from the outset, was revived in 1944. Wide opposition to the Missouri Valley Authority existed even within the Missouri basin. Shortly after becoming president, Truman, in his 'Twenty One Point Message' advocated in 1945, an MVA similar to the TVA, and called for regional development of the Columbia, Missouri, and Arkansas rivers and the Central Valley of California. Interagency rivalry, among other reasons, including the antagonism between the irrigation (upstream) and navigation (downstream) interest groups blocked the MVA. Critics noted that the MVA, as in the case of TVA, threatened private enterprise, state sovereignty, exceeded the bounds of congressional control.[84]

The State, Energy, Conservation, and the Environment

The State's role in resource allocation increased with the shift from wood to other energy sources; this function can be accomplished either through the market or administratively. For many but by no means all purposes the several sources of non-renewable energy (coal, oil, and natural gas) are interchangeable. Consequently, price and regulatory changes introduced for any single fuel necessarily have repercussions on the others because of short-term price competition among the fuels.

Precisely because these fossil-derived energy sources constitute non-renewable resources, at various times the specter of scarcity has loomed large on the distant

---

82 McCraw 1971, pp. vii, 53, and passim.
83 Hausman and Neufield 2002, p. 1050 note 1.
84 Kathka 1990, pp. 241-242; Lawson 1982, pp. 17-24.

and ever receding horizon and has been met with the response of conservation. The 'conservation movement' found many adherents who claimed that the 'special interests' only masked a desire to reduce supply so as to increase price. By no means all of one mind, the oil industry preached *laissez faire* ideology but acted pragmatically in furthering self-interest by controlling the market and increasing its profits. In the energy industry, the number of producers of bituminous (soft) coal, oil, and natural gas has been quite large. Producers could not control output, and thereby pricing, without government help. Yet, under virtually all circumstances, oil independents as well as soft coal producers have been opposed to government regulations.[85]

Historically, the United States has been an energy-rich nation, endowed with enough coal, oil, and natural gas so that, up to World War II, it exported these commodities. In addition, both private and public enterprises utilized waterpower, sometimes at enormous sources such as Niagara Falls and the Grand Coulee Dam and others too small to be notable individually. For this reason, the Federal Power Commission (1920), renamed the Federal Energy Regulatory Agency (1977), has dealt with the waterpower question. The primary concern remained fostering the development of available sources of hydroelectric power, so-called clean energy. The preservation of unspoiled natural beauty in response to environmental concerns surfaced only later.[86]

The conservation movement developed around the turn of the century. In 1909, State control of oil output resulted when the federal government withdrew public land from exploration. President Woodrow Wilson set aside a naval oil reserve in 1915. During the depression of the 1930s, the demand for oil dropped, just at the very time that new major sources of supply came on stream, leading to a calamitous price decline and chaotic conditions in the oil fields. State and federal legislation combined to limit oil production in most of the oil producing states. The East Texas oil strike in 1930 and the 1930s depression fostered the Texas Railroad Commission's adoption of production quotas in accordance with market demand. The Commission reduced allowable production levels to maintain producer prices. The Connally Act (1935) supplemented state prorating legislation; it forbade the shipment in interstate commerce of oil produced in violation of state laws. The so-called conservation laws effectively stabilized the price of petroleum. Prorating endured for several decades, expiring in 1972 only when the Organization of Petroleum Exporting Countries (OPEC) dramatically increased the price of oil.[87]

While the long-term demand for oil moved inexorably upward, in the short run demand fluctuated with the business cycle. Furthermore, the United States gradually needed to supplement domestic production with imports, especially from lower-cost foreign supply sources, such as Mexico, Venezuela, and the Middle East. Concern over the impact of oil imports on the domestic oil industry intensified after World War II. The 1953-1954 recession depressed the demand for

---

85   Pratt 1980, p. 212; Clark 1987, pp. 385-386.
86   Keller 1990, p. 77.
87   Wright 1996, pp. 1397-1399.

oil sufficiently so that the oil producing states clamored for protection from lower-cost imports. Voluntary import limitations were introduced in 1955 and, when this proved ineffective, mandatory limits followed in 1959. The multinational oil companies doubted the importance of encouraging domestic drilling from a strategic point of view. Limiting oil imports protected the domestic oil industry, although at the expense of the consumers. Particularly hard hit were the states located in non-energy producing areas, such as those in New England, while the oil importation policy benefited the oil independents rather than the oil multinationals, which furnished the imports.[88]

The Natural Gas Act (1938) extended of the authority the Federal Power Commission (FPC) to include natural gas pipelines, utility systems, and producers selling natural gas interstate. The Federal Power Commission regulated price, rate of return, entry, and supply.[89] A shortage of natural gas developed during the 1970s, allegedly because the regulators fixed the price too low; under pricing of natural gas increased demand and therefore its share of energy consumption. Bowing to the inevitable, the Natural Gas Policy Act (1978) acknowledged the market by deregulating natural gas in 1981.[90]

Since the 1960s environmental and health concerns have become manifest, resulting in a totally different type of regulation. In the early years, the vocal anxiety of the electorate induced the federal government to enact an entire series of legislation such as the National Environmental Policy Act (1973), the Energy Policy and Conservation Act (1975), and the Clean Air Act (1976). Environmental policy restricted sulfur emission from coal-fired power plants. Although at higher cost, oil replaced coal to obtain cleaner air. Even hydroelectric power became increasingly less popular with the realization of the harm done to wild rivers. Public policy reversed itself to such a degree that a few dams have been decommissioned to restore rivers to their pristine condition.

The most striking change that has taken place in the history of regulatory agencies has been the shift from economic to social and environmental regulation since the 1960s. Neither the ends nor the means can be calculated only according to economic criteria of maximizing the income of individuals or the firm's profitability. Instead, one must consider private gains and costs versus pecuniary and non-pecuniary social gains and costs. Laws concerned with consumer and environmental protection and consumer health and safety, for instance, have resulted in the Consumer Product Safety Commission, the Occupational Safety and Health Administration, and the Environmental Protection Administration. Even this expansion of the administrative state and the marked departure from either *laissez faire* or the prior development of regulation appeared without ideological qualms or reservations.[91]

---

88 Nash 1968, pp. 202-206; Barber 1981, pp. 252, 257; Vietor 1984, p. 131.
89 Moreover, in *Phillips Petroleum Company versus Wisconsin* (1954), the Supreme Court gave the FPC the power to control field prices of natural gas.
90 Vietor 1994, pp. 117, 124-128.
91 Vogel 1981, p. 155.

Transport Infrastructure

While the railroad controls as enacted and administered acted as a straitjacket, there continued to be those observers with keener hindsight than foresight. Since it might lessen the presumably excessive economic power of the railroads, inter-modal competition, therefore, lingered as an ideal, and, indeed, a fervent hope. Such dreams motivated the federal government's participation with Canada in the construction of the St. Lawrence Seaway linking the Great Lakes with the St. Lawrence River. Prompted partially by supposedly high railroad rates and long advocated by Presidents Herbert Hoover, Franklin D. Roosevelt, and Harry S. Truman, this inter-modal competitive project came to fruition during the presidency of Dwight D. Eisenhower during the 1950s.

With the passage of the St. Lawrence Seaway Development Act (1954), construction started immediately and the waterway opened in 1959. Interest politics rather than *laissez faire* ideology delayed the development of this long-sought venture in State ownership. The states and cities on the Great Lakes, which stood to benefit from a low cost-all water route, favored the St. Lawrence Seaway and the associated hydropower. The vested interest opposition comprised: the railroads and the railroad unions, the coalmine owners and miner unions, and the Atlantic and Gulf seaports. If the Interstate Commerce Commission allowed lower rates, they argued that the railroads could supply the transportation services at a competitive cost. Since for decades the State had planned, controlled, and owned canals, the *laissez faire* argument remained dormant. History has vindicated those who long had questioned the economic feasibility of the waterway. Predictably, mid western cities, for instance, Chicago, gained while those on the Atlantic and Gulf, such as New York and New Orleans, lost.[92]

Trade Policy

Tariff policy fluctuated greatly from World War I through World War II. Tariff levels had tended upward from the founding of the nation at the end of the eighteenth century; an alliance between the manufacturing North and the agricultural West during the second half of the nineteenth century succeeded in pushing the tariff upward, especially between 1860 and 1932. However, the adoption of the income tax in 1913 provided an alternative source of federal revenue, which made the tariff even more contentious. In the aftermath of World War I, both the Fordney-McCumber Act (1922) and the Hawley-Smoot Act (1930) elevated the tariff still further. Beginning with the Reciprocal Trade Agreement Act (1934), followed by the General Agreement on Tariffs and Trade, GATT (1947), changed to the World Trade Organization, WTO, the United States switched from being a high tariff country to a low tariff proponent.

The economics profession overwhelmingly had opposed the Hawley-Smoot tariff. For one, this tariff predictably provoked tariff retaliation by other countries. For another, just as pressure politics had raised tariffs, especially on specific

---

92   Willoughby 1961, p. 284 and passim.

products, pressure politics in conjunction with the great crash and the 1930s depression generated a reaction. Economists became convinced that the tariff had benefited owners and workers of specific protected industries at the expense of the economy as a whole, that is, those sectors not protected. This reaction gave rise to the Reciprocal Trade Agreement Act (1934) to restore a liberal, market-driven international political economy. After World War II this effort was reinforced when a consensus developed not to repeat the depression of the 1930s.

After World War II, the change of the product mix and the greater reliance on exports contributed to converting the United States from a historically high tariff nation to one bent on expanding world trade as a general policy. During the depression, world trade had collapsed even more sharply than world gross product. The Export-Import Bank was founded in 1934 to promote American exports, especially farm products (through loans, guarantees, and insurance) by offsetting the alleged help foreign governments were giving their exporters through exchange controls and tariffs. In early 1945, this Bank was transformed into an independent agency. Since World War II, the Bank has promoted freer trade through the Organization for Economic Cooperation and Development (OECD). As an export credit agency, the Bank has worked to offset imperfections in the market and to fulfill political goals.[93]

In the immediate post World War II era the United States contributed the Marshall Plan (1947) to restore the damaged world economy, but the Marshall Plan also fostered United States exports. Even the most nationalistic groups realized that a new era of international economic interdependence had commenced. While the United States and its trade partners had largely adopted free trade, occasionally skirmishes occur when either the United States or its trading partners attempt to protect certain sectors or industries. 'When industries become globally concentrated, visible hands rather than anonymous market ones emerge to guide trade.'[94]

Social Policy

Taxation and Welfare With the inauguration of President Theodore Roosevelt in 1901, the United States truly entered the twentieth century. The end of the frontier, the rise of big business, socialism (defined in the broadest possible way) and imperialism marked this transition. Combined, these made the responses to the political-economic issues and controversies before the New Deal, different from those during the New Deal (1933-1938) and since. Such nineteenth century issues and controversies as the tariff, banking and currency, public lands, and development policy, specifically internal improvement continued during the twentieth century before the New Deal. The tariff and banking and currency policies were carried over from the earlier period and new issues and controversies

---

93   Becker and McClenahan 2003, pp. ix, 1, 2, 8, 289, 295-296.
94   Yoffie 1993, p. 3.

came to the fore such as progressive taxation, social legislation, and the public control of business.

Since the New Deal perhaps the most critical issues have been the role of the State in coping with economic fluctuations and the scope of welfare policies. The twentieth century has witnessed the avowed use of taxation to redistribute income and wealth. As distinct from revenue raising, the passage of the Sixteenth Amendment to the Constitution (1913) inaugurated the graduated income tax; in addition, the use of an excise tax on specific products and services (e.g., liquor and tobacco) has affected consumption. The Wealth Tax Act (1935) increased the marginal income tax rate and commenced the estate tax.

Until early in the twentieth century, social legislation remained in the hands of the individual states. Having been regulated by the federal government since 1887, not surprisingly, the railroad industry was the first to have its labor relations governed by federal legislation. The Adamson or Eight Hour Act (1916) provided for an eight-hour day and for time and a half for overtime in interstate railroads. The Railway Labor Act (1926) established the National Mediation Board for railroad labor. Owing to the National Labor Relations Act and the Social Security Act, both in 1935, as well as the Fair Labor Standards Act (1938), the federal government took center stage by extending its reach from a single sector to all sectors of the economy. The Occupational Health and Safety Act of 1970 reflected concerns with another aspect of work-related quality of life issues.

Social and Labor Legislation   During the nineteenth century the federal government displayed only rudimentary interest in social and labor legislation and the several states could not fill the gap although notable exceptions existed. The first state to industrialize, Massachusetts, led in responding to industrialization. Certain industrially advanced states enacted workmen's compensation laws during the first decades of the twentieth century. There was a setback in *Lochner vs. New York* (1905), when the Supreme Court overturned a state law establishing maximum hours for men, ruling that the statute contravened the liberty of contract, and thus the Fourteenth Amendment of the Constitution, because no government had the right to interfere with the freedom of contract.

While Oliver Wendell Holmes's famous dissenting opinion criticized the majority on the grounds that the Constitution did not prescribe *laissez faire*, the 5-4 majority declared that *laissez faire* theory limited the police power of the State. Classical political economy, that is, *laissez faire*, coupled with a national market, made the task of enacting social and labor legislation on a state-by-state basis not only onerous but also competitively uneconomic. When southern and western states lagged, northeastern states encountered competitive difficulty in leading.[95]

Sometimes known as the 'Third American Revolution', The New Deal federalized the process of enacting social and labor legislation. The 1930s saw the passage of the National Labor Relations Act (1935), the Social Security Act (1935), and the Fair Labor Standards Act (1938). What once had been the

---

95   Hovenkamp 1991, p. 101; Abrams 1964, p. 291.

minority became the majority, both in the public at large, the political branch of government, and later in the courts. This time economic individualism, that is, *laissez faire*, commanded few adherents. While formerly impractical on a state-by-state basis, social and labor legislation now became thoroughly economically viable through national action.

Housing Policy In accordance with nineteenth-century economic liberalism, historically the United States at all levels, federal, state, and local, left housing substantially to the market. Nevertheless, the powerful forces of urbanization, immigration, and industrialization brought sporadic legislation during the second half of the nineteenth century. The largest urban center, New York, exemplifies this process; thus, the Tenement House Law of 1867 was designed to remove the worst of the eyesores for the benefit of the poorest in particular and society in general.

Since this pioneering venture in social control hardly made a dent in solving social problems, during the Progressive Era New York reformers and conservative business interests, with a sense of *noblesse oblige*, combined to produce the Tenement Housing Act of 1901, followed by the first zoning law in 1916. These laws consciously rejected the *laissez faire* market as a means of providing socially acceptable housing for the very poor, maintaining that no one, regardless of means, should have to live without minimal space, light, and sanitation. Thus a morality of social responsibility replaced agrarian individualism even though *laissez faire* precluded much more than a first step. In a free market, the poorest could hardly pay rents which would enable landlords to earn a profit, and unfortunately privately subsidized housing could not provide enough housing to help those unable to pay market rents for socially acceptable housing.

The federal government's role has been immeasurably expanded since the New Deal with, for instance, the Home Owners Loan Act (1933), the Federal Housing Authority (1934), and the Federal National Mortgage Association (1938). Since World War II, the federal government has enacted the Housing and Home Financial Agency Act (1946) and the Housing Acts (1949 and 1968). Collectively, this legislation moved beyond tenement house reform to facilitate either better quality and subsidized rental housing or home ownership.

Advocates justified state action on public housing to cope with slum conditions because of the social costs of neighborhood effects. The Progressive Era established minimum housing standards for the poor. On an exceedingly small scale, deemed inadequate considering the magnitude of the problem, during the New Deal the federal government took steps to ameliorate the housing problem. With the intention of supplementing private efforts, the federal government subsidized housing with rents calibrated to income. The New Deal through the Housing Act of 1937 provided minimal housing without the amenities that the middle class had come to expect. Some opposed, although unsuccessfully, State competition with private property owners.

After World War II, through the Housing Acts of 1949 and 1954, urban renewal and redevelopment through the power of eminent domain became the chosen instrument for slum clearance and renewal. It seems that even staunch defenders of *laissez faire* recognized fairly early that they, too, shared a common interest in curbing human blight and its associated side effects just as they might have an interest in limiting industrial pollution. While some critics on ideological grounds, argued that the State should not enter into competition with the private sector in the housing market, advocates supported housing legislation aimed at the protection of a fraction of the population. Thus, such ideological resistance was overcome; however, the United States has been a middle class nation with a very high percentage of single home ownership reinforced by the fact that the mortgage interest has been tax deductible. There has been some privatization of public housing since 1980; consequently, the State provides housing for only two percent of the population whereas in comparable economies the share is almost 20 percent.[96]

Conclusions

The United States has had a mixed economy, that is, one with relatively few State-owned enterprises. Unlike other public utilities, waterworks became publicly owned and operated circa 1890; furthermore, there was considerable purchase of waterworks during 1897-1915. The railroads and other means of transportation as well as electric power, gas, and telecommunications have become minutely regulated although, towards the end of the twentieth century, there has been some tendency towards deregulation. For the most part, prices have been left to seek their own level and therefore goods and services have been allocated in accordance with the dictates of the market, that is, costs, profits, and consumer preferences.

Admittedly, agriculture constitutes a unique example. State policy typically has been intended to circumscribe the power of large-scale enterprises competing among the few whereas in the case of agriculture competition among the many has been responsible for the 'farm problem' and its ongoing solution. International trade warrants particular mention. While the United States flourished for a century or more with protection, since the 1930s it has embarked on a course of almost free trade, although the justification hardly harks back to Adam Smith. Instead, the United Stats has become the world economic leader and since World War II has recognized that protection no longer serves its interests or those of its major trade partners. Nonetheless, this omnibus proposition is riddled with exceptions and contradictions prompted by special interests. The beet sugar growers remain protected at the expense of both foreign cane sugar growers and domestic consumers. Similarly, cotton textile manufacturers receive protection against Third World low wage producers. Likewise, imports of Japanese manufactured automobiles have been hampered so as to transfer production to the United States automobile manufacturers and, incidentally, the Japanese automobile transplants.

During the nineteenth century, under free market conditions, observers assumed that when the poor would have the right to vote, they would claim a larger

---

96   Lubove 1962, pp. 3, 25, 135, 155, 237, 245; Friedman 1968, pp. 8, 15, 43, 105, 125, 161, 184, 192.

slice of the pie. The second assumption was that the United States was a very socially mobile society. Both assumptions proved to be wrong. While from 1929 to 1947, the gap between the rich and the poor narrowed, during the 1970s and 1980s this gap has been steadily increasing. For a short period of time during the second half of the 1990s because of a tight labor market the gap narrowed marginally. 'But even in the prosperous 1990s, the richest, most prosperous country in the world had a lot of people living on the edge of desperation.'[97] Economic liberalism has made Americans wealthier but strengthened inequality. One may thus be surprised that the U.S. share of GDP devoted to 'social welfare' is not much lower than that of the Continental European countries. During the 1990s the chances of climbing the socio-economic ladder in the United States were comparable to that in Britain although different from most Continental countries where the chances for socio-economic mobility have greatly increased.[98]

In short, at every juncture the State has added to the scope of activity. If *laissez faire* lingered at the fringes at the opening of the twentieth century, it vanished under the impact of two world wars and the intervening depression of the 1930s. Still, the more things change, the more they remain the same. The United States epitomizes the mixed economy centered on the market. In practice, the *laissez faire* ideology has remained strong among business people and others.[99] It seems that Anglo-American individualism propelled the economy to its heights but in the main left behind a segment of society. Some contend that there is a concentration of power among a small number of corporations that are not necessarily responding to the shareholders but to the political order made up of the State and interests groups.[100] A U.S. prominent political economist has argued that 'rational individuals will not act to achieve their common or group interest', but an interest group small enough and sufficiently cohesive, can achieve gains contrary to the public good.[101]

Choices had to be made regarding what economic functions the State should perform and what should be left to individuals and the market. Prices, rates of return, growth rates, and similar measurable economic entities in the United States have constituted part of the choice. Since World War II the federal government has furnished more than half the funds for research and development. Virtually all government intrusions into the economy have been included under the rubric 'economic'. Both proponents and opponents played by the same set of rules, that is, loosely defined models in which gains or losses derived from efficiency or

---

97   Rivlin 2002, p. 8.
98   See also: Christopher Shea 'Class Truce: Why the Poor Won't Soak the Rich', in the *Boston Sunday Globe*, 17 November 2002.
99   When 39 pharmaceutical multinationals sued South Africa for manufacturing generic medications against Aids, it was clear that the patent rights were more important than the life or death of five million Africans tested as HIV positive. A Monsanto director acknowledged that between the product and the markets one forgot society.
100   Lodge 1986, p. 85.
101   Olson 1965, p. 2.

fairness could be calculated, according to the economic criteria, in however arbitrary a fashion.[102]

France

Following its defeat in the Franco-Prussian War of 1870 and the proclamation of the Third Republic, various unstable coalitions governed France. Aiming to have the laic State in control, the republican governments were united in anti clericalism.[103] In the aftermath of the War, in 1871 France agreed to an indemnity to Prussia, which it paid rapidly by borrowing to rid France of the German occupation; indeed, France completed payment by 1875, well ahead of schedule.

By the beginning of the twentieth century France dropped from the second during the 1870s to fourth place as an industrial power behind Britain, the United States, and Germany. Protectionist trade policies in addition to increased international competition and a booming domestic demand, apparently played a role in the decline of foreign trade from about 40 percent of gross national product in 1860 to about 12 percent in 1913.

France was under partial or total German occupation during 1870-1871, 1914-1917, and 1940-1944 while Britain has not been invaded since 1066. France recovered rapidly domestically from the 1870 debacle (see Chapter III). During the 1920s France adhered to a protectionist policy that continued through the depression years of the1930s. Also, the 1920s is the only decade when the State's expenditures declined; for the remainder of the twentieth century, government expenditures increased for up to five percent each decade.

While not subscribing entirely to Keynesian theory, policy makers did not hesitate to utilize monetary and fiscal policies to combat the 1930s economic depression. In the aftermath of World War II, the French nationalized basic industries (partially privatized in the 1980s and the 1990s), and introduced indicative economic planning. Since World War II France has witnessed marked advances in labor and social legislation. Following the centuries long trend, the French rejected administrative regionalization although enthusiastically embracing

---

102 As in the nineteenth century when the State fostered and accelerated the Transportation Revolution, during the twentieth-century, the State induced and helped the Computer Revolution. Further computer innovation between the mid-1950s to mid-1960s owed much to federal government finance, which supplied research funding and, in addition, constituted the prime customer. Flamm 1988, pp. vii, 12, 29, 41, 80, 86, 253.

103 Even before the French Revolution the State had attempted to subordinate the Church if only for fiscal reasons. Post-1871 legislation progressively led to laicization of the school system, followed in 1904 by prohibiting opening religious schools; by 1900 there were more Catholic than public secondary schools. In 1905 France instituted the separation of Church and State, but even so, by 1935 Catholic schools enrolled half of French elementary pupils. Parenthetically, in 2004 France banned all conspicuous religious symbols from public schools.

inter-European economic and political cooperation and thereby transferring limited sovereign power to the European Union.

World War I and Its Aftermath

As the nineteenth century closed, nationalism became increasingly rampant. France suffered a tremendous loss of life and one third of its national wealth during World War I; while on the winning side, the aftermath brought no rejoicing and no settlement. Not until the early 1920s did France regain the pre-war level of industrial output; protectionism, as demanded by industry, intensified. In 1919 the government abrogated all prewar bilateral trade treaties and during the 1920s protection characterized the French commercial policy.[104]

With a huge debt burden, France expected to recoup reparations from the defeated Germany but the immediate post-World War I period left the German economy in shambles, even though there was no combat on German territory. Since Germany could not and/or would not make good its peace treaty obligations but also because of domestic inflation, the French franc slid against the US dollar. By 1928, the franc stabilized at one-fifth its pre war parity. This impoverished many of the *petite* bourgeoisie that had invested their savings in French government bonds. Furthermore, at the urging of the government, many Frenchmen had bought Russian bonds that had lost all value as a result of the Russian Revolution of 1917. Wages failed to keep up with inflation in both the private and public sectors; furthermore, the security and prestige derived from working for the State seemed to have diminished.

Yet, between 1924 and 1929 output grew by an annual rate of five percent compared to 2.4 percent immediately before the war. By 1928, the intellectual left alleged that this recovery had been achieved on the backs of the workers. While praising the increase in output, many criticized the modern corporation as a form of collectivism that destroyed the foundations of capitalism, that is, private property, the owner-manager, and small-scale enterprise. Other critics encouraged by Mussolini's apparent success in Italy, preached Fascism asserting that the State should be the defender of the working class but under an authoritarian government.[105]

The World Depression: French Style Contra Cyclical Policies

France recovered enough from the war only to have the economy strangled by the breakdown of the world economy. The European financial debacle began when Austria's largest bank, the *Kreditanstalt*, collapsed in May 1931. By September 1931, the Bank of England encountered difficulties and had to be rescued by the United States, which forced Britain to abandon the gold standard two years later France still confronted the financial and economic crisis. Policy makers attempted

---

104 Kuisel 1981, p. 63.
105 Bertrand de Jouvenel (1928), *L'économie dirige: le programme de la nouvelle génération*, Paris, cited by Kuisel 1981, p. 81.

conservative economic solutions, with no avail. Anticipating the later intellectual critique, traditional liberal economists dreaded the adoption of State intervention in the market, fearing that all government intervention could lead towards socialism.[106]

France tried to recover from the 1930s depression after enduring the post World War I recovery process. With substantial unemployment,[107] few options existed; public policies put the State in the forefront of trying to resolve the chaos created by the great depression.[108] In the face of the grave economic debacle, the State took a leading role, using the banking system that it controlled. In 1932 these banks financed businesses in difficulty such as the *Compagnie Internationale des wagons lit* and the automaker Citroen. The State ordered the *Banque de France* to discount commercial paper of enterprises on the verge of bankruptcy. Moreover, and it came to the rescue of the epidemic of collapsing banks.[109]

John Maynard Keynes published the *General Theory* in 1936, but while his key economic precepts were spreading, during the early 1930s, French policy makers were not happy with Keynesian short-term solutions. While Keynes emphasized the short run, these policy makers sought long run solutions to counteract short run cyclical economic downturns. This may explain why the 'Political Left' joined the old classical economics (as interpreted by Marx) in preaching that the market forces alone could bring about the demise of capitalism and the hegemony of the proletariat.[110]

In contradiction, in 1936 the State under the Socialist Leon Blum and the Popular Front government responded with massive interventionist measures, including the long expected nationalization of railroads as well as the armaments and aviation industries, but no large-scale public works program. The Bank of France was placed under government control (by appointing government trusted directors), allegedly to break the power of the 'two hundred families'. The Blum government deviated in thought and in fact from the previous never-applied liberal doctrine. While not accepting Keynesian theory, the State followed many Keynesian precepts regarding deficit spending, monetary reform, and reducing unemployment. Counter cyclical measures also included: the 40 hour week, the three weeks vacation, collective bargaining (later replaced by mandatory

---

106 During the 1950's, the Austrian economist Ludwig von Mises told his New York University classes that government intervention meant Socialism and eventually Communism; see, for instance, Mises 1949, pp. 712-729.

107 Reliable comparable unemployment statistics during the 1930s do not exist. Even the data and consequently opinions on recovery differ. While each country showed some signs of recovery by the mid-1930s, recovery resulted mainly from public spending on war preparation with Germany in the lead. See: Garraty 1986, pp. 216-217; Kindleberger 1986, p. 240.

108 While the governments of many advanced economies probably feared a Communist revolution, enacted welfare legislation was not much different than that predicted by Karl Marx and Friedrich Engels in *The Communist Manifesto* in the mid-nineteenth century. Marx and Engels 1948.

109 Gueslin 1997, p. 125.

110 Rosanvallon 1989, pp. 588-589.

arbitration), compulsory education until 14 years of age, and the devaluation of the franc.[111]

Inter-war Social Legislation

In 1929, the Chamber of Deputies passed the Social Security Act, revised in 1930 that covered old age pensions, workers disability, and national health insurance. France preceded the United States (1935) but not Britain, by a few years with such legislation. Germany's return of Alsace and Lorraine to France created problems of homogenization of social policies and became an inducement for change. The inhabitants of these two regions had benefited from the social security legislation, which Bismarck had introduced in Germany during the 1880s.

During the 1930s unions were willing and eager to have social security and enterprises did not object in an atmosphere of the apparent collapse of the capitalist system. Despite these anxieties, the labor unions were not weakened but strengthened and became partners of the State, while the State gained power by becoming the ultimate social arbiter of the labor-management compact. Advocates of *laissez faire* believed that allowing the State to take action would be a step away from collectivism.

Proponents of state intervention were not happy with contra cyclical policies adopted during the Great Depression. During the mid-1930s traditional economic liberals were afraid that by adopting a program copied from the German Finance Minister Hjalmar Schacht (1877-1970), France might turn into a Fascist State. By accepting economic planning, policy makers and technocrats believed that they were empowering the capitalists to control the State. A French political economist observed that 'the problem is no longer to decide whether or not the French economy will be managed, the only choice is between shilly-shallying...and firm direction provided by one, good pilot'.[112]

France probably suffered less during the thirties than many other countries (at least as compared to Britain and perhaps the United States) because it relied more than the United States and Britain on small-scale enterprises and less on foreign trade and therefore proved less vulnerable to the vicissitudes of the market. Policies introduced after 1936 to remedy the consequences of the Great Depression of 1929-1937 did not immediately improve the livelihood of the workers but in the long run facilitated social change. Social legislation included the eight-hour day, the 48-hour week (later to 40 hours) with no reduction in wages, and paid vacations. It is understandable that business groups opposed all these laws vehemently as counter productive to employment and business profitability but during the 1930s radical solutions gained popularity.[113]

---

111 Gueslin 1997, pp. 128-130.
112 Michel Debré (1938), 'Pour une administration de l'économie française', *Science politique*, No. 8, June, p. 269, cited by Kuisel, 1981, p. 127.
113 Gueslin 1997, p. 119.

Business Concentration, Protection, and Planning

Extreme nationalist 'beggar thy neighbor' policies adopted by every nation, including France diminished international trade but did not benefit anyone. Now the State encouraged the formation of cartels among large enterprises and initiated the rescue of failed major banks and the flagship passenger line *Compagnie Générale Transatlantique*. By changing the composition of the board of directors of the Bank of France, replacing them with trusted political allies, the government curtailed the independence of the ultra-conservative leaning central bank.

The Popular Front government (1936-1937) toyed with the idea of planning. The neo-liberals (modified *laissez faire* backers) thought that planning emerged when capitalism confronted increasing concentration, whereas for the socialists planning was part of the self-destruction of capitalism. The difference between the two groups was nationalization, that is, private versus public ownership, but the Popular Front was not in power long enough to initiate a process of nationalization. By 1938 industrial production recovered only five percent from the depths of the depression. In part owing to preparations for war, as elsewhere, economic conditions ameliorated in France during the late thirties.[114]

The Sad Vichy Interlude and the Immediate Aftermath

In 1940 the Third Republic disintegrated as never before in modern history. Defeated by the Germans, France lived under Nazi German occupation (completely in the North, partially in the South) for four years. During this traumatic time, while some Frenchmen collaborated with the enemy, most Frenchmen lost their freedom. The collaborationist government, with its capital in Vichy in central France, adhered to the conqueror's philosophy and actions; policy makers of the Vichy regime flirted with the fascist corporate State. This institutional change involved State control of agricultural mutual cooperatives with poor results while in the industrial sectors the State organized 230 corporate units by 1944, all dissolved at the end of the war. It appears that the Fascist system never had a firm hold on the French society.[115]

Towards the end of the war and the Vichy regime, the uprising of the *maquis*, the Resistance movement, harassed the Germans with some success and obtained a considerable following among the French people. The political objective of the Resistance was to replace the Third Republic with a more 'socially concerned' institutional framework. The Fourth Republic born this way lasted from 1944 to 1958 when, with General Charles de Gaulle, the Fifth Republic was born. During1944-1958, governments presented a dichotomy of economic principles. The 'Political Left', originating in part with the *maquis*, advocated such State intervention in the economy as business regulation, nationalization, planning, and social welfare legislation. The 'Liberals', the so-called Gaullists, were

---

114　Catherine and Gousset 1965, pp. 153-156; Kuisel 1981, pp. 95-96, 105, 120.
115　Gueslin 1997, p. 137.

philosophically inclined towards market forces but in practice followed policies that made the 'Interventionist State' the norm.

Immediately after World War II State intervention in the economy responded to the material destruction. However, there was a cultural break in the popular view of the State; the Resistance movement, controlled in large part by the Communist Party, now a major political force, nourished a strong anti-capitalist bias and a contempt for the prewar ruling class. A new generation of policy makers adopted social reform and enjoyed their newly entrusted power; the State was *them* and, therefore could not be the enemy. Nationalization and planning were not only accepted but became the consensus. While still in Algiers, in 1943, de Gaulle explained that all resources of the nation should be put to work for the general welfare and not for the pleasure of a few individuals. By 1946, the State enterprises employed 1,200,000 people (about four percent of the employed labor force) and were responsible for one quarter of industrial investments.[116]

Dirigisme

Believing that the institutions of the discredited Third Republic no longer represented the will of the people, immediately after the war, France adopted a new Constitution for the Fourth Republic. The preamble of the 1946 Constitution stated: 'The Nation guarantees...medical care, maternal assistance, rest and leisure. Anyone who for reasons beyond his control is incapable to work, has the right to obtain from the collectivity the means of a convenient existence.'[117]

When the postwar euphoria era subsided, policy makers were confused and confusing in an attempt to strike a political balance. Having preserved the multiparty system not different from under the Third Republic, the government changed often. Despite this unsettled situation, and the widespread ravages of the war, the index of industrial production reached the 1938 mark by 1951. Having achieved recovery relatively rapidly, France had to select paths to attain a steady and high rate of growth and assure welfare for most of its citizens. All over Western Europe, the debate at the time centered between a modified *laissez faire* and a modified form of socialism. France chose *dirigisme* that could be defined as State planning and controls in the development process.

State Enterprises and Privatization

Irrespective of who held power after World War II, France followed a *étatiste* policy. Following liberation, in addition to implicit ideology, the explicit reasons for nationalization of private enterprises were to: 1. Restructure certain sectors such as credit institutions so as to be less affected by the business cycles; 2. Take over the assets of industrialists who during the occupation collaborated with the enemy such as the automobile manufacturer Louis Renault; 3. Assure continuous functioning for the sectors of strategic economic importance such as energy and

---

116 Rosanvallon 1989, pp. 591-2; Kuisel, pp. 202-211.
117 Rosanvallon 1989, p. 552.

Cultural Continuity in Advanced Economies

civil aviation. In addition, nationalization appeared to have wide support and policy makers argued that State-owned companies would facilitate macro policy and planning.[118]

France nationalized coal, gas, electricity, the Bank of France, and private banks and insurance companies. In a highly atypical case, Renault, who had built the leading French automobile company, was incarcerated after liberation on charges of collaboration with the Nazis, and died while awaiting trial. The French government confiscated its remaining industrial property, and organized the state-controlled *Régie nationale des usines Renault in* 1945. At the close of the twentieth century the State still owned over 40 percent of the company's stock.

Some other companies were nationalized after World War II and privatized later; Saint-Gobain, Thompson, and Rhone-Poulenc were nationalized in 1982. Saint-Gobain originated with *les manufactures royales* and became famous for producing high quality glass and was privatized in 1986. Thompson has been producing electric equipment since the late nineteenth century when it acquired patents from General Electric. Rhone-Poulenc, a chemical and pharmaceutical company was formed through mergers and privatized in 1993.

Since 1944 there has been a lively debate on the cost and benefit of the nationalization of industrial enterprises and on the role of the State as an entrepreneur in productive business. Some maintain that, tongue in cheek, the mines of capitalists become the mines of the miners; what they mean in reality is that, they become the mines of the ministry. Others argue that nationalized companies give the State another instrument with which to implement social policies. The institutional climate of opinion of the immediate post-World War period encouraged the latter view and re-enforced the historical *dirigisme* of France.[119]

Nationalized companies offered enviable tenured jobs and positions, that is, good wages, salaries, benefits and working conditions, to both technical workers and managers. It would seem that a *rapprochement* between workers and management was possible. Yet, the nationalized enterprises (large-scale enterprises with strong labor unions) were nuclei of agitation to raise wages and fueled wage-push inflation. Some suggested that the power of labor unions exceeded that of the managers.[120]

The French State became a major producer and employer and the public at large assumed that the State would set an example by running enterprises in a business-like fashion. In the decade immediately after the war, these State economic enterprises, SEEs, did not accomplish the objectives of the working class of diminishing the rate of unemployment since the SEEs operated on a 'market oriented basis'. However, those people who were employed by the SEEs fared well, and most of the State-run firms were profitable.

The Fourth Republic instituted indicative planning, which forecasts the future of the economy and thus gives enterprises an indication of what and how much to

---

118 Gueslin 1997, pp. 141-142.
119 Catherine and Gousset 1965, pp. 189-197.
120 Dupeux 1969, p. 127.

produce, reducing risk and uncertainty. On the financial front, the nationalization of the major banks did not perceptibly alter the relationship with the central bank, the *Banque de France*. The nationalized financial entities as well as the manufacturing enterprises assisted the government in its planning process.[121]

While state enterprises were frequently criticized for mismanagement, technological adventurism, and politicization, they displayed an unexpected dynamism and served as balancing tools in business cycles. Before parliament legislated it, Renault conceded a fourth week of vacation to its workers. By lowering electric energy prices, the State Electric Corporation, EDF, contributed to the growth of private enterprises. Some state economic enterprises gained in reputation at home and abroad despite State interferences such as intrusive regulations and non-business demands by the government.[122]

Role and Size of the Bureaucracy

Cognizant of France's place in history, since World War II the State has subsidized and operated industries, for example, aluminum, to help maintain that alleged place. 'In France, where the State had been the caretaker of society, government control of the allocation of domestic credit and Marshall Plan funds permitted the bureaucracy to stake out a new role as architect of the renovation.'[123] To enhance the quality of the bureaucracy, in 1948 the State founded the National School of Public Administration, another elite higher education institution, akin to those founded a century or more before.

According to a French economic historian, the State not only strengthened the bureaucracy but also has been the leader in modernizing the economy. This required: 1. An economic and industrial education of the nation through the creation, in addition to the General Commissariat for Planning, of the General Commissariat of Productivity, unique in advanced economies; 2. The strategy of big projects by having the State concentrate on struggling sectors but also in internationally competitive sectors as exemplified by the development of the airbus (aircraft industry) to compete with the United States enterprises and the now defunct *Concorde* (an inefficient and unprofitable supersonic airplane); 3. The necessity to comply with an open economy as a result of France's joining the Common Market. This affected mostly agriculture and the steel sector that lost their protective wall.[124]

The data on public sector employment are revealing. Public employment increased from circa 100,000 in 1800 to about 500,000 in 1900 and about 2.5 million in 1985.[125] During this two-century span, the increment was from one public employee for every 200 citizens to one for every 24. In the early 1950s, the

---

121 Dupeux 1969, pp. 129-130.
122 Gueslin 1997, p. 156.
123 Zysman, 1979, p. 12.
124 Rosanvallon 1989, pp. 603-616.
125 Another estimate of all-inclusive public employment stood at 4.5 million in 1975 or the State employed one in five workers. Gueslin 1997, p. 9.

French State had a payroll of 2.8 million blue and white-collar workers accounting for about 15 percent of the active labor force; the share of public employment increased to 25 percent in 1995, one of the largest shares in western European countries.[126] Furthermore, the composition of these employees changed drastically. While the number of public school teachers was negligible in 1800, there were more than one million public school teachers in France by 2000.[127]

Post World War II Social Legislation

Article 22 of the 1948 United Nations Declaration of Human Rights states that 'all persons, while members of society have the right to Social Security' originates with the famous British Beveridge Report. Issued in Britain during World War II and adopted by many Western European countries, this Report assumed that the inspiration for effort would be enhanced if people were guaranteed a better life at the war's conclusion. Moreover, the general acceptance of Keynesian economic policies minimized the debate about the social role of the State.

Although State *dirigisme* developed gradually over the century, it became the conventional practical wisdom. As elsewhere in the industrial world, since 1945 modified Keynesian interventionist policies have become accepted by almost everyone in France. Traditional differences between right and left have been erased creating a broad 'center' *dirigiste* policymaking. Observers contend that the State as a provider of social benefits has not been a necessary characteristic of the *dirigiste* State. First, the State has not financed social security; instead, it has been financed by obligatory contributions of the employer and employee; second, by being universal it has increased efficiency of the social security system. Public policy makers have assumed that by assuring social security, welfare assistance would be less needed.[128]

Taxation

Fiscal policies have often been used as a social policy instrument. In 1954 the value added tax was introduced; different from a sales tax, there is no double taxation because the tax is applicable at every stage of production. Within the scope of economic planning, many enterprises were given such tax privileges as rapid depreciation and tax postponement or reduction. The increase in social

---

126 OECD 1997.
127 In 1984, the French public sector employed 1,050,000 teachers, 208,000 at the Ministry of Finance, 47,000 in the judiciary, and 513,000 at the post office (PTT) Rosanvallon 1989, pp. 493-494.
128 Rosanvallon 1989, pp. 556-561. All political parties have supported a supplementary contribution to the public social security in private non-taxable saving accounts, CREF, *Complément retraite de la fonction publique*, for civil servants and the professions. Private employers and labor unions have argued for the same privilege for the wage earners in industry. This has been a departure from the principle the State as the only source of social security.

security contribution was reluctantly accepted by the public and by business. From 1954 to 1973 the social security contribution grew from 7.4 percent to 13.5 percent, approaching the prevailing rates in the United States.

After the 1970s, liberal economic advisers to the State attempted unsuccessfully to lessen the State's influence in the economy by lowering the tax burden. By 1991 total State revenue accounted for 43.8 percent of gross national product compared with 35.6 percent in 1970. Most of the tax increase was due to social security contributions that climbed from 12.9 to 19.5 percent of the GNP during the period.[129]

Centralization

Since at least the seventeenth century, France's economic, political, administrative, and intellectual locus has been centralized, with everything revolving around Paris.[130] For this reason, Paris has always lived beyond its own resources and therefore has been both envied and resented by the provinces, which exercised a considerable degree of autonomy before the Revolution. Since the reign of Louis XIV, France has had a strong centralized administrative State centered in Paris. During 1870-1939 the French built a second empire but its stature as a world power in many ways diminished while the attraction of Paris, as more than merely a French capital, magnified.

Charles de Gaulle, President of France (1958-1969), saw himself above the political battle and reacted against the weak executive of the Third Republic. Under de Gaulle's aegis, after 1945 the power of the executive was expanded, but the drive for decentralization was not that successful. Indeed, in 1969 the new strong executive, de Gaulle, resigned from the presidency partly because the voters rejected two of his pet institutional reforms; one referendum was on the grater autonomy for French regions, and the other concerned the introduction of workers participation on corporate boards.[131] It appears that a policy of *dirigisme* is apt to encourage centralization because of the controls from the top.[132]

At the end of the twentieth century, the debate on regionalization still raged in the major French newspapers indicating that the dichotomy between the center and periphery is as strong as ever. The continuation of the Office of the Regional and Territorial Management Office, *Délégation a l'aménagement du territoire et à l'action régionale (Datar)*, created decades ago, was in doubt rather than being

129 Gueslin 1997, pp. 156-157, 204. While in 1983 the tax burden in France was 48.8 percent of the gross national product, in Britain 42.1 percent, in Germany the tax burden was 45.1 percent, and in the United States 31.5 percent.
130 Paris has historically been used to glorify first the monarchy and then France as an abstract entity. Both Germany and Italy have been and are polycentric because unification occurred during the nineteenth century long after regional economic and cultural institutions had become well established.
131 Catherine and Gousset 1965 pp. 206-208.
132 Teyssier 1995, pp. 159-163.

strengthened at the same time that the European Union assumed many tasks of the member countries.[133]

State Intervention through European Economic Integration

Immediately after World War II coal mining and the steel industry were struggling. Some of the steel plants had become obsolete and France had to import the coal. In conjunction with the Marshall Plan the State aimed at restructuring these industries to enable them to weather stiff foreign competition. In 1950, the French Premier Robert Schuman proposed to establish of a super-national agency, the European Coal and Steel Association (ESCA) to plan the allocation and distribution of coal, iron, and steel. The ESCA was signed in 1951 by the participating countries: Benelux France, Germany, and Italy; the individual states ceded some of their natural sovereignty to a cartel controlled by appointed bureaucrats. In 1957, based on ESCA experience, the European Economic Community (EEC), established a common market among the above named countries (and later enlarged as the European Union). This seems to have been the starting point for the creation of a supra-national State. This new entity, slowly but definitely, surmounted trade impediments (tariffs, quotas) among the participating states and, as the need arose, set standardized protection for certain sectors and products. Steel and agriculture have been especially contentious internationally. Both have been overtly or covertly subsidized by the individual states or by the supra-national body.

As in the U.S, French farming has been subsidized since at least the Great Depression. In 1948, the State abandoned the assumption of agricultural self-sufficiency and in order to help farmers (probably for electoral reasons) attempted to develop agriculture for export. The results were dismal although by 1960, farm support increased from 3.5 to 6.5 percent of the State budget. Only in the mid-1960s, did the State create agencies to reorganize farms on a commercial basis. The State encouraged and subsidized investment in new technology and equipment on enlarged tracts of land. By controlling credit, through the State-owned bank, the *Crédit agricole*, the State encouraged and has supervised the organization of agricultural cooperatives. With the creation of the EEC, farm subsidies were shifted from the national State to the new Common Market, that is, the European Commission in Brussels. By 2000, during the process of the internationalization of State intervention, almost half of all the European Union's expenditures were dedicated to farm support.[134]

133 During 2002 a debate took place in France about the future of Datar. See for example, Jean-Louis Gigou, 'Datar pas morts', and Pierre Richard, 'La France avance: et l'état', Le Monde, February 1, 2002.
134 See also: Gueslin 1997, pp. 160, 181.

French-Type Economic Planning

Jean Monnet (1888-1979), an economist and public official, was not only a key individual in dealing with France's post World War II recovery but also was instrumental in the process that created first the customs union among Belgium, Netherlands, and Luxembourg, the Benelux, the ESCA (Monnet was its first president) and, finally, established the foundation of the European Union. Appointed by de Gaulle to oversee France's economic recovery as Commissioner General for Planning (1947-1955), Monnet bore primary responsibility for the introduction of national economic planning in post-1945 France. 'Jean Monet [was] a *grand commis* in the best tradition of the Old Regime.'[135]

In 1947 a contingent of bureaucrats and economists prepared a National Balance document. This work was the precursor of the first rudimentary input-output table published in 1956 by the Service of Economic Studies that became the Forecasting Directorate by 1962. This table improved in usefulness with the development of computing techniques applied to macro economic models to derive public policies. Applications of these models have been based on data supplied by INSEE (National Institute of Statistics). There has been a consensus among policy makers that the system has been working satisfactorily in providing information and analysis.

In France, 'the efforts to organize markets by making long-term forecasts, and by dividing orders among various suppliers had its origin in the period preceding the First World War'.[136] The planning process has been an exercise *à la française* that has made the State a partner in the market place; the Plan has expanded the bureaucracy (and the number of bureaucrats with a vested interest in planning) over the last half a century from six committees to over 100 committees. The Plan has been based on a model, containing about 1600 equations and 4000 exogenous parameters, made possible by the computer revolution.[137]

The Monnet Plan for the modernization of the French economy, PME, *Plan de Modernisation et de Equipement*, called for channeling the post-war recovery effort towards long-term goals with the State taking a leading role 'through cheap investment capital, accelerated depletion allowances, special tax reduction and outright grants'.[138] Indeed, in the 1950s half and even by 1980s one-third of all industrial investments originated with the State. The nationalized companies played an important role in the process of planning by having control of resource allocation. In essence, France has had an *économie dirigiste* that fused indicative planning with some State coercion. While the plan, a macro-forecasting tool has been voluntary, the State had some not so subtle instruments to implement the plan. It could intervene financially through macro budget policies, credit control through the banking system it owned and/or controlled, and through direct investment in State enterprises. Also, the State has had the power of legislation,

---

135 Landes 1969, p. 530.
136 Caron 1970, p. 340.
137 Caron 1981, pp. 248-249; Kuisel 1981, p. 213.
138 Cohen 1969, p. 21.

licensing, and zoning as well as other micro policies such as direct subsidies, tax privileges, credit at lower than market interest rate, and State procurement.[139]

De Gaulle contended that the Plan would unify the nation ideologically by making it possible to coordinate economic policies. Those who favored planning contended that planning has been a modification of *laissez faire* and not a replacing the market; by preventing market imbalances and by decreasing business uncertainty, planning has diminished risks and could increase profits of private enterprises. However, some critics argued that the Plan did not influence French economic growth in the sixties and the seventies. Others disagreed citing a poll taken during the Fifth Plan in which 80 percent of the 2000 enterprises polled were aware of the objectives of both in making long-term plans; these enterprises relied on the plan for sales projections and for scheduling production.[140] According to one economic historian, '...French planning...became an agent of economic growth rather than a step towards socialism...French planning became neo-liberal, rather than socialist-syndicalism, in character'.[141]

True enough, immediately after the Second World War, the British briefly attempted to condition the market via a plan based on the Beveridge Report. Even the United States has had what some would consider an annual plan. The 1946 Employment Act directs the President to appoint an advisory body, the Council of Economic Advisers, which reports to him on the condition of the economy and recommend appropriate alternative policies that, however, the President is free to ignore. Although much stronger than under the Third Republic, French presidents have still not been as strong as United States presidents; conversely, the State bureaucracy has autonomous power in France unmatched in the United States.

French planning has more force since the government, through active or passive actions, such as authorizing charters or selective contracts and subsidies, can induce but not compel enterprises to comply with the plan. One French economist claimed that the State exploits, controls, and commands; in short, the State touches everything.[142] While the State used intervention and planning, it also sought the cooperation of the private interests in forging economic policies. 'The result was a Gallic style of economic management that blended state direction, corporatist bodies, and market forces.'[143]

Market Liberalization and Privatization

In the post-World War II era, the French tended to hold economic liberalism responsible for recurrent economic ills. Indeed, *laissez faire* and the economic liberalism of the nineteenth and twentieth centuries has lost whatever mass appeal it may have had. 'There was a certain continuity between the *Ancien Régime* and the liberal order ...the interventionist reflex of the State was in some ways as old as

---

139 Gueslin 1997, pp. 153-154, 157, 209.
140 Caron 1981, pp. 47, 248-249.
141 Kuisel 1981, p. 246.
142 Bleton 1966, p. 177.
143 Kuisel 1981, p. 248.

Colbert and the monarchy'.[144] However, some observers maintain that immediately after World War II, public policies have been *dirigiste* in name only and that they were confusing and contradictory. This can be illustrated best in the implementation of monetary policy. Also, price setting and rationing were abandoned even though inflation plagued the economy soon after. In contrast, nominally less interventionist, the British maintained food rationing until 1954; Britain could not feed itself and therefore had to rely on substantial food imports paid with scarce foreign exchange, which contributed to the delayed retention of rationing.[145]

At the end of the twentieth century, the trend within the European Union has been for market liberalization, privatization, and increased competitiveness. French policy makers have always worked under the assumption that a partnership between the State and the market exists. By the 1990s, there were no state economic enterprises besides public utilities where the State owned 100 percent of the capital stock. An observer remarked that in France there is no difference between State capitalism and private capitalism.[146] Policy makers and the bureaucrats have continued to harbor misgivings regarding the resulting modified *laissez faire* model. For instance, the French have considered the privatization and/or deregulation of railroads and other public utilities on pragmatic rather than on ideological grounds. They cite alleged unhappy outcomes in the process of deregulation and privatization both in the European Union and in the United States.

The French point to the U.S. where the Baby Bell companies gained control of 90 percent of the telephone market six years after deregulation. They insist that this also could happen in France in all natural monopolies sectors with potentially great harm to the public. The California energy crisis when black outs during the summer of 2001 were common, brought about by, among other reasons, partial deregulation of the sector, has been another consideration. Also, after privatization, the British railroads have been probably the worst in the European Union while the public French railroads have been considered among the best.[147]

French policy makers have been pragmatic rather than ideological, as in the case of railroads, in the belief that public services can be best delivered by the State. An example of the lack of ideology in public polices is the handling of break up the broadcasting public monopoly. Under Valery Giscard d'Estaing (1974-1981), a *laissez faire* President, the State-owned radio and television gained autonomy, but only under Francois Mitterand (1981-1994), a Socialist President, were private TV and radio legalized.[148]

---

144 Kuisel 1981, pp. 9-10.
145 Dupeux 1969, p. 38.
146 Gueslin 1997, p. 209, citing a reporter for the newspaper, *Le Monde*, in 1985.
147 See also, Eric Le Boucher 'La dernière hypocrisie française', *Le Monde*, 18 February 2002.
148 Teyssier 1995, pp. 248-250, 322-324.

Conclusions

It appears that in France the State *has been* the bourgeoisie for centuries. After the 1789 Revolution and a century of changes from Terror to Empire, Restoration, Second Empire, and Third Republic, the *haute bourgeoisie* in charge of administration and finance preserved the order of the State. By World War I, the actual control of the State shifted from the inflation-impoverished *haute bourgeoisie* to the *petite bourgeoisie*. The State was 'governed not by and for "the people" but by and for the middle class'.[149] Since the 1789 Revolution, the peasant proprietors have worked in close harmony with the bourgeoisie. Together they spread the bourgeois mentality, defended property and the *status quo*, fearful of change, and undisputed supporters of the State's activities in the market.

George Pompidou, President of France (1969-1974), asserted in the 1970s that for a thousand years, the State and France have been one. Different from de Gaulle, Pompidou feared that administrative regionalization would weaken the powers of the central *état*. The State has always been supposed to organize, enlarge, and defend not only against the external menaces but also against the collective egoism, the rivalry of interest groups.[150] While the French have been defenders of property rights, they expect the State to protect these rights and to lead in economic policies that will bring economic and social stability. As practiced in France, *dirigisme* has been a unifying force, regardless of the political party in power.

This is why it was relatively easy to move from a protectionist policy to the elimination of all tariffs among the member states of the Common Market (now the European Union). More difficult has been the implementation of a program of liberalization that included deregulation and privatization required by the Union. Apparently ideology has not played a role as much as pragmatism in continuing to have the State active in the marketplace. As Francois Caron, a noted French economic historian puts it, the ideological justification for French *étatisme* has changed over two centuries but the permanence of State actions has been enduring. The French bureaucracy has been claiming that the 'public good' has overwhelmed particular interests. While aiming at industrial decentralization, the State has used its power to centralize decision-making. The French have not perceived a contradiction between favoring the development of free enterprise and the State's defense of the welfare state.[151]

Germany

A French economist and businessman, Michel Albert, recently suggested that for historical and cultural reasons, Germany developed a unique form of capitalism, the *Rhenish* model different from that of American capitalism. 'The *Rhenish*

---

149 Guerard 1969, p. 459.
150 Teyssier 1995, pp. 183-184.
151 Caron 1995, pp. 415-416.

model, contrary to the American entrepreneurial spirit, values collective success and long-term performance over short-term profit and individual success.'[152] Albert contends that over the last two centuries the German cultural environment treated business as a *social* venture and not only as a source of short-term profits for individuals. It appears that the *Rhenish* model includes a reliance on the State not only as a moderator but also as a partner in the market place.[153]

During the second half of the nineteenth century, since German industries had to compete with the well-established British counter parts, business welcomed the State's protection. Between 1900 and 1914 the State encouraged large-scale enterprise and condoned cartelization while the German economics profession advocated a major role for the State not only in the economy but also in coping with the 'social question'. At the beginning of the twentieth century, free trade ideas advanced by German economists did not appeal to German businessmen. The defenders of liberal economics had 'begun to be seen as Anglophile academics unversed in the reality of business world'.[154] Later, one witnessed a continuation of the weak economic liberalism initiated under Bismarck; this type of liberalism sustained a State paternalism generally not practiced in Britain and the U.S.

Under the empire Germany experienced a prolonged industrial expansion hand in hand with a State-supported export-led economy. Even though careful pre-war economic planning had been in place World War I was traumatic in many ways because the war lasted longer than anticipated. The immediate post-war period burdened Germany with reparations and with the economy in turmoil climaxed by hyperinflation. The subsequent economic expansion came to a halt at the beginning of 1930s, the great depression, only to be succeeded by an authoritarian Nazi regime under which big industry in partnership with the State controlled the economy.

The World War II catastrophic defeat forced Germany to make hard choices to restore the economy. The country remained divided for almost half a century between the western Federal Republic of Germany and eastern German Democratic Republic.[155] The Federal Republic of Germany was decentralized in *Länder*, regions with increased fiscal autonomy. Also, immediately after World War II, as in other European countries, the State enlarged public ownership of business only to partially privatize it over the next half century. With the State's acquiesces, cartels succeeded to survive; on the other hand, the State granted workers a voice in business decisions through representation on big business corporate boards. Twentieth century Germany continued to solidify the welfare state initiated during the late nineteenth century by Bismarck.

---

152 Bark and Gress 1993b, p. 783, quoting Michel Albert (1991) *Capitalisme contre-capitalisme*, Seuil, Paris.
153 Bark and Gress 1993b, pp. 782-786.
154 Nicholls 1994, p. 17.
155 Here, we do not examine the German Democratic Republic; our discussion refers only to the Federal Republic of Germany.

Industrial Expansion and Imperialism before 1914

In the later part of the nineteenth century, Germany as France and Italy attempted to catch up with Britain on colonization wanting participation in the new imperialism. Before 1914, the German ruling classes, the *Junkers* and the industrialists, all opted for the new imperialism, even though the *Junkers* were afraid that an expansionary policy would cause them to lose their privileges and hegemony within the State. Yet, generally business leaders and government policy makers thought that only by sustaining the momentum of economic expansion could the status quo be maintained. Ultimately, German imperialism was a continuation of a political culture immersed in traditional values that glorified power politics. It is probably correct to say that 'beleaguered elites always tend to resort to aggression and, in extreme cases, diversionary war in order to uphold their ascendancy'.[156] While the bourgeoisie was increasingly vocal in pre-1914 German society, Germany was still governed by the traditional ruling class.[157]

Economists are still debating whether economic growth contributes to political and social stability or vice versa. While hardly a democracy, in the same sense as Britain or France, the German State responded to social problems (see Chapter III), creating an environment favorable to economic growth. Generalizing about cause and effect can be hazardous and misleading. Did the Prussian-German unification wars foster or hinder economic growth? The answer lies somewhere in between; the wars destroyed resources but in the aftermath provided an incentive for expanding production partially because of public procurement needs and an extended market.

The State was ever present in encourage and supporting domestic initiatives that helped Germany become an industrial power. Industrial magnates were not enchanted with free markets. The older established Ruhr steel and coal industrialists sought protective tariffs and price fixing through cartels while the newer export oriented electrical and chemical companies aimed at a market organized by the State for the benefit of producers. 'Neither was advocating sovereignty of the consumer.'[158] By 1913 half the electric products traded in the world markets were of German origin. One of the two companies that manufactured these products was A.E.G., the *Allgemeine Elektrizität Gesellschaft*, General Electric Company, founded by Emil Rathenau at the end of the nineteenth century and directed by his son, Walther Rathenau (1867-1922).

For the anticipated war that started in1914, Germany counted on a short conflict. Expecting a dearth of both war and civilian inputs, Walther Rathenau joined the government and proposed planning the war economy so that stockpiled supplies would be in place for the war effort.[159] While other combatant countries

---

156 Mommsen 1995, p. 77.
157 Mommsen 1995, p. 171; Wehler 1972, pp. 117-118, 173-174; Berghahn 1982, p. 51; Carr 1991, p. 175.
158 Nicholls 1994, p. 21.
159 While not siding with the Socialists, Walther Rathenau, argued, in his published professional writings, that the era of unfettered capitalism was over and that the State

also rationalized resources for war, Germany was the exception that prudently *planned* the allocation of resources *before* the war since it expected an Allied blockade once war started as well as a two-front war. The German planned war economy consisted of allocating available supplies from the center, with military needs receiving the highest priority.[160] Until 1916 this system worked well and no shortages were evident. After two years of warfare, when shortages became acute, the population became restless and began to criticize the State and its bureaucrats paving the way for the revolutionary climate of 1918-1920.[161]

World War I Aftermath

Following the debacle of World War I, the German economy could not easily recover from loss of people, territory, and resources. The Constitution was thoroughly revised by 1919 when the German empire became the Weimar Republic and Germany became a democracy; the Constitution promised an equal voice and equal rights for employers and employees alike and made provisions for taking private property into public ownership. Indeed, Karl Kautsky (1854-1938), a socialist theoretician and historian chaired a socialization committee that recommended the nationalization of coal, land, and electric power.

Instead, the coal industry was reorganized into a new cartel, the *Reichskohlenverband*, the State Coal Group, which supervised the production and consumption of coal. The *Reichskohlenrat*, the State Coal Council, included miners, merchants, and consumers, who reported to the Ministry of Economic Affairs. Similar reorganizations established cartels in other industries. Yet the German government rejected the proposal of the Minister of Economic Affairs to continue the wartime economic planning designed by Rathenau. Despite the post-war uprisings, the German social and political structure did not change substantially; the power of the *Junker* and industrial barons remained intact. As one historian puts it, '...the mental attitudes of the Wilhelmian period lingered on under the democratic veneer'.[162]

War Reparations, Hyper Inflation, and the 'Rentenmark'

By 1922, run away inflation added to the havoc and utter collapse of the German economy, which had both domestic and international roots. Industrial production lagged due to labor unrest, scarcity of supplies especially coal and iron to meet the

---

had to assume a new role in allocation of resources. After World War I, he became Minister of Reconstruction and was assassinated in 1922.

160 Insofar as it was possible, German wartime planning became a model for other combatants.

161 Carr 1991, pp. 167, 218-220.

162 Behind the façade, the State appeared to disintegrate. The brutalization of political life from 1919 to 1922 is exemplified by 376 political murders, of which 356 have been attributed to right-wing extremists and culminated in 1922 with the assassination of Rathenau. Carr 1991, pp. 256-257, 265, 269-270.

demands of heavy industry, and above all the lack of internal and external confidence in the Weimar Republic. Authoritarian government had been ingrained for centuries and the change towards an unstable representative republic confused the public at large as well as their policy makers.

Hyperinflation had a ratchet effect feeding on itself in geometric progression. Germany could not face paying reparations—the treasury was empty or would not, arguing that it constituted extortion. Furthermore, to compel Germany to pay reparations, the French had temporary occupied the coal rich Ruhr. Futile attempts to meet war reparations commitments depleted the treasury and weakened Germany's credit standing and fueled inflation. In 1923, the State intervened with a psychological trick by introducing a new currency, the *Rentenmark*, backed by State-owned real estate. Psychology worked; inflation declined within bounds and one year later the government could transform the currency to one backed by gold.

By the end of the 1920s, the German national income had risen above the 1913 level. The German breed of capitalism-favored cartels with fixed production quotas, assigned markets, and fought for lower wages and higher prices. Not different from pre-war policies, the State encouraged these oligopolistic practices in basic industries. 'The new Republican government, dominated by Marxists social democrats and Roman Catholic center party politicians, was not inclined temperamentally to leave economic matters to the free play of market forces.'[163] The efficiency of German manufacturing was reduced by the tension in industrial relations. In some well-organized branches of industry, such as the metallurgical and chemical industries, management-labor collusion was detrimental to the public interest; therefore, when prices were rigged, the State intervened by regulating prices. Big business reacted to this interference by organizing various *Verbande*, trade associations, headed by the Association of German Industry.[164]

Economic Depression: 1929-1932

The weak post-World War I Weimar governments attempted to appease all sections of society but in the words of a contemporary Austrian political economist and student of German economy, Ludwig von Mises, fell into *Interventions-spiralen*, intervention spirals. Mises was a strong advocate of State neutrality in business cycles.[165] Like many other contemporary economists, Mises thought that the State fell prey to private interest groups fighting for restraints in competition and securing rents (returns beyond competitive levels) for themselves, *Der Staat als Beute*. Mises opposed unemployment benefits or any form of welfare programs; he claimed that the unhampered forces of demand and supply would eventually restore equilibrium.[166]

---

163   Nicholls 1994, p. 46.
164   Hardach 1980, pp. 30-35.
165   Mises 1962, p. 84; L. von Mises, *Die Ursachen der Wirtschaftskrise*. Tübingen 1931,
      p. 18, cited by Nicholls 1994, pp. 30-31.
166   Mises 1978, pp. 77-82.

It appears that Mises did not question how people would endure without the means of subsistence. 'It was this blind spot when faced with massive human suffering which rendered *laissez faire* economics—or paleo-liberalism, as its more moderate liberal critics came to describe it, unpalatable to most Germans.'[167] German moderate liberal economists, such as Walter Eucken, Wilhelm Ropke, and Alexander Rustow, argued that when there is no entrepreneurial initiative the State must initiate the mobilization of the economic forces of the private economy to help capitalism survive.[168]

The 1931 bankruptcy of the major commercial Austrian bank, the *Kreditanstalt*, rippled throughout the entire world financial structure. Germany was especially affected because of the extraordinarily close connection between the post-World War I truncated Austria and Germany. The ensuing inherent of interlocked industry-banks inefficiency delayed recovery from the depression (1929-1932). When the *Deutsche Bank*, one of the largest private commercial banks failed later that year, the entire financial system collapsed; in a rescue effort, the State injected cash by purchasing equity in the banks but to no avail.[169]

While the collapse had complex international origins, the weakness of the German banking system and the entire economy, did not help. Before the crash, American rescue plans (Dawes 1924 and Young 1929) and loans of private financial intermediaries attempted to keep the German economy afloat. As a result of the heritage of its nineteenth century banking structure, the large German banks financed industrialization. As mentioned in Chapter III, the State had encouraged a symbiosis between banking and industry with interlocking directorates. Since banking problems wee reflected in the industrial sector, the State was forced to intervene in the acute financial crisis to rescue the 'real' economy.

During the contraction of the early thirties when the State lacked financial capability, and the banks became insolvent, factories shut their gates.[170] To be sure, in the 1930s, most industrialized countries experienced a banking crisis and the State intervened. For instance in the United States, the Reconstruction Finance Corporation (RFC) in 1932, attempted to salvage the banks and, in March 1933, the federal government declared a bank holiday briefly closing all banks. Also, as we will see further, the Italian State created the *Istituto per la Ricostruzione Industriale* (IRI), the Institute for Industrial Reconstruction, which took over shares of the banks and *indirectly* became a large share holder in Italian industry.

Nazism and its Aftermath

The interaction between private and public economic and political power (*Vermachung der Wirtschaft*) eventually brought the concentration of all economic and political power in the Nazi State.[171] The depression brought in its wake the

---

167   Nicholls 1994, p. 30.
168   Nicholls 1994, pp. 39, 52, 55.
169   Moss 1997, pp. 229-273.
170   Hardach 1980, pp. 40-41; Kindleberger 1993, pp. 361-365.
171   Giersch, Paque, and Schmieding 1992, p. 27.

rise of Hitler with dire consequences. Nazism introduced the Corporate State in which the State, overtly or covertly, controlled resource allocation. 'The Nazi philosophy for the type of the economy they introduced reflected Germany's historical legacy, ...[that] favored establishment of strict social and political structures under the leadership of an elite group.'[172]

The Nazi philosophy rejected class antagonism and thus, upon coming to power in 1933, liquidated the trade unions and forced all workers to join the *Deutsche Arbeitsfront, DAF*, the German Labor Front, a State-sponsored institution that had no independent bargaining power. This Labor Front was used as propaganda and offered subsidized recreational facilities to members through its affiliated association *Kraft durch Freude*, Strength through Joy, which regimented labor in cohorts without individual liberty and civil rights.

The Nazis transformed the German limited market economy into a thoroughly State regulated economy, by controlling consumption, investment, and labor supply. By capping wages to limit money income, the State controlled domestic consumption and thus inflation. Following an autarchic model, investments aside from armaments were directed to the production of substitute materials. The labor supply was increased by recruiting women and after the start of World War II, slave labor from conquered European countries. The State had two rich revenue sources: before the war, before and after the 1938 *Kristallnacht*, the State plundered the Jews and other 'undesirable' minorities; during World War II, from 1938 to 1945, Germany transferred income and wealth from conquered territories.[173] The Nazis did not accept either central planning or the market economy but just muddled through with one aim, that is, German absolute power and hegemony everywhere.

The Nazis did not hesitate to use the 'inferior' races, an estimated 4.5 million Poles and Russians, as slave laborers when labor shortages developed due to mobilization, in line with the ideology that the Aryan race has to dominate and be supported by lesser races. The industrial establishment by then either lost control of its own enterprises or cooperated happily in these profitable ventures. Under the Nazis, the State was supreme authorizing more extraordinary measures than any other regime.

Neo-liberalism

Immediately after World War II an ideological vacuum emerged in defeated Nazi Germany. Initially, the four major allied victors Britain, France, the United States, and the Soviet Union divided Germany into four zones.[174] In the British zone, the German economic administration under the control of the Social Democrats was enthusiastic for planning, state control, and centralization. The American Zone

---

172   Angresano 1995, p. 151.
173   While World War II started on September 1, 1939, the previous year, at Munich, France and Britain gave Czechoslovakia, the most industrialized central European country to Hitler.
174   Note that in Britain the 'interventionist' Labor Party won the 1945 election.

was divided in three *Länder*, provinces, each one having its own economic ministry, hostile to centralization. To be sure, unfettered capitalism was in particularly in disrepute in Germany, and more generally in Western Europe. Many Europeans felt betrayed by an economic system that brought about the Nazi disaster, and held capitalist greed responsible for the depression and the war. German political parties saw a free market economy as impossible.[175]

Eventually the British and the U.S. zones, the 'Bizone', combined in a joint administration. When it became clear that the Soviet Union would retain its zone, the French joined with the 'Bizone' to form West Germany; the zone controlled by the Soviet became East Germany shortly afterwards. In *de facto* control of West Germany, the United States was confronted with a dilemma. In principle, it wanted to introduce a modified *laissez faire* economy. Tempered by the precarious conditions of the West German economy as well as by the historical background of the formerly powerful German cartels, policy makers opted for a strong public sector. The Marshall Plan (1948-1952) gave an immediate psychological boost to the economy and the new German leadership accepted public policies based on a limited market economy. This approach initiated a new symbiosis between big business and the State that continued for the rest of the century.[176]

Neo-liberalism emerged from the Nazi ashes; most were convinced that unhampered *laissez faire* was unacceptable. Neo-liberalism preached *laissez faire* with the State playing a central role in the overall economy and especially in charge of transfer payments. Also, in 1960 the *Reichstag*, the German parliament, formed the Council of Economic Experts, which was designed to be a group autonomous of the government and thus different from the United States Council of Economic Advisers.[177]

Ordoliberalism

Some German economic historians identified the postwar liberalism, as *ordoliberalism*; they attempted to establish a link between the German neo-liberal economic order and the medieval 'ordo', that is, 'the natural and harmonious state of affairs to be detected by scholarly discussions and to be approached in reality by appropriate policies'. The neo-liberals developed the concept of the *Soziale Marktwirtschaft*, the social market economy based on the 'conscious development of a fundamentally free, but also socially responsible, social and economic order, secured by a strong state'. One contemporary German economist, Rustow, contended, 'a strong state is needed to protect capitalism from capitalists'.[178] Another German economist, Wilhelm Eucken maintained that the State is bound to

---

175 Bark and Gress 1993a, pp. 193-197.
176 Polster and Voy 1991b, pp. 178-180, 185-189.
177 Radkau 1974, pp. 483-501; Hardach 1980, pp. 144-147; Giersch, Paque and Schmieding 1992, p. 139.
178 Heinz Lampert (1990) Die Wirtschaftund Sozialordnung der Bundesrepublik Deutschland. Tenth Edition, Olzog, Munich, quoted by Bark and Gress 1993a, p. 207; see also: Voy, Polster and Thomasberger 1991, p. 17.

provide conditions for 'a viable and humane economic order'. The State should be an ally of the capitalist process, not its master.[179]

The German *ordoliberals* demanded minimal *laissez faire* liberalism, *Nachtwächter Staat*. They wanted a strong State that could maintain a liberal economic order, but intervening only slightly in the market process. Traditional liberals such as Mises opted for the gold standard while Hayek viewed economic planning as 'the road to serfdom'.[180] German economists such as Ropke, Rustow and Eucken viewed Mises and Hayek as ultra liberals who did not belong to the main stream of modern liberalism.[181]

The German neo-liberals should be distinguished from the Anglo-American free market liberals; the conviction on the Continent was that societies unprotected by the State power are vulnerable to recurring economic crisis. This was also the view of Ludwig Erhard (1897-1977), a convinced neo-liberal economist Economics Minister in the immediate post-World War II period and later Prime Minister. German *ordoliberal* economists argued that it was no longer a question of freedom versus regulation but instead of choosing between State regulation and regulation by private groups. Since markets are imperfect, they claimed that the market works in a semi-automatic fashion and required 'sensible management' (*sinnvolle Bedienung*).[182]

The furthest departure from *laissez faire* in Germany has been the adoption of restrictive farm policies. As everywhere in Europe and the United States since the Great Depression, Germany has continued through the twentieth century to protect and subsidize agriculture. Erhard attempted to free the agricultural markets but to no avail. As we mentioned earlier in this chapter, since their inception, the European Union's farm policies have leaned towards protection; agricultural financial support has constituted almost half of the EU budget. Liberal economists have argued that by supporting artificially high food prices and subsidies to farmers there is a transfer of income from the industrial to the agricultural sector. As elsewhere in the industrialized world, the farm sector has been shrinking for a century and a half in Germany but the farm bloc has constituted a powerful interest group that no government can ignore with impunity.

Business Concentration

Another powerful interest group to reckon with has been the cartels. From the beginning of industrialization in the mid-nineteenth century until the end of World War II, the State not only tolerated but also legalized cartels. In 1897, the *Reichsgericht*, the Imperial Supreme Court, ruled that cartel contracts were legal. This conclusion originated with the tradition of price fixing and monopolies of the

---

179 Overy 2003, pp. 266-267.
180 Hayek 1944, p. 33; Mises 1980, pp. 429-434, 500.
181 Nicholls 1994, p. 29.
182 Giersch, Paque, and Schmieding 1992, pp. 28-29; Nicholls 1994, pp. 302-303, 390;
     Peacock and Willgerodt 1989, pp. 1-12; Bark and Gress 1993a, p. 207; Polster and
     Voy 1991b, p. 176.

fifteenth and sixteenth centuries when German princes offered exclusive trading privileges for ready cash.

In the 1920s the massive efforts of vertical integration undertaken by industry aimed at controlling the production, allocation, and marketing of iron and steel as well as the products manufactured from them. This was more than a response to State regulations dictated by World War I. 'Vertical concentration during the inflation, [was] extremely important in strengthening the economic and political power of heavy industry and of promoting collaboration between rival sectors of big business.'[183]

After World War II the U.S. Administration was in a quandary regarding cartels in its zone. The Americans assumed that the cartel habit was ingrained in German big business, and did not expect results from their 1947 decree against cartelization. The United States was determined to break up the German steel industry into 24 smaller units under Allied control. Also, it wanted to eliminate steel and coal vertical concentration so characteristic of pre-war German industry.[184] While the iron and steel industry has continued to be basic to the German economy, the core of German export industries has remained metallurgical-mechanical, electrical, and chemical products.

By the 1950s the German economic authority under Erhard was given responsibility for 'de-concentration' and decartelization. Erhard was a neo-liberal in the sense that he believed in *Sociale Marktwirtschaft*, which may mean either 'regulated free market economy' or 'socially conscious free market economy'.[185] As such, Erhard opposed monopolies and in 1952 he attempted to legislate cartels out of existence against strong opposition from big industry. When the law finally passed in 1957, Erhard could not recognize his ideas because a multitude of loopholes allowed the continuation of cartels although on a more limited scale than before the war. Although Erhard did not eliminate cartels entirely, he succeeded in breaking the power of the steel-coal cartels; the large coal and steel cartels were split into twenty-eight companies. Furthermore, the main commercial banks, the *Deutsche Bank*, the *Dresdner Bank*, and the *Commerzbank* were divided into thirty regional companies, and *I. G. Farben* was broken up into four companies.[186] Some argue that the anti-cartel movement was a farce since the export-led economic expansion relied on industrial concentration and State intervention; this development had a firm tradition in German economic history.[187]

---

183 Feldman 1977, p. 279.
184 Abromeit 1990, pp. 61-83; Fear 1997b, pp. 183-226; One should note that German steel and coal, came upon hard times during the 1980s.
185 Hardach 1980, p. 143; Graf 1992, p. 13.
186 Fulbrook 1992, p. 158; Nicholls 1994, pp. 15, 18, 72, 168, 326, 329, 337; Polster and Voy 1991a, p. 70.
187 Graf 1992, p. 16. Examples abound: IG-Farben has increased production and profits beyond those before break up. The banks again interlocked with industry, coal and steel as well as Siemens, AEG and Grundig have been again cartelized and have controlled the electronics market. A Nazi collaborator, Alfred Krupp left the Allied prison and put in charge of his industrial empire. Graf 1992, p. 16.

By the mid-1960s, the State approved 300 cartels compared with 3,000 in 1930. Some sectors, such as agriculture, housing, transportation, banking, and insurance were completely exempted from anti-cartel policy and the State facilitated cartel arrangements for these sectors. Different from the United States where mergers have stimulated 'business conglomerates', that is, large-scale managerial enterprises, or in Britain, France, and Italy where the family enterprise predominated, in Germany the large-scale enterprise has predominated which the State encouraged. German academics and the State have always had a benevolent attitude towards economic concentration in general and cartels in particular.[188] As mentioned above, the first federal anti trust legislation in the United States was enacted in 1890 (Sherman Act), while in Britain, France, and Italy only after World War II.

In 1956 Friedrich Lutz, a noted German economist argued that the German academic view of cartels has remained steadfast with old liberals but changed with the neo-liberals, the *ordoliberals*. The traditional, some would say extreme, liberals led by Hayek and Mises, maintained that any monopoly impedes trade and decreases the efficiency of the market but opposed any legislation against cartels. The *ordoliberals* realized that in a capitalist system business concentration will occur, and that necessarily moderating legislation is needed to sustain the market. The philosophy of the German 'social market economy' has been based on this pragmatic view.[189]

State Economic Enterprises and Privatization

The State has been quite directly involved in the marketplace; by the late 1960s the State had an ownership interest in over three thousand enterprises, even after some privatization. Erhard successfully experimented with privatization in the 1960s by selling shares of the Volkswagen automobile corporation to its workers with great success. Attempts to repeat the experiment in that decade received a tepid response from the public and they were abandoned.[190] By 2000, the State still owned a substantial, but a minority, interest in Volkswagen. In certain sectors, such as the utilities, the role of the State has been more obvious; one might expect the public ownership of transportation, gas, and electric power and distribution enterprises but a process of privatization has occurred in the late twentieth century.

While reluctant to be overtly subservient to the government, big business stood ready to seek government financial and other support as a right. But usually the State totally or partially owned enterprises have had enough autonomy in the market place. As elsewhere, for instance Italy, the objectives of German public enterprises often have been in conflict. There has been a dichotomy between the objective of profit making enterprise and State directed macro social policies such as the maintenance and creation of jobs and the development of sectors with high growth potential. Also, the State has not shied away from public investments

---

188   Hardach 1980, pp. 148-150; Polster and Voy 1991a, pp. 67-68.
189   Lutz 1989, pp. 152-155.
190   Nicholls 1994, pp. 357-358.

designed to encourage growth and bring about economic, political, and social stability.

During the last half of the twentieth century a wide program of privatization took place. The State became a minority shareholder in many enterprises but being a major minority holder, it succeeded in retaining control. The partially or totally owned companies have been managed in a business-like fashion as private enterprises, and, by and large, have been efficient and competitive. Some non-competitive public enterprises have been granted administrative independence such as the *Deutsche Bundesbahn* (German Federal Railroads), and the *Deutsche Bundespost* (German Federal Postal Service). In both cases, however, the deficits have been supported by the Federal budget as necessary public services. Also, regulation has ranged from the very stringent in sectors such as railroads, postal services, agriculture and utilities to a milder regulation of other sectors such as transportation, education and health.[191]

Codetermination

After World War II, organized labor regained its independence but in a sense lost firepower through a new policy of *Mitbestimmung*, codetermination, or workers participation in large enterprises; this policy allows labor to participate in corporate decisions, thereby allegedly weakening workers independence. On the other hand, codetermination may improve work quality and managers cannot follow their own goals without reference to the workers' welfare. As early as 1949, the Allied occupation authority granted the trade unions in the steel and coal industries in the British Zone the right of codetermination. The neo-liberals argued that *Mitbestimmung* constitutes an infringement of the entrepreneur in his responsibility to shareholders and a deviation from *laissez faire* policies. However, the West German government viewed it differently, passing legislation in 1952 that instituted codetermination in large enterprises. The State has condoned and has encouraged codetermination as an experiment in labor management relations. By the end of the twentieth century Germany was still debating the principle of codetermination.[192]

Some economists perceive codetermination as an extension of Bismarck's attitude based on his paternalistic philosophy; note that the Work Councils have existed in Germany since 1891. After the Nazi cataclysm, Germany desired to revert to Bismarck's search for social peace with the State an important partner, that is, the social market economy. The consensus seemed to be that the self-regulating market economy could not possibly solve labor market failures. The State reluctantly interfered with market forces until the mid-1960s. As some economists interpret the pre-mid 1960s period, the relationship between the private

---

191 Smith, Burgerand and Funk 1994, pp. 461, 474-475, 492; Berghahn 1982, p. 382; Polster and Voy 1991, pp. 214-216; Voy and Polster 1991, pp. 143-146.
192 CPB 1997, pp. 280-281; Fulbrook 1992, pp. 158-160; Giersch, Paque, and Schmieding 1992, p. 85; Overy 2003, p. 267.

sector and the State left little room for the State; nevertheless, the presence of the State in the market place was palpable and effective.[193]

The State has sided with those who see a positive role in workers joining in corporate decision making which could soften the antagonistic relationship between labor and management. The counter argument is that workers lose their autonomy and that codetermination is akin to the corporate State implemented by Fascist governments between the two world wars. While in such a State, workers were prevented from joining in labor unions; Fascist ideology assumed labor-management cooperation, and not antagonism. However, it appears that the German experiment with codetermination during the second part of the twentieth century has been a success, that is, it has lessened labor-management conflicts and minimized work hours lost through labor disputes.

Social Welfare

The public sector has been quite prominent in social welfare policy. German social security expenditures were 31 percent of the federal budget in 1993, similar to France but somewhat higher than Britain with 27.8 percent. As noted in Chapter III, in the 1870s, Germany was in the forefront among the industrialized countries in introducing social legislation. Bismarck implemented social security for the disabled, the aged, and the unemployed, and pioneered in universal health insurance backed entirely or partially by the State. After World War II, Germany further expanded these policies. It appears that social policies decisions have not depended entirely on the political orientation of the times.

After World War II, the prevailing views have been dominated by the idea of *Soziale Marktwirtschaft*, a social market economy, however defined. German economic historians argued that by the 1970s the welfare State slowly but definitely changed from a provider of emergency welfare to a 'collective provision for existence', *kollektive Daseinsvorsorge*, translated as public assistance from cradle to the grave. Critics have viewed enlarging the welfare state as counter productive; the high unemployment rate after the 1980s often has stemmed from generous welfare payments. Also, they have argued that a large public sector creates vested interests for the bureaucrats, who divert to their clients resources from productive endeavors. Yet, it appears that social expenditures have brought political and social stability and confidence in the government.[194]

The role of the State in Germany and the United States has differed considerably. In the United States, by and large, adjustments have been left to the market; individual adaptability ranks high and government intervention have been frequently opposed. For the most part, the unemployed individual is supposed to shift from one occupation to another or move from one part of the country to another. In Germany cooperation and negotiation between the State and private agents have prevailed. Social security shields individuals from the vagaries of the market as the State has a more active role in economic adjustment. For instance,

---

193   Hardach 1980, pp. 154-155.
194   Bark and Gress 1993b, pp. 86-89.

health care accessibility is no longer an issue for most industrialized countries except the United States where some form or another of private insurance covers two-thirds of the population and fifteen percent of the population is not covered by any health care insurance.[195] Furthermore, in the United States health care is tied to employment with employers partly footing the bill for health insurance coverage and in most cases health care coverage is withdrawn upon employment termination.

In Germany, health care insurance has been universal and is the responsibility of the State, even though individuals contribute to the system and can obtain allegedly superior care from private providers. The most significant changes in social security were legislated in 1972. Pension payments were separated from contributions to make sure that retired workers could maintain their standard of living while employed. In addition, there were improvements in health and accident insurance, better unemployment benefits, and rent control as well as subsidies to encourage savings and investments. Through these policies, West Germany succeeded in establishing the Welfare State at among the highest historical levels in Europe. By 2003, budgetary pressure forced the government to reverse and cut some of the State welfare provisions, not a very popular measure.

In the post World War II environment, the United States mitigated its competitive model, which is still far removed from the German cooperative model. The German model calls for the various actors in the economy to cooperate, with the State as a moderator. As mentioned above, in large enterprises labor-management relations have been governed by a pact of codetermination that allows labor to have a voice in management policy decisions. Not different from the United States, the locus of policy making has been based on the principle of subsidiarity, defined as the relationship between State and its citizens, State and the market, and has ranked responsibility from localities through *Länder*, single German states, and the Federal Administration.[196]

During the second half of the twentieth century, the German institutional framework, similar to France and Italy but different from Britain and the United States, has included job protection to the extent that it transformed labor input from a variable to a fixed cost, thus establishing a very rigid labor market, allegedly increasing the unemployment rate. Within the framework of the European Union, Germany has attempted to make adjustments to achieve a more flexible labor market. German business has been opposed to a proposed decrease of the weekly hours from 40 to 35. Yet, in the middle 1990s when autoworkers were faced with legislation limiting their income, Volkswagen workers voluntarily accepted a decrease in working hours with a partial loss of take home pay; the loss was equally divided between the enterprise and labor.

---

195 CPB 1997, p. 522.
196 CPB 1997, pp. 139-145, 154-159, 190; Bark and Gress 1993b, pp. 244-247.

Conclusions

Perhaps the last half of the twentieth century has been the most successful period of the Germany economy but not necessarily as a market economy. The *Soziale Marktwirtschaft* has featured the pragmatic acceptance of a regulated market. Some historians note that in Germany as in the rest of the industrialized world, substantial inequality in private income and wealth has persisted despite redistributive legislation and social protection, limited diffusion of economic power, and the strong influence of the State. It appears that after World War II, Germany experienced rapid economic progress with moderate success in solving social problems even though the State, as a moderator and as an active actor, has played a significant role in this process. The State's role in the economy was a main factor in social progress. The symbiosis between business and State has been reinforced by international events. 'Rearmament also enhanced the tightening nexus between business and the state. In West Germany, as in other post-war Western states, the warfare and welfare states increasingly merged into one another.'[197]

While industrial concentration and sectoral domination by cartels have continued to be present, Germany has instituted labor management co-determination thus lessening entrepreneurial independence. Labor and political interest groups have been controlling the rigid labor market that has made labor a quasi fix cost of production. By the end of the twentieth century, there have been a plethora of State entrepreneurial activities and regulations affecting business. Regardless of the political composition of governments and vicissitudes of wars, depression, and Nazism, the State has played a key role in having Germany enter the twenty-first century as the third economic power after the United States and Japan.

Italy

Italy entered the twentieth century with a broad band of interventionist policies. Having assisted significantly with railroad construction during the nineteenth century, Italy nationalized the railroads in 1905. The State also subsidized the shipyards directly and indirectly through procurement for the State-owned merchant marine and the navy and, above all, protected the mechanical and textile industries with high tariffs. In addition, under Giovanni Giolitti (1842-1928), an Italian statesman who dominated the political scene between 1900-1914 and served as Prime Minister during 1892-1893, 1903-1905, and 1906-1909, Italy enacted extensive social legislation. Before World War I, the 'liberal' (*laissez faire*) Giolitti government, with a helping hand especially from Francesco Nitti (1868-1953), professor of finance, Minister of Agriculture and subsequently Minister of

---

197 Ossip K. Fleitheim (1964) *Eine Welt Oder Keine?* EWG, Frankfurt, pp. 241-242, cited by Graf 1992, p. 19.

Industry, Labor, and Social Programs, created an important institutional framework for State intervention.

In order to improve workers pensions, in 1912 the government sought a role in the insurance sector by organizing the National Insurance Institute, *L'istituto nazionale delle assicurazioni (INA)*. Giolitti proposed to make life insurance a State monopoly but the parliament modified the proposed law beyond recognition, and then postponed its implementation for 10 years, only to be enacted by Mussolini in the 1920s. It appears that certain public policy decisions were not different under economic and political liberals from the later Fascist counterpart; life insurance however, never became a State monopoly. The policy of State monopoly of life insurance was followed in 1914 by a consortium to subsidize industrial enterprises, and in 1917, a veterans aid agency to assist army veterans re-entering the labor market. After World War I, Nitti also masterminded a number of State financial agencies. By the 1920s if not earlier the so-called liberal government could no longer be associated readily with *laissez faire*.[198]

If one considers the military and railway expenditures between 1896 and 1908, the State accounted for one third of the demand for mechanical industry products. Before World War I, the State was responsible for 15 to 20 percent of the GNP, a ratio higher than in many other leading European economies. Due to the lack of entrepreneurs, the State was relatively a more important factor in Italy than in other European countries in the development process. As elsewhere, the State intervened even more significantly during World War I in the management of supplies and the increase of production. The 'liberals', that is, those who had preached *laissez faire* of yesteryear, became promoters of State intervention and at times encouraged the nationalization of industries deemed strategic.[199]

In particular, during the twentieth century the State became involved repeatedly in banking. It did so during the financial crisis of the early1920s and during the depression of the1930s, the State took over most of the banks only to privatize them at the end of the century. Since these universal banks owned a large share of the basic industries, which per force became public assets, the State inevitably became an industrial entrepreneur by proxy. Fascist economic policies favored the role of the State in the market place; to defend the internal market, the Fascist State pursued mercantilist polices which aided heavy industry, damaged agriculture as an unintended consequence, and kept consumer goods prices high.

World War II was partially fought on Italian soil bringing in its wake much destruction, displacement, and misery. During the immediate post-war era the northern part of Italy, less damaged by the war, experienced rapid recovery and by 1960s an 'economic miracle' occurred. When labor unions demanded participation in this economic expansion, the State added to an array of social programs. The State remained a substantial owner of large economic enterprises and until the 1990s, while professing to privatize its holdings, expanded them by design or by

---

198 Barca 1997, pp. 9-10; Cafagna 1989, pp. 316-317; A. Scialoja (1971) 'L'Istituto nazionale delle assicurazioni e il progetto giolittiano di un monopolio di stato delle assicurazioni sulla vita', *Quaderni Storici*, 18, cited by Zamagni 1993, p. 191.
199 Zamagni 1981, p. 160; Brosio and Marchese 1986, pp. 202-203; De Rosa 1974, p. 32.

default.   The attempt to use these enterprises to solve southern Italy's underdevelopment problems failed; instead, State policy created conditions of perpetual dependency with the South psychologically expecting the dole.[200]

Italy joined the European Common Market, now the European Union (EU), in 1958, as a founding member.   The enlarged market brought notable economic benefits by freeing and expanding trade among the EU member states.   Like France and Germany, while successful in liberalizing capital markets, Italy encountered economic and political problems in liberalizing the labor markets, limiting social benefits (such as welfare, medical insurance, pensions), and privatizing strategic sectors.   The European Union as a whole as well as each individual State has professed economic liberalism, but by the end of the twentieth century, because of interest groups pressures, half of the EU budget has been allocated to farm support.

Banking

At the end of the nineteenth century, the *Banca Commerciale Italiana* and the *Credito Italiano*, two leading commercial banks, were founded with German financial backing to facilitate the participation of German capital in Italian industry and trade and to replace French capital.   These banks followed typical German banking practices, that is, they acted both as both commercial and investment banks, and appointed representatives to the boards of directors of the industrial enterprises in which they invested.

Alberto Beneduce (1877-1944) was instrumental in 1919 in founding the *Consorzio per Opere Pubbliche, Crediop*, a Public Works Credit Consortium.   As an adviser to Nitti, Beneduce proposed the establishment of *Crediop* and also became its first president.   He aimed to capture private funds for public works by issuing non-tax bearing government bonds, thus crowding out private banks.[201] Before and during Fascism, Beneduce forged the Italian financial system and succeeded in having the banks under the State's aegis but at a price.[202]

Italian banks, that is, 'mixed' banks or universal rather than functionally specialized, provided all banking services including short-term and long-term credit similar to French and German banks and therefore markedly different from British and U.S. banks.[203] The development of banking institutions and the growth of state economic enterprises, SEEs, have been closely related.   Banks owned shares in industrial enterprises, which the State rescued when they failed during the 1930s; in practice this meant that, as a consequence, the State assumed control of non-banking enterprises.

---

200 For a detailed analysis of southern underdevelopment problems after World War II, see Schachter and Engelbourg 1995, pp. 585-601.
201 Zamagni 1993, pp. 236-237.
202 De Cecco 1997, p. 403.
203 Zamagni 1993, p. 147. Shortly before World War I, Italian banks succeeded in freeing themselves first from French and then from German domination.

Because of their universal nature, the banks were often tempted to take unusually high risks, anticipating high returns not associated with commercial banks. These banks immersed themselves in politics to secure subsidies, tax exemptions, tariff protection, and government contracts for their clients. In this way, they hoped to increase their profits or to shift the losses of risky enterprises to the taxpayers.[204] Luigi Einaudi (1874-1961), professor of public finance, journalist, representative of the free trade school in Italy, governor of the Bank of Italy (1945-1946), treasury minister in 1947, and second president of the Italian Republic, in the early 1920s despaired of the close relationship between banking and industry, which had been already doled tariff protection and government procurement. Einaudi was aghast that 'when the problem became that of forcing the state to take over losses running into the billions of lira, the same people proclaimed themselves partners of the government'.[205]

With the cessation of hostilities, in 1918 Italy terminated the war economy. While connected with the worldwide financial and economic downturn, the Italian post-war depression was provoked by the banking crisis of 1920-1921, which started with the bankruptcy of the *Banca italiana di sconto*.[206] This bank was tied to the mechanical industry conglomerate, Ansaldo, which, in turn, faced bankruptcy. Ansaldo products ranged from boiler and steel plates for the navy to railroad locomotives; the State did not hesitate to foot the bill in order to prevent the entire economy from collapsing. In the United States and Great Britain the steel and mechanical industries had government contracts mainly for defense, however, the proportions differ since in Italy the steel and mechanical industries *depended* on wartime government contracts. After the nationalization of the railroads in 1905, the Italian government's procurement from Ansaldo increased to such a magnitude that the Ansaldo could survive only by the government's grace.

Long before the 1930s depression, the relationship between the banks and the State had been synchronized for their mutual benefit. As one would expect, the banks encouraged private enterprises to invest in new ventures; unfortunately, when these investments failed the State often bailed the banks out. To a certain extent, the State played a role in decreasing investment risk and uncertainty that might well have been caused by the relative weakness of the Italian banks and the economy but served as a prop for the banks.

Founded in 1893 to reorganize and regulate the banking system, the Bank of Italy became the central bank in charge of national monetary policy but not until in 1926 the sole bank of issue. At unification in 1861, Italy had five banks of issue and added one in 1870. In 1893, the *Banca Romana* liquidated and then the two Tuscan banks of issue merged with the Sardinia National Bank to form the Bank of

---

204 Einaudi, Bye and Rossi 1955, pp. 191-192.
205 Einaudi 1933, pp. 18-19.
206 Originally, the *Figli di Weil Schott & Company* became the *Società Bancaria Milanese*, SBM; in turn, SBM bought the bankrupt *Banco di Sconto e Sette* of Turin. In 1904, it changed the name *to Società Bancaria Italiana*, SBI, and in 1914 became *Banca Italiana di Sconto*, BIS Zamagni 1993, p. 146; see also Kindleberger 1993, pp. 144-146.

Italy. In preparation for the reevaluation of the lira, the State deprived the Bank of Naples and the Bank of Sicily of the right of issue in 1926. Finally, in 1936, Italy nationalized the Bank of Italy. The major banks became state-owned and the State has been the principal source of investment and the keystone for financial intermediation.[207]

The Fascist Economic Policy

Before, and probably even during Fascism, the State's actions were not centrally coordinated; policies were adopted in an *ad hoc* fashion to achieve certain short-term goals. It is not the coordination that changed drastically but rather the Fascist permanent war economy (1922-1943) made it necessary to augment the State's role in the market.[208] Nevertheless, a noted Italian economist argued, 'We can detect a strong continuity between the Fascist years and the experience of wartime economic dirigisme'.[209]

As a key element of autarky and fearing isolation and foreign dependency for its food supplies but also as a grandiose gesture to gain prestige, Italy initiated '*la battaglia del grano*, the grain battle, in 1925. Fearing isolation, this State initiative sought self-sufficiency in providing bread for the masses although with an increased cost for the State. Like most European countries, then, and at other times in the twentieth century, Italy did not have a comparative advantage in grains. In the North, the farms approached the yields of other Western European countries but in the South grain yield per man-hour was merely one-sixteenth that of the United States. Under these circumstances, the self-sufficiency policy backfired because it grossly and predictably misallocated resources.[210]

On the one hand, in the short run since previously grain constituted one quarter of all imports this eased the pressure on the balance of payments and the national currency. Note that in the 1920s Mussolini in Italy, as Churchill in Britain, set an artificially high rate of exchange (4.44 lire one dollar and $4.85 equaled one British pound) that discouraged exports. On the other hand, it diminished household expenditures because of the scarcity of consumer goods and the higher prices paid for grain products, even though the State attempted to impose a ceiling on grain prices.[211]

Different from some European countries such as Britain, the State has played a role of mediator and pacifier among social classes, the oligopolies, labor unions, and the public at large. State intervention in the Italian economy was not just an accident; rather, it was the basis of the nascent Italian State and perhaps inherited from Piedmont before the unification. Regardless of ideology, it seems that most Italians have accepted the role assumed by the State. Under Fascism, the role of

---

207 Kindleberger 1993, p. 139.
208 De Rosa 1974, pp. 33-35; Kindleberger 1993, pp. 349-350.
209 De Cecco 2002, p. 74. World War I 'economic planning' influenced the New Deal policies in the United States.
210 Schachter 1965, passim.
211 Petri 2002, pp. 240-249.

the State as a moderator was biased; as in any dictatorial absolutist regime, there could be only one power center.[212]

Corporativismo integrale

Under Fascism the State attempted to control the economy by integrating the financial sector so that it became difficult to distinguish between private monopolies and the State. Under the so-called *corporativismo integrale* (integral corporate) the State delegated its market intervention to the corporate trade association controlled by the large enterprises. In a notable speech, Mussolini in 1936 presented his plan for the Italian economy asserting that heavy industry (essential for future wars) should be the basis of the Fascist State. It appears that his ultimate aim was to eliminate the distinction between the State and private corporations.

Since his 1922 *coup d'état*, the March on Rome, Mussolini had contended that the collaboration between the State and the private corporations would be in the best interests of the country.[213] During the nineteen twenties, Alfredo Rocco (1875-1935), a leading Fascist political theoretician and Minister of Justice (1924-1932), maintained that cooperation among classes, the tenet of the corporate State, should replace antagonism.

In a totalitarian state, even during peacetime, a permanent war economy exists. Fascist Italy constitutes a classic example, controlling prices, wages, giving preference to heavy industry for present and future wars, and neglecting the rest of the economy. This allowed a deterioration of the quality of life especially since Italy was already far behind other Western European countries.[214] On the one hand, it represented the best illustration of the autarkic inefficient State, perhaps an aberration after century-long relative political liberalism. On the other hand, as expressed by Mussolini, the concept of the State under Fascism became the goal: '...the State is not only a living reality of the present. It is also linked with the past and above all with the future, and thus transcending the brief limits of individual life, it represents the immanent spirit of the nation'.[215]

According to Rocco, Fascists use individuals as instruments for the benefit of the State, instruments who can be removed, changed or subordinated when no longer serviceable to the State. Rocco's Law of Corporations, enacted in 1926, assumed that in the Corporate State the main objective was to discipline labor and no action should take place outside of the State.[216] Rocco maintained that, while

---

212 Fascism succeeded in reversing the laic nature of the Italian State by expanding religion in the schools and in all public affairs. Hoping to reinforce and legitimize the Fascist State, in 1929, Mussolini signed a concordat with the Vatican, reinstating many rights of the Church denied since unification. Kelikian 2002, pp. 57-58.

213 Grifone 1975, pp. 26, 54-55; Petri 2002, pp. 104-111.

214 Covino, Gallo and Mantovani 1976, pp. 232-237.

215 Benito Mussolini, 'The Political and Social Doctrine of Fascism', in *International Conciliation*, January 1935, pp. 13-14, quoted by Welk 1938, p. 33.

216 Alfredo Rocco 1926, p. 404, in 'The Political Doctrine of Fascism', *International*

individuals come and go, the State remains as a continuing institution. To Fascists 'economic liberty is merely a concession, made to the individual by society in the interest of the social group'.[217]

Mussolini was determined to remove power from the labor unions, which were mainly dominated by the Socialist and the Communist parties. In the early 1920s, Mussolini first banned opposing parties and then, decided to control the labor market through State employment offices, although not very efficiently nor with enough resources. These employment offices decided to strengthen the employed and to put less emphasis on the unemployed, who were powerless and without a choice but to starve. The Fascist regime subordinated the unions since no totalitarian system can withstand competing institutions.[218]

In the field of higher education the State as in most other European countries, historically has had a quasi monopoly.[219] Public funding for higher education succeeded in bureaucratizing and politicizing the university system. Furthermore, Fascism required an oath of allegiance to the system, which virtually all professors signed; those who did not sign effectively resigned their positions.[220] Under Fascism, and even afterwards, Italy had no analogous competitive capabilities such as private/independent institutions to those existing in the United States. Before World War II there were no more than a few small private universities in Italy, and besides, the State controlled all institutions of higher education.

The State and 'La Comunità'

Economic pioneering may not always pay off but someone must be willing to bear the initial risks. Some Italian economists contend that capital accumulation in Italy has been a continuous process initiated by the State.[221] In a 1939 article in *La Stampa,* a leading Turin newspaper, Adriano Olivetti (1901-1960), a maverick but highly successful manufacturer of typewriters, calculators, and later computers, observed that the financial community enjoyed a good bargain at the expense of

---

Conciliation, October, pp. 395-407, cited by Welk 1938, p. 34.

217 Welk 1938, pp. 35.

218 Examples of the state-controlled unions in the former Soviet Union confirm this view; the State subordinated labor unions in 1926.

219 Public universities have always dominated the Italian system of higher education. Only a small fraction of higher education institutions, such as Bocconi University, *Universita Cattolica del Sacro Cuore*, and Luis University (created by *Confindustria,* the Italian National Association of Manufacturers) have been privately operated but heavily subsidized by the State. Also, there have been a number of small off shore campuses of American universities, especially in Rome and Florence, attracting American students and with a small core (compared with the large student population in the Italian public universities) of Italian students.

220 Barca 1997, p. 37. The United States underwent a similar experience in the 1950s when Senator Joseph McCarthy hunted Communists in academia. The similarity stops there; the United States has countervailing institutions. McCarthy had some success in public universities, but most private universities stood firm.

221 Bonelli 1979, p. 1231.

the public at large. When the corporations earned profits, they retained the earnings or distributed dividends to the shareholders and, echoing the 1933 comment of economist Einaudi, when corporations showed losses the State rushed to their rescue. This was part of the Fascist logic in defending the interests of the moneyed classes as well as in participating in the allocation of scarce resources.[222]

During the late nineteenth century, Adriano's father, Camillo Olivetti, who founded the enterprise advocated a type of utopian socialism, believing that capitalist societies have the tendency to concentrate wealth. After World War II, his son Adriano followed in his father's footsteps by encouraging the creation of community centers that could mediate between the individual and the State so that individuals could retain their independence with the State offering physical and social protection. He contended that a partnership should develop between the State and industry but policy decisions should take place at the local level.[223]

Adriano Olivetti launched *La Comunità* movement in 1948 to which he devoted a large part of his time and wealth. The movement was dedicated to social, cultural and political betterment through organizing cultural centers, libraries, and community assistance centers. While hardly a great political force, nevertheless, it influenced the Italian social fabric. On one hand, his philosophy vaguely reminds one of the early utopians, Proudhon and Fourier; on the other hand, the closest applications of *La Comunità* philosophy have occurred in only a few localities and had almost no effect on central government policies.[224] It appears that there was no mass appeal for Olivetti's philosophy, although not because of a diminished role of the State at the center but instead because its populist framework sounded too much like a repackaging of Rocco's Fascist philosophy of cooperation. One must not discount the antagonism of the established labor unions and left leaning political parties, weary of labor being co-opted by management.

Reforms and Planning

World War II (1939-1945) was partially fought on Italian soil between 1943 and 1945 and in its wake brought much misery. By the time the Marshall Plan ended in 1952, Italy regained its prewar industrial output level. To be sure, Italian recovery took place in the North where industries were fueled by cheap migratory labor from southern Italy, productivity growth, and State assistance such as easy credit and tax exemptions. During the 'Italian miracle' of the 1960s economic growth surpassed everyone's expectations due to the rapid increase in productivity and capital accumulation owed to high profit margins but none of this reflected in salaries and wages.

---

222 Grifone 1975, p. 97.
223 Caizzi 1962, pp. 32, 33, 322-333, 360-375.
224 As mentioned above, a similar philosophy has been practiced in the post World War II Germany. There has been a federal system (as advocated by Adriano Olivetti) coupled with workers co-determination, that is, workers have been included on the boards of directors of large enterprises.

International and domestic factors caused a slowdown of the 'miracle'; the early 1970s energy crises, the end of the gold standard, and strengthening of the currency lowered Italy's competitiveness. Domestically, labor demanded an enlarged share of the economic gains, that is, organized labor claimed a lager return on their increased productivity. When some labor demands were met, economic growth continued but at a lower level than before. By the end of the 1960s, the Italian government responded by formulating key objectives for the State: *riforme* and *programmazione*, reforms and planning. Reforms were directed to change the Italian social structure to adjust for the problems created by rapid economic growth. The second objective, that is, *programmazione*, was intended to adjust the market to social goals.

As a result of enacting social programs, public expenditure increased from 33 percent of the GNP in the 1960s to 41 percent in 1975 and to a whopping 52 percent in 1996. This rapid expansion originated with the increased demands for social welfare, health, improved compensation for civil servants, and continued subsidies to State enterprises in order to create employment without regard to enterprise profitability. Because of these expenditures, the public debt increased and concomitantly interest payments *and* interest rates rose; the Italian government seemed to approve expenditures without regard to budgetary constraints. The State attracted savings that otherwise would have gone to private enterprises thus slowing down the economy further.[225]

State Economic Enterprises

The dichotomy between Anglo-America and Continental Europe is evident State-business relationship; the Anglo-Saxons favored regulation, the Continentals relied often on Sate business participation.[226] State Economic Enterprises (SEE) are usually have been established as a palliative solution for market failure and/or as a political action. Examples abound, in the fifteenth century Venice built the *Arsenale*, in the seventeenth century Colbert established *les manufactures royales*, and Frederick II founded enterprises partially or wholly owned by the State. The United States established a mixed public-private federal bank in 1791 and Britain nationalized the telegraph during the nineteenth century.

Twentieth century witnessed State participation in business enterprises followed by privatization. In the mid-century, the apparent collapse of the capitalist system during the Great Depression in Continental countries forced the State to partake in business enterprises to save the short run calamity. Even in the United States, the State invested in the Tennessee Valley Authority, while Britain waited until after World War II for a vast program of nationalization, followed by privatization in the 1980s. In Continental Europe, State participation in business was wider before and after World War II, consequently after 1980, the movement

---

225   Rossi 2000, pp. 10-20.
226   'Regulation was the policy instrument favored in the United States. Elsewhere, public sector operation of the firms was the preferred alternative.' Galambos and Baumol 2000, p. 305.

of privatization has been slower and more difficult to implement. Between 1963 and 1990, while the economic index of State participation definitely declined in Britain it remained about the same in France and Germany and increased in Italy.[227]

During the banking crisis of the Great Depression, Italy had little or no choice but to intervene massively in the economy to surmount this colossal market failure. Italy organized the *Istituto per la ricostruzione industriale* (IRI), The Institute for Industrial Reconstruction in 1933 a holding company, to rescue the commercial banks, which held industrial securities. The development of IRI as the major umbrella state economic enterprise, SEE, although triggered by the Great Depression and encouraged by the very nature of the Fascist corporate state, stemmed from the principle of close cooperation between the State as well as the private sector and an explicit rejection of *laissez faire*. Along with the banks, IRI acquired the banks' shares and credits in industrial companies, regardless of whether these industries were profitable or not. There was a similarity between IRI and the 1932 United States Reconstruction Finance Corporation (RFC), which rescued failing banks and other large-scale enterprises.

As elsewhere, government agencies seemed to become self-perpetuating and endured long after their original justification. They frequently gave rise to constituencies, such as directors, personnel, and suppliers, which have had a vested interest in their perpetuation.[228] The Italian government's intention to have IRI, ostensibly a temporary institution, to cope with the financial and industrial collapse during the 1930s depression, simply did not materialize. Many of its holdings either were unattractive to private investors or there were insufficient private funds to repurchase the stocks of these banks and industrial enterprises. Ultimately, the Italian government viewed certain enterprises as militarily strategic and also vested internal interests chose to keep them under direct government control.[229]

Although similar, IRI and the United States RFC were hardly identical. Secured by collateral, RFC loans were commercial transactions and not grants. The RFC provided emergency financing for life insurance companies, building and loan societies, railroads, and farm mortgage associations. Itself the successor of the World War I, WFC (World Finance Corporation), during World War II the RFC built and equipped industrial buildings in addition to lending to private companies before being dismantled in the 1950s. Unlike IRI, the RFC did not manage or interfere with management; in keeping with the U.S. tradition, vis-à-vis the railroads during the nineteenth century, the State (RFC) bailed out private enterprises but did not attempt to substitute its judgment for that of the enterprise. While President Franklin Delano Roosevelt might have nationalized banks and

---

227 The economic weight of SEE was calculated as a percent of total enterprise accounting for shares of employment, gross investment, and value added. Indices for 1963 and 1990 were respectively: Britain 10 and 4, France 19 and 18, Germany 11 and 10, and Italy 12 and 19. Toninelli, pp. 21-22.
228 See for example Finoia 2001, pp. 685-690.
229 Galambos and Baumol 2000, pp. 304-306; Toninelli 2000, pp. 5-10.

other sectors, he preferred to save capitalism from itself whereas Mussolini did not care either way.

In 1937, the State gave IRI a permanent charter as a public holding company and continued to expand. By 1939, largely driven by the severity of the depression, as well as military needs and the Fascist ideology, IRI controlled 80 percent of Italy's shipping and shipyards, 75 percent of iron, and 50 percent of steel production. In addition, IRI controlled 100 percent of the armaments industry, 80 percent of the locomotive production, and 30 percent of electric generation, the entire telephone company, various mechanical companies, and a minority share of other industries. Moreover, it had a controlling interest in the major banks.[230] By the mid-1930s Italy had the highest percentage of state enterprises in Western Europe. By the end of the twentieth century, while greatly reduced, IRI remained the largest single entity in the Italian economy.[231]

In 1953, the *Ente Nazionale Idrocarburi*, ENI, the National Petroleum Agency, was organized as a state holding company assembling several petroleum and natural gas drilling and refining and petrochemical enterprises. Probably an exception, ENI's creation was clearly an overt State decision to compete with the private sector and achieve energy independence from the seven sisters, the corporations that controlled the international oil markets.[232]

The ENI saga is synonymous with the legendary Enrico Mattei (1902-1962) who was put in charge of dismantling the Fascist AGIP enterprise; instead, Mattei built ENI as an energy empire. ENI has been an extension of AGIP, *Azienda Generale Italiana Petroli*, (Italian General Agency for Petroleum), established in 1926 by the Fascist government's autarkic policy. With all odds against him, Mattei succeeded in establishing a profitable State enterprise. ENI eventually discovered natural gas deposits beneath the Po Valley and later in Basilicata, Abruzzi, and Sicily. 'By the beginning of the 1960s the image of ENI was that of a pivotal element of the "Italian economic miracle", a company run in the best interest of the nation.'[233] One could also view the formation of ENI as an illustration of nationalism, which at other times and places, has generated state enterprises.

After Mattei's accidental death in 1963, ENI continued efficient operation and attempted to create a State monopoly in the field; by 1969 Italy had the largest oil refinery capacity in Europe with 130 million tons a year. Economic power can corrupt as much as political power; during the 1970s and 1980s ENI leadership and others were involved in scandals involving corruption and bribery of politicians for company and personal gains. By the 1990s ENI was scheduled for privatization.[234]

230 Petri 2002, p. 101.
231 Romeo 1963, passim; Marsan 1980, pp. 85-98; Posner and Woolf 1967, pp. 23-24; Schachter 1986, pp. 12-15.
232 Tolliday 2000, p. 245; Carnevali 2000, p. 252.
233 Amatori 1997b, p. 262.
234 Schachter 1986, pp. 12-15; Di Scala 1998, p. 309; Mack Smith 1997, p. 450.

Between 1950 and the 1970s, other SEEs were established, the *Ente autonomo di gestione per il finanziamento dell'industria meccanica*, EFIM Agency for Managing and Financing Mechanical Industry and in 1971, the State initiated *Gestioni e partecipazioni industriali*, GEPI, Agency for Management and Industrial Participation, with the mission of taking over the management of weak private enterprises and restoring them to financial health. After World War II, IRI retained a legal structure, which enabled it to function as an ordinary joint stock corporation with respect to asset management, taxation, and personnel procedures. IRI operated like a private investment trust; it owned stock in industrial undertakings in which private shareholders also might have owned stock. The SEEs have been faced with a conflict between the social role of the public enterprise and profit maximization for the benefit of private shareholders. Conflicts sometimes have risen when the SEEs have been used as instruments for implementing overall government policies.[235]

While before the 1960s the SEEs were owned by the State, operational controls were in the hands of professional managers and technocrats or 'public entrepreneurs'. Since the 1960s the State has moved from indirect to direct control of SEEs; undermining the autonomy of the professional managers and technocrats previously in charge. The party in power used positions (*poltrone*, literally, chairs) in the enterprises for political ends to reward supporters, defend local interests, and rescue ailing firms.[236] The inherent contradiction between the multiple and conflicting nature of the objectives and the instruments selected to attain the goals of the SEEs has never been fully resolved. The conflict can be viewed from the single enterprise and the State points of view. The enterprise has viewed the commercial need profitability. State 'control insures the enterprise' conformity with government guidelines...diminishing or nullifying entrepreneurial responsibility. As a result, confusion has prevailed'.[237]

Between 1930 and 1970, the State through ownership and/or control of big business attempted the difficult task of reconciling the economic goals of state enterprises with social goals. Through the end of the twentieth century, through IRI or otherwise, the Italian State has aided large-scale enterprises. It has been estimated that by the 1990s more than 40 percent of Italy's GNP has been produced, owned, or controlled by the state economic enterprises that competed with the sector's private enterprises.[238]

'*Lo stato imprenditore*': The State as an Entrepreneur

In 1958, as in 1914 or 1938, Italy was the least developed nation among the founders of the six-nation European Economic Community or the Common Market. After World War II, Italy unsuccessfully attempted to adopt an American modified *laissez faire* model of capitalism but as during the previous century, the

---

235 Prodi and di Giovanni 1992, pp.31-55; De Rosa 1986, pp. 231-244.
236 Tolliday 2000, p. 242.
237 Cassese 1981, p. 147.
238 Mack Smith 1997, p. 464.

State played a critical role in forging economic progress. Italy underwent a strong economic spurt between 1951 and 1971.[239] During the so-called 'economic miracle', the State continued to expand its ownership of large-scale enterprises while small and medium enterprises remained private.[240] The State bought the telephone system in 1957, privatized in 1995; the State nationalized electric power production in 1963 and vowed to privatize this sector during the 1990s. Since World War II, in Italy, as in France, since state economic enterprises have been prime employers in large-scale industries the State has intervened in the labor market, even if unintentionally, in a sense, the State became a price maker leaving private enterprise as the price taker.

Especially after World War II, one had witnessed a strange 'Italian style' capitalism: the market has been controlled by the private giants such as FIAT (mainly automobiles) and Pirelli (mostly tires) and the public giants such as IRI and ENI and then about 75,000 small (less than 100 employees) enterprises and few in between. One could not tell if FIAT was part of the State (FIAT's policies affected public economic policies) or IRI played the game of the so-called market. As long as this arrangement helped to achieve increases in productivity and employment, not many objected.

Regardless of the party in power, the private business sector traditionally accepted *lo stato imprenditore* (the State as entrepreneur) for the services supplied and the laboring class acknowledged as a source of secure employment.[241] The growth of SEEs originated with Fascism from rescuing failing enterprises to avoid unemployment and the creation of power centers tied to the governing parties. Only after the 'miracle' lost its momentum in the late 1960s and early 1970s (the energy crisis, the end of the U.S. backed gold standard) and was replaced by inflation, slow growth, and greater unemployment, especially in the South, were voices raised.[242]

Until the 1990s, the SEEs performance has been a bellwether for the Italian economy. Owing to the large share of total industrial investment that these enterprises have represented (by law SEEs were constrained to invest 40 to 60 percent of their total outlays in the South), the SEEs have been the keystones of southern industrialization. The SEEs invested in capital-intensive industries resulting in increased productive capacity but without a commensurate increase in employment. While these investments induced backward linkages during construction, only weak forward linkages were forthcoming during operation. In the 1970s, policy makers finally realized that it was difficult to reconcile the conflict between the social role assigned to SEEs partially owned by the State and

239 For example, Italy produced 18,500 refrigerators in 1951 and 3.2 million in 1967.
240 Zamagni 2002, p. 55.
241 From 1945 to the late 1980s Italy was governed by circa 40-plus Christian Democratic led coalition governments. After 1962, the Socialist Party became a power broker as well.
242 Castronovo 1997, pp. 33-106; Amatori and Colli 1999, pp. 281-290; Crepax 2002, p. 187.

their private character as joint stock corporations.[243] The process of privatization of these enterprises, begun in the 1980s, has attempted to resolve this problem.

Public Utilities and Privatization

Even in the absence of the French indicative model of planning, the State has been able to exercise considerable influence over the pace and direction of the Italian economy. The enlarged public sector and the SEEs have influenced prices and volume in surface and air transport networks, and (until recently) in telecommunications, postal service and electricity. 'The supposed existence of a natural monopoly in these public utilities has led to the creation of public legal monopolies.'[244] Since the 1930s state enterprises have crowded out the available private ventures. During the late twentieth century efforts to privatize Italian public enterprises have not been entirely effective. The capital market has continued to be rudimentary until liberalized in the1980s. Still the capital market has remained quite thin because of the peculiarity of the Italian large enterprise system, which has been divided among family alliances (FIAT automobiles, Pirelli tires, and Falck steel), the mixed or former state enterprises, and medium-small enterprise networks that eventually became industrial giants in their respective sectors, for instance, Benetton (clothing).

Benetton has been the outstanding example of the major economic expansion in the 1970s attributed to the high technology cottage industry of the so-called 'Third Italy'.[245] By mid 1990s, families owned about half of the Italian enterprises compared with Germany 16.9, France 27.7 and Britain 13.3 percent. Furthermore, small business was still predominant; 59 percent of the factories employed less than 100 workers compared with Germany 30, France 29 while in Britain 25 percent and in the United States 23 percent of the factories employed less than 100 workers.[246] While hostile takeovers have occurred, this has not been a standard practice; cooperation rather than antagonism among the giants has prevailed. Rather than keeping their distance, large companies called upon the State for mediation especially in labor management disputes or support for enterprises in trouble.[247]

Financial Markets

Until the end of the twentieth century, Italian capitalism was characterized by a very thin stock market; a limited number of companies were listed with a small volume of transactions compared with other major European stock markets. Note

---

243 Schachter and Engelbourg 1988, p. 518.
244 Padoa Schioppa Kostoris 1993, p. 43.
245 Allum 2000, p. 21.
246 Amatori 1997b, p. 249; Zamagni 1990, p. 438; Zanetti and Alzona 1998, p. 55.
247 Amatori and Brioschi 1997, p. 149; note that in 1992 Italy had 220 companies quoted on the national stock market, France 443, and Germany 649 compared with the United States 1678 and Britain 1946. De Cecco and Ferri 1996, pp. 32-33.

that the London Stock Exchange began operations in 1773, the Paris Bourse in 1724, the New York Stock Exchange in 1792, and the Frankfurt Bourse in 1797.[248] The Italian stock market (*Il mercato dei valori*), founded as a vehicle to sell government bonds, opened in Milan in 1808 under the aegis of Napoleon's Kingdom of Italy (1804-1814). Different from continental European countries, the London and New York stock exchanges originated without significant State intervention and have had economic viability. A critical difference between institutions has prevailed. British and American exchanges have had an independent existence and originated through the voluntary action of the participants. On the Continent exchanges owe their origin to the initiative of the State without regard to ordinary economic criteria.

Shares in Italian corporations have been largely owned either by a few families, syndicated groups, or the State. This particular type of capitalism does not separate ownership and control, characteristic in most of the capitalist world. When the processes of privatization began, during the 1990s, both in the private and public sectors, this characteristic impeded a smooth and efficient privatization. It took quite a while to attract small investors; with better regulation as well as regulatory enforcement during the 1990s bull market, public participation in the stock market expanded. Indeed, by the end of the 1990s, the Milan stock market has become one of the important exchanges in Europe.[249]

In the private sector Italian enterprises have preferred cooperative arrangements often sanctioned by the central government; cooperation also frequently has meant bank loans to private businesses guaranteed by the State. The 'Third Italy' that sustained economic expansion since the 1980s, has consisted of government support of small cooperatives to share resources in a competitive market. 'The government sponsorship of collective action in Italy is a reinforcement of a socialist ethos that has been the dominant attitude among small producers in Emilia-Romagna and Tuscany for nearly a century.'[250]

Labor Markets

Between the 1950s and the 1980s the Italian State was the most important actor in the market; it had a direct hand in the financial and labor markets. The Italian labor market has presented contradictions; it has provided safeguards for selected segments of the labor force and no protection for others, and in this way encouraged the development of a secondary labor market of the underground economy.[251]

---

248 Sir Thomas Gresham (Gresham's Law states that bad money drives away good money from the market), having observed the Antwerp exchange, established an exchange in London (1571) as a private venture, which became a direct predecessor of the London Royal Exchange.
249 Crepax 2002, p. 336.
250 Langlois and Robertson 1995, p. 126.
251 Padoa Schioppa Kostoris 1993, p. 131.

In sharp contrast to Britain and the United States where there is limited protection for workers in terms of recruitment or dismissals, Italian labor markets remained rigid; employers have continued to have problems in dismissing workers and union rules makes it difficult for the enterprise to make independent hiring choices. At the end of the twentieth century, a debate has been ongoing in Italy on job protection and on job creation with no conclusive outcome. In the late 1990s the unemployment rate has hovered around eight percent (higher in the South); those employed in the secondary markets have not been counted.

The Planning Experience

The State has had an overt distrust of economic planning; the only proposed plan was the never implemented 1954 Vanoni Plan. The Minister of Finance, Ezio Vanoni, modeled his economic indicative plan on the French experience. However, Italy lacked the French public technocrats as well as the institutional environment conducive to the plan's implementation. Perhaps as a reaction to the over centralized and corrupt Fascist regime, a sense of discipline or consensus as to ends and means has been lacking throughout the post-war years.

The absence of economic planning perhaps points to lost opportunities but also to more flexibility that facilitated the Italian miracle of the 1950s and 1960s. This is somewhat akin to the controversy concerning the absence of a United States central bank from 1836 to 1913; some scholars bemoan the absence of a central bank citing the extreme cyclical fluctuations during that period while others have rebutted this view noting the rapid growth as well as the failure of the Federal Reserve to respond effectively during 1929-1932 crisis. Italy has fared well since World War II compared with the Fascist era (1922-1943) or with its economic/political rivals and even, to the surprise of many, surpassed in per capita income Britain during the 1980s.[252]

Laissez Faire and State Intervention

As one of the six founders of the Common Market, Italy has increasingly opened its economy to the winds of fortune. Nearly all political factions nominally favor the market economy; 'what emerges instead are measures that, far from fostering more individual responsibility, increase the "demand" for state intervention that characterizes individuals and institutions in this (twentieth) century'.[253] It has been suggested that since World War II the State has been playing a mediating role that has backfired when bureaucrats have become responsive primarily to political needs and secondarily to economic development while pursuing their own agenda. The local *Mezzogiorno* bureaucracy has been expanding and gaining in influence and control of public funds, 'the bureaucracy is necessary to the political

---

252 Based on the 1982 Input-Output Table, ISTAT, the National Institute of Statistics revised the national income accounts; the revised statistics resulted in an increase of about 18 percent in gross national product.

253 Savona 1995, p. 87.

equilibrium of the *Mezzogiorno*, since it is responsible for distributing public expenditure in a way that preserves the political status quo'.[254]

Italian political economists view the State as an integral part of Italian culture.[255] In Italy, different from Britain and the United States but, similar to France and Germany, governments have been composed of multi-party coalitions. This institutional arrangement has resulted in shorter government life spans, with less political stability and probably a lack of long run policies.[256] Even so, or in spite of it, the Italian 'economic miracle' occurred in the 1950s and 1960s and the per capita income by the end of the twentieth century has been among the highest in the world. The State has attained consensus in all affairs through wheeling and dealing, a kind of pseudo solidarism. In spite of all the frivolity through the 'art of *arrangiarsi*' (improvisation) and muddling through, Italy achieved relatively high marks for economic performance.[257]

Ordinary and Special Agencies

Early in the twentieth century policy makers adopted a peculiar model to solve specific problems: the creation of special agencies or commissions that to all intents and purposes, although nominally limited in time continued indefinitely. The peculiarity consisted in dividing the tasks between the 'ordinary' and 'extraordinary' bureaucracy with little coordination between them. But the State tried to retain control of all sides by overt or covert funding, or other means.

Other arrangements have been unique to Italy; while approved by parliament, the State budget often did not constitute a framework for expenditures. Since the regionalization of 1970, regions and localities have been responsible for one side of the fiscal process, expenditures; however, the other side of the fiscal process, revenues, has remained the prerogative of the central government. Theoretically this should work were it not for the local cronyism and the lack of solid budgetary controls.[258]

The Mezzogiorno

This confused structure is best epitomized by the relationship of the State with the *Mezzogiorno* that has remained Italy's Achilles heel. While other nations have less developed regions, Italy's has continued as the classic example of regional disparity, providing the standard by which all others are judged. After decades of

254 Graziani 1979, p. 65.
255 'The nation's Catholic roots and the strong showing of the Communist Party before the collapse of the Soviet Union tempted some analysts to call the ideology Cathocommunism.' Padoa Schioppa Kostoris 1993, p. 229.
256 Some argue that until the 1990s the frequent changes of governments were more in form than in substance. The Christian Democrats continued as the dominant party for about forty years, insuring political stability.
257 Padoa Schioppa Kostoris 1993, p. 229.
258 D'Antone 1997, p. 616; Castronovo 1995, pp. 510-511.

doing relatively little (despite the 1904 and 1906 laws favoring southern development), since 1950 Italy has attempted to decrease the socio-economic gap between the South and the rest of the nation. The southern population has not viewed the State as a representative of the common good or of law and moral order.[259] The cultural environment has continued to persist with a tenuous relationship between the periphery and the center, '... the policies of the center are dependent on the local structures, whatever they happen to be, and the local capitalist *cum* tradition is dependent on the economy of the center'.[260]

Initially, the State concentrated its efforts in the agricultural sector through land redistribution and reclamation but the (northern) Italian miracle attracted a migration of people to the North, as well as to Germany and other foreign countries. The State attempted to create adequately financed institutions such as the Fund for the South (*Cassa per il Mezzogiorno*), with accomplishments that have been still debated two decades after the *Cassa* demise. A change in emphasis occurred in 1957; the objective became industrialization through incentives for large multinationals and investments of State enterprises. By their very nature, these capital-intensive behemoths did not generate much employment but exerted pressure on the State and the finances and management of the state enterprises. Southerners have loved this panacea since it has allowed more sinecures through the public bureaucracy. Also, the cultural milieu did not change greatly with the creation of large steel and chemical plants, 'cathedrals in the desert' with little backward or forward linkages.

While in the North, social relations have been based on checks and balances between the counter positions of management and labor, in the South, where the number of industrial workers was still limited by the end of the twentieth century, the relationship has been paternalistic and bureaucratic and directed by power brokers, based upon by the amount of public resources one can control. Public spending has been directed mainly to income maintenance and support for consumption. Extraordinary assistance to the South became inefficient and hardly yielded results commensurate with the fiscal effort.[261]

In addition, the central government has provided capital funds, subsidized interest, offered free or token-priced sites, tax and tariff concessions, and, at times, an assured market. The would-be entrepreneurs, granted any or all of these incentives, with little risk or uncertainty, have proceeded in business ventures with little or no reference to economic viability. On the contrary, the incentive for business has been to maximize short-term profits at the expense of long-term growth even though that would have meant the demise of the venture.[262] The growth of a private firm is motivated by economic considerations, yet in Italy many such firms have grown in order to be in a better position to bargain with the political powers. Hence, some define Italian capitalism as 'political' in contrast

---

259 Schachter 1965, pp. 114-115.
260 Schachter and Engelbourg 1988, p. 517.
261 Engelbourg and Schachter 1986, p. 585; Viesti 2001, pp. 426-427.
262 Arlacchi 1983, pp. 114-5; Schachter and Engelbourg 1988, p. 516.

with American defined as 'managerial', the British 'personal', and the German as 'cooperative'.[263]

During 1950-1984 the State, through the *Cassa per il Mezzogiorno* as well as through various ministries, supplied capital, subsidized enterprises, furnished infrastructure, and adopted other policies.[264] The South achieved a rate of economic growth comparable to that elsewhere in Italy but it also succeeded through this process in developing a strong State dependency, resented but embraced by everyone.[265] During the 1990s *status quo* prevailed with steadfast labor market disequilibrium when the unit labor costs in the South approached northern unit costs, although without much improvement in relative productivity.

Some economists blame these disequilibria on the excessive *dirigistic* regulation in favor of the South. The State has aimed to provide equal opportunities by means of administrative and legal instruments, negating the reaction of the market. Through the reduction of real-wage differentials, the strengthening of the safety net in the South, and by ignoring the weight of the underground economy (larger than in any western European country), rather than equalizing opportunities, the State has reinforced this disequilibrium. 'Social spending in Italy is marked by the preponderance of pensions and the low incidence of unemployment benefits and of welfare benefits for persons of working age.'[266]

Since the 1960s, the ratio of fixed investment to regional gross product has been higher in the Mezzogiorno than in the Center-North, yet the southern rate of value added growth has lagged behind the rest of the country. An additional shortcoming is that public expenditures have lacked a multiplier effect because such funds have been used more to increase household disposable income rather than gross domestic product. It seems that public policies in Italy have all along confused short-term welfare with long-term economic growth goals. This has a political ring since in a democracy voters elect officials who respond to their immediate, often ill-advised, selfish needs.

Conclusions

In the 1950s, an outstanding Italian economic historian best expressed the culture: 'The State cannot be sheltered in a Political Economy book. We all have to worry more about the problems the country has than about the integrity of some doctrines that call themselves infallible.'[267] While criticizing the specifics, both economists and the public at large have justified the reliance on the public purse. Even Luigi Einaudi, an internationally renowned economist as well as a persuasive advocate of traditional *laissez-faire* economics, never favored allowing the Mezzogiorno to

263 Amatori 1997b, pp. 257-258.
264 While the State terminated the Cassa in the 1980s, other forms of transfers to the South have survived.
265 Schachter and Engelbourg 1995, passim.
266 Sacconi and Biagi 2001, p. 451.
267 Luzzatti 1952, p. 306.

sink or swim without State aid. The Italian institutional arrangement is replete with contradictions. 'The Italian development model is based on liberalism without rules for an authentic free market, public intervention without an inkling of planning and a principle of solidarity without the existence of a social State.'[268]

As another Italian political economist put it, 'there is scarce autonomy of civil society from the State in our country, which has been described as "clientele dependence" and whose traits were evident since the first post-Unitarian decades'.[269] Public finances have become a competitive game among social groups with everyone aiming to obtain more from the State, consequently the distributive role of the State lost any coherence.[270] It is true that this role of the State constitutes merely a continuation of the culture Italy has developed, at least since unification.

On the one hand, the Italians have viewed the State as a *sportello pagatore*, a paying window, always ready to finance individuals, corporations, labor unions or any political organized and potent group. On the other hand, the State has participated directly in the market creating some grave distortions and exacerbating others. The State's regional policy definitely has constituted the antithesis of *laissez faire*. During the twentieth century, the Italian system has developed into an extreme variant of the welfare state characteristic of Continental European nations. The development of an advanced industrial Italy during the twentieth century would probably not have been possible without strong government intervention.[271]

During the twentieth century four political movements have been instrumental in initiating strong public intervention in Italy: Giolitti, the liberal statesman, at the beginning of this century (see Chapter III), Mussolini, the Fascist dictator, during the inter-war period; the Christian Democrats after 1948; and the post-Christian Democratic period since the 1990s. Allegedly Italian *étatisme* (a state-backed market economy) encouraged industrial development, although with the advance of high technology and the globalization of markets, one could question the continuance of *étatisme*. Corporative behavior depends on internal political cohesion that has not apparently existed in Italy. Yet an observer despaired that 'the new liberal path is also not viable given that it would exacerbate rather than resolve the current problems, challenging the advanced industrial state'.[272]

The Twentieth Century: Concluding Remarks

By the end of the twentieth century, Britain and the United States have pursued economic policies more like those of the Continental European nations than since the beginning of the century. Two major wars and the intervening worldwide catastrophic depression assigned an important role to the State, even in the most

268 Castronovo 1997, p. 99.
269 Paci 1989, p. 220.
270 Brunetta and Tonti 1991, passim.
271 Paci 1989, p. 217; Amatori 1997b, p. 274; Arcelli and Micossi 1997, pp. 295-360.
272 Locke 1995, p. 188.

laissez faire countries. Though this variation from non-interventionism was supposed to be temporary, it inevitably left permanent footprints. The industrial structure as well as the per capita income differentials has converged and the vulnerability to economic cycles has decreased through enactment of built-in stabilizers. The power of big business to affect supply prices and to influence the political process has persisted, and globalization of the markets resulted from free trade mandated by international agreements.

While for the last three centuries, Britain has been the traditional home of the market-driven economy, the long-term decline of the British economy induced, among other things, intermittent cycles of regulation and deregulation as well as the more dramatic nationalization and privatization. The decline stemmed as much from diminished international competitiveness as the first industrialized State as from its loss of the empire. Britain witnessed the disappearance of invisible income from foreign investment as a result of World War I and World War II. In a departure from economic liberalism, many utilities were nationalized before and after World War II. Owing to the depressed conditions of coal and cotton, Britain intervened to align supply with demand. While during the depression of the 1930s Britain, like other countries, adopted the worldwide beggar thy neighbor policy, thus breaking with its free trade tradition, it returned to free trade by the end of the century along with its major trading partners.

The United States, like Britain, succumbed to the pressure of the depression and World War II by deviating from rigorous *laissez faire* policies. While state-owned enterprises have been scarce in the United States, selected sectors of the economy have been closely regulated. Antitrust legislation has been followed by fair trade, minimum wages, health and safety, and environmental regulations. Different from Britain, the United States had a high tariff history; it elevated the tariffs still further during the depression in 1930s, only to switch to reciprocal trade agreements by 1934; the United States opted to become a general low tariff country during the second half of the twentieth century. Also, during this period a movement towards deregulation has been successful in eliminating some market rigidities but has increased business concentration as well as market failures.

In France, Germany, and Italy the State has not only regulated but also has owned and operated economic enterprises thus enabling these nations to participate more directly and intentionally in the economy. The main characteristic of France and Germany has been the continuity of the bureaucracy, which has acted as a stabilizer for economic policy; this has not been true in Italy because of both *clientelismo* and widespread State dependency. France has been reluctant to privatize because the public and political elites have believed that the State can and should be able to do better than private enterprise in certain sectors.

While the social welfare systems of these five countries have somewhat converged, the Anglo-Americans view social transfers as a State concession to the public, the Continentals as a State mandated obligation. One need only recall that the first country to legislate social security and national health insurance was Germany under Bismarck in the late nineteenth century. France and Italy as well as Britain were slower to adopt these programs, but during the second half of the twentieth century these countries adopted an entire array of social legislation. The

United States enacted social security legislation in 1935, but has remained the only advanced industrial country that by the end of the twentieth century lacked universal health insurance.

All European countries (including Britain) have developed education as a quasi-State-monopoly. Perhaps this stems from the monarchical origins of many educational institutions. Nonetheless, the so-called British 'public schools' date from the sixteenth century or even earlier and originated with royal charters and financing; these ancient and honorable preparatory schools have been much more important than the number of students would indicate since they educated the future leaders of British society. Most of Continental and British higher education has been public; in contrast, the United States has had a significant private/independent academia.

While nominally accepting free trade, a cardinal feature of *laissez faire*, Continental countries have intervened in the economy much more comprehensively than Britain or the United States. In Continental European countries, different from the United States but not from Britain, the nineteenth century meaning of economic liberalism has remained unchanged to denote free trade and a minimalist State. Some critics have perceived interventionist of economic policy as antithetical to democracy.

Since the presidency of Theodore Roosevelt at the opening of the century, United States economic liberals have advocated an active role for the State in the economy. Those U.S. economic liberals have become ideologically closer to the Continental Europe defenders of the Interventionist State than to the general cultural milieu of Anglo-American countries. The Continental European culture has vouched for the welfare state by accepting the social compact developed over centuries, different from Britain and the U.S. culture that has been based more on economic and social individualism.

Chapter 6

Conclusions

Over the past three centuries, Britain and the U.S. as well as Continental Europe (represented by France, Germany, and Italy) with the timing varying considerably, achieved universal suffrage and developed democratic political institutions based on majority rule. Britain's two seventeenth century revolutions and nineteenth century political liberalism resulted in wider inclusion. Rugged individualism has been manifest in the United States while majority rule arrived during the seventeenth century; by 1775 wide suffrage resulted from broad property ownership. Enfranchisement spread to one state after another, supplemented by critical amendments to the Constitution.

France underwent the classic political revolution in 1789 but needed another century and several additional revolutions before achieving universal electoral suffrage and ministerial responsibility derived from majority rule. Economic policy as illustrated by *dirigisme* and *Colbertisme* during the seventeenth century remained firm throughout the twentieth century, regardless of the political persuasion of the particular government in power. *Cameralism* has influenced public policies in Germany for over three centuries. This has been sustained by Bismarck's social legislation that has represented a policy signature to this day. Italian economic liberalism generally has meant a belief in State dependency; *laissez faire* policies were attempted in some of the Italian states before unification and later in unified Italy but met only with mixed success.

Occasionally, and especially in Britain and the United States, *laissez faire* crystallized into an ideology, regardless of the specific circumstances, which Adam Smith would have had difficulty recognizing. *Laissez faire* acquired a firm hold on the climate of informed opinion in Britain and the United States that it never attained in France, Germany, and Italy. This did not preclude the United States from maintaining a high protective tariff until the 1930s or promoting canals and railroads. Economic policy in the former two, however much they may have differed from each other, surely have been dissimilar from that of France, Germany, and Italy. While there has been continuity of thought and action, policy responses of necessity have not been identical because of the particular historical circumstances of each nation.[1]

Both the Anglo-Americans and the Continental European countries have had various degrees of mixed economies and public policies have played a significant

---

1   See for example Lerner 1963, pp. 149-166.

role in influencing private economic activity. Britain and the U.S. have envisaged the individual as illustrated by Smith's *economic man*, the prime actor in the economy, who maximizes his/her economic welfare for the benefit of all. Yet, Smith acknowledged that businessmen gather habitually to benefit themselves at the expense of the consumer.[2] During and after the 1930s both Britain and the United States have often resorted to Keynesian countercyclical policies to correct market failures, which neo-classical economists have criticized.

Even before gaining independence from Britain the *frontier spirit* had become dominant in the United States.[3] The colonists adventured to seek a better economic life that in itself gave them, and later the immigrants and their heirs, the notion of individual economic freedom. Some contend that English colonists brought the ideas of both economic and political freedom with them; others rebut that in both Virginia and Massachusetts, the initial colonizing impulse embodied a communal sense. Different from Continental Europeans at the time, the freedom of occupation was implicit, market-based decision-making came soon after.

On the other hand, the United States, which drew so heavily on British example in so many ways, found it expedient to pursue State involvement in the economy by focusing on internal improvements to expand the market. For example, the State supported the construction of capital-intensive infrastructure such as roads, canals, and railroads; in foreign trade, a protective tariff prevailed from the 1790s until the 1930s. Also, the self-interest of many economic actors has led them to press the State for rent-seeking preferential treatment.

The institutionalization of anti-State feelings has remained deeply ingrained in the individualism of British and U.S. culture, while the adoration of *l'état* has lingered as a feature of the French, German, and Italian cultures. Centuries of tradition have left their mark on both sides. The nature of the British island economy may well have justified a greater reliance on the market; in addition, Britain has not been invaded since 1066. Historically, the specific patterns of State intervention have varied but have maintained approximately the same relationships.

Under these circumstances, cultural divergences and consequent policy differences have occasionally appeared in the European Union. To no one's surprise, when the members of the European Union signed the Maastricht Treaty in 1991, Britain initially refused to adhere to clauses on social policies although

---

2   Although cognizant of the Newcastle Coal Vend an effective combination of producers that monopolized London's coal market, Smith could not be aware of large-scale managerial enterprise, high overhead cost, and oligopoly. Not until the 1930s, with the innovative contributions of Edward H. Chamberlin of the United States and Joan Robinson of Britain did political economy successfully accommodate monopolistic competition and imperfect competition into the corpus of economic theory as other than minor and transitory aberrations.

3   The *frontier* conferred the opportunity of becoming an owner-occupier and the State was too weak to help or hinder settlers; Indian removal and public land policies were driven by western settlers and not by eastern city dwellers.

concurring by the end of the century. Despite the process of economic and political integration that has taken place in Western Europe since World War II, intellectually and institutionally the Anglo-American culture has continued to differ from the Continental culture.

The end of the twentieth century has brought a new dimension in the role of the State between the *laissez faire* advocates in Britain and the United States and those who see a permanent distortion of values in the capitalist world.[4] A strong movement of *anti-mondialization* has been growing on the assumption that liberal economic policies destroy people and the planet earth. This movement with strong roots in Continental Europe has been assuminng that free trade, rather than bringing prosperity and increased benefits through the application of the Ricardian comparative advantage, marginalizes the poor as well as lesser-developed countries.[5] This contention is in accord with List, the nineteenth century German economist, who argued that free trade could be accomplished only among equals.[6] Even in this case, Britain and the United States have been more at ease with the *laissez faire* proposition of a minimalist State than the Continental European nations.

The British mercantilist society of the eighteenth century viewed individual *economic* freedom as the essence of *economic* improvement in the free market place.[7] True, the Thirteen Colonies revolted against the British but adopted British mercantilism as soon as they gained independence, hardly consonant with *laissez faire*. While such statesmen as Alexander Hamilton, Henry Clay, and Abraham Lincoln all staunchly supported a pivotal role for the State, during the nineteenth century the Jacksonian free enterprise spirit promoted individualism, and rejection of the institutional State evolved further. In the U.S., there has been a continuous preaching of the liberty of individual action with policies that often have ignored the alleged needs of society.[8] Continental Europeans have contended that freedom, which does not include assurance of health care, being adequately fed, housed, and educated is not freedom at all. In Britain and the United States, freedom is construed to mean freedom from the State. France, Germany and Italy have been

---

4   Marxism as a credo embraced most of Continental Europe during the nineteenth and
     twentieth centuries only to peter out with the devolution of the Soviet Union.
5   This seems akin to the anti-mechanization movement during the late eighteenth and
     the early nineteenth centuries, as best represented by the British Luddites.
6   In the United States Henry Carey (1837-1840) and in Germany Friedrich List (1841)
     rebutted David Ricardo's (1817) trade theory as inapplicable to the circumstances of
     nations trying to play catch up with the first industrial nation, Britain, for which
     laissez faire might make more sense; instead of a free trade policy, these economic
     writers have advocated a protective tariff especially for infant industries.
7   This view can be traced through *Thatcherism* the best twentieth century representation
     of a Social Darwinist philosophy. Margaret Thatcher the Conservative British Prime
     Minister (1979-1990) and Ronald Reagan, President of the United States (1980-1988)
     represented the hard core of British and U.S. non-interventionism.
8   See, for example, John Kenneth Galbraith, *The Affluent Society*, 1958.

weary to accept even a modified Social Darwinism prevalent in Britain and the U.S.

As one might expect, the process of policy making of both Anglo-Americans and Continentals cannot be traced on a smooth trend line. Notwithstanding social welfare policies initiated since the 1930s depression, 'liberal' policies and a minor role for the State could be generally observed in Britain and the United States. *Étatisme* and a 'social contract', an unwritten implicit pact between the citizens and the State, for achieving economic welfare, has predominated in France, Germany, and Italy. However, some aberrations from the cultural trend should be noted.

Despite Smith's critique, during the eighteenth century Britain often instituted mercantilist policies when it was deemed necessary for the national interest as well as for individual self-interest. In the nineteenth century, Britain nationalized selected public utilities such as the telegraph. The coming of the railroad and the steamship accompanied by other forms of large-scale enterprise dramatically altered the economic landscape and established national and, indeed international markets. The construction of capital-intensive railroads required the mobilization of funds on a massive and unprecedented scale, which everywhere, except Britain, warranted State promotion to accelerate the process of industrialization.[9]

During the twentieth century two world wars coupled with probably the deepest economic depression in the history of capitalist nations placed extraordinary demands on the nation states. Regulation, followed by nationalization, frequently *ad hoc*, appealed as a remedy for the alleged failings of the market. Declining agriculture (as a share of economic activity) and certain high overhead cost sectors, for instance, the railroads, tended to be the focus of the State's attention everywhere, while other sectors relied on path dependence to enable them to flourish in the market.

Immediately after the World War II, Britain nationalized and several decades later privatized several basic industries. Some minor deviations from *laissez faire* occurred early in U.S. history such as the establishment of the First and the Second United States Banks (while private, the State owned a controlling minority interest). Also, the State built roads and canals early in the nineteenth century and later aided railroad construction, which was followed by regulation. Significantly more changes occurred during the Progressive Era (1901-1917), the New Deal (1933-1938), and the Great Society (1963-1968) but some would have liked to bury these changes in the dustbin of history.

The departures from the trend have been few in France, for example, the Le Chapelier Law (1789-1791) that, in the spirit of Smithian *laissez faire* philosophy as well as that of the philosophy of the Enlightenment preached free competition and prohibited collective bargaining; the Le Chapelier Law forbade guilds and

---

9   Giant enterprises have affected prices and production and therefore the allocation of resources and income distribution between and among countries as well as the various sectors of each nation's economy.

Chambers of Commerce as well as labor associations. During the July Monarchy (1830-1848), the French government attempted to copy British free trade policies with little success. Only in the post-World War II era, in conjunction with other Western European nations, did France opt for free trade by initiating and joining the Common Market and the European Union (EU) and participating in the World Trade Organization (WTO). However, at the end of the twentieth century France has not been ready to completely privatize and deregulate the economy as well as to dismantle or substantially limit the welfare state.

Over the last three centuries Germany and Italy rarely deviated from interventionist policies; economic liberalism in contrast to *étatisme* has been an ideal philosophy rather than a policy guideline. In Germany, the emerging bourgeoisie preached *laissez faire*, while at the same time seeking State support for railroad construction since, as a poor country, a functioning domestic capital market hardly existed. Furthermore, nationalism, that is, the desire to create a unified national State, overshadowed the *theoretical* political and economic freedom of trade ideas. As it happened in France, Germany opted for free trade when it participated in forming the EU and in joining the WTO; in addition it has pursued policies within the scope of the social market economy.

Like Germany, pre-unification Italy contained a dozen widely disparate political units. In Austrian Lombardy as well as Tuscany (led by an Austrian prince), in the mid-eighteenth century, the public administration defended *laissez faire* asserting that the State should not interfere in individual economic affairs. In 1786, under Austrian control, Lombardy adopted freedom of grain trade and the Kingdom of The Two Sicilies briefly rejected protective tariffs. After unification in the mid-nineteenth century, Camilo Cavour of Piedmont remained a free trade advocate, but Italian economic liberalism of the 1860s has been constrained by emerging nationalism and the weakness of the economy; liberalism had little success in withstanding the pressures for State assistance. Post-World War II Italy went through the same process of trade liberalization as France and Germany as founding partners in the EU and members in the WTO. Domestically, a period of rapid economic growth and nationalization was followed by a relative economic slowdown and attempts at privatization and deregulation, with the State always remaining a social partner in the market place.

Over the last three centuries, with few exceptions, the political economic model adopted and sustained by the Anglo-Americans and the Continentals definitely have had a *continuum*. It is significant that these two sets of nations attempted to realize the welfare of their citizens with different approaches. The resulting outcomes cannot be correlated with given policies, which indicates that any model, given the proper cultural milieu, resources and their efficient use, level of knowledge and technology, and some would add political stability, has the potential to achieve given public policy objectives, but not necessarily social objectives.

Bibliography

Abel, Wilhelm (1967), *Geschichte der deutschen Landwirtschaft vom frühen Mittelalter bis' zum 19. Jahrhundert*, Eugen Ulmer, Stuttgart, 2nd Edition.

Abrams, Richard A. (1964), *Conservatism in a Progressive Era: Massachusetts Politics 1900-1912*, Harvard University Press, Cambridge.

Abromeit, Heidrun (1986), *British Steel, An Industry between the State and the Private Sector*, St. Martin's Press, New York.

Abromeit, Heidrun (1990), 'Government-Industry Relations in West Germany', in Martin Chick (ed), *Government, Industries and Markets*, Edward Elgar, Brookfield, Vermont, pp. 61-83.

Ackley, G. (1987), 'The Size and Economic Role of the Government', in Giancarlo Gandolfo and Ferruccio Marzano (eds), *Keynesian Theory Planning Models and Quantitative Economics: Essays in Memory of Vittorio Marama*, Dott. A. Giuffre, Milan, pp. 387-408.

Acton, Harold (1956), *The Bourbons of Naples (1734-1825)*, St. Martin's Press, New York.

Adam, Jean Paul (1972), *Instauration de la politique des chemins de fer en France*, Presses Universitaires de France, Paris.

Adams, William James (1989), *Restructuring the French Economy*, Brookings Institution, Washington, DC.

Aftalion, Florin (1990), *The French Revolution: An Economic Interpretation*, Cambridge University Press, Cambridge.

Albert, William (1972), *The Turnpike Road System in England 1663-1840*, Cambridge University Press, Cambridge.

Aldcroft, Derek H. (1970), *The Inter-War Economy: Britain 1919-1939*, B. T. Batsford, London.

Aldcroft, Derek H. (1975), *British Transport since 1914: An Economic History*, David and Charles, Newton Abbot.

Allum, Percy (2000), 'Italian Society Transformed', in Patrick McCarthy (ed), *Italy since 1945*, Oxford University Press, New York, pp. 10-41.

Amatori, Franco (1997a), 'Reflections on Global Business and Modern Italian Enterprises by a Stubborn "Chandlerian"', *Business History Review*, 71, pp. 309-318.

Amatori, Franco (1997b), 'Italy: The Tormented Rise of Organizational Capabilities between Government and Families', in Alfred D. Chandler Jr., Franco Amatori, Takashi Hikino (eds), *Big Business and the Wealth of Nations*, Cambridge University Press, Cambridge, pp. 246-276.

Amatori, Franco and Francesco Brioschi (1997), 'Le grandi imprese private: famiglie e coalizioni', in Fabrizio Barca (ed), *Storia del capitalismo italiano*, Donizelli, Rome, pp. 119-154.

Amatori, Franco and Andrea Colli (1999), *Impressa e industria in Italia dall'Unita a oggi*, Marsilio, Venice.

Ambrosoli, Mauro (1997), *The Wild and the Town*, Cambridge University Press, Cambridge.

Angresano, James (1995), *Comparative Economics*, Prentice Hall, Upper Saddle River, NJ, Second Edition.

Anzilotti, Antonio (1964), *Movimenti e contrasti per l'unita italiana*, Giuffre, Milan.

320 *Cultural Continuity in Advanced Economies*

6ent, The Experience of

Appleby, Joyce Oldham (1978), *Economic Thought and Ideology in Seventeenth Century England*, Princeton University Press, Princeton.

Arcelli, Mario and Stefano Micossi (1997), 'La politica economica negli anni Ottanta (e nei primi anni Novanta)', *Economia Italiana*, 1-2, January-August, pp. 295-360.

Arlacchi, Pino (1983), *La mafia imprenditrice*, Il Mulino, Bologna.

Ashby, Eric and Mary Anderson (1981), *Politics of Clean Air*, Clarendon Press, Oxford.

Ashton, T.S. (1955), *An Economic History of England: The Eighteenth Century*, Methuen and Co, London.

Asprey, Robert B. (1986), *Frederick the Great, the Magnificent Enigma*, Ticknor and Fields, New York.

Aymard, Maurice (1978), 'La transizione dal feudalismo al capitalismo,' in *Storia d'Italia: Annali*, Giulio Einaudi, Turin, Vol. 1, pp. 1131-1192.

Badaloni, Nicola (1973), 'La cultura', in Ruggiero Romano and Corrado Vivanti (eds), *Storia d'Italia, Dal primo settecento all'unita*, Einaudi, Turin, Vol. III, pp. 699-986.

Bagwell, Philip S. (1974), *The Transport Revolution from 1770*, Harper and Row, New York.

Ball, Edward (1994), 'No More Jobs for the Boys', in Jonathan Michie and John Grieve Smith (eds), *Unemployment in Europe*, Academic Press, London, pp. 116-129.

Barbagallo, di Francesco (1999), 'Da Crispi a Giolitti, lo stato, la politica, i conflitti sociali', in Giovanni Sabbatucci and Vittorio Vidotto (eds), *Storia d'Italia, Liberalismo e democrazia, 1887-1914*, Laterza, Bari, Vol. 3, pp. 3-134.

Barber, William J. (1981), 'The Eisenhower Energy Policy: Reluctant Intervention', in Crawford D. Goodwin (ed), *Energy Policy in Perspective*, Brookings Institution, Washington, DC, pp. 205-286.

Barca, Fabrizio (1997), 'Compromesso senza riforme nel capitalismo italiano', in Fabrizio Barca (ed), *Storia del capitalismo italiano*, Donizelli, Rome, pp. 4-118.

Bark, Dennis L. and David R. Gress (1993a), *A History of West Germany: From Shadow to Substance 1945-1963*, Blackwell, Oxford, Vol. 1.

Bark, Dennis L. and David R. Gress (1993b), *A History of West Germany: Democracy and Discontents 1963-1991*, Blackwell, Oxford, Vol. 2.

Barone, Giuseppe (1999), 'La modernizzazione italiano dalla crisi allo sviluppo', in Giovanni Sabbatucci and Vittorio Vidotto (eds), *Storia d'Italia, Liberalismo e democrazia, 1887-1914*, Laterza, Bari, Vol. 3, pp. 249-362.

Bartrip, P. W. (1983), 'State Intervention in Mid-Nineteenth Century Britain; Fact or Fiction', *Journal of British Studies*, XXIII, Fall, pp. 63-83.

Baumol, William J. (1987), 'Rebirth of a Fallen Leader: Italy and the Long Period Data', in Giancarlo Gandolfo and Ferruccio Marzano (eds), *Keynesian Theory, Planning Models and Quantitative Economics: Essays in Memory of Vittorio Marama*, Dott. A. Giuffre, Milan, pp. 138-157.

Becker, William H. and William M. McClenahan Jr. (2003), *The Market, the State, and the Export Import Bank of the United States, 1934-2000*, Cambridge University Press, Cambridge.

Behrens, C. B. A. (1985), *Society, Government and the Enlightenment: The Experience of Eighteenth-Century France and Prussia*, Harper and Row, New York.

Bendix, Richard (1977), *Max Weber, An Intellectual Portrait*, University of California Press, Berkeley.

Berghahn, Volker R. (1982), *Modern Germany*, Cambridge University Press, London.

Berghahn, Volker R. (1994), *Imperial Germany 1871-1914*, Berghahn Books, Providence-Oxford.

Bianchini, Marco (1991), 'I fattori della distribuzione (1350-1850)', in Ruggiero Romano (ed), *Storia dell'economia italiana: L'età moderna: verso la crisi*, Giulio Einaudi,

Turin, Vol. II, pp. 187-211.

Blackbourn, David (1997), *The Long Nineteenth Century, Fontana History of Germany 1780-1918*, Fontana Press, London.

Bleton, Pierre (1966), *Le capitalisme français*, Les Editions ouvrières, Paris.

Bloch, Camille (1974), *L'assistance de l'état en France a la vieille de la révolution 1764-1790*, Slatkin-Megariotis Reprints, Geneva.

Bohme, Helmut (1966), *Deutschland Weg zur Großmacht*, Kiepenheuer & Witsch, Berlin.

Bohme, Helmut (1972), 'Bismarck Schutzzollpolitik und die Festigung der konservativen Staates', in Helmut Böhme, (ed), *Probleme der Reichgrundungszeit 1848-1879*, Kiepenheuer & Witsch, Berlin, pp. 328-354.

Bohme, Helmut (1978), *An Introduction to the Social and Economic History of Germany*, St. Martin's Press, New York.

Bonelli, Franco (1978) 'Il capitalismo italiano: linee generali d'interpretazione', in Ruggiero Romano (ed), *Storia d'Italia: Dal feudalismo al capitalismo*, Giulio Einaudi Turin, Vol. 1, pp. 1193-1256.

Borchardt, Knut (1985), *Grundriss der deutschen Wirtschaftsgeschichte*, Vandenhoeck and Ruprecht, Göttingen.

Borchardt, Knut (1991), 'Protectionism in Historic Perspective', in Knut Borchardt (ed), *Perspectives in Modern German Economic History and Policy*, Cambridge University Press, Cambridge, pp. 1-15.

Bordo, Michael D. (1987), *The New Palgrave: A Dictionary of Economics*, Macmillan, London, 3, Vol. IV, p. 143.

Bottiglieri, Bruno (1991), 'La funzione dello stato', in Ruggiero Romano (ed), *Storia dell'economia italiana: L'età contemporanea, un paese nuovo*, Giulio Einaudi, Turin Vol. III, pp. 280-329.

Bowen, Frank C. (1930), *A Century of Atlantic Travel*, Little, Brown, Boston.

Brebner, J. Bartlett (1948), 'Laissez-Faire and State Intervention in Nineteenth Century Britain', *Journal of Economic History*, Supplement VIII, pp. 59-73.

Brewer, John and Eckhart, Helmuth (1999), 'Introduction: Rethinking Leviathan', in John Brewer and Eckhart Hellmuth (eds), *Rethinking Leviathan, The Eighteenth-Century State in Britain and Germany*, Oxford University Press, Oxford, pp. 1-21.

Briggs, Asa (1965), *Victorian Cities*, Harper and Row, New York.

Broder, Andre (1976), 'Le commerce extérieur: l'échec de la conquête d'une position internationale', in Fernand Braudel and Ernest Labrousse (eds), *Histoire économique et sociale de la France: L'avènement de l'ère industrielle (1789-années 1880)*, Presse Universitaire de France, Paris, Tome III, Vol. I, pp. 305-346.

Brophy, M. James (1998), *Capitalism, Politics, and Railroads in Prussia, 1830-1870*, Ohio State University Press, Columbus.

Brosio, G. and C. Marchese (1986), *Il potere di spendere: Economia e storia della spesa pubblica dall'unificazione ad oggi*, Il Mulino, Bologna.

Brown, Richard (1991), *Society and Economy in Modern Britain 1700-1850*, Routledge, London.

Bruhat, Jean (1976), 'L'affirmation du monde du travail urbain', in Fernand Braudel and Ernest Labrousse (eds), *Histoire économique et sociale de la France: L'avènement de l'ère industrielle (1789-annes 1880)*, Presse Universitaire de France, Paris, Vol. III, pp. 769-828.

Brunetta, R. and L Tronti (1991), *Welfare State e redistribuzione*, Franco Angeli, Milan.

Bryer, R. A. (1990), 'The First Nationalization of the UK Iron and Steel Industry: A Test of Socialist Principles', in Martin Chick (ed), *Governments, Industries and Markets: Aspects of Government-Industry Relations in the UK, Japan, West Germany and the USA since 1945*, Edward Elgar, Brookfield, Vermont, pp. 84-109.

Busch, Otto (1981), *Militarsystem und Sozialleben in alten Preußen: 1713-1807*, Verlag Ullstein, Frankfurt/M.

Cafagna, Luciano (1989), *Dualismo e sviluppo nella storia d'Italia*, Marsilio, Venice.

Cain, Louis (1978). *Sanitation Strategy for a Lakefront Metropolis: The Case of Chicago*, Northern Illinois University Press, De Kalb.

Cain, P. J. (1972), 'Railway Combination and Government, 1900-1914', *Economic History Review*, Vol. 25, pp. 623-641.

Cain, P. J. (1980) 'Private Enterprise or Public Utility? Output, Pricing, and Investment in English and Welsh Railways 1870-1914', *Journal of Transport History*, 1, pp. 9-28.

Cairncross, Alec (1992), *The British Economy since 1945: Economic Policy and Performance*, Blackwell, Oxford.

Caizzi, Bruno (1962), *Camillo e Adriano Olivetti*, UTET, Turin.

Cameron, Rondo E. (1961), *France and the Economic Development of Europe 1800-1914, Conquests of Peace and Seeds of War*, Princeton University Press, Princeton.

Cameron, Rondo E. (1967), 'Banking in the Early Stages of Industrialization: A Study in Comparative Economic History', in Rondo Cameron in collaboration with Olga Crisp, Hugh T. Patrick and Richard Tilly (eds), *France 1800-1870*, Oxford University Press, New York, pp. 100-128.

Cameron, Rondo E. (1997), *A Concise Economic History of the World*, Oxford University Press, New York.

Cameron, Rondo E. and Larry Neal (2003), *A Concise Economic History of the World*, Oxford University Press, New York.

Cammarano, Fulvio (1995), 'La costruzione dello stato e la classe dirigente', in Giovanni Sabbatucci and Vittorio Vidotto (eds), *Storia d'Italia, Il nuovo stato e la società civile*, Laterza, Bari, Vol. II, pp. 3-112.

Campolieti, Giuseppe (1999), *Il re lazzarone: Ferdinando IV di Borbone amato dal popolo e condannato dalla storia*, Arnoldo Mondadori, Milan.

Campolieti, Giuseppe (2001), *Il re bomba: Ferdinando II, il Borbone di Napoli che per primo lotto contro l'unita d'Italia*, Arnoldo Mondadori, Milan.

Candeloro, Giorgio (1973), *Storia dell'Italia moderna, Le origini del Risorgimento*, Feltrinelli, Milan, Vol. I, 8th edition.

Capone, Alfredo (1981), *Destra e sinistra da Cavour a Crispi*, UTET, Turin.

Caracciolo, Alberto (1973), 'La storia economica', in Romano Ruggiero and Corrado Vivanti (eds), *Storia d"Italia: Dal primo settecento all'unita*, Giulio Einaudi, Turin, Vol. 3, pp. 511-698.

Carnevali, Francesca (2000), 'State Enterprise and Italy's "Economic Miracle"': The Ente Nazionale Idrocarburi, 1945-1962', *Enterprise and Society*, June, 1, pp. 249-278.

Caron, Francois (1970), 'French Railroad Investment 1850-1914', in Rondo Cameron, *Essays in French Economic History*, Richard D. Irwin, Homewood, Illinois, pp. 315-340.

Caron, Francois (1973), *Histoire de l'exploitation d'un grand réseau: la compagnie du chemin de fer du nord 1846-1937*, Mouton, Paris.

Caron, Francois (1981), *Histoire économique de la France: XIXe-XXe Siècles*, Armand Colin, Paris.

Caron, Francois (1983), 'France', in Patrick O'Brien (ed), *Railways and the Economic Development of Western Europe*, St. Martin's Press, New York, pp. 28-48.

Caron, Francois (1984), 'La France des patriotes de 1851 a 1918', in Jean Favier (ed), *Histoire de France*, Librairie Artheme Fayard. Paris, Tome 5.

Caron, Francois (1995), *Histoire Economique de la France, XIXe-XXe siècle*, Armand Colin, Paris.

Carpanetto, Dino and Giuseppe Ricuperati (1986*)*, *L'Italia del settecento, crisi,* *transformazioni, lumi*, Laterza, Bari.

Carpanetto, Dino and Giuseppe Ricuperati (1987), *Italy in the Age of Reason*, Longman, London.

Carr, William (1991), *A History of Germany 1815-1990*, Edward Arnold, London, Fourth Edition.

Cassese, Sabino (1981), 'Public Control and Corporate Efficiency', in Raymond Vernon and Yair Aharoni (eds), *State Owned Enterprises in the Western Economies*, St. Martin's Press, New York, pp. 145-156.

Castronovo, Valerio (1980), *L'industria italiana dall'ottocento ad oggi*, Arnoldo Mondadori, Milan.

Castronovo, Valerio (1995), *Storia economica d'Italia*, Einaudi, Turin.

Castronovo, Valerio (1997), 'I cinquant'anni della repubblica italiana', *Economia Italiana*, 1-2, January-August, pp. 33-106.

Catherine, Robert and Pierre Gousset (1965), *L'état e l'essor industriel: du dirigisme colbertien an l'économie concertée*, Editions Berger-Levrault, Paris.

Chaloner, W. H. (1953), 'Francis Egerton, Third Duke of Bridgewater', *Explorations in Entrepreneurial History*, V, March, pp. 181-185.

Chandler, Alfred D. Jr. (1980), 'Government versus Business, an American Phenomenon', in John T. Dunlop (ed), *Business and Public Policy*, Division of Research, Graduate School of Business Administration, Harvard University, Boston, pp. 1-11.

Channon, Geoffrey (2001), *Railways in Britain and the United States, 1830-1940*, Ashgate, Aldershot.

Checkland, Sidney (1983), *British Public Policy 1776-1939*, Cambridge University Press, Cambridge.

Clapham, John (1949), *Concise Economic History of Britain to 1750*, Cambridge University Press, Cambridge.

Clapham, John (1963), *A Concise Economic History of Britain: From the Earliest Times to 1750*, Cambridge University Press, Cambridge.

Clapham, John (1968), *The Economic Development of France and Germany 1815-1914*, Cambridge University Press, Cambridge.

Clark, John G. (1987), *Energy and the Federal Government*, University of Illinois Press, Urbana.

Clayton, James (ed) (1970), *The Economic Impact of the Cold War*, Harcourt, Brace and World, New York.

Clough, Shepard Bancroft (1939), *France: A History of National Economics 1789-1939*, Charles Scribner's Sons, New York.

Clough, Shepard Bancroft (1964), The Economic History of Modern Italy, Columbia University Press, New York.

Coase, R. H. (1950), *British Broadcasting: A Study in Monopoly*, Harvard University Press, Cambridge.

Coats, A. W. (1960), 'The First Decades of the American Economic Association', *American Economic Review*, Vol. 50, September, pp. 555-574.

Coats, A. W. (1987), 'American Economic Association', in John Eatwell (ed), *New Palgrave: A Dictionary of Economics*, Macmillan, London, pp. 87-88.

Cobban, Alfred (1971), *The Social Interpretation of the French Revolution*, Cambridge University Press, Cambridge.

Cochrane, Eric W. (1961), *Tradition and Enlightenment in the Tuscan Academies*, University of Chicago Press, Chicago.

Cochrane, Eric W. (1973), *Florence in the Forgotten Centuries 1527-1800*, University of Chicago Press, Chicago.

Cohen, Jon and Giovanni Federico (2001), *The Growth of the Italian Economy, 1820-1960*,

Cambridge University Press, Cambridge.

Cohen, Stephen (1969), *Modern Capitalist Planning: The French Model*, Harvard University Press, Cambridge.

Coornaert, Emile (1970), 'French Guilds under the Old Regime', in Rondo Cameron (ed), *Essays in French Economic History*, Richard D. Irwin, Homewood Illinois, pp. 123-127.

Coppini, Paolo (1994), 'Il Piemonte sabaudo e l'unificazione, 1849-1861', in Giovanni Sabbatucci and Vittorio Vidotto (eds), *Storia d'Italia: Le premesse dell'unita Dalla fine del settecento al 1862*, Laterza, Bari, Vol. 1, pp. 337-430.

Court, W. H. B. (1954), A *Concise Economic History of Britain: From 1750 to Recent Times*, Cambridge University Press, Cambridge.

Covino, Renato, Gianpaolo Gallo and Enrico Mantovani (1976), 'L'industria dell'economia di guerra alla ricostruzione, in P. Ciocca and G. Toniolo (eds), *L'economia italiana nel periodo fascista*, Il Mulino, Bologna, pp. 171-270.

CPB, Netherlands Bureau for Economic Policy Analysis (1997), *Challenging Neighbours: Rethinking German and Dutch Economic Institutions*, Heidelberg, Springer.

Craig, Gordon A. (1978), *Germany, 1866-1945*, Oxford University Press, Oxford.

Cranmer, Jerome H. (1961), 'Improvements Without Public Funds: The New Jersey Canals', in Carter Goodrich (ed), *Canals in American Economic Development*, Columbia University Press, New York, pp. 115-166.

Crepax, Nicola (2002), *Storia dell'industria in Italia: uomini, imprese prodotti*, Il Mulino, Bologna.

Crouch, R. L. (1967), 'Laissez Faire in Nineteenth Century Britain: Myth or Reality?' *Manchester School*, XXV, pp. 199-215.

Crouzet, Francois (1985), *De la supériorité de l'Angleterre sur la France*, Librairie Academique Perrin, Paris.

Crouzet, Francois (1987), *L'économie britannique et blocus continental*, Economica, Paris.

Crouzet, Francois (2001), *A History of the European Economy 1000-2000*, University Press of Virginia, Charlottesville.

D'Antone, Leandra (1997), '"Straordinarita" e stato ordinario', in Fabrizio Barca (ed), *Storia del capitalismo italiano*, Donizelli, Rome, pp. 579-616.

Daumard, Adeline (1976a), 'L'état libéral et le libéralisme économique', in Fernand Braudel and Ernest Labrousse (eds), *Histoire économique et sociale de la France: L'avènement de l'ère industrielle (1789–annes 1880)*, Presse Universitaire de France, Paris, Tome III, Vol. I, pp. 137-161.

Daumard, Adeline (1976b), 'Caractères de la société bourgeoisie', in Fernand Braudel and Ernest Labrousse (eds), *Histoire économique et sociale de la France: L'avènement de l'ère industrielle (1789–annes 1880)*, Presse Universitaire de France, Paris, Tome III, Vol. II, pp. 829-840.

Daumard, Adeline (1976c), 'Diversité des milieux supérieurs et dirigeants', in Fernand Braudel and Ernest Labrousse (eds), *Histoire économique et sociale de la France: L'avènement de l'ère industrielle (1789–annes 1880)*, Presse Universitaire de France, Paris, Tome III, Vol. II, pp. 931-960.

Daunton, W. J. (1985), *Royal Mail*, Athlone Press, London.

Davis, David Brion (1984), *Slavery and Human Progress*, Oxford University Press, New York.

Dawson, William Harbutt (1912), *Industrial Germany*, Collins Clear Type Press, London and Glasgow.

De Cecco, Marcello (1997), 'Splendore e crisi del sistema Beneduce: note sulla struttura finanziaria e industriale dell'Italia dagli anni venti agli anni sessanta', in Fabrizio Barca (ed), *Storia del capitalismo italiano*, Donizelli, Rome, pp. 389-404.

De Cecco, Marcello (2002), 'The Economy from Liberalism to Fascism', in Adrian

Lyttelton (ed), *Liberal and Fascist Italy, 1900-1945*, Oxford University Press, New York, pp. 62-82.

De Cecco, Marcello and G. Ferri (1996), *Le banche d'affari in Italia*, Il Mulino, Bologna.

De Francesco, Antonino (1994), 'Ideologie e movimenti politici', in Giovanni Sabbatucci and Vittorio Vidotto (eds), *Storia d'Italia, Le premesse dell'unita: dalla fine del settecento al 1862*, Laterza, Bari, Vol. 1, pp. 229-336.

De Grand, Alexander (2001), *The Hunchback's Tailor: Giovanni Giolitti and Liberal Italy from the Challenge of Mass Politics to the Rise of Fascism, 1882-1922*, Praeger, Westport, Connecticut.

De Rosa, Luigi (1974), *La rivoluzione industriale in Italia e il Mezzogiorno*, Laterza e figli, Bari.

De Rosa, Luigi (1982), *Storia del Banco di Roma*, Banco di Roma, Rome, Vol. I.

De Rosa, Luigi (1986), 'Italy's Second Industrial Revolution', in Frank J. Coppa (ed), *Studies in Modern Italian History*, Peter Lang, New York, pp. 231-244.

De Ruggiero, Guido (1961), 'Storia del liberalismo europeo', in A. Fanfani Director, *Economia e storia, L'economia italiana dal 1861 al 1961*, A. Giuffre, Milan, pp. 614-655.

Descimon, Robert and Alain Guery (1989), 'Un état des temps modernes?' in Jacques Le Goff (ed), *L'état et les pouvoirs*, Andres Burguiere et Jacques Revel (eds), *Histoire de la France*, Editions du seuil, Paris, Vol. II, pp. 183-360.

Di Scala, Spencer M. (1998), *Italy from Revolution to Republic: 1700 to the Present*, Westview Press, Boulder, Colorado.

Dobbin, Frank (1994), *Forging Industrial Policy: the United States, Britain and France in the Railway Age*, Cambridge University Press, New York.

Dorfman, Joseph (1949), *The Economic Mind in American Civilization, 1865-1918*, Viking Press, New York, Vol. III.

Dorfman, Joseph (1959), 'Principles of Freedom and Governmental Intervention in American Economic Expansion', *Journal of Economic History*, XIX, pp. 570-584.

Dorwart, Reinhold (1971), *The Prussian Welfare State before 1740*, Harvard University Press, Cambridge.

Doukas, Kimon A. (1945), *The French Railroads and the State*, Columbia University Press, New York.

Duby, George and Robert Mandrou (1958), *Histoire de la civilisation française*, Armand Colin Mouton, Paris, Vol. 2.

Dunlavy, Colleen A. (1994), *Politics and Industrialization: Early Railroads in the United States and Prussia*, Princeton University Press, Princeton.

Dunnett, Peter S. (1980), *The Decline of he British Motor Car Industry: The Effects of Government Policy, 1945-1979*, Croom Helm, London.

Dupeux, George (1969), *La France de 1945 a 1965*, Librairie Armand Colin, Paris.

Durkheim, E. (1975), 'Une révision de l'idée socialiste', *Revue philosophique*, 1899, reprinted in *Texte*, Edition de Minuit, Paris, Vol. III.

Dyos, H. J. and D. H. Aldcroft (1969), *British Transport*, Leicester University Press, Leicester.

Economist, The (1999) June 5th.

Edwards, Richard C. (1970), 'Economic Sophistication in Nineteenth-Century Congressional Tariff Debates', *Journal of Economic History*, XXX, pp. 802-838.

Eichholtz, Dietrich (1962), *Junker und Bourgeoisie vor 1848 in der preußischen Eisenbangeschiechte*, Akademie-Verlag, Berlin.

Einaudi, Luigi (1933), *La condotta economica e gli efetti sociali della guerra italiana*, Laterza, Bari.

Einaudi, Mario, Maurice Bye, Ernesto Rossi (1955), *Nationalization in France and Italy*,

Cornell University Press, Ithaca, New York.

Engelbourg, Saul and Leonard Bushkoff (1996), *The Man who found Money: John Stewart Kennedy and the Financing of the Western Railroads*, Michigan State University Press, East Lansing.

Engelbourg, Saul and Gustav Schachter (1986), 'Two "South's"', The United States and Italy since the 1860s', *Journal of European Economic History*, Vol. 15, No. 3, Winter, pp. 563-589.

Engelbourg, Saul and Gustav Schachter (1999), 'Intellectual and Institutional Continuum in Advanced Economies: The Anglo-Saxons vs. the Continentals', *Journal of European Economic History*, Vol. 28, No. 3, Winter, pp. 631-671.

Fabricant, Solomon (1950), 'The Quantitative Study of Government Activity', *Journal of Economic History*, Supplement, X, pp. 4-18.

Falasca, Chiara (1997), 'Review of Adolfo Bernadello, "La prima ferovia fra Venezia e Milano"', *Business History Review*, 71, pp. 501-504.

Farnie, D. A. (1969), *East and West of Suez: The Suez Canal in History, 1854-1956*, Clarendon Press, Oxford.

Fear, Jeffrey (1997a), 'German Capitalism', in Thomas K. McCraw (ed), *Creating Modern Capitalism*, Harvard University Press, Cambridge, pp. 133-182.

Fear, Jeffrey (1997b), 'August Thyssen and German Steel', in Thomas K. McCraw (ed), *Creating Modern Capitalism*, Harvard University Press, Cambridge, pp. 183-226.

Federico, Giovanni (1996), 'Italy, 1860-1940: A Little Known Success Story', *Economic History Review*, XLIX, November, pp. 764-786.

Federico, Giovanni and Antonio Tena (1998), 'Was Italy a Protectionist Country?', *European Review of Economic History*, 2, 1, April, pp. 73-97.

Federico, Giovanni and Gianni Toniolo (1991), 'Italy', in Richard Sylla and Gianni Toniolo (eds), *Patterns of European Industrialization: The Nineteenth Century*, Routledge, London, pp. 197-217.

Fehrenbacher, Don E. (2001), *The Slaveholding Republic: An Account of the United States Government's Relations to Slavery*, Oxford University Press, New York.

Feinstein, Charles (1983), *The Managed Economy: Essays in British Policy and Performance since 1929*, Oxford University Press, New York.

Feldman, Gerald D. (1977), *Iron and Steel in the German Inflation 1916-1923*, Princeton University Press, Princeton.

Fenoaltea, Stefano (1973), 'Riflessioni sull'esperienza industriale italiana dal risorgimento alla prima guerra mondiale', in Gianni Toniolo (ed), *Lo sviluppo economico italiano 1861-1940*, Laterza, Bari, pp.121-156.

Fenoaltea, Stefano (1983), 'Italy', in Patrick O'Brien (ed), *Railways and the Economic Development of Western Europe 1830-1914*, St. Martin's Press, New York, pp. 49-120.

Ferrier, R. W. (1982), *The History of the British Petroleum Company, The Developing Years 1901-1932*, Cambridge University Press, Cambridge, Vol. 1.

Findlay, Ronald (1992), 'The Roots of Divergence: Western Economic History in Comparative Perspective', *American Economic Review*, 82, 2, pp. 158-161.

Finoia, Massimo (2001), 'Continuity of Economic Policy and Economic Thought in Italy between the First and Second World Wars', *Journal of European Economic History*, 30, No. 3, Winter, pp. 675-693.

Fischer, Wolfram (1972), *Wirtschaft und Gesellschaft im Zeitalter der Industrialisierung*, Vandenhoeck & Ruprecht, Göttingen.

Flamm, Kenneth (1988), *Creating the Computer: Government, Industry, and High Technology*, Brookings Institution, Washington DC.

Fogel, Robert F. (1960), *The Union Pacific Railroad: A Case in Premature Enterprise*, John Hopkins Press, Baltimore.

Fogel, Robert F. (1991), 'The Conquest of High Mortality and Hunger in Europe and America: Timing and Mechanisms', in Patrice Higonnet, David S. Landes, Henry Rosovsky (eds), *Favorites of Fortune: Technology, Growth and Economic Development since the Industrial Revolution*, Harvard University Press, Cambridge, pp. 33-71.

Fohlen, Claude (1970), 'The Industrial Revolution in France', in Rondo Cameron (ed), *Essays in French Economic History*, pp. 201-225, Richard D. Irwin, Homewood, Illinois.

Foreman-Peck, James (1987), 'Natural Monopoly and Railway Policy in the Nineteenth Century', *Oxford Economic Papers XXXIX*, pp. 699-718.

Foreman-Peck, James (1989), 'Competition and Nationalization in the Nineteenth-Century Telegraph System', *Business History*, XXXI, July, pp. 81-101.

Foreman-Peck, James and Robert Millward (1994), *Public and Private Ownership of British Industry 1820-1890*, Clarendon Press, Oxford.

Foreman-Peck, James, Sue Bowden and Alan McKinlay (1995), *The British Motor Industry*, Manchester University Press, Manchester.

Fraser, Derek (1973), *The Evolution of the British Welfare State*, Barnes and Noble, New York.

Freedeman, Charles E. (1979), *Joint Stock Enterprise in France 1807-1867, From Privileged Company to Modern Corporation*, University of North Carolina Press, Chapel Hill.

Freeman, Richard (2004), 'Are European Labor Markets as Awful as All That?', *CES IFO Forum*, Vol. 5, 1, Spring, pp. 34-39.

Fremdling, R. (1980), 'Freight Rates and the State Budget: The Role of the Nationalized Prussian Railways 1880-1913', *Journal of European Economic History*, 9, pp. 21-39.

Fremdling, Rainer (1983), 'Germany', in Patrick O'Brien (ed), *Railways and the Economic Development of Western Europe*, St. Martin's Press, New York, pp. 121-147.

Freyer, Tony (1992), *Regulating Big Business: Antitrust in Great Britain and America, 1880-1990*, Cambridge University Press, Cambridge.

Friedman, Lawrence M. (1968), *Government and Slum Housing*, Rand McNally, Chicago.

Fulbrook, Mary (1992), *The Divided Nation: A History of Germany 1918-1990*, New York, Oxford University Press.

Gaeta, Franco (1982), *La crisi di fine secolo e l'età giolittiana*, UTET, Turin.

Gagliardo, John G. (1967), *Enlightened Despotism*, Crowell, New York.

Gagliardo, John G. (1969), *From Pariah to Patriot: The Changing Image of the German Peasant, 1770-1840*, University Press of Kentucky, Lexington.

Gagliardo, John G. (1980), *Reich and Nation*, Indiana University Press, Bloomington.

Gagliardo, John G. (1991), *Germany under the Old Regime 1600-1790*, Longman, New York.

Galambos, Louis and William Baumol (2000), 'Conclusion', in Pier Angelo Toninelli (ed), *The Rise and Fall of State-Owned Enterprise in the Western World*, Cambridge University Press, Cambridge, pp. 303-309.

Galbraith, J. K. (1958), *The Affluent Society*, Houghton Mifflin, Boston.

Garnet, Robert N. (1985), *The Telephone Enterprise*, John Hopkins University Press, Baltimore.

Garraty, John A. (1986), *The Great Depression*, Harcourt, Brace, Jovanovich, New York.

Geiger, Reed G. (1994), *Planning the French Canals: Bureaucracy, Politics, and Enterprise under the Restoration*, University of Delaware Press, Newark, NJ.

Geremia, Giusto (1961), 'La previdenza sociale in Italia nell'ultimo secolo, in A. Fanfani Director, *L'economia italiana dal 1861 al 1961*, A. Giuffre, Milan, pp. 614-655.

Gerschenkron, Alexander (1962), *Economic Backwardness in Historical Perspective*,

Harvard University Press, Cambridge.

Gerschenkron, Alexander (1965), 'Osservazioni sull' saggio di sviluppo industriale dell'Italia', in A. Gerschenkron (ed), *Il problema storico dell'arretratezza economica*, Giulio Einaudi, Turin.

Gerschenkron, Alexander (1968), *Continuity in History and Other Essays*, Belknap Press of Harvard University Press, Cambridge.

Giersch, Herbert, Karl-Heinz Paque, Holger Schmieding (1992), *The Fading Miracle: Four Decades of Market Economy in Germany*, Cambridge University Press, New York.

Gilbert, Bentley (1970), *British Social Policy 1914-1939*, Cornell University Press, Ithaca, New York.

Gilbert, Mark F. and Robert Nilsson (1999), *Historical Dictionary of Modern Italy*, Scarecrow Press, Lanham, Maryland & London.

Goodrich, Carter (1950a), 'Introduction', *Journal of Economic History*, Supplement X, 3, pp. 1-3.

Goodrich, Carter (1950b), 'The Revulsion against Internal Improvements', *Journal of Economic History*, 10, November, pp. 145-169.

Goodrich, Carter (1960), *Government Promotion of American Canals and Railroads 1800-1890*, Columbia University Press, New York.

Goodrich, Carter (ed) (1961), *Canals in American Economic Development*, Columbia University Press, New York.

Goodrich, Carter (1968), 'State in—State out', *Journal of Economic Issues*, 2, pp. 365-383.

Goodrich, Carter (1970), 'Internal Improvements Reconsidered', *Journal of Economic History*, 30, June, pp. 289-311.

Gordon, Lincoln (1938), *The Public Corporation in Great Britain*, Oxford University Press, London.

Goubert Pierre (1970), 'Le tragique xvii siècle', in Fernand Braudel and Ernest Labrousse (eds), *Histoire économique et sociale de la France: Des derniers temps de l'age seigneurial aux préludes de l'age industriel*, Presses Universitaires de France, Paris, Tome 2, (1660-1789), pp. 321-360.

Goulemot, Jean Marie and Michel Launay (1968), *Le siècle des Lumières*, Editions du seuil, Paris.

Gourvish, T. R. (1980), *Railways and the British Economy 1830-1914*, Macmillan, London.

Grab, Alexander I. (1985), 'The Politics of Subsistence: The Liberalization of Grain Commerce in Austrian Lombardy under Enlightened Despotism', *Journal of Modern History*, 57, pp. 185-216.

Graebner, William (1974), 'Grand Expectations: The Search for Order in the Bituminous Coal, 1890-1917', *Business History Review*, Spring 1948, pp. 49-72.

Graf, William D. (1992), 'Internationalization and Exoneration: Social Functions of Transnationalizing West Germany Political Economy in the Post-war Era', in William D. Graf (ed), *The Internationalization of the German Political Economy: Evolution of a Hegemonic Project*, St. Martin's Press, New York, pp. 8-24.

Grampp, William D. (1965), *Economic Liberalism*, Random House, New York.

Grantham, George (1997), 'The French Cliometric Revolution: A Survey of Cliometric Contributions to French Economic History', *European Review of Economic History*, December, 1, pp. 352-405.

Graziani, Augusto (1979), 'Il Mezzogiorno nel quadro dell'economia italiana', in A. Graziani and E. Pugliese (eds), *Investimenti e disoccupazione nel Mezzogiorno*, Il Mulino, Bologna, pp. 7-65.

Greaves, Julian J. (2002), 'Competition, Collusion and Confusion: The State and Reorganization of the British Cotton Industry: 1931-1939', *Enterprise and Society*, 3, March, pp. 48-79.

Green George D. (1980), 'Financial Intermediaries', in Glenn Porter (ed), *Encyclopedia of American Economic History*, Charles Scribner's Sons, New York, Vol. II, pp. 707-726.

Greenfield, Kent Roberts (1965), *Economics and Liberalism in the Risorgimento: A study of Nationalism in Lombardy, 1814-1848*, John Hopkins Press, Baltimore, Revised edition of the 1934 original.

Gregg, Pauline (1969), *The Welfare State: An economic and Social History of Great Britain from 1945 to the Present Day*, University of Massachusetts Press, Amherst.

Grifone, Pietro (1975), *Capitalismo di stato ed imperialismo fascista*, Gabriele Mazzotta Editore, Milan.

Groenewegen, Peter (1987), 'Anne Robert Jacques Turgot', in John Eatwell (ed), *The New Palgrave: A Dictionary of Economics*, Vol. 3, pp. 216-218, Stockton Press, New York.

Grove, J. W. (1962), *Government and Industry in Britain*, Longman, London.

Guerard, Albert (1969), *France, A Modern History*, New edition revised and enlarged by Paul A. Gagnon, University of Michigan Press, Ann Arbor.

Guerri, Giordano Bruno (1992), *Gli italiani sotto la chiesa*, Arnoldo Mondadori, Milan.

Gueslin, André (1997), *L'état, l'économie et la société française XIXe-XXe siècle*, Hachette, Paris.

Gunn, Roy L. (1988), *The Decline of Authority: Public Economic Policy and Political Development in New York, 1800-1860*, Cornell University Press, Ithaca, NY.

Hadfield, Charles (1968), *The Canal Age*, David and Charles, Abbot Newton, UK.

Hales, E. Y. (1960), *Revolution and Papacy 1769-1846*, Hanover House, Garden City, NJ.

Hall, Peter A. (1986a), 'The State and Economic Decline', in Bernard Elbaum and William Lazonick (ed), *The Decline of the British Economy*, Clarendon Press, Oxford, pp. 266-302.

Hall, Peter A. (1986b), *Governing the Economy: The Politics of State Intervention in Britain and France*, Oxford University Press, New York.

Hallgarten, George W. F. (1974), 'Von Bismarck bis zum Ende der Weimarer Republik', in George W. F. Hallgarten and Joachim Radkau (eds), *Deutsche Industrie und Politik von Bismarck bis Heute*, Europäische Verlagsanstalt, Frankfurt am Main, pp. 19-224.

Halperin, Sandra (1997), *In the Mirror of the Third World – Capitalist Development in Modern Europe*, Cornell University Press, Ithaca, New York.

Hamerow, Theodore S. (1958), *Restoration, Revolution, Reaction: Economics and Politics in Germany 1815-1871*, Princeton University Press, Princeton.

Handlin, Oscar (1943), 'The Development of American Laissez-Faire: Laissez-Faire Thought in Massachusetts, 1790-1880', *Journal of Economic History*, Supplement III, pp. 55-65.

Handlin, Oscar and Mary Flug Handlin (1969), *Commonwealth, A Study of the Role of the Government in the American Economy: Massachusetts, 1774-1861*, Harvard University Press, Cambridge.

Hanlon, Gregory (2000), *Early Modern Italy 1550-1800*, St. Martin's Press, New York.

Hannah, Leslie (1977), 'A Pioneer of Public Enterprise: The Central Electricity Board and the National Grid', in Barry Supple (ed), *Essays in British Business History*, Clarendon Press, Oxford, pp. 207-226.

Hannah, Leslie (1979), *Electricity before Nationalization: A Study of Development of the Electricity Supply Industry in Britain to 1948*, John Hopkins University Press, Baltimore.

Hardach, Karl (1980), *The Political Economy of Twentieth Century Germany*, University of California Press, Berkeley.

Hartz, Louis (1948), *Economic Policy and Democratic Thought, Pennsylvania 1770-1860*, Harvard University Press, Cambridge.

Hassinger, Herbert (1978), 'Politische Kräfte und Wirtschaft 1350-1800', in Hermann

Aubin and Wofgang Zorn (eds), *Handbuch der Deutschen Wirtschaft und Sozialgeschichte*, Vol. 1, *Von der Frühzeit bis zum Ende des 18. Jahrhunderts*, Ernest Klett Verlag, Stuttgart, pp. 608-657.

Hausman, William and John L. Neufeld (2002), 'The Market for Capital and the Origins of State Regulation of Electric Utilities in the United States', *Journal of Economic History*, 62, December, pp. 1050-1074.

Hawke, R. and J. P. P. Higgins (1981), 'Transport and Social Overhead Capital', in Roderick Floud and Donald McCloskey (eds), *The Economic History of Britain since 1700*, Cambridge University Press, Cambridge, Vol. I, pp. 227-252.

Hawke, R. and J. P. P. Higgins (1983), 'Britain', in Patrick O'Brien (ed), *Railways and the Economic Development of Western Europe*, St. Martin's Press, New York.

Hayek, Friedrich A. (1944), *The Road to Serfdom*, University of Chicago Press, Chicago.

Hayward, Jack (1986), *The State and the Market Economy: Industrial Patriotism and Economic Intervention in France*, New York University Press, New York.

Hayward, Keith (1971), *The British Aircraft Industry*, Manchester University Press, Manchester.

Hayward, Keith (1983), *Government and British Civil Aerospace*, Manchester University Press, Manchester.

Hayward, Keith (1989), *The British Aircraft Industry*, Manchester University Press, Manchester.

Hearder, Harry (1983), *Italy in the Age of Risorgimento 1790-1870*, Longman, London.

Heath, Milton Sydney (1954), *Constructive Liberalism: The Role of the State in Economic Development in Georgia to 1860*, Harvard University Press, Cambridge.

Heffter, Heinrich (1950), *Die Deutsche Selbstverwaltung im 19' Jahrhundert*, K. F. Koehler Verlag, Stuttgart.

Hegel, Georg Wilhelm Friedrich (1953), *Reason in History, A General Introduction to the Philosophy of History*, Bobbs-Merrill Educational Publishing, Indianapolis, Indiana, Originally published in 1837.

Hegel, Georg Wilhelm Friedrich (1954), 'The Constitution of Germany', in Carl J. Fredrich (ed), *The Philosophy of Hegel*, Modern Library, New York, pp. 527-539, originally published in 1802.

Henderson, W. O. (1958), *The State and the Industrial Revolution in Prussia, 1740-1870*, Liverpool University Press, Liverpool.

Henderson, W. O. (1968), *Studies in the Economic Policies of Frederick the Great*, Reprint of London, Frank Cass, 1963, August M. Kelley, New York.

Henning, Friedrich Wilhelm (1974), *Das vorindustrielle Deutschland 800 bis 1800*, Ferdinand Schoeningh, Paderborn, Germany.

Hennock, E. P. (1973), *Fit and Proper Persons*, Edward Arnold, London.

Henrich, Frederick K. (1943), 'The Development of American Laissez Faire: A General View of the Age of Washington', *Journal of Economic History*, Supplement III, 51-54.

Higgs, Robert (1987), *Crisis in Leviathan: Critical Period in the Growth of American Government*, Oxford University Press, New York.

Hobsbawm, Eric J. (1968), *Industry and Empire*, Pantheon, New York.

Hochfelder, David (2000), 'A Comparison of the Postal Telegraph Movement in Great Britain and the United States, 1866-1900', *Enterprise and Society*, Vol. 1, December, pp. 739-761.

Hochfelder, David (2002), 'Constructing an Industrial Divide: Western Union, AT&T, and the Federal Government', 1876-1971, *Business History Review*, Vol. 76, Winter, pp. 705-732.

Hoffmann, Stanley [and others] (1963), *In Search of France*, Harvard University Press, Cambridge.

Hoffmann, Walter G., Franz Grumbach and Helmut Hesse (1965), *Das Wachstum der Deutschen Wirtschaft seit der Mitte des 19' Jahrhunderts*, Springer Verlag, Berlin, Heidelberg, New York.

Hogwood, Brian W. (1979), *Government and Shipbuilding*, Saxon House, Hants, UK.

Hollander, S. C. (1966), 'United States of America', in Basil S. Yamey (ed), *Resale Price Maintenance*, Weidenfeld and Nicholson, London, pp. 67-100.

Holmes, Colin, J. (1976), 'Laissez Faire in Theory and Practice: Britain 1800-1875', *Journal of European Economic History*, Vol. 5, pp. 671-688.

Horwitz, Morton (1977), *The Transformation of American Law, 1780-1860*, Harvard University Press, Cambridge.

Hovenkamp, Herbert (1991), *Enterprise and American Law, 1836-1937*, Harvard University Press, Cambridge.

Huber, Ernst Rudolf (1957), *Deutsche Verfassungsgeschichte seit 1789*, Vol. I, *Reform und Restauration bis 1830*, W. Kohlhammer Verlag, Stuttgart.

Hughes, Jonathan R. T. (1976), *Social Control in the Colonial Economy*, University of Virginia Press, Charlottesville.

Hughes, Jonathan R. T. (1991), *The Governmental Habit Redux: Economic Controls from Colonial Times to the Present*, Princeton University Press, Princeton.

Hughes, Michael (1992), *Early Modern Germany 1477-1806*, University of Pennsylvania Press, Philadelphia.

Hume, David (1967), 'On the Original Contract', in Ernest Barker (ed), *Social Contract*, Oxford University Press, New York, pp. 147-168.

Huneke, William (2003), 'Railroads', *Oxford Encyclopedia of Economic History*, Oxford University Press, Oxford, Vol. 4, pp. 329-338.

Hurst, James Willard (1970), *The Legitimacy of the Business Corporation in the Law of the United States 1780-1970*, University Press of Virginia, Charlottesville.

Hutchins, John G. B. (1947), *The American Maritime Industries and Public Policies*, Harvard University Press, Cambridge.

ISTAT (2000), *Rapporto sull'Italia*, Edizione 2000, Bologna.

Jensen, Merrill (1956), *The New Nation: A History of the United States during the Articles of the Confederation 1781-1789*, Alfred A. Knopf, New York.

John, Richard R. (1995), *Spreading the News: The American Postal System from Franklin to Morse*, Harvard University Press, Cambridge.

John, Richard R. (2000), 'Recasting the Information Infrastructure for the Industrial Age', in Alfred D. Chandler Jr. and James W. Cortada (eds), *A Nation Transformed by Information*, Oxford University Press, New York, pp. 55-106.

Johnson, E. A. J. (1962), 'Federalism, Pluralism, and Public Policy', *Journal of Economic History*, Vol. 22, pp. 427-444.

Johnson, E. A. J. (1973), *The Foundation of American Economic Freedom: Government and Enterprise in the Age of Washington*, University of Minnesota Press, Minneapolis.

Johnson, P. (1994), 'The Welfare State', in R. Floud and D. McCloskey (eds), *The Economic History of Britain since 1700*, Cambridge University Press, Cambridge, Vol. III, pp. 284-317.

Jones, Colin (2002), *The Great Nation: France from Louis XV to Napoleon, 1715-1799*, Columbia University Press, New York.

Jones, Geoffrey (1981), *The State and the Emergence of the British Oil Industry*, Macmillan, London.

Kalla-Bishop, P. M. (1971), *Italian Railways*, David & Charles, Newton Abbot.

Kathka, David A. (1990), 'Missouri River', in Richard Kirkendall (ed), *The Harry S. Truman Encyclopedia*, G.K. Hall & Co, Boston, pp. 241-242.

Kaufmann, Richard de (1900), *La politique française en matière de chemins de fer*, Librairie polytechnique, Paris.

Kelikian, Alice A. (2002), 'The Church and Catholicism', in Adrian Lyttelton (ed), *Liberal and Fascist Italy 1900-1945*, Oxford University Press, New York, pp. 44-61.

Kellenbenz, Hermann (1976), *Rise of the European Economy*, Holmes and Meier, New York.

Kellenbenz, Hermann (1977), *Deutsche Wirtschaftsgeschichte: Von den Anfangen bis' zum Ende des 18. Jahrhunderts*, Verlag C. H. Beck, Munich, Vol. I.

Keller, Morton (1990), *Regulating a New Economy: Public Policy and Economic Change in America*, Harvard University Press, Cambridge.

Kennedy, Robert Dawson (1991), 'The Statist Evolution of Rail Governance in the United States', in John L. Campbell, J. Rogers Hollingsworth, and Leon L. Lindberg (eds), *Governance of the American Economy*, Cambridge University Press, Cambridge, pp. 138-181.

Kieve, Jeffrey (1973), *The Electric Telegraph in the U.K.: A Social and Economic History*, David & Charles, Newton Abbot.

Kindleberger, Charles P. (1976), 'The Historical Background: Adam Smith and Industrial Revolution', in Thomas Wilson and Andrew S. Skinner (eds), *The Market and the State: Essays in Honour of Adam Smith*, Clarendon Press, Oxford, pp. 1-25.

Kindleberger, Charles P. (1983), 'Standards as Public, Collective and Private Goods', *Kyklos*, 36, pp. 377-396.

Kindleberger, Charles P. (1986), *The World in Depression 1929-1939*, University of California Press, Berkeley.

Kindleberger, Charles P. (1993), *A Financial History of Western Europe*, Oxford University Press, New York, Second Edition.

Kindleberger, Charles P. (1995), *The World Economy and National Finance in Historical Perspective*, University of Michigan Press, Ann Arbor.

Kirby, M. W. (1973), 'Government Intervention in Industrial Organization in the Nineteen Thirties', *Business History*, vol. XV, pp. 160-173.

Kirby, M. W. (1977), *The British Coal Mining Industry, 1870-1946*, Macmillan, London.

Kirkaldy, Adam W. (1914), *British Shipping*, Kegan, Trench, Trubner, London.

Kirkland, Edward C. (1961), *Industry Comes of Age 1860-1897*, Holt, Rinehart and Winston, New York.

Kisser, Edgar and Julian Kane (2001), 'Revolution and State Structure: The Bureaucratization of Tax Administration in Early Modern England and France', *American Journal of Sociology*, July, pp. 183-223.

Kitchen, Martin (1978), *The Political Economy of Germany 1815-1914*, Croom Helm, London.

Kitson Clark, G. S. R. (1967), *An Expanding Society Britain 1830-1900*, University Press, Cambridge, Cambridge.

Klang, Daniel M. (1977), *Tax Reform in Eighteenth Century Lombardy*, Columbia University Press, New York.

Klippel, Diethelm (1999), 'Reasonable Aims of Civil Society: Concerns of the State in German Political Theory in the Eighteenth and Early Nineteenth Centuries', in John Brewer and Eckhart Hellmuth (eds), *Rethinking Leviathan, The Eighteenth-Century State in Britain and Germany*, Oxford University Press, Oxford, pp.71-98.

Knight, Arthur (1974), *Private Enterprise and Public Intervention: The Courtlauds Experience*, George Allen & Unwin, London.

Koehn, Nancy F. (1994), *The Power of Commerce: Economy and Government in the First British Empire*, Cornell University Press, Ithaca, NY.

Komlos, John (2000), 'The Industrial Revolution as the Escape from the Malthusian Trap', *Journal of European Economic History*, 29, 2-3, Fall and Winter, pp. 307-331.

Koselleck, Reinhart (1967), *Preußen zwischen Reform und Revolution: Allgemeines Landrecht, Verwaltung und soziale Bewegung von 1791 bis 1848*, Ernst Klett Verlag, Stuttgart.

Kriedte, Peter (1996), 'Trade', in Sheilagh Ogilvie (ed), *Germany, A New Social and Economic History*, Vol. 2, 1630-1800, Arnold, London, pp. 100-133.

Kuisel, Richard F. (1981), *Capitalism and the State in Modern France*, Cambridge University Press, New York.

Kujovich, Mary Yeager (1970), 'The Refrigerator Car and the Growth of the American Dressed Meat Industry', *Business History Review*, 44, Winter, pp. 460-482.

Labracherie, Pierre (1967), *Napoléon III et son temps*, Julliard, Paris.

Labrousse, Ernest (1970), 'Les «bons prix» agricole du xviii siècle', in Fernand Braudel and Ernest Labrousse (eds), *Histoire économique et sociale de la France: Des derniers temps de l'age seigneurial aux préludes de l'age industriel 1660-1789*, Presses Universitaires de France, Paris, Tome II, Vol.2, pp. 367-416.

Landes, David S. (1968), *The Unbound Prometheus: Technological Change and Industrial Development in Western Europe from 1750 to the Present*, Cambridge University Press, Cambridge.

Lane, Frederic C. (1973), *Venice, A Maritime Republic*, Johns Hopkins University Press, Baltimore.

Lane, Peter (1978), *The Industrial Revolution*, Harper and Row, New York.

Langins, Janis (2004), *Conserving the Enlightenment: French Military Engineering from Vauban to the Revolution*, MIT Press, Cambridge.

Langlois, Richard W. and Paul L. Robertson (1995), *Firms, Markets and Planned Economic Change*, Routledge.

Larson, John Lauritz (1984), *Bonds of Enterprise: John Murray Forbes and Western Development in America's Railway Age*, Harvard University Press, Cambridge.

Larson, John Lauritz (1990), 'Liberty by Design: Freedom, Planning and John Quincy Adams' American System', in Mary O. Furner and Barry Supple (eds), *The State and Economic Knowledge*, Cambridge University Press, Cambridge, pp. 73-102.

Larson, John Lauritz (2000), *Internal Improvement*, University of North Carolina Press, Chapel Hill.

Laurent, Robert (1976), 'Les cadres de la production agricole: propriété e modes d'exploitation', in Fernand Braudel and Ernest Labrousse (eds), *Histoire économique et sociale de la France: L'avènement de l'ère industrielle (1789–annes 1880)*, Presse Universitaire de France, Paris, Tome 3, Vol. II, pp. 629-662.

Lawson, Michael L. (1982), *The Pick-Sloan Plan and the Missouri River Sioux, 1944-1980*, University of Oklahoma Press, Norman.

Lee, W. R. (1988), 'Economic Development and the State in Nineteenth Century Germany', *Economic History Review*, 41, pp. 346-367.

Lee, W. R. (ed), (1991), *German Industry and German Industrialization*, Routledge, London.

Leon, Pierre (1970a), 'Les nouvelle élites', in Fernand Braudel and Ernest Labrousse (eds), *Histoire économique et sociale de la France: Des derniers temps de l'age seigneurial aux préludes de l'age industriel (1660-1789)*, Presses Universitaires de France, Paris, Tome II, pp. 601-650.

Leon, Pierre (1970b), 'Morcellement et émergence du monde ouvrier', in Fernand Braudel and Ernest Labrousse (eds), *Histoire économique et sociale de la France: Des derniers temps de l'age seigneurial aux préludes de l'age industriel (1660-1789)*, Presses Universitaires de France, Paris, Tome II, pp. 651-692.

Leon, Pierre (1976a), 'L'épanouissement d'un marche national', in Fernand Braudel and Ernest Labrousse (eds), *Histoire économique et sociale de la France: L'avènement de l'ère industrielle (1789–annes 1880)*, Presse Universitaire de France, Paris, Tome III, Vol.1, pp. 275-304.

Leon, Pierre (1976b), 'La dynamisme industriel', in Fernand Braudel and Ernest Labrousse (eds), *Histoire économique et sociale de la France: L'avènement de l'ère industrielle (1789–annes 1880)*, Presse Universitaire de France, Paris, Tome III, Vol. II, pp. 581-618.

Leon, Pierre (1976c), 'L'impulsion technique,' in Fernand Braudel and Ernest Labrousse (eds), *Histoire économique et sociale de la France: L'avènement de l'ère industrielle (1789–annes 1880)*, Presse Universitaire de France, Paris, Tome III, Vol. II, pp. 475-502.

Lerner, Max (1963), 'The Triumph of Laissez Faire', in Arthur M. Schlesinger, Jr. and Morton White (eds), *Paths of American Thought*, Houghton Mifflin, Boston, pp. 147-166.

Letwin, William (1989), 'American Economic Policy, 1865-1939', *Economic History of Europe*, Cambridge University Press, Cambridge, Vol. VIII, pp. 641-690.

Levasseur, Emile (1904), *Histoire des classes ouvrières et de l'industrie en France de 1789 a 1870*, A. A. Rousseau, Paris, Vol. 2, Second Edition.

Leveque, Pierre (1989), 'La France et le pouvoir politique de 1789 a nos jours', in André Burguiere and Jacques Revel (eds), *Histoire de la France: L'état et les pouvoir*, Editions du seuil, Paris, Vol. II, pp. 361-490.

Levy-Leboyer, Maurice (1968), 'Le rôle historique de la monnaie de banc', *Annales, Economies, Société, Civilisation*, Vol. 28, pp. 1-8.

Levy-Leboyer, Maurice (1976), 'Le crédit et la monnaie: l'évolution institutionnelle', in Fernand Braudel and Ernest Labrousse (eds), *Histoire économique et sociale de la France: L'avènement de l'ère industrielle (1789–annes 1880)*, Presse Universitaire de France, Paris, Tome III. Vol.1, pp. 391-430.

Levy-Leboyer, Maurice and Michel Lescure (1991), 'France', in Richard Sylla and Gianni Toniolo (eds), *Patterns of European Industrialization: The Nineteenth Century*, Routledge, London and New York, pp. 153-174.

Lewchuk, Wayne (1986), 'The Motor Vehicle Industry', in Bernard Elbaum and William Lazonick (eds), *The Decline of the British Economy*, Clarendon Press, Oxford, pp. 135-161.

Libecap, Gary D. (1992), 'The Rise of Chicago Packers and the Origin of Meat Inspection and Antitrust', *Economic Inquiry*, No. 30, April, pp. 242-262.

Lindert, Peter H. (1994), 'The Rise of Social Spending', *Explorations in Economic History*, January, Vol. 31, pp. 1-37.

Lindert, Peter H. (1998), 'Poor Relief before the Welfare State: Britain versus the Continent, 1780-1880', *European Review of Economic History*, 2, 2, August, pp. 101-140.

Lindert, Peter H. (2003), 'Voice and Growth: Was Churchill Right'? *Journal of Economic History*, 63, pp. 315-350.

Lipartito, Kenneth (1989), *The Bell System and Regional Business*, Johns Hopkins University Press, Baltimore.

Lipson, E. (1959), *The Growth of English Society: A Short Economic History*, Henry Holt, New York.

List, Friedrich (1991), *The National System of Political Economy*, August M. Kelley, Fairfield NJ, originally published in German in 1840.

Locke, John (1967), 'An Essay Concerning the True Original, Extent and End of Civil Government', in Ernest Barker (ed), *Social Contract*, Oxford University Press, New York, pp. 3-143.

Locke, John (1975), *Two Treatises of Government*, Dutton, New York, first published in

1690.

Locke, Richard M. (1995), *Remaking the Italian Economy*, Cornell University Press, Ithaca, NY.

Lodge, George C. (1986), *The New American Ideology*, New York University Press, New York.

Lorenz, Eduard and Frank Wilkinson (1986), 'The Shipbuilding Industry 1880-1965', in Bernard Elbaum and William Lazonick (eds), *The Decline of the British Economy*, Clarendon Press, Oxford, pp. 109-134.

LoRomer, David C. (1987), *Merchants and Reform in Livorno 1814-1868*, University of California Press, Berkeley.

Lubove, Roy (1962), *The Progressives and the Slums: Tenement House Reform in New York City, 1890-1917*, University of Pittsburgh Press, Pittsburgh.

Luthy, Herbert (1955), *The State of France*, Secker & Warburg, London.

Lutz, Friedrich, A. (1989), 'Observations on the Problem of Monopoly', in Alan Peacock and Hans Willgerodt (eds), *Germany's Social Market Economy*, St. Martin's Press, New York, pp. 152-170.

Luzzatti, L. (1952), *L'ordine sociale*, Zanichelli, Bologna, Vol. IV.

Luzzatto, G. (1967), *Per una storia economica d'Italia*, Laterza, Bari.

Mack Smith, Denis (1997), *Modern Italy: A Political History*, University of Michigan Press, Ann Arbor.

Malanimo, Paolo (1991), 'I fattori della produzione', in Ruggiero Romano (ed), *Storia dell'economia italiana: L'età moderna: verso la crisi*, Giulio Einaudi, Turin, Vol. II, pp. 169-186.

Mangoni, Luisa (1999), 'Gli intellettuali alla prova dell'Italia unità, in Giovanni Sabbatucci and Vittorio Vidotto (eds), *Storia d'Italia: Liberalismo e democrazia, 1887-1914*, Laterza, Bari, Vol. 3, pp. 443-528.

Marchi, Vittorio (1984), *Un porto Europeo ed intercontinentale in Toscana*, Editrice Nuova Fortezza, S. Giovanni in Persiceto.

Marlow, John (1964), *The Making of the Suez Canal*, Cresset Press, London.

Marsan, V. Ajmone (1980), 'The Italian Holding System in Italian Economic Development', in William J. Baumol (ed), *Public and Private Enterprise in the Western Economies*, St. Martin's Press, New York, pp. 85-98.

Marx, Karl and Friedrich Engels (1948), *The Communist Manifesto*, International Publishers, New York, first edition published in 1848.

Mason, Edward S. (1960), 'Role of Government in Economic Development', *American Economic Review*, LI, 2, May, pp. 636-641.

Mason, Joseph D. (2003), 'The Political Economy of Reconstruction Finance Corporation Assistance during the Great Depression', *Explorations in Economic History*, 40, pp. 101-121.

Matson, Cathy D. (1996), 'The Revolution, the Constitution and the New Nation', in Stanley L Engerman and Robert Gallman, (eds), *Cambridge Economic History of the United States*, Cambridge University Press, New York, Vol. I, pp. 363-401.

Matson, Cathy D. and Peter S. Onuf (1990), *A Union of Interests: Political and Economic Thought in Revolutionary America*, University Press of Kansas, Lawrence.

Matthews, Derek (1986), 'Laissez-faire and the London Gas Industry in the Nineteenth-Century: Another Look', *Economic History Review*, XXXXIX, pp. 244-263.

Maurois, André (1948), *Histoire de la France*, Editions de la Maison Française, Paris, Vol. 2.

Mayeur, Jean-Marie (1973), *Le débuts de la Troisième République 1871-1898*, Editions du Seuil, Paris.

McCraw, Thomas K. (1971), *TVA and the Power Fight, 1922-1939*, J. P. Lippincott,

Philadelphia.

McCraw, Thomas K. (1984), 'Business and Government: The Origins of the Adversary Relationship', *California Management Review*, Winter, 26, pp. 35-52.

McCraw, Thomas K. (1996), 'Competition and Fair Trade: History and Theory', *Research in Economic History*, 16, pp. 185-239.

McCurdy, Charles (1978), 'American Law and the Marketing Structure of the Large Corporation', *Journal of Economic History*, 38, September, pp. 631-649.

McCusker, John J. (1996), 'British Mercantilist Policies and the American Colonies', in Stanley L. Engerman and Robert E. Gallman (eds), Cambridge Economic History of the United States, Cambridge University Press, Cambridge, UK, Vol. 1, pp. 357-362.

McCusker, John J. and Russell R. Menard (1991) *The Economy of British North America, 1607-1789*, University of North Carolina Press, Chapel Hill.

McKay, John P. (1976), *Tramways and Trolleys*, Princeton University Press, Princeton.

McKinney Schweitzer, Mary (1980), 'Economic Regulation and the Colonial Economy: The Maryland Tobacco Inspection Act of 1747', *Journal of Economic History*, XL, September, pp. 551-569.

Meriggi, Marco (1994), 'Società, istituzioni e ceti dirgenti', in Giovanni Sabbatucci and Vittorio Vidotto (eds), *Storia d'Italia, le premesse dell'unita, dalla fine dell settecento al 1861*, Laterza, Bari, Vol. 1, pp. 119-228.

Meuvret, Jean (1971), *Etude histoire économique*, Librairie Armand Colin, Paris.

Mierzejewski, Alfred C. (1999), *The Most Valuable Asset of the Reich: A History of the German National Railway,* University of North Carolina Press, Chapel Hill, Vol. 1.

Millward, Robert (2004), 'European Governments and Infrastructure Industries, c. 1840-1914', *European Review of Economic History*, 8, April, pp. 3-28.

Milward, Alan S. and S. B. Saul (1977), *The Development of the Economies of Continental Europe 1850-1914*, Harvard University Press, Cambridge.

Mises, Ludwig von (1949), *Human Action, A Treatise in Economics*, Yale University Press, New Haven, Connecticut.

Mises, Ludwig von (1962), *The Free and Prosperous Commonwealth*, Van Nostrand, Princeton.

Mises, Ludwig von (1978), *Liberalismus: A Socio-Economic Exposition*, Sheed Andrews and McMeel, Kansas City.

Mises, Ludwig von (1980), *The Theory of Money and Credit, Indiana*, Liberty Classics, Indianapolis, first published in 1934.

Mitchell, B. R. (1998), *International Historical Statistics: Europe 1750-1993*, Macmillan, London.

Mokyr, Joel (1983), *Why Ireland Starved*, George Allen & Unwin, London.

Mokyr, Joel (1990), *The Lever of Riches*, New York, Oxford University Press, London.

Mommsen, Wilhelm (1972), 'Bismarcks kleindeutscher Staat und das grossdeutsche Reich', in Helmut Bohme (ed), *Probleme der Reichgrundungszeit 1848-1879*, Kiepenheuer & Witsch, Berlin, pp. 355-368.

Mommsen, Wolfgang J. (1981) (ed), *The Emergence of the Welfare State in Britain and Germany*, Croom Helm, London.

Mommsen, Wolfgang J. (1995), *Imperial Germany 1867-1918: Politics, Culture and Society in an Authoritarian State*, Arnold, London.

Montanelli, Indro (2001), *L'Italia giacobina e carbonara (1789-1831)*, Superbur, Biblioteca Universale Rizzoli, Milan.

Morris, Richard B. (1946), *Government and Labor in Early America*, Columbia University Press, New York.

Moss, David A. (1997), 'The Deutsche Bank', in Thomas K. McCraw (ed), *Creating Modern Capitalism*, Harvard University Press, Cambridge, pp. 229-263.

Mowat, Charles Loch (1955), *Britain between the Wars 1918-1940*, University of Chicago Press, Chicago.

Mueller, Milton L. Jr. (1997), *Service: Competition, and Monopoly in the Making of the American Telephone System*, MIT Press, Cambridge.

Munch, Paul (1996), 'The Growth of the Modern State', in Sheilagh Ogilvie (ed), *Germany, A New Social and Economic History*, 1630-1800, Arnold, London, Vol. 2, pp. 196-232.

Musson, A. E. (1972), 'The "Manchester School" and Exploitation of Machinery', *Business History*, XIV, January, pp. 17-50.

Musgrave, Peter (1999), *The Early Modern European Economy*, St. Martin's Press, New York.

Myers, Margaret G. (1970), *Financial History of the United States*, Columbia University Press, New York.

Nash, Gerald D. (1964), *State Government and Economic Development: A History of Administrative Policies in California*, Berkley Institute of Government Studies, Berkley.

Nash, Gerald D. (1968), *United States Oil Policy 1890-1964: Business and Government in Twentieth Century America*, University of Pittsburgh Press, Pittsburgh.

Nef, John U. (1932), *Rise of the British Coal Industry*, George Routledge and Sons, London.

Nettels, Curtis P. (1938), *The Roots of American Civilization*, Appleton-Century-Crofts, New York.

Nettels, Curtis P. (1962), *The Emergence of a National Economy 1775-1815*, Holt, Rinehart and Winston, New York.

Nicholls, A. J. (1994), *Freedom with Responsibility, The Social Market Economy in Germany 1918-1963*, Clarendon Press, Oxford.

Nielsen, Randall (1997), 'Storage and English Government Intervention in Early Modern Grain Markets', *Journal of Economic History*, 57, March, pp. 1-33.

Nipperdey, Thomas (1993), *Deutsche Geschichte, 1866-1918: Machstaat vor der Demokratie*, C. H. Brock, Munich, Vol. II.

Noether, Emiliana Pasca (1951), *Seeds of Italian Nationalism 1700-1815*, Columbia University Press, New York.

Nonnenmacher, Tomas (2001), 'State Promotion and Regulation of the Telegraph Industry, 1845-1860', *Journal of Economic History*, No. 61, March, pp. 19-36.

Norberg, Kathryn (1994), 'The French Fiscal Crisis of 1788 and the Financial Origins of the Revolution of 1789', in Philip T. Hoffman and Kathryn Norberg (eds), *Fiscal Crisis, Liberty, and Representative Government, 1450-1789*, Stanford University Press, Stanford, pp. 253-298.

Nye, John (1991), 'The Myth of Free Trade Britain and Fortress France', *Journal of Economic History*, March, Vol. 51, pp. 23-46.

O'Brien, P. K. (1959), 'British Income and Property in the Early Nineteenth Century', *Economic History Review*, n. s. XII, 2, pp. 255-267.

O'Brien, Patrick and Caglar Keyder (1978), *Economic Growth in Britain and France, 1780-1914: Two Paths to the Twentieth Century*, G. Allen and Unwin, London.

OECD (1981), *Historical Statistics: 1960-1980*, Paris.

OECD (1987), *Economic Outlook*, Paris.

OECD (1989), *Economic Outlook*, Paris.

OECD (1990a), *Economic Outlook*, Paris.

OECD (1990b), *Historical Statistics: 1960-1988*, Paris.

OECD (1991), *Economic Outlook*, Paris.

OECD (1997), *Historical Statistics: 1960-1995*, Paris.

Ogilvie, Sheilagh (1996), 'The Beginning of Industrialization', in Sheilagh Ogilvie (ed), *Germany, A New Social and Economic History*, Arnold, London, Vol. 2, 1630-1800, pp. 263-308.

338 *Cultural Continuity in Advanced Economies*

Ogilvie, Sheilagh (2003), *A Bitter Living, Women, Markets and Social Capital in Early Modern Germany*, Oxford University Press, Oxford.

O'Grada, Cormac (1988), *Ireland Before and After the Famine*, Manchester University Press, Manchester.

O'Grada, Cormac (1999), *Black '47 and Beyond*, Princeton, University Press, Princeton.

Okun, Mitchell (1986), *Fair Play in the Market Place: The First Battle for Pure Food and Drugs*, Northern Illinois University Press, De Kalb, Il.

Oliva, Gianni (1998), *I Savoia: Novecento anni di una dinastia*, Arnoldo Mondadori, Milan.

Olson, Mancur Jr. (1965), *The Logic of Collective Action*, Harvard University Press, Cambridge.

Overton, Richard C. (1965), *Burlington Route: A History of the Burlington Lines*, Alfred A. Knopf, New York.

Overy, Richard (2003), 'Economy and State in Germany in the Twentieth Century', in Sheilagh Ogilvee and Richard Overy (eds), *Germany, A New Social and Economic History, Since 1800*, Vol. 3, Arnold, London, pp. 251-278.

Owen Smith, Eric (1994), *The German Economy*, Routledge, London.

Owen Smith, Eric, Stephen Burger and Lothar Funk (1994), 'Industry, Trade and Economic Policy', in Eric Owen Smith, *The German Economy*, Routledge, London, pp. 416-536.

Oxford Encyclopedia of Economic History (2003), Oxford University Press, Oxford.

Paci, Massimo (1989), 'Public and Private in the Welfare System', in Peter Lange and Marino Regini (eds), *State, Market, and Social Regulation*, Cambridge University Press, New York, pp. 217-234.

Padoa Schioppa Kostoris, Fiorella (1993), *Italy and the Sheltered Economy: Structural Problems in the Italian Economy*, Clarendon Press, Oxford.

Papa, Antonio (1973), *Classe politica e intervento pubblico nell'età Giolittiana: la nazionalizzazione delle ferrovie*, Guida Editore, Naples.

Parent, Antoine and Christophe Rault (2004), 'The Influences Affecting French Assets Abroad Prior to 1914', *Journal of Economic History*, 64, June, pp. 328-362.

Parks, Robert J. (1972), *Democracy's Railroads: Public Enterprise in Jacksonian Michigan*, Kennikat Press, Port Washington, NY.

Parris, Henry (1960), 'The Nineteenth-Century Revolution in Government: A Reappraisal', *Historical Journal*, 3, pp. 17-32.

Parris, Henry (1965), *Government and the Railways in Nineteenth Century Britain*, Routledge, London.

Pawson, Eric (1977), *Transport and the Economy: The Turnpike Roads of Eighteenth Century Britain*, Academic Press, New York.

Pawson, Eric (1979), *The Early Industrial Revolution: Britain the Eighteenth Century*, Harper and Row, New York.

Peacock, Alan and Hans Willgerodt (1989), 'Overall View of the German Liberal Movement', in Alan Peacock and Hans Willgerodt (eds), *German Neo-Liberals and the Social Market Economy*, St. Martin's Press, New York, pp. 1-15.

Perini, Leandro (1991), 'La funzione dello stato', in Ruggiero Romano (ed), *Storia dell'economia italiana: L'età moderna: verso la crisi*, Vol. II, Giulio Einaudi, Turin, pp. 285-309.

Perkins, Edwin J. (1994), *American Public Finance and Financial Services 1700-1815*, Ohio State University Press, Columbus.

Persson, Karl Gunnar (1996), 'The Seven Lean Years, Elasticity, Traps, and Intervention in Grain Markets in Pre-Industrial Europe', *Economic History Review*, XLIX, pp. 667-691.

Pescosolido, Guido (1994), 'L'economia e la vita materiale', in Giovanni Sabbatucci and Vittorio Vidotto (eds), *Storia d'Italia: le premesse dell'unita, dalla fine dell' settecento al 1861*, Laterza, Bari, Vol. 1, pp. 3-118.

Pescosolido, Guido (1995), 'Arretratezza e sviluppo, in Giovanni Sabbatucci and Vittorio Vidotto (eds), *Storia d'Italia: Il nuovo stato e la società civile*, Laterza, Bari, Vol. 2, pp. 217-328.

Petri, Rolf (2002), *Storia economica d'Italia: Dalla grande guerra al miracolo economico (1918-1963)*, Il Mulino, Bologna.

Petrusewicz, Marta (1996), *Latifundum, Moral Economy and Material Life in a European Periphery*, University of Michigan Press, Ann Arbor.

Peyret, Henry (1949), *Histoire des chemins de fer en France et dans le monde*, Société d'éditions françaises et Internationales, Paris.

Pflanze, Otto (1963), *Bismarck and the Development of Germany: The Period of Unification, 1815-1871*, Princeton University Press, Princeton.

Piquet, Caroline (2004), 'The Suez Company's Concession in Egypt, 1854-1956', *Enterprise and Society*, 5, March, pp. 107-127.

Polanyi, Karl (1944), *The Great Transformation*, Rinehart, New York.

Pollard, Sidney and Paul Robertson (1979), *The British Shipbuilding Industry: 1870-1914*, Harvard University Press, Cambridge.

Pollins, Harold (1971), *Britain's Railways*, David and Charles, Newton Abbot.

Polster, Werner and Klaus Voy (1991a), 'Die Entfaltung der Industriewirtschaft—zum Strukturwandel von Wirtschaft und Erwerbesarbeit in der Industriegesellschaft', in Klaus Voy, Werner Polster, and Claus Thomasberger (eds), *Marktwirtschaft und politische Regulierung*, Metropolis-Verlag, Marburg, Vol. 1, pp. 25-86.

Polster, Werner and Klaus Voy (1991b), 'Von der politischen Regulierung zum Selbstregulierung der Markte—Die Entwicklung von Wirtschafts-Ordnungs-Politik in der Bundesrepublik', in Klaus Voy, Werner Polster, and Claus Thomasberger (eds), *Marktwirtschaft und politische Regulierung*, Metropolis-Verlag, Marburg, Vol. 1, pp. 169-226.

Poole, Keith T. and Howard Rosenthal (1993), 'The Enduring 19th Century Battle for Economic Regulation: The Interstate Commerce Act Revisited', *Journal of Law and Economics*, No. 36, October, pp. 837-860.

Posner, M. V. and S. Woolf (1967), *Italian Public Enterprise*, Harvard University Press, Cambridge.

Pounds, Norman J. G. (1959), 'Economic Growth in Germany', in Hugh J. Aitken (ed), *The State and Economic Growth*, New York, Social Science Research Council, pp. 189-200.

Pratt, Joseph A. (1980), 'Natural Resources and Energy', in *Encyclopedia of American Economic History*, Charles Scribner's Sons, New York, Vol. I, pp. 202-213.

Price, Roger (1987), *A Social History of Nineteenth Century France*, Holmes and Meier, New York.

Prodi, Romano and Daniele di Giovanni (1992), 'Forty-Five Years of Industrial Policy in Italy: Protagonists, Objectives and Instruments', in Mario Baldassarri (ed), *Industrial Policy in Italy*, St. Martin's Press, New York, pp. 31-55.

Puffert, Douglas J. (2000), 'The Standardization of Track Gauge on the American Railways, 1830-1890', *Journal of Economic History*, 60, December, pp. 933-960.

Puffert, Douglas J. (2002), 'Path Dependence in Spatial Networks: The Standardization of Railway Track Gauge', *Exploration in Economic History*, 39, pp. 282-314.

Quinn, M.A. (1985), 'Cens', in Samuel F. Scott and Barry Rothaus (eds), *Historical Dictionary of the French Revolution, 1789-1799*, Greenwood, Westport, Ct., pp. 162-163.

Radkau, Joachim (1974), 'Von der nationalsozialistischen Machtergreifung bis zur Gegenwart', in George W. F. Hallgarten and Joachim Radkau (eds), *Deutsche Industrie und Politik von Bismarck bis Heute*, Europäische Verlagsanstalt, Frankfurt am Main, pp.

225-527.

Rae, Thomas I. (1974), *The Union of 1707: Its Impact on Scotland*, Blackie and Son, Glasgow.

Reader, W. J. (1977), 'Imperial Chemical Industries and State, 1926-1945', in Barry Supple (ed), *Essays in British Business History*, Clarendon Press, Oxford, pp. 227-243.

Recktenwald, H. C. (1987), 'Cameralism', in John Eatwell, (ed), *The New Palgrave: A Dictionary of Economics*, Stockton Press, New York, Vol. 1, pp. 313-314.

Remond, Rene (1997), *Il XIX secolo: 1815-1914*, Rizzoli, Milan.

Richards, Leonard L. (2000), *The Free North and Southern Domination, 1780-1860*, Louisiana State University Press, Baton Rouge.

Rifkin, Jeremy (2004), *The European Dream*, Jeremy P. Tarcher/Penguin, New York.

Rivlin, Alice M. (2002), 'Challenges to Capitalism', *Regional Review of the Federal Reserve Bank of Boston*, 12, 3, Q3, pp. 4-10, Boston.

Robbins, Lord (1976), *Political Economy: Past and Present*, Macmillan, London.

Romano, Ruggiero (1991a), 'Linee di sintesi', in Ruggiero Romano (ed), *Storia dell'economia italiana: L'età moderna: verso la crisi*, Giulio Einaudi, Turin, Vol. II, pp. 337-344.

Romano, Ruggiero (1991b), 'Linee di sintesi', in Ruggiero Romano (ed), *Storia dell'economia italiana: L'età contemporanea, un paese nuovo*, Giulio Einaudi, Turin, Vol. III, pp. 363-375.

Romeo, Rosario (1963), *Breve storia della grande industria in Italia*, Rocca San Casiano.

Romeo, Rosario (1984), *Vita di Cavour*, Laterza, Bari.

Rosa, Alberto Asor (1975), 'La cultura', in Romano Ruggiero and Corrado Vivanti (eds), *Storia d'Italia: Dall'unita ad oggi*, Giulio Einaudi Turin, Vol. 4, pp. 861-1664.

Rosanvallon, Pierre 1989, 'Etat et société (du xix siècle a nos jours)', in Jacques Le Goff (ed), *L'état et les pouvoir*, in a compendium of André Burguiere and Jacques Revel, *Histoire de la France*, Editions du seuil, Paris, Vol. II, pp. 489-617.

Rosenberg, Hans (1978), *Machteilen und Wirtschaftskonjukturen*, Vandenhoeck & Ruprecht, Göttingen.

Ross, George W. (1965), *The Nationalization of Steel*, McGibbon & Kee, London.

Rossi, Salvatore (2000), *La politica economica italiana 1968-2000*, Laterza, Bari.

Rousseau, Jean-Jacques (1966), *Du Contrat Social*, Flammarion, Paris.

Rousseau, Jean-Jacques (1967), 'The Social Contract', in Ernest Barker (ed), *Social Contract*, Oxford University Press, Oxford, pp. 169-307.

Rubin, Julius (1961), 'An Innovating Public Improvement: The Erie Canal', in Carter Goodrich (ed), *Canals and American Economic Development*, Columbia University Press, New York, pp. 15-66.

Rule, John (1992), *The Vital Economy: England's Developing Economy, 1714-1815*, Longman, London.

Saboul, Albert (1976a), 'Le choc révolutionnaire 1789-1797', in Fernand Braudel and Ernest Labrousse (eds), *Histoire économique et sociale de la France: L'avènement de l'ère industrielle (1789—annes 1880)*, Presse Universitaire de France, Paris, Tome III, Vol. 1, pp. 1-64.

Saboul, Albert (1976b), 'La reprise économique et la stabilisation sociale, 1797-1815', in Fernand Braudel and Ernest Labrousse (eds), *Histoire économique et sociale de la France: L'avènement de l'ère industrielle (1789—annes 1880)*, Presse Universitaire de France, Paris, Tome III, Vol. 1, pp. 65-136.

Sacconi, Maurizio and Marco Biagi (2001), 'The White Paper on the Labour Market in Italy, Proposal for An Active Society and Quality Employment (Executive Summary)', *Review of Economic Conditions in Italy*, No. 3, September-December, pp. 447-459.

Saladino, Salvatore (1970) *Italy from Unification to 1919: Growth and Decay of a Liberal*

Regime, Thomas Crowell, New York.

Salomone, William A. (1960), *Italy in the Giolittian Era: Italian Democracy in the Making 1900-1914*, University of Pennsylvania Press, Philadelphia.

Saloutos, Theodore (1946), 'Efforts of Crop Control in Seventeenth Century America', *Journal of Southern History*, 12, pp. 45-66.

Salsbury, Stephen (1967), *The State, the Investor and the Railroad*, Harvard University Press, Cambridge.

Salvatorelli, Luigi (1970), *The Risorgimento: Thought and Action*, Harper and Row, New York.

Salvemini, Gaetano (1915), *Mazzini*, Francesco Battiato, Catania.

Sargent, Thomas J. (1993), *Bounded Rationality in Macro Economics*, Clarendon Press, Oxford.

Sauvy, Alfred (1967), *Histoire économique de la France entre les deux guerres*, Librairie Artheme Fayard, Paris.

Savona, Paolo (1995), 'State and Market; Guarantees and Freedom: The Principle of Individual Responsibilities in a New Society', *Review of Economic Conditions in Italy*, January-June, No.1, pp. 79-90.

Schachter, Gustav (1965), *The Italian South: Economic Development in Mediterranean Europe*, Random House, New York.

Schachter, Gustav (1973), 'Development in Economic Science Since 1965', *The American Journal of Economics and Sociology*, Vol. 32, No. 3 July, pp. 331-335.

Schachter, Gustav (1986), 'Italian Public Enterprises', paper, Joint Congrip-Stato e Mercato Conference on *The State and Social Regulation in Italy*, April 14-18, The Rockefeller Foundation, Bellagio Study and Conference Center, Bellagio, pp. 1-15.

Schachter, Gustav (1991), 'Francois Quesnay: Interpreters and Critics Revisited', *American Journal of Economics and Sociology*, July 50, No. 3, pp. 313-322.

Schachter, Gustav and Saul Engelbourg (1988), 'The Steadfastness of Economic Dualism in Italy', *Journal of Developing Areas*, July, pp. 515-526.

Schachter, Gustav and Saul Engelbourg (1995), 'Economic Growth Through Dependency in the Mezzogiorno 1950-1990', in Ilaria Zilli (ed), *Studi in onore di Luigi De Rosa: il novecento*, Edizioni scientifiche italiane, Rome, Vol. III, pp. 585-601.

Schaeper, Thomas J. (1995), 'Merchants, Manufacturers and Mercantilism in Old Regime France', in Ilaria Zilli (ed), *Studi in onore di Luigi De Rosa: il novecento*, Edizioni scientifiche italiane, Rome, Vol. II, pp. 755-775.

Scheiber, Harry N. (1973), 'Property Law, Expropriation, and Resource Allocation by Government: the United States, 1789-1910', *Journal of Economic History*, XXXIII, March, pp. 232-251.

Schmoller, Gustav (1967), *The Mercantile System and its Historical Significance*, Arthur M. Kelley, New York, first US edition 1897.

Schram, Albert (1997), *Railways and the Formation of the Italian State in the Nineteenth Century*, Cambridge University Press, Cambridge.

Scoville, Warren (1950), *Capitalism and French Glassmaking, 1640-1789*, University of California Press, Berkeley.

Sears, Marian V. (1966), 'Michigan Bureaucrat Promotes the State's Economic Growth', *Explorations in Entrepreneurial History*, 2nd ser., III, pp. 200-219.

Sée, Henri (1926), *Les origines du capitalisme moderne*, Librairie Armand Colin, Paris.

Sée, Henri (1942), *Histoire économique de la France: Les temps modernes,(1789-1914)*, Librairie Armand Colin, Paris.

Sée, Henri (1967) *France économique et sociale au XVIIIe siècle*, Librairie Armand Colin, Paris, originally published in 1927.

Sheehan, James J. (1989), *German History: 1770-1866*, Clarendon Press, Oxford.

Sibalis, M. D. (1985), 'Le Chapelier, Isac-Rene-Guy', in Samuel F. Scott and Barry Rothaus (eds), *Historical Dictionary of the French Revolution, 1789-1799*, Greenwood, Westport CT., pp. 576-578.

Sinclair, Upton (1946), *The Jungle*, Robert Bentley, Cambridge.

Smith, Adam (1937), *An Inquiry in the Nature and Causes of the Wealth of Nations*, Modern Library, New York, originally published in 1776.

Smith, Cecil O. Jr. (1990), 'The Longest Run: Public Engineers and Planning in France 1820-1850', *American Historical Review*, 95, pp. 657-692.

Somers, Frans (1998), *European Union Economies*, Addison Wesley Longman, New York.

Spengler, Joseph J. (1949), 'Laissez Faire and Intervention', *Journal of Political Economy*, 57, pp. 438-441.

Splawn, Walter M. V. (1928), *Government Ownership and Operation of Railroads*, Macmillan, New York.

Stachura, Peter D. (2003), 'Social Policy and Social Welfare in Germany From the Mid-nineteenth Century to the Present', in Sheilagh Ogilvee and Richard Overy (eds), *Germany, A New Social and Economic History: Since 1800*, Arnold, London, Vol. 3, pp. 227-250.

Stampp, Kenneth M. (1956), *The Peculiar Institution*, Alfred A. Knopf, New York.

Steinmetz, George (1996), 'The Myth of an Autonomous State: Industrialists, Junkers, and Social Policy in Imperial Germany', in Geoff Eley (ed), *Society, Culture and the State in Germany, 1870-1930*, University of Michigan Press, Ann Arbor, pp. 257-318.

Stone, Alan (1991), *Public Service Liberalism*, Princeton University Press, Princeton.

Stover, John F. (1997), *American Railroads*, University of Chicago Press, Chicago.

Studenski, Paul and Herman E. Krooss (1952), *Financial History of the United States*, McGraw-Hill Book Company, New York.

Taylor, A. J. P. (1965), *English History 1914-1945*, Oxford University Press, New York.

Taylor, Arthur J. (1972), *Laissez-faire and State Intervention in Nineteenth Century Britain*, Macmillan, London.

Taylor, George Rogers (1951), *The Transportation Revolution 1815-1860*, Holt, Rinehart and Winston, New York.

Taylor, Rosemary C. R. (1984), 'State Intervention in Postwar European Health Care: The Case Prevention in Britain and Italy', in Stephen Bornstein, et al (eds), *The State in Capitalist Europe*, George Allen & Unwin, London, pp. 91-111.

Teyssier, Arnaud (1995), *La 5e république (1958-1995), de De Gaulle à Chirac*, Pygmalion Gérard Matelot, Paris.

Thomas, Brinley (1985), 'Food Supply in the United Kingdom during the Industrial Revolution', in Joel Mokyr (ed), *The Economics of the Industrial Revolution*, Rowman and Allanheld, Totowa, NJ, pp. 137-150.

Thomasson, Melissa A. (2002), 'From Sickness to Health: The Twentieth-Century Development of U.S. Health Insurance', *Explorations in Economic History*, 39, pp. 233-253.

Thompson, Robert L. (1947), *Wiring a Continent*, Princeton University Press, Princeton.

Tilly, Richard H. (1966), *Financial Institutions and Industrialization in the Rhineland, 1815-1860*, University of Wisconsin Press, Madison.

Tilly, Richard H. (1991), 'Germany', in Richard Sylla and Gianni Toniolo (eds), *Patterns of European Industrialization: The Nineteenth Century*, Routledge, London, pp. 175-196.

Tipton, Frank B. Jr. (1976), *Regional Variations in the Economic Development of Germany during the Nineteenth Century*, Wesleyan University Press, Middletown, CT.

Tipton, Frank B. Jr. (2003), 'Government and the Economy in the Nineteenth Century', in Sheilagh Ogilvee and Richard Overy (eds), *Germany, A New Social and Economic History: Since 1800*, London, Arnold, Vol. 3, pp. 106-151.

Tocqueville, de Alexis (1955), *The Old Regime and the French Revolution*, Doubleday, Garden City, original published in 1856.

Tolliday, Steven V. (1986). 'Steel and Rationalization Policies, 1918-1959', in Bernard Elbaum and William Lazonick, (eds), *The Decline of the British Economy*, Clarendon Press, Oxford, pp. 82-108.

Tolliday, Steven V. (2000), 'Introduction: Enterprise and State in the Italian "Economic Miracle"', *Enterprise and Society*, June, 1, pp. 241-248.

Tomlinson, Jim (1981), *Problems of British Economic Policy 1870-1945*, Methuen, London.

Toninelli, Pier Angelo (2000), 'The Rise and Fall of Public Enterprise', in Pier Angelo Toninelli (ed), *The Rise and Fall of State-Owned Enterprise in the Western World*, Cambridge University Press, Cambridge, pp. 3-24.

Toniolo, Gianni (1990), *An Economic History of Liberal Italy 1850-1918*, Routledge, London.

Trebilcock, Clive (1981), *The Industrialization of the Continental Powers 1780-1914*, Longman, New York.

Tribe, K. (1987), 'Friedrich List', in John Eatwell (ed), *The New Palgrave: A Dictionary of Economics*, Macmillan, London, 3, pp. 216-218.

Tribe, Kenneth (1988), *Governing Economy: The Reformation of German Economic Discourse 1750-1840*, Cambridge University Press, Cambridge.

Tulard, Jean (1985), 'Les Revolutions de 1789 a 1851', in Jean Favier, Director, *Histoire de France*, Librairies Artheme Fayard, Paris, Vol. IV.

Tyler, David Budlong (1939), *Steam Conquers the Atlantic*, Appleton-Century, New York.

United States Council of Economic Advisers (1997), *Economic Report to the President*, Washington, DC.

United States Department of Commerce (1975), *Historical Statistics of the United States*, Washington, DC.

United States Department of Commerce (2001), *Statistical Abstracts of the United States*, Washington, DC.

Vaizey, John (1974), *The History of British Steel*, Weidenfeld and Nicholson, London.

Valsecchi, Franco (1959), *L'Italia nel settecento dal 1714 al 1788*, Mondadori, Milan.

Vannutelli, Cesare (1961), 'Occupazione e salari', in A. Fanfani Director *L'economia italiana dal 1861 al 1961*, A. Giuffre, Milan, pp. 560-596.

Vaussard, Maurice (1963), *Daily Life in Eighteenth Century Italy*, Macmillan, New York.

Venturi, Franco (1980), *Venezia nel secondo settecento*, Editrice Tirrenea Stampatori, Turin.

Viesti, Gianfranco (2001), 'Government Decentralization and the Regional Question in Italy', *Review of Economic Conditions in Italy*, 3, September-December, pp. 417-446.

Vietor, Richard H. K. (1984), *Energy Policy in America since 1945*, Cambridge, University Press, Cambridge.

Vietor, Richard H. K. (1994), *Contrived Competition: Regulation and Deregulation in America*, Cambridge University Press, Cambridge.

Vietor, Richard H. K. (2000), 'Government Regulation of Business', in Stanley L. Engerman and Robert E. Gallman, (eds), *Cambridge Economic History of the United States, Twentieth Century*, Cambridge University Press, Cambridge, III, 969-1012.

Vivanti, Corrado (1991), 'Cita e campagna', in Ruggiero Romano, (ed), *Storia dell'economia italiana: L'età moderna: verso la crisi*, Giulio Einaudi, Turin, Vol. II, pp. 243-283.

Vogel, David (1981), 'The "New" Social Regulation in Historical and Comparative Perspective', in Thomas K. McCraw (ed), *Regulations in Perspective, Historical Essays*, Boston Division of Research, Graduate School of Business Administration, Harvard University, Cambridge, pp. 155-185.

Voy, Klaus and Werner Polster (1991), 'Konjunkturen Akkumulationsprozess und

Geldwert—Gesamtwirtschaftliche Entwiklungslinien in der Bundesrepublik', in Klaus Voy, Werner Polster, and Claus Thomasberger (eds), *Markwirtschaft und politische Regulierung*, Metropolis-Verlag, Marburg, Germany, Vol. 1, pp. 87-168.

Voy, Klaus and Werner Polster and Claus Thomasberger (eds) (1991), *Markwirtschaft und politische Regulierung*, Metropolis-Verlag, Marburg, Germany, Vol. 1, pp. 11-20.

Vries, P. H. H. (2002), 'Governing Growth: A Comparative Analysis of the Role of the State in the Rise of the West', *Journal of World History*, 13,1, pp. 67-138.

Waley, Daniel (1988), *The Italian City-Republics*, Longman, New York.

Wallace, Lillian P. (1966), *Leo XIII and the Rise of Socialism*, Duke University Press, Durham, North Carolina.

Ward, J. R. (1974), *The Finance of Canal Building in Eighteenth-Century England*, Oxford University Press, London.

Weber, Max (1958), *The Protestant Ethic and the Spirit of Capitalism*, Charles Scribner's Sons, New York.

Wehler, Hans-Ulrich (1972), *Bismarck und der Imperialismus*, Kiepenheuer u. Witsch, Cologne.

Wehler, Hans-Ulrich (1989), *Deutsche Gesellschaft Geschichte vom Feudalismus des Alten Reiches bis zur Defensiven Modernisierung der Reformara 1700-1815*, C. H. Beck, Munich, Vol. I.

Weiss, John (1982), *The Making of Technological Man: The Social Origin of French Engineering Education*, MIT Press, Cambridge.

Welk, William G. (1938), *Fascist Economic Policy*, Harvard University Press, Cambridge.

Wells, John (1991), 'Britain in the 1990s; The Legacy of Thatcherism', in John Cornwall (ed), *The Capitalist Economies*, Edward Elgar, Hauts, England, pp. 71-200.

Wengenroth, Ulrich (1997), 'Germany, Capitalism Abroad—Cooperation at Home, 1870-1990', in Alfred D. Chandler, Jr., et al (eds), *Big Business and the Wealth of Nations*, Cambridge University Press, Cambridge, pp. 139-175.

Whisler, Timothy R. (1999), *The British Motor Car Industry 1945-1994*, Oxford University Press, Oxford.

White, Henry Kirke (1973), *History of the Union Pacific Railroad*, August M. Kelley Publishers, Clifton, New Jersey.

Wiebe, Robert H. (1962), *Businessmen and Reform: A Study of the Progressive Movement*, Harvard University Press, Cambridge.

Williams, William Appleman (1958), 'The Age of Mercantilism 1763-1828', *William and Mary Quarterly*, XV October, pp. 419-437.

Willoughby, William R. (1961), *The St. Lawrence Waterways: A Study in Politics and Diplomacy*, University of Wisconsin Press, Madison.

Wilson, Charles (1968), *England's Apprenticeship 1603-1763*, St. Martin's Press, New York.

Winch, Donald (1970), *Economics and Policy: A Historical Study*, Walker, New York.

Winthrop Papers (1931), 'Sir John Eliot's Copy of the New England Tracts', Massachusetts Historical Society, Boston, II, 145-147.

Woodham-Smith, Cecil (1989), *The Great Hunger: Ireland 1845-1849*, Old Town Books, New York.

Woolf, Stuart J. (1973), 'La storia politica e sociale', in Ruggiero Romano and Corrado Vivanti (eds), *Storia d'Italia: Dal primo settecento all'unita*, Einaudi, Turin, Vol. III, pp. 3-508.

Woolf, Stuart J. (1979), *A History of Italy: 1760-1860: The Social Constraints of Political Change*, Methuen and Co., London.

Woolf, Stuart J. (1991), *A History of Italy 1760-1860*, Routledge, London.

Wright, Gavin (1996), 'Natural Resources', *in Encyclopedia of the United States in the*

Twentieth Century, Charles Scribner's, New York, pp. 1383-1406.

Yoffie, David B. (1993), 'Introduction: From Competitive Advantage to Regulated Competition', in David B. Yoffie (ed), *Beyond Free Trade: From Comparative Advantage to Regulated Competition*, Harvard Business School Press, Boston, pp. 1-25.

Young, Arthur (1942), *Travels in France and Italy*, J. M. Dent & Sons, Ltd., London.

Youngson, A. J. (1960), *The British Economy 1920-1957*, Harvard University Press, Cambridge.

Zamagni, Vera (1981), *Lo stato italiano e l'economia*, Le Monnier, Florence.

Zamagni, Vera (1990), *Dalla periferia all centro*, IL Mulino, Bologna.

Zamagni, Vera (1993), *The Economic History of Italy 1860-1990*, Oxford University Press, Oxford.

Zamagni, Vera (2002), 'Evolution of the Economy', in Patrick McCarthy (ed), *Italy since 1945*, Oxford University Press, New York, pp. 42-68.

Zanetti, G. and G, Alzona (1998), *Capire le privatizzazioni*, Il Mulino, Bologna.

Zorn, Wolfgang (1978), 'Sozialgeschichte', in Hermann Aubin and Wolfgang Zorn (eds), *Handbuch der Deutschen Wirtschafts-und Sozialgeschichte: Von der Frühzeit bis zum Ende des 18. Jahrhunderts*, Ernest Klett Verlag, Stuttgart, Vol. 1, pp. 574-607.

Zorzi, Alvise (2001), *La Repubblica del leone: Storia de Venezia*, Bompiani, Bologna.

Zweiniger-Bargielowska, Ina (2000), *Austerity in Britain*, Oxford University Press, Oxford.

Zysman, John (1979), *Political Strategies for Industrial Order*, University of California Press, Berkeley.

Index